CLASSIC TEXTS SERIES

ALGEBRA FOR BEGINNERS

HALL & KNIGHT

arihant
SUCCESS AND NOTHING LESS

arihant
SUCCESS AND NOTHING LESS

ARIHANT PRAKASHAN (Series), MEERUT

卐 Administrative & Production Offices

Regd. Office

'Ramchhaya' 4577/15, Agarwal Road, Darya Ganj, New Delhi -110002
Tele: 011- 47630600, 43518550

卐 Head Office

Kalindi, TP Nagar, Meerut (UP) - 250002
Tel: 0121-7156203, 7156204

卐 Sales & Support Offices

Agra, Ahmedabad, Bengaluru, Bareilly, Chennai, Delhi, Guwahati, Hyderabad, Jaipur, Jhansi, Kolkata, Lucknow, Nagpur & Pune.

卐 **PRICE** ₹185.00

卐 PO No. : TXT-59-T066426-08-25

Published by Arihant Publications (India) Ltd.

For further information about the books published by Arihant, log on to www.arihantbooks.com or e-mail at info@arihantbooks.com

Follow us on

PREFACE

THE present work has been undertaken in order to supply a demand for an easy introduction to our *Elementary Algebra for Schools*, and also to meet the wishes of those who, while approving of the order and treatment of the subject there laid down, have felt the want of a beginners' text-book in a cheaper form.

The order we adopted in our Elementary Algebra differed in some important particulars from that of previous text-books. It was an innovation and an experiment; but our own long experience, backed by the cordial support of friends and colleagues, emboldened us to hope that our treatment would eventually win general acceptance. And we have not been disappointed. The favourable reception of six editions of our text-book, and its adoption in so many of the principal English and Colonial schools, furnish ample proof that no objection has been urged against our treatment of the subject, whilst numbers of teachers, previously unknown to us, have favoured us with expressions of distinct approval. We have, therefore, felt no hesitation in compiling this little book on similar lines.

Our order has been determined mainly by two considerations: first, a desire to introduce as early as possible the practical side of the subject and some of its most interesting applications, such as easy equations and problems; and secondly, the strong opinion that all reference to compound expressions and their resolution into factors should be postponed until the usual operations of Algebra have been exemplified in the case of simple expressions. By this course the beginner soon becomes acquainted with the ordinary algebraical processes without encountering too many of their difficulties; and he is learning at the same time something of the more attractive parts of the subject.

As regards the early introduction of simple equations and problems, the experience of teachers favours the opinion that it is not wise to take a young learner through all the somewhat mechanical rules of Factors, Highest Common Factor, Lowest Common Multiple, Involution, Evolution, and the various types of Fractions, before making some effort to arouse his interest and intelligence through the medium of easy equations and problems. Moreover, this view has been amply supported by all the best text-books on Elementary Algebra which have been recently published.

With so much evidence in favour of a more suitable order we venture to suggest that a revision of the prescribed limits of Algebra in some of the more elementary examinations would be welcomed by teachers; or at any rate that some more definite indication of the required range should be given than " Algebra up to Simple Equations," which figures in so many examinations as the limit of the learner's first stage.

We have endeavoured to provide a first course of Algebra suitable for all classes of Indian students; with this object some prominence has been given to problems involving Indian Currency, Weights, and Measures. Also, in order to meet the requirements of students preparing for entrance to the Indian Universities, we have treated the subject of Ratio and Proportion very fully with numerous examples and illustrations; while the Miscellaneous Examples at the end of the book have been taken entirely from papers set to matriculation candidates during the last few years.

H. S. HALL
S. R. KNIGHT

CONTENTS

I.	Definitions. Substitutions	1
II.	Negative Quantities. Addition of Like Terms	7
III.	Simple Brackets Addition	10
IV.	Subtraction	15
	Miscellaneous Examples I	18
V.	Multiplication	20
VI.	Division	31
VII.	Removal and Insertion of Brackets	38
	Miscellaneous Examples II	42
VIII.	Revision of Elementary Rules	44
IX.	Simple Equations	53
X.	Symbolical Expression	61
XI.	Problems Leading to Simple Equations	66
XII.	Highest Common Factor, Lowest Common Multiple of Simple Expressions. Fractions Involving Simple Expressions only	73
XIII.	Simultaneous Equations	79
XIV.	Problems Leading to Simultaneous Equations	87
XV.	Involution	91
XVI.	Evolution	93
XVII.	Resolution into Factors Converse Use of Factors	95
	Miscellaneous Examples III	117
XVIII.	Highest Common Factor of Compound Expressions	119
XIX.	Multiplication and Division of Fractions	125
XX.	Lowest Common Multiple of Compound Expressions	129
XXI.	Addition And Subtraction of Fractions	132
XXII.	Miscellaneous Fractions	141
XXIII.	Harder Equations	148
XXIV.	Harder Problems	155
	Miscellaneous Examples IV	160
XXV.	Quadratic Equations	163
XXVI.	Problems Leading to Quadratic Equations	174
XXVII.	Ratio and Proportion	178
	Miscellaneous Examples V	192
	Answers	202

APPENDIX ON EASY GRAPHS

1-7.	Axes, Coordinates, Plotting a Point	223
	Examples I	226
8- 9.	Graph of a Function. Straight Lines	228
	Examples II	231
10-15.	Linear Graphs. Application to Simultaneous Equations	233
	Examples III	235
6-18.	Measurement on Different Scales	235
	Examples IV	237
19-21.	Graphs of Statistics. Practical Applications	238
	Examples V	245
22-28.	Graphs of Quadratic Functions. Roots of Equations. Turning Points. Maxima and Minima. Equation of a Circle	251
	Examples VI	255
29-31.	Infinite and Zero Values. Asymptotes	257
32-33.	Combination of Two Graphs	260
	Examples VII	263
34-36.	Miscellaneous Applications of Graphs	264
	Examples VIII	273
	Answers	277

METRIC MEASURES

Money

100 Paise	=	1 Rupee.
		Thus Rs. 5.45 Stands For 5 Rupees 45 Paise.

Weight

10 milligrams (mg)	=	1centigram (cg)
10 centigrams	=	1 decigram (dg)
10 decigrams	=	1 gram (g)
10 grams	=	1 decagram (dag)
10 decagrams	=	1 hectogram (hg)
10 hectogram	=	1 kilogram (kg)
100 kilograms	=	1 quintal (q)
1000 kilograms	=	1 tonne (t)

Length

10 millimetres (mm)	=	1 centimetre (cm)
10 centimetres	=	1 decimetre (dm)
10 decimetres	=	1 metre (m)
10 metres	=	1 decametre (dam)
10 decametres	=	1 hectometre (hm)
10 hectometres	=	1 kilometre (km)

Area

100 sq decimetres	=	1 sq metre = 1 centiare
100 sq metres	=	1 sq decametre = 1 are
100 centiares	=	1 are
100 ares	=	1 hectare
100 hectares	=	1 sq kilometre

ALGEBRA

CHAPTER I

DEFINITIONS. SUBSTITUTIONS

1. ALGEBRA treats of quantities as in Arithmetic, but with greater generality; for while the quantities used in arithmetical processes are denoted by *figures* which have one single definite value, algebraical quantities are denoted by *symbols* which may have any value we choose to assign to them.

The symbols employed are letters, usually those of our own alphabet; and, though there is no restriction as to the numerical values a symbol may represent, it is understood that in the same piece of work it keeps the same value throughout. Thus, when we say " let $a = 1$," we do not mean that a must have the value 1 always, but only in the particular example we are considering. Moreover, we may operate with symbols without assigning to them any particular numerical value at all; indeed it is with such operations that Algebra is chiefly concerned.

We begin with the definitions of Algebra, premising that the symbols $+, -, \times, \div$, will have the same meanings as in Arithmetic.

2. An **algebraical expression** is a collection of symbols; it may consist of one or more **terms**, which are separated from each other by the signs + and –. Thus $7a + 5b - 3c - x + 2y$ is an expression consisting of five terms.

Note. When no sign precedes a term the sign + is understood.

3. **Expressions** are either **simple** or **compound.** A *simple expression* consists of *one* term, as $5a$. A *compound expression* consists of *two or more* terms. Compound expressions may be further distinguished. Thus an expression of *two* terms, as $3a - 2b$, is called a **binomial** expression; one of *three* terms, as $2a - 3b + c$, a **trinomial**; one of *more than three* terms a **multinomial**.

4. When two or more quantities are multiplied together the result is called the **product**. One important difference between the notation of Arithmetic and Algebra should be here remarked. In Arithmetic the product of 2 and 3 is written 2×3, whereas in Algebra the product of a and b may be written in any of the forms $a \times b$, $a \cdot b$, or ab. The form ab is the most usual. Thus, if $a = 2$, $b = 3$, the product $ab = a \times b = 2 \times 3 = 6$; but in Arithmetic 23 means " twenty-three," or $2 \times 10 + 3$.

5. Each of the quantities multiplied together to form a product is called a **factor** of the product. Thus 5, a, b are the factors of the product $5ab$.

6. When one of the factors of an expression is a numerical quantity, it is called the **coefficient** of the remaining factors. Thus in the expression $5ab$, 5 is the coefficient. But the word coefficient is also used in a wider sense, and it is sometimes convenient to consider any factor, or factors, of a product as the coefficient of the remaining factors. Thus in the product $6abc$, $6a$ may be appropriately called the coefficient of bc . A coefficient which is not merely numerical is sometimes called a **literal coefficient**.

Note. When the coefficient is unity it is usually omitted. Thus we do not write $1a$, but simply a.

7. If a quantity be multiplied by itself any number of times, the product is called a **power** of that quantity, and is expressed by writing the number of factors to the right of the quantity and above it. Thus $a \times a$ is called the *second power* of a, and is written a^2;

$a \times a \times a$ .... *third power* of a, ... a^3; and so on.

The number which expresses the power of any quantity is called its **index** or **exponent**. Thus 2, 5, 7 are respectively the indices of a^2, a^5, a^7.

Note. a^2 is usually read " a squared "; a^3 is read " a cubed "; a^4 is read " a to the fourth "; and so on.

When the index is unity it is omitted, and we do not write a^1, but simply a. Thus, a, $1a$, a^1, $1a^1$ all have the same meaning.

8. The beginner must be careful to distinguish between *coefficient* and *index*.

Example 1. What is the difference in meaning between $3a$ and a^3?

By $3a$ we mean the product of the quantities 3 and a.

By a^3 we mean the third power of a; that is, the product of the quantities a, a, a.

Thus, if $a = 4$,

$$3a = 3 \times a = 3 \times 4 = 12;$$
$$a^3 = a \times a \times a = 4 \times 4 \times 4 = 64.$$

Example 2. If $b = 5$, distinguish between $4b^2$ and $2b^4$.

Here $4b^2 = 4 \times b \times b = 4 \times 5 \times 5 = 100$;

whereas $2b^4 = 2 \times b \times b \times b \times b = 2 \times 5 \times 5 \times 5 \times 5 = 1250$.

Example 3. If $x = 1$, find the value of $5x^4$.

Here $5x^4 = 5 \times x \times x \times x \times x = 5 \times 1 \times 1 \times 1 \times 1 = 5$.

Note. The beginner should observe that every power of 1 is 1.

9. In arithmetical multiplication the order in which the factors of a product are written is immaterial. For instance, 3×4 means 4 sets of 3 units, and 4×3 means 3 sets of 4 units; in each case we have 12 units in all. Thus

$$3 \times 4 = 4 \times 3.$$

In a similar way, $3 \times 4 \times 5 = 4 \times 3 \times 5 = 4 \times 5 \times 3$;

and it is easy to see that the same principle holds for the product of any number of arithmetical quantities.

In like manner in Algebra ab and ba each denotes the product of the two quantities represented by the letters a and b, and have therefore the same value. Again, the expressions $abc, acb, bac, bca, cab, cba$ have the same value, each denoting the product of the three quantities a, b, c. It is immaterial in what order the factors of a product are written; it is usual, however, to arrange them in alphabetical order.

Fractional coefficients which are greater than unity are usually kept in the form of improper fractions.

Example 4. If $a = 6$, $x = 7$, $z = 5$, find the value of $\frac{13}{10}axz$.

Here $\frac{13}{10}axz = \frac{13}{10} \times 6 \times 7 \times 5 = 273$.

EXAMPLES I. a

If $a = 5, b = 4, c = 1, x = 3, y = 12, z = 2$, find the values of

1. $2a$. **2.** a^2. **3.** $3z$. **4.** z^3.

5. c^4. **6.** $4c$. **7.** $4b^2$. **8.** c^3.

9. x^3. **10.** $3x$. **11.** $7y^2$. **12.** $8a^3$.

13. $6z^5$. **14.** $5z^6$. **15.** $7c^6$.

If $a = 6, p = 4, q = 7, r = 5, x = 1$, find the values of

16. ap. **17.** $3pq$. **18.** $3qx$. **19.** $5p^3$.

20. $8aqx$. **21.** pqr. **22.** $8aqr$. **23.** $7qrx$.

24. $2apx$. **25.** $7x^4$. **26.** $3p^4$. **27.** $8r^4$.

28. $9apqx$. **29.** $6x^7$. **30.** x^{10}.

If $h=5$, $k=3$, $x=4$, $y=1$, find the value of

31. $\frac{1}{9}k^3$. **32.** $\frac{1}{6}kx$. **33.** $\frac{1}{7}y^7$. **34.** $\frac{1}{10}hkx$.

35. $\frac{1}{10}y^5$. **36.** $\frac{1}{8}x^4$. **37.** $\frac{1}{27}k^5$. **38.** $\frac{1}{125}h^6$.

39. $\frac{1}{6}y^8$. **40.** $\frac{1}{8}hkxy$.

10. When several different quantities are multiplied together a notation similar to that of Art. 7 is adopted. Thus, *aabbbbcddd* is written $a^2b^4cd^3$. And conversely $7a^3cd^2$ has the same meaning as $7\times a\times a\times a\times c\times d\times d$.

Example 1. If $c=3$, $d=5$, find the value of $16c^4d^3$.

$$\text{Here } 16c^4d^3=16\times3^4\times5^3=(16\times5^3)\times3^4.$$
$$=2000\times81=162000$$

Note. The beginner should observe that by a suitable combination of the factors some labour has been avoided.

Example 2. If $p=4$, $q=9$, $r=6$, $s=5$. find the value of $\frac{32qr^3}{81p^s}$.

$$\text{Here } \frac{32qr^3}{81p^s}=\frac{32\times9\times6\times6\times6}{81\times4\times4\times4\times4\times4}=\frac{3}{4}.$$

11. If one factor of a product is equal to 0, the product must be equal to 0, *whatever values the other factors may have*. A factor 0 is usually called a *zero factor*.

For instance, if $x=0$, then ab^3xy^2 contains a zero factor. Therefore, $ab^3xy^2=0$ when $x=0$, whatever be the values of a, b, y.

Again, if $c=0$, then $c^3=0$; therefore $ab^2c^3=0$, whatever values a and b may have.

Note. Every power of 0 is 0.

EXAMPLES I. b

If $a=3$, $b=2$, $p=10$, $q=1$, $x=0$, $z=7$, find the value of

1. $3bp$. **2.** $8ax$. **3.** $5pqz$. **4.** $6aqz$.

5. bpz. **6.** $3b^2q$. **7.** az^2. **8.** q^2x^3.

9. qz^2. **10.** $5b^3px^4$. **11.** a^3p^4x. **12.** $8p^3q^5$.

13. b^3a^3. **14.** px^4z^3. **15.** $8a^4q^5$.

If $k = 1$, $l = 2$, $m = 0$, $p = 3$, $q = 4$, $r = 5$, find the value of

16. $\frac{3k^2}{p^2}$. **17.** $\frac{5l^3}{qr}$. **18.** $\frac{m}{3k^2}$. **19.** $\frac{3m^2}{4l}$.

20. $\frac{16p^3}{9q^2}$. **21.** $\frac{5m^3}{k^5}$. **22.** $\frac{6l^4}{3q^3}$. **23.** $\frac{8r^3}{25lq^2}$.

24. $\frac{9mq}{4p^2}$. **25.** $\frac{81q^4r^2}{400p^5}$. **26.** $\frac{mq}{l^p}$. **27.** $\frac{q^k}{l^p}$.

28. $\frac{kr^k}{q^l}$. **29.** $\frac{5m^r}{k^p}$. **30.** $\frac{k^r}{r^k}$.

12. We now proceed to find the numerical value of expressions which contain more than one term. In these each term can be dealt with singly by the rules already given, and by combining the terms the numerical value of the whole expression is obtained.

13. We have already, in Art. 8, drawn attention to the importance of carefully distinguishing between *coefficient* and *index*; confusion between these is such a fruitful source of error with beginners that it may not be unnecessary once more to dwell on the distinction.

Example When $c = 5$, find the value of $c^4 - 4c + 2c^3 - 3c^2$.

Here $c^4 = 5^4 = 5 \times 5 \times 5 \times 5 = 625$;

$$4c = 4 \times 5 = 20,$$

$$2c^3 = 2 \times 5^3 = 2 \times 5 \times 5 \times 5 = 250,$$

$$3c^2 = 3 \times 5^2 = 3 \times 5 \times 5 = 75.$$

Hence the value of the expression
$= 625 - 20 + 250 - 75 = 780$.

14. The beginner must also note the distinction in meaning between the *sum* and the *product* of two or more algebraical quantities. For instance, ab is the *product* of the two quantities a and b, and its value is obtained by *multiplying* them together. But $a + b$ is the *sum* of the two quantities a and b, and its value is obtained by *adding* them together.

Thus if $a = 11$, $b = 12$,
the *sum* of a and b is $11 + 12$, that is 23;
the *product* of a and b is 11×12, that is, 132.

15. By Art. 11 any term which contains a *zero factor* is itself zero, and may be called a *zero term*.

Example If $a = 2, b = 0, x = 5, y = 3$, find the value of

$$5a^3 - ab^2 + 2x^2y + 3bxy.$$

The expression $(5 \times 2^3) - 0 + (2 \times 5^2 \times 3) + 0$

$$= 40 + 150 = 190.$$

Note. The two zero terms do not affect the result.

16. In working examples the student should pay attention to the following hints.

1. Too much importance cannot be attached to neatness of style and arrangement. The beginner should remember that neatness is in itself conducive to accuracy.
2. The sign = should never be used except to connect quantities which are equal. Beginners should be particularly careful not to employ the sign of equality in any vague and inexact sense.
3. Unless the expressions are very short the signs of equality in the steps of the work should be placed one under the other.
4. It should be clearly brought out how each step follows from the one before it; for this purpose it will sometimes be advisable to add short verbal explanations; the importance of this will be seen later.

EXAMPLES I. c

If $a = 4, b = 1, c = 3, f = 5, g = 7, h = 0$, find the value of

1. $3f + 5h - 7b$.
2. $7c - 9h + 2a$.
3. $4g - 5c - 9b$.
4. $3g - 4h + 7c$.
5. $3f - 2g - b$.
6. $9b - 3c + 4h$.
7. $3a - 9b + c$.
8. $2f - 3g + 5a$.
9. $3c - 4a + 7b$.
10. $3f + 5h - 2c - 4b + a$.
11. $6h - 7b - 5a - 7f + 9g$.
12. $7c + 5b - 4a + 8h + 3g$.
13. $9b + a - 3g + 4f + 7h$.
14. $fg + gh - ab$.
15. $gb - 3hc + fb$.
16. $fh + hb - 3hc$.
17. $f^2 - 3a^2 + 2c^3$.
18. $b^3 - 2h^3 + 3a^2$.
19. $3b^2 - 2b^3 + 4h^2 - 2h^4$.

CHAPTER II

NEGATIVE QUANTITIES. ADDITION OF LIKE TERMS

17. IN his arithmetical work the student has been accustomed to deal with numerical quantities connected by the signs + and – ; and in finding the value of an expression such as $1\frac{3}{4}+7\frac{2}{3}-3\frac{1}{8}+6-4\frac{1}{5}$, he understands that the quantities to which the sign + is prefixed are *additive*, and those to which the sign – is prefixed are *subtractive*, while the first quantity, $1\frac{3}{4}$, to which no sign is prefixed, is counted among the additive terms. The same notions prevail in Algebra; thus in using the expression $7a+3b-4c-2d$ we understand the symbols $7a$ and $3b$ to represent additive quantities, while $4c$ and $2d$ are subtractive.

18. In Arithmetic the sum of the additive terms is always greater than the sum of the subtractive terms; if the reverse were the case the result would have no arithmetical meaning. In Algebra, however, not only may the sum of the subtractive terms exceed that of the additive, but a subtractive term may stand alone, and yet have a meaning quite intelligible.

Hence all algebraical quantities may be divided into **positive quantities** and **negative quantities**, according as they are expressed with the sign + or the sign –; and this is quite irrespective of any actual process of addition and subtraction.

This idea may be made clearer by one or two simple illustrations.

(i) Suppose a man were to gain Rs. 100 and then lose Rs. 70, his total *gain* would be Rs. 30. But if he first gains Rs. 70 and then loses 100, the result of his trading is a *loss* of Rs. 30.

The corresponding algebraical statements would be

$$\text{Rs. } 100-\text{Rs. } 70 = +\text{Rs. } 30$$
$$\text{Rs. } 70-\text{Rs. } 100, = -\text{Rs. } 30,$$

and the negative quantity in the second case is interpreted as a *debt*, that is, a sum of money opposite in character to the positive quantity, or *gain*, in the first case; in fact it may be said to possess a subtractive quality which would produce its effect on other transactions or perhaps wholly counterbalance a sum gained.

(ii) Suppose a man starting from a given point were to walk along a straight road 100 kilometres forwards and then 70 kilometres backwards, his distance from the starting-point would be 30 kilometres. But if he first walks 70 kilometres forwards and then 100 kilometres backwards, his distance from the starting-point would be 30 kilometres, but *on the opposite side of it*. As before we have 100 kilometres – 70 kilometres = + 30 kilometres,

70 kilometres – 100 kilometres = – 30 kilometres.

In each of these cases the man's *absolute distance* from the starting-point is the same; but by taking the positive and negative signs into account, we see that –30 is a distance from the starting-point *equal in magnitude but opposite in direction* to the distance represented by + 30. Thus the negative sign may here be taken as indicating *a reversal of direction*.

(iii) The freezing point of the Centigrade thermometer is marked zero and a temperature of 15°C. means 15° above the freezing point, while a temperature 15° below the freezing point is indicated by – 15°C.

19. Many other illustrations might be chosen ; but it will be sufficient here to remind the student that a subtractive quantity is always opposite in character to an additive quantity of equal *absolute value*. In other words *subtraction is the reverse of addition*.

20. DEFINITION. When terms do not differ, or when they differ only in their numerical coefficients, they are called **like**, otherwise they are called **unlike**. Thus $3a, 7a; 5a^2b, 2a^2b; 3a^3b^2 - 4a^3b^2$ are pairs of like terms; and $4a, 3b; 7a^2, 9a^2b$ are pairs of unlike terms. In the present chapter we shall only consider the addition of like terms.

The rules for adding like terms are

Rule I. *The sum of a number of like terms is a like term.*

Rule II. *If all the terms are positive, add the coefficients.*

Example. Find the value of $8a + 5a$.

Here we have to increase 8 like things by 5 like things of the same kind, and the aggregate is 13 of such things;

for instance, 8 kg + 5 kg = 13 kg.

Hence also, $8a + 5a = 13a$.

Similarly, $8a + 5a + a + 2a + 6a = 22a$.

Rule III. *If all the terms are negative, add the coefficients numerically and prefix the minus sign to the sum.*

Example. To find the sum of $-3x, -5x, -7x, -x$.

Here the word *sum* indicates the aggregate of 4 subtractive quantities of like character. In other words, we have to *take away* successively 3, 5, 7, 1 like things, and the result is the same as taking away 3 + 5 + 7 + 1 such things in the aggregate.

Thus the sum of $-3x, -5x, -7x, -x$ is $-16x$.

Rule IV. *If the terms are not all of the same sign, add together separately the coefficients of all the positive terms and the coefficients of all the negative terms; the difference of these two results, preceded by the sign of the greater, will give the coefficient of the sum required.*

Example 1. The sum of $17x$ and $-8x$ is $9x$, for the difference of 17 and 8 is 9, and the greater is positive.

Example 2. To find the sum of $8a, -9a, -a, 3a, 4a, -11a, a$.

The sum of the coefficients of the positive terms is 16.

The sum of the coefficients of the negative terms is 21.

The difference of these is 5, and the sign of the greater is negative; hence the required sum is $-5a$.

We need not, however, adhere strictly to this rule, for the terms may be added or subtracted in the order we find most convenient. This process is called **collecting terms.**

21. When quantities are connected by the signs + and –, the resulting expression is called their **algebraical sum.**

Thus $11a-27a+13a=-3a$ states that the algebraical sum of $11a, -27a, 13a$ is equal to $-3a$.

22. The sum of two quantities numerically equal but with opposite signs is zero. Thus the sum of $5a$ and $-5a$ is 0.

EXAMPLES II

Find the sum of

1. $2a, 3a, 6a, a, 4a$.

2. $4x, x, 5x, 6x, 8x$.

3. $6b, 11b, 8b, 9b, 5b$.

4. $6c, 7c, 3c, 16c, 18c, 101c$.

5. $2p, p, 4p, 7p, 6p, 12p$.

6. $d, 9d, 3d, 7d, 4d, 6d, 10d$.

7. $-2x, -6x, -10x, -8x$.

8. $-3b, -13b, -19b, -5b$.

9. $-y, -4y, -2y, -6y, -4y$.

10. $-17c, -34c, -9c, -6c$.

11. $-21y, -5y, -3y, -18y$.

12. $-4m, -13m, -17m, -59m$.

13. $-4s, 3s, s, 2s, -2s, -s$.

14. $11y, -9y, -7y, 5y, 7y$.

15. $3x, -10x, -7x, 12x, 2x$.

16. $8ab, -6ab, 5ab, -4ab$.

17. $2xy, -4xy, -3xy, xy, 7xy$.

18. $5pq, -8pq, 8pq, -4pq$.

19. $abc, -3abc, 2abc, -5abc$.

20. $-xyz, -2xyz, 7xyz, -xyz$.

Find the value of

21. $-9a^2+11a^2+3a^2-4a^2$.

22. $b^3-2b^3+7b^3-9b^3$.

23. $-11a^3+3a^3-8a^3-7a^3+2a^3$.

24. $2x^3-3x^3-6x^3-9x^3$.

25. $a^2b^2-7a^2b^2+8a^2b^2+9a^2b^2$.

26. $a^2x-11a^2x+3a^2x-2a^2x$.

27. $2p^3q^2-31p^3q^2+17p^3q^2$.

28. $7m^4n-15m^4n+3m^4n$.

29. $9abcd-11abcd-41abcd$.

30. $13pqx-5xpq-19qpx$.

CHAPTER III

SIMPLE BRACKETS. ADDITION

23. WHEN a number of arithmetical quantities are connected together by the signs + and –, the value of the result is the same in whatever order the terms are taken. This also holds in the case of algebraical quantities.

Thus $a - b + c$ is equivalent to $a + c - b$, for in the first of the two expressions b is taken from a, and c added to the result; in the second c is added to a, and b taken from the result. Similar reasoning applies to all algebraical expressions. Hence we may write the terms of an expression in any order we please.

Thus it appears that the expression $a - b$ may be written in the equivalent form $-b + a$.

To illustrate this we may suppose, as in Art. 18, that a represents a gain of a pounds, and $-b$ a loss of b pounds: it is clearly immaterial whether the gain precedes the loss or the loss, precedes the gain.

24. Brackets ( ) are used to indicate that the terms enclosed within them are to be considered as one quantity. The full use of brackets will be considered in Chap. VII; here we shall deal only with the simpler cases.

$8 + (13 + 5)$ means that 13 and 5 are to be added and their sum added to 8. It is clear that 13 and 5 may be added separately or together without altering the result.

Thus $$8 + (13 + 5) = 8 + 13 + 5 = 26\,.$$

Similarly, $a + (b + c)$ means that the sum of b and c is to be added to a.

Thus $$a + (b + c) = a + b + c\,.$$

$8 + (13 - 5)$ means that to 8 we are to add the excess of 13 over 5; now if we add 13 to 8 we have added 5 too much, and must therefore take 5 from the result.

Thus $$8 + (13 - 5) = 8 + 13 - 5 = 16\,.$$

Similarly, $a + (b - c)$ means that to a we are to add b, diminished by c.

Thus $$a + (b - c) = a + b - c.$$

In like manner; $a + b - c + (d - e - f) = a + b - c + d - e - f$.

By considering these results we are led to the following rule:

Rule. *When an expression within brackets is preceded by the sign +, the brackets can be removed without making any change in the expression.*

25. The expression $a-(b+c)$ means that from a we are to take the sum of b and c. The result will be the same whether b and c are subtracted separately or in one sum. Thus

$$a-(b+c)=a-b-c.$$

Again, $a-(b-c)$ means that from a we are to subtract the excess of b over c. If from a we take b we get $a-b$; but by so doing we shall have taken away c too much, and must therefore add c to $a-b$. Thus

$$a-(b-c)=a-b+c.$$

In like manner, $$a-b-(c-d-e)=a-b-c+d+e.$$

Accordingly the following rule may be enunciated :

Rule. *When an expression within brackets is preceded by the sign –, the brackets may be removed if the sign of every term within the brackets be changed.*

26. Addition. When two or more *like* terms are to be added together we have seen that they may be collected and the result expressed as a *single* like term. If, however, the terms are *unlike* they cannot be collected; thus in finding the sum of two unlike quantities a and b, all that can be done is to connect them by the sign of addition and leave the result in the form $a+b$.

27. We have now to consider the meaning of an expression like $a+(-b)$. Here we have to find the result of taking a negative quantity $-b$ together with a positive quantity a. Now $-b$ implies a decrease, and to add it to a is the same in effect as to subtract b ; thus

$$a+(-b)=a-b\,;$$

that is, the algebraical sum of a and $-b$ is expressed by $a-b$.

28. It will be observed that in Algebra the word *sum* is used in a wider sense than in Arithmetic. Thus, in the language of Arithmetic, $a-b$ signifies that b is to be subtracted from a, and bears that meaning only; but in Algebra it is also taken to mean the sum of the two quantities a and $-b$ without any regard to the relative magnitudes of a and b.

Example 1. Find the sum of $3a-5b+2c$, $2a+3b-d$, $-4a+2b$.

$$\begin{aligned}\text{The sum } &= (3a-5b+2c)+(2a+3b-d)+(-4a+2b)\\ &= 3a-5b+2c+2a+3b-d-4a+2b\\ &= 3a+2a-4a-5b+3b+2b+2c-d\\ &= a+2c-d,\end{aligned}$$

by collecting like terms.

The addition is, however, more conveniently effected by the following rule:

Rule. *Arrange the expressions in lines so that the like terms may be in the same vertical columns; then add each column, beginning with that on the left.*

$$\begin{array}{rrrr} 3a & -5b & +2c & \\ 2a & +3b & & -d \\ -4a & +2b & & \\ \hline a & & +2c & -d \end{array}$$

The algebraical sum of the terms in the first column is a, that of the terms in the second column is zero. The single terms in the third and fourth columns are brought down without change.

Example 2. Add together $-5ab + 6bc - 7ac; 8ab + 3ac - 2ad;$
$-2ab + 4ac + 5ad; bc - 3ab + 4ad.$

$$\begin{array}{llll} -5ab & +6bc & -7ac & \\ 8ab & & +3ac & -2ad \\ -2ab & & +4ac & +5ad \\ -3ab & +bc & & +4ad \\ \hline -2ab & +7bc & & +7ad \end{array}$$

Here we first rearrange the expressions so that like terms are in the same vertical columns, and then add up each column separately.

EXAMPLES III.a

Find the sum of

1. $3a + 2b - 5c; -4a + b - 7c; 4a - 3b + 6c.$
2. $3x + 2y + 6z; x - 3y - 3z; 2x + y - 3z.$
3. $4p + 3q + 5r; -2p + 3q - 8r; p - q + r.$
4. $7a - 5b + 3c; 11a + 2b - c; 16a + 5b - 2c.$
5. $8l - 2m + 5n; -6l + 7m + 4n; -l - 4m - 8n.$
6. $5a - 7b + 3c - 4d; 6b - 5c + 3d; b + 2c - d.$
7. $2a + 4b - 5x; 2b - 5x; -3a + 2y; -6b + 8x + y.$
8. $7x - 5y - 7z; 4x + y; 5z; 5x - 3y + 2z.$
9. $a - 2b + 7c + 3; 2b - 3c + 5; 3c + 2a; a - 8 - 7c.$
10. $5 - x - y; 7 + 2x; 3y - 2z; -4 + x - 2y.$
11. $25a - 15b + c; 4c - 10b + 13a; a - c + 20b.$
12. $2a - 3b - 2c + 2x; 5x + 3b - 7c; 9c - 6x - 2a.$
13. $3a - 5c + 2b - 2d; b + 2d - a; 5c + 3f + 3e - 2a - 3b.$

14. $p - q + 7r; 6q + r - p; q - 3p - r; 6q - 7p$.

15. $17ab - 13kl - 5xy; 7xy; 12kl - 5ab; 3xy - 4kl - ab$.

16. $2ax - 3by - 2cz; 2by - ax + 7cz; ax - 4cz + 7by; cz - 6by$.

17. $3ax + cz - 4b\,y\,; 7by - 8ax - cz; -3by + 9ax$.

18. $3 + 5cd\,; 2fg - 3st; 1 - 5cd\,; -4 + 2st - fg$.

19. $5cx + 3fy - 2 + 2s\,; -2fy + 6 - 9s\,; -3s - 4 + 2cx - fy$.

20. $-3ab + 7cd - 5qr\,; 2ry + 8qr - cd\,; 2cd - 3qr + ab - 2ry$.

29. Different powers of the same letter are unlike terms; thus the result of adding together $2x^3$ and $3x^2$ cannot be expressed by a single term, but must be left in the form $2x^3 + 3x^2$.

Similarly, the algebraical sum of $5a^2b^2$, $-3ab^3$, and $-b^4$ is $5a^2b^2 - 3ab^3 - b^4$. This expression is in its simplest form and cannot be abridged.

Example. Find the sum of $6x^3 - 5x, 2x^2, 5x, -2x^3, -3x^2, 2$.

$$\begin{aligned} \text{The sum} &= 6x^3 - 5x + 2x^2 + 5x - 2x^3 - 3x^2 + 2 \\ &= 6x^3 - 2x^3 + 2x^2 - 3x^2 - 5x + 5x + 2 \\ &= 4x^3 - x^2 + 2. \end{aligned}$$

This result is in *descending* powers of x.

30. In adding together several algebraical expressions containing terms with different powers of the same letter, it will be found convenient to arrange all expressions in *descending* or *ascending* powers of that letter. This will be made clear by the following examples.

Example. 1. Add together $3x^3 + 7 + 6x - 5x^2; 2x^2 - 8 - 9x;$ $4x - 2x^3 + 3x^2; 3x^3 - 9x - x^2; x - x^2 - x^3 + 4$.

$$\begin{array}{rrrr} 3x^3 & -5x^2 & +6x & +7 \\ & 2x^2 & -9x & -8 \\ -2x^3 & +3x^2 & +4x & \\ 3x^3 & -x^2 & -9x & \\ -x^3 & -x^2 & +x & +4 \\ \hline 3x^3 & -2x^2 & -7x & +3 \end{array}$$

In writing down the first expression we put in the first term the highest power of x, in the second term the next highest power, and so on till the last term in which x does not appear. The other expressions are arranged in the same way, so that in each column we have *like powers of the same letter.*

Example 2. Add together

$$3ab^2 - 2b^3 + a^3; 5a^2b - ab^2 - 3a^3; 8a^3 + 5b^3. 9a^2b - 2a^3 + ab^2.$$

$$\begin{array}{rrrr} -2b^3 & +\,3ab^2 & & +\,a^3 \\ & -ab^2 & +\,5a^2b & -\,3a^3 \\ 5b^3 & & & +\,8a^3 \\ & ab^2 & +\,9a^2b & -\,2a^3 \\ \hline 3b^3 & +\,3ab^2 & +\,14a^2b & +\,4a^3 \end{array}$$

Here each expression contains powers of two letters and is arranged according to *descending* powers of b, and *ascending* powers of a.

EXAMPLES III. b

Find the sum of the following expressions:

1. $x^2 + 3xy - 3y^2; -3x^2 + xy + 2y^2; 2x^2 - 3xy + y^2.$

2. $2x^2 - 2x + 3; -2x^2 + 5x + 4; x^2 - 2x - 6.$

3. $5x^3 - x^2 + x - 1; 2x^2 - 2x + 5; -5x^3 + 5x - 4.$

4. $a^3 - a^2b + 5ab^2 + b^3; -a^3 - 10ab^2 + b^3; 2a^2b + 5ab^2 - b^3.$

5. $3x^3 - 9x^2 - 11x + 7; 2x^3 - 5x^2 + 2; 5x^3 + 15x^2 - 7x; 8x - 9.$

6. $x^5 - 5x^3 + 8x; 7x^5 + 4x^3 + 5x; 8x^3 - 9x; 2x^5 - 7x^3 - 4x.$

7. $4m^3 + 2m^2 - 5m + 7; 3m^3 + 6m^2 - 2; -5m^2 + 3m; 2m - 6.$

8. $ax^3 - 4bx^2 + cx; 3bx^2 - 2cx - d; bx^2 + 2d; 2ax^3 + d.$

9. $py^2 - 9qy + 7r; -2py^2 + 3qy - 6r; 7qy - 4r; 3py^2.$

10. $5y^3 + 20y^2 + 3y - 1; -2y + 5 - 7y^2; -3y^2 - 4 + 2y^3 - y.$

11. $2 - a + 8a^2 - a^3; 2a^3 - 3a^2 + 2a - 2; -3a + 7a^3 - 5a^2.$

12. $1 + 2y - 3y^2 - 5y^3; -1 + 2y^2 - y; 5y^3 + 3y^2 + 4.$

13. $a^2x^3 - 3a^3x^2 + x; 5x + 7a^3x^2; 4a^3x^2 - a^2x^3 - 5x.$

14. $x^5 - 4x^4y - 5x^3y^3; 3x^4y + 2x^3y^3 - 6xy^4; 3x^3y^3 + 6xy^4 - y^5.$

15. $a^3 - 4a^2b + 6abc; a^2b - 10abc + c^3; b^3 + 3a^2b + abc.$

16. $ap^5 - 6bp^3 + 7cp; 5 - 6cp + 5bp^3; 3 - 2ap^5; 2cp - 7.$

17. $c^7 - 2c^5 + 11c^6; -2c^7 - 3c^6 + 5c^5; 4c^6 - 10c^5; 4c^7 - c^6.$

18. $4h^3 - 7 + 3h^4 - 2h; 7h - 3h^3 + 2 - h^4; 2h^4 + 2h^3 - 5.$

19. $3x^3 + 2y^2 - 5x + 2; 7x^3 - 5y^2 + 7x - 5; 9x^3 + 11 - 8x + 4y^2;$
$6x - y^2 - 18x^3 - 7.$

20. $x^2 + 2xy + 3y^2; \quad 3z^2 + 2yz + y^2; \quad x^2 + 3z^2 + 2xz; \quad z^2 - 3xy - 3yz;$
$xy + xz + yz - 6z^2 - 4y^2 - 2x^2.$

CHAPTER IV

SUBTRACTION

31. THE simplest cases of subtraction have already come under the head of addition of *like* terms, of which some are negative. [Art. 20.]

Thus
$$5a - 3a = 2a,$$
$$3a - 7a = -4a,$$
$$-3a - 6a = -9a.$$

Since subtraction is the reverse of addition,
$$+b - b = 0;$$
$$\therefore \quad a = a + b - b.$$

Now subtract $-b$ from the left-hand side and erase $-b$ on the right; we thus get
$$a - (-b) = a + b.$$

This also follows directly from the rule for removing brackets [Art. 25.]

Thus
$$3a - (-5a) = 3a + 5a = 8a,$$
and
$$-3a - (-5a) = -3a + 5a = 2a.$$

32. In dealing with expressions which contain unlike terms we may proceed as in the following example.

Example. Subtract $3a - 2b - c$ from $4a - 3b + 5c$.

The difference $= 4a - 3b + 5c - (3a - 2b - c)$ $= 4a - 3b + 5c - 3a + 2b + c$ $= 4a - 3a - 3b + 2b + 5c + c$ $= a - b + 6c.$	The expression to be subtracted is first enclosed in brackets with a minus sign prefixed, then on removal of the brackets the like terms are combined by the rules already explained in Art. 20.

It is, however, more convenient to arrange the work as follows, the signs of all the terms in the lower line being changed.

$$\begin{array}{r} 4a - 3b + 5c \\ -3a + 2b + c \\ \hline a - b + 6c \end{array}$$

The like terms are written in the same vertical column, and each column is treated separately.

by *addition*.

Rule. *Change the sign of every term in the expression to be subtracted, and add to the other expression.*

NOTE. It is not necessary that in the expression to be subtracted the signs should be *actually* changed; the operation of changing signs ought to be performed mentally.

Example 1. From $5x^2 + xy$ take $2x^2 + 8xy - 7y^2$.

$$\begin{array}{l} 5x^2 + xy \\ 2x^2 + 8xy - 7y^2 \\ \hline 3x^2 - 7xy + 7y^2 \end{array}$$

In the first column we combine mentally $5x^2$ and $-2x^2$, the algebraic sum of which is $3x^2$. In the last column the sign of the term $-7y^2$ has to be changed before it is put down in the result.

Example 2. Subtract $3x^2 - 2x$ from $1 - x^3$.

Terms containing different powers of the same letter being *unlike* must stand in different columns.

$$\begin{array}{llll} -x^3 & & & +1 \\ & 3x^2 & -2x & \\ \hline -x^3 & -3x^2 & +2x & +1 \end{array}$$

In the first and last columns, as there is nothing to be subtracted, the terms are put down without change of sign. In the second and third columns each sign has to be changed.

The rearrangement of terms in the first line is not *necessary*, but it is convenient, because it gives the result of subtraction in descending powers of x.

EXAMPLES (IV)

Subtract

1. $a + 2b - c$ from $2a + 3b + c$.
2. $2a - b + c$ from $3a - 5b - c$.
3. $3x + y - z$ from $x - 4y + 3z$.
4. $x + 8y + 8z$ from $10x - 7y - 6z$.
5. $-m - 3n + p$ from $-2m + n - 3p$.
6. $3p - 2q + r$ from $4p - 7q + 3r$.
7. $a - 7b - 3c$ from $-4a + 3b + 8c$.
8. $-a - b - 9c$ from $-a + b - 9c$.

Subtract

9. $3x - 5y - 7z$ from $2x + 3y - 4z$.
10. $-4x - 2y + 11z$ from $-x + 2y - 13z$.

11. $-2x-5y$ from $x+3y-2z$.
12. $3x-y-8z$ from $x+2y$.
13. $m-2n-p$ from $m+2n$.
14. $2p-3q-r$ from $2q-4r$.
15. $ab-2cd-ac$ from $-ab-3cd+2ac$.
16. $3ab+6cd-3ac-5bd$ from $3ab+5cd-4ac-6bd$.
17. $-xy+yz-zx$ from $2xy+zx$.
18. $-2pq-3qr+4rs$ from $qr-4rs$.
19. $-mn+11np-3pm$ from $-11np$.
20. x^2y-2xy^2+3xyz from $2x^2y+3xy^2-xyz$.

From

21. x^3-3x^2+x take $-x^3+3x^2-x$.
22. $-2x^3-x^2$ take x^3-x^2-x.
23. a^3+b^3-3abc take b^3-2abc.
24. $-8+6bc+b^2c^2$ take $4-3bc-5b^2c^2$.
25. $3p^3-2p^2q+7pq^2$ take $p^2q-3pq^2+q^3$.
26. $7+x-x^2$ take $5-x+x^2+x^3$.
27. $-4+x^2y-xyz$ take $-3-2x^2y+11xyz$.
28. $-8a^2x^2+5x^2+15$ take $9a^2x^2-8x^2-5$.
29. p^3+r^3-3pqr take r^3+q^3+3pqr.
30. $1-3x^2$ take x^3-3x^2+1.
31. $2+3x-7x^2$ take $3x^2-3x-2$.
32. x^3+11x^2+4 take $8x^2-5x-3$.
33. a^3+5-2a^2 take $8a^3+3a^2-7$.
34. $x^4+3x^3-x^2-8$ take $2x^4+3x^2-x+2$.
35. $1-2x+3x^2$ take $7x^3-4x^2+3x+1$.
36. x^2yz+y^2zx take $-3y^2zx-2xyz^2-x^2yz$.
37. $4a^3x^2-3ax^4+a^5$ take $3a^3x^2+7a^2x^3-a^5$.
38. $1-x+x^5-x^4-x^3$ take $x^4-1+x-x^2$.
39. $-8mn^2+15m^2n+n^3$ take $m^3-n^3+8mn^2-7m^2n$.
40. $1-p^3$ take $2p^3-3pq^2-2q^3$.

33. The following exercise contains miscellaneous examples on the foregoing rules.

MISCELLANEOUS EXAMPLES I

1. When $x=2$, $y=3$, $z=4$, find the value of the sum of $5x^2, -3xy, z^2$. Also find the value of $3z^x + 3xy$.
2. Add together $3ab+bc-ca$, $-ab+ca$, $ab-2bc+5ca$. From the sum take $5ca+bc-ab$.
3. Subtract the sum of $x-y+3z$ and $-2y-2z$ from the sum of $2x-5y-3z$ and $-3x+y+4z$.
4. Simplify
   (1) $3b-2b^2-(2b-3b^2)$.
   (2) $3a-2b-(2b+a)-(a-5b)$.
5. Subtract $8c^2+8c-2$ from c^3-1.
6. When $x=3$, $a=2$, $y=4$, $z=0$, find the value of
   (1) $2x^2-3ay+4xz^3$.
   (2) $\dfrac{5a^3x}{3y}$.
7. Add together $3a^2-7a+5$ and $2a^3+5a-3$, and diminish the result by $3a^2+2$.
8. Subtract $2b^2-2$ from $-2b+6$, and increase the result by $3b-7$.
9. Find the sum of $3x^2-4x+8$, $2x-3-x^2$, and $2x^2-2$, and subtract the result from $6x^2+3$.
10. What expression must be added to $5a^2-3a+12$ to produce $9a^2-7$?
11. Find the sum of $2x$, $-x^3$, $3x^2$, 2, $-5x$, -4, $3x^3$, $-5x^2$, 8; arrange the result in ascending powers of x.
12. From what expression must the sum of $5a^2-2$, $3a+a^2$, and $7-2a$ be subtracted to produce $3a^2+a-5$?
13. When $x=6$, find the numerical value of the sum of $1-x+x^2$, $2x^2-1$, and $x-x^2$.
14. Find the value of $6ax+(2by-cz)-(2ax-3by+4cz)-(cz+ax)$, when $a=0$, $b=1$, $c=2$, $x=8$, $y=3$, $z=4$.
15. Subtract the sum of x^3-3x^2, $2x^2-7x$, $8x-2$, $5-3x^3$, $2x^3-7$ from x^3+x^2+x+1.

16. What expression must be taken from the sum of $p^4-3p^3, 2p+8, 2p^2$, $2p^3-3p^4$, in order to produce $4p^4-3$?

17. What is the result when $-3x^3+2x^2-11x+5$ is subtracted from zero?

18. By how much does $b+c$ exceed $b-c$?

19. Find the algebraic sum of three times the square of x, twice the cube of x, $-x^3+x-2x^2$, and x^3-x-x^2+1.

20. Take p^2-q^2 from $3pq-4q^2$, and add the remainder to the sum of $4pq-p^2-3q^2$ and $2p^2+6q^2$.

21. Subtract $3b^3+2b^2-8$ from zero, and add the result to b^4-2b^3+3b.

22. By how much does the sum of $-m^3+2m-1$, m^2-3m, $2m^3-2m^2+5$, $3m^3+4m^2+5m+3$, fall short of $11m^3-8m^2+3m$?

23. Find the sum of $8x^5-4x^3y^2$, $7x^4y-xy^4$, $3x^3y^2+2x^2y^3+5xy^4$, $y^5-4xy^4+x^3y^2$, $x^5-y^5+x^3y^2+xy^4-x^2y^3+3x^4y$, and arrange the result in descending powers of x.

24. To what expression must $3x-4x^3+7x^2+4$ be added so as to make zero? Give the answer in ascending powers of x.

25. Subtract $7x^2-3x-6$ from unity, and $x-5x^2$ from zero, and add the results.

26. When $a=4, b=3, c=2, d=0$, find the value of

(1) $3a^2-2bc-ad+3b^2cd$.

(2) $\dfrac{2b^2c}{9a}$.

27. Find the sum of $a, -3a^2, 4a, -5a, 7, -18a, 4a^2, -6$, and arrange the result in descending powers of a.

28. Add together $4+3x^2+x^3$, x^3-x^2-11, x^3-2x^2+7, and subtract $2x^3+x^2-7$ from the result.

29. If $a=5x-3y+z$, $b=-2x+y-3z$, $c=x-5y+6z$, find the value of $a+b-c$.

30. If $x=2a^2-5a+3$, $y=-3a^2+a+8$, $z=5a^2-6a-5$, find the value of $x-(y+z)$.

CHAPTER V

MULTIPLICATION

34. MULTIPLICATION in its primary sense signifies repeated addition.

Thus $3 \times 5 = 3$ taken 5 times

$$= 3 + 3 + 3 + 3 + 3.$$

Here the multiplier contains 5 units, and the number of times we take 3 is the same as the number of units in 5.

Again $a \times b = a$ taken b times

$$= a + a + a + a \ldots, \text{ the number of terms being } b.$$

Also $3 \times 5 = 5 \times 3$; and so long as a and b denote positive whole numbers it is easy to shew that

$$a \times b = b \times a.$$

Hence

$$abc = a \times b \times c = (a \times b) \times c = b \times a \times c = bac$$
$$= b \times (a \times c) = b \times c \times a = bca.$$

Similarly we can shew that the product of three positive integral quantities a, b, c is the same in whatever order the factors are written.

Example. $2a \times 3b = 2 \times a \times 3 \times b = 2 \times 3 \times a \times b = 6ab$.

35. When the quantities to be multiplied together are not positive whole numbers, the definition of multiplication has to be modified. For example, to multiply 3 by $\frac{4}{7}$, we perform on 3 that operation which when performed on unity gives $\frac{4}{7}$; that is, we must divide 3 into 7 equal parts and take 4 of them.

By taking multiplication in this sense, the statement $ab = ba$ can be extended so as to include every case in which a and b stand for positive quantities.

It follows as in the previous article that the product of a number of positive factors is the same in whatever order the factors are written.

36. Since, by definition, $a^3 = aaa$, and $a^5 = aaaaa$;

$$\therefore \quad a^3 \times a^5 = aaa \times aaaaa = aaaaaaaa = a^8 = a^{3+5};$$

that is, the index of a in the product is the sum of the indices of a in the factors of the product.

Again, $5a^2 = 5aa$, and $7a^3 = 7aaa$;

$\therefore$ $5a^2 \times 7a^3 = 5 \times 7 \times aaaaa = 35a^5$.

When the expressions to be multiplied together contain powers of different letters, a similar method is used.

Example. $5a^3b^2 \times 8a^2bx^3 = 5aaabb \times 8\,aabxxx = 40a^5b^3x^3$.

Note. The beginner must be careful to observe that in this process of multiplication *the indices of one letter cannot combine in any way with those of another.* Thus the expression $40a^5b^3x^3$ admits of no further simplification.

37. Rule. *To multiply two simple expressions together, multiply the coefficients together and prefix their product to the product of the different letters, giving to each letter an index equal to the sum of the indices that letter has in the separate factors.*

The rule may be extended to cases where more than two expressions are to be multiplied together.

Example 1. Find the product of x^2, x^3, and x^8.

The product $= x^2 \times x^3 \times x^8 = x^{2+3} \times x^8 = x^{2+3+8} = x^{13}$.

The product of three or more expressions is called the **continued product**.

Example 2. Find the continued product of $5x^2y^3$, $8y^2z^5$, and $3xz^4$.

The product $= 5x^2y^3 \times 8y^2z^5 \times 3xz^4 = 120x^3y^5z^9$.

38. By definition, $(a+b)\,m = m + m + m + \ldots$ taken $a+b$ times

$= (m+m+m+\ldots$ taken a times$)$,

together with $(m+m+m+\ldots$ taken b times$)$,

$= am + bm$.

Also $(a-b)\,m = m + m + m + \ldots$ taken $a-b$ times,

$= (m+m+m+\ldots$ taken a times$)$,

diminished by $(m+m+m+\ldots$ taken b times$)$,

$= am - bm$.

Similarly, $(a-b+c)\,m = am - bm + cm$.

Thus, it appears that *the product of a compound expression by a single factor is the algebraic sum of the partial products of each term of the compound expression by that factor.*

Examples. $3\,(2a+3b-4c) = 6a + 9b - 12c$.

$(4x^2 - 7y - 8z^3) \times 3xy^2 = 12x^3y^2 - 21xy^3 - 24xy^2z^3$.

EXAMPLES V. a

Find the value of

1. $5x \times 7$.
2. $3 \times 2b$.
3. $x^2 \times x^3$.
4. $5x \times 6x^2$.
5. $6c^3 \times 7c^4$.
6. $9y^2 \times 5y^5$.
7. $3m^3 \times 5m^5$.
8. $4a^6 \times 6a^4$.
9. $3x \times 4y$.
10. $5a \times 6b^2$.
11. $4c^2 \times 5d^5$.
12. $3p^4 \times 5q^5$.
13. $6ax \times 5ax$.
14. $3qr \times 4qr$.
15. $ab \times ab$.
16. $3ac \times 5ad$.
17. $a^3x \times a^4x^3$.
18. $3x^3y^2 \times 4y^5$.
19. $a^3b^5 \times a^5b^4$.
20. $a^4 \times 3a^5b^3$.
21. $a^2 \times a^3b \times 5ab^4$.
22. $pr^4 \times 6p^3r \times 7pr^5$.
23. $6x^3y \times xy \times 9x^4y^2$.
24. $7a^2 \times 3b^3 \times 5c^4$.
25. $6xy^2 \times 7yz^2 \times xz^3$.
26. $3abcd \times 5bca^2 \times 4cabd$.

Multiply

27. $ab - ac$ by a^2c.
28. $x^2y - x^3z + 4yz^5$ by x^3yz^3.
29. $5a^2 - 3b^2$ by $3\,ab^2c^4$.
30. $a^2b - 5ab + 6a$ by $3a^3b$.
31. $a^2 - 2b^3$ by $3x^2$.
32. $2ax^3 - b^3y + 3$ by a^2xy.
33. $7p^2q - pq^2 + 1$ by $2p^2$.
34. $m^2 + 5mn - 3n^2$ by $4m^2n$.
35. $xy^2 - 3x^2z - 2$ by $3yz$.
36. $a^3 - 3a^2x$ by $2a^2bx$.

39. Since $(a-b)\,m = am - bm$, [Art. 38.]

by putting $c-d$ in the place of m, we have

$$\begin{aligned}(a-b)(c-d) &= a(c-d) - b(c-d)\\ &= (c-d)\,a - (c-d)\,b\\ &= (ac-ad) - (bc-bd)\\ &= ac - ad - bc + bd.\end{aligned}$$

If we consider each term on the right-hand side of this result, and the way in which it arises, we find that

$$\begin{aligned}(+a)\times(+c) &= +ac.\\ (-b)\times(-d) &= +bd.\\ (-b)\times(+c) &= -bc.\\ (+a)\times(-d) &= -ad.\end{aligned}$$

These results enable us to state what is known as the **Rule of Signs** in multiplication.

Rule of Signs. *The product of two terms with like signs is positive; the product of two terms with unlike signs is negative.*

40. The rule of signs, and especially the use of the negative multiplier, will probably present some difficulty to the beginner. Perhaps the following numerical instances may be useful in illustrating the interpretation that may be given to multiplication by a negative quantity.

To multiply 3 by -4 we must do to 3 what is done to unity to obtain -4. Now -4 means that unity is taken 4 times and the result made negative: therefore $3\times(-4)$ implies that 3 is to be taken 4 times and the product made negative.

But 3 taken 4 times gives $+12$;

$$\therefore \qquad 3\times(-4)=-12.$$

Similarly, -3×-4 indicates that -3 is to be taken 4 times, and the sign changed; the first operation gives -12, and the second $+12$.

Thus $$(-3)\times(-4)=+12.$$

Hence, *multiplication by a negative quantity indicates that we are to proceed just as if the multiplier were positive, and then change the sign of the product.*

Example 1. Multiply $4a$ by $-3b$.

By the rule of signs the product is negative; also $4a\times 3b=12ab$;

$$\therefore \qquad 4a\times(-3b)=-12\,ab.$$

Example 2. Multiply $-5ab^3x$ by $-ab^3x$.

Here the absolute value of the product is $5a^2b^6x^2$, and by the rule of signs the product is positive;

$$\therefore \quad (-5ab^3x)\times(-ab^3x)=5a^2b^6x^3.$$

Example 3. Find the continued product of $3a^2b, -2a^3b^2, -ab^4$.

$3a^2b\times(-2a^3b^2)=-6a^5b^3;$

$-(6a^5b^3)\times(-ab^4)=+6a^6b^7.$

This result, however, may be written down at once; for

$$3a^2b\times 2a^3b^2\times ab^4=6a^6b^7.$$

and by the rule of signs the required product is positive.

Thus the complete product is $6a^6b^7$.

Example 4. Multiply $6a^3-5a^2b-4ab^2$ by $-3ab^2$.

The product is the algebraical sum of the partial products formed according to the rule enunciated in Art. 37;

thus $(6a^3-5a^2b-4ab^2)\times(-3ab^2)=-18a^4b^2+15a^3b^3+12a^2b^4.$

EXAMPLES V. b

Multiply together

1. $a, -2.$
2. $-3, 4x.$
3. $-x^2, -x^3.$
4. $-5m, 3m^3.$
5. $-4q, 3q^2.$
6. $-4y^3, -4y^3.$
7. $-3m^3, 3m^3.$
8. $4x^4, -4x^4.$
9. $-3x, -4y.$
10. $-5a^2, 4x.$
11. $-3p^2, -4q^5.$
12. $3ab, -4ab.$
13. $3a^2, -b^2, 2ab.$
14. $-a, -b, -c^2.$
15. $3a^2, -2b, -4c^3, -d.$
16. $-3ab, -4ac, 3bc.$
17. $-2a^3, -3a^2b, -6.$
18. $-2p, -3q, 4s, -t.$

Multiply

19. $-ab+ac-bc$ by $-ab.$
20. $-3a^2-4ax+5x^2$ by $-a^2x^3.$
21. $a^2c-ac^3+c^4$ by $-a^3c.$
22. $-2ab+cd-ef$ by $-3x^2y^2.$

41. To further illustrate the use of the rule of signs, we add a few examples in substitution where some of the symbols denote negative quantities.

Example 1. If $a=-4$, find the value of a^3.

Here $a^3=(-4)^3=(-4)\times(-4)\times(-4)=-64$.

By repeated applications of the rule of signs it may easily be shewn that any *odd* power of a negative quantity is *negative,* and any *even* power of a negative quantity is *positive.*

Example 2. If $a=-1, b=3, c=-2$, find the value of $-3a^4bc^3$.

Here $-3a^4bc^3=-3\times(-1)^4\times3\times(-2)^3$

$=-3\times(+1)\times3\times(-8)$
$=72.$

We write down at once, $(-1)^4=+1$, and $(-2)^3=-8$.

EXAMPLES V.c

If $a=-1, b=0, c=-2, n=1, q=-3$, find the value of

1. $3c.$
2. $-5a.$
3. $an.$
4. $(-a)^2.$
5. $-3c^2.$
6. $(-q)^4.$

7. $-2a^3$.
8. $-ac$.
9. ab.
10. $-acn$.
11. $-3a^4$.
12. $4(-c)^3$.
13. $2abc^2$.
14. $-c^2$.
15. $-(a)^4$.
16. $-3a^2q$.
17. $-a^3n^2$.
18. ac^3.
19. $-a^3c^2$.
20. c^3q^2.

If $a=-3, c=1, k=0, x=5, y=-1$, find the value of

21. $3a-2y+4k$.
22. $-4c-3x+2y$.
23. $-4a+5y-x$.
24. $ac-3cy-yk$.
25. $2ay-kx+4k^2$.
26. $a^2-2c^2+3y^2$.
27. $-a^2-ay+3y^2$.
28. $ax-yx-cy$.
29. $c^2-y^2-c^3+y^3$.
30. a^3-x^2-2y.
31. $c^2y^2-2ac^2+ck^2$.
32. $acy-y^4+2a^2$.

Multiplication of Compound Expressions

42. *To find the product of $a+b$ and $c+d$.*

From Art. 38, $(a+b)m=am+bm$;
replacing m by $c+d$, we have

$$\begin{aligned}(a+b)(c+d)&=a(c+d)+b(c+d)\\&=(c+d)a+(c+d)b\\&=ac+ad+bc+bd.\end{aligned}$$

Similarly it may be shewn that

$$\begin{aligned}(a-b)(c+d)&=ac+ad-bc-bd;\\(a+b)(c-d)&=ac-ad+bc-bd;\\(a-b)(c-d)&=ac-ad-bc+bd.\end{aligned}$$

43. When one or both of the expressions to be multiplied together contain more than two terms a similar method may be used. For instance,

$$(a-b+c)m=am-bm+cm;$$

replacing m by $x-y$, we have

$$\begin{aligned}(a-b+c)(x-y)&=a(x-y)-b(x-y)+c(x-y)\\&=(ax-ay)-(bx-by)+(cx-cy)\\&=ax-ay-bx+by+cx-cy.\end{aligned}$$

44. The preceeding results enable us to state the general rule for multiplying together any two compound expressions.

Rule. *Multiply each term of the first expression by each term of the second. When the terms multiplied together have like signs, prefix to the product the sign +, when unlike prefix –; the algebraical sum of the partial products so formed gives the complete product.*

45. It should be noticed that the product of $a+b$ and $x-y$ is briefly expressed by $(a+b)(x-y)$, in which the brackets indicate that the expression $a+b$ taken as a whole is to be multiplied by the expression $x-y$ taken as a whole. By the above rule, the value of the product is the algebraical sum of the partial products $+ax, +bx, -ay, -by$; the sign of each product being determined by the rule of signs.

Example 1. Multiply $x+8$ by $x+7$.

$$\begin{aligned}\text{The product} &= (x+8)(x+7)\\ &= x^2+8x+7x+56\\ &= x^2+15x+56.\end{aligned}$$

The operation is more conveniently arranged as follows:

$$\begin{array}{r} x+8\\ x+7\\ \hline x^2+8x\qquad\\ +7x+56\\ \hline \text{by addition,}\quad x^2+15x+56\end{array}$$

We begin on the left and work to the right, placing the second result one place to the right, so that like terms may stand in the same vertical column.

Example 2. Multiply $2x-3y$ by $4x-7y$.

$$\begin{array}{r} 2x-3y\qquad\\ 4x-7y\qquad\\ \hline 8x^2-12xy\qquad\\ -14xy+21y^2\\ \hline \text{by addition,}\quad 8x^2-26xy+21y^2.\end{array}$$

EXAMPLES V.d

Find the product of

1. $a+7, a+5$.
2. $x-3, x+4$.
3. $a-6, a-7$.
4. $y-4, y+4$.
5. $x+9, x-8$.
6. $c-8, c+8$.
7. $k+5, k-5$.
8. $m-9, m+12$.
9. $x-12, x+11$.
10. $a-14, a+1$.
11. $p-10, p+10$.
12. $d+7, d+7$.
13. $x-4, -x+4$.
14. $-y+3, -y-3$.
15. $-a+4, -a+5$.
16. $x-10, -x+8$.
17. $-k+4, -k-7$.
18. $-y-7, -y-7$.
19. $2a-5, 3a+2$.
20. $x-7, 2x+5$.
21. $3x-4, 2x+3$.
22. $3y-5, y+7$.
23. $5m-4, 7m-3$.
24. $7p-2, 2p+7$.
25. $x-3a, 2x+3a$.
26. $3a-2b, 2a+3b$.
27. $5c+4d, 5c-4d$.
28. $a-2x, 3a+2x$.
29. $7b+c, 7b-2c$.
30. $2a-5c, 2a+5c$.
31. $3x-5y, 4x+y$.
32. $2y-3z, 2y+3z$.
33. $xy+2b, xy-2b$.
34. $2x-3a, 2x+3b$.
35. $3x-4y, 2a+3b$.
36. $mn-p, 2xy+3z$.

46. We shall now give a few examples of greater difficulty.

Example 1. Find the product of $3x^2-2x-5$ and $2x-5$.

$$\begin{array}{l} 3x^2-2x-5 \\ 2x-5 \\ \hline 6x^3-4x^2-10x \\ \qquad -15x^2+10x+25 \\ \hline 6x^3-19x^2 \qquad\quad +25. \end{array}$$

Each term of the first expression is multiplied by $2x$, the first term of the second expression; then each term of the first expression is multiplied by -5; like terms are placed in the same column and results added.

Example 2. Multiply $a-b+3c$ by $a+2b$.

$$\begin{array}{l} a-b+3c \\ a+2b \\ \hline a^2-ab+3ac \\ \qquad\quad 2ab \quad -2b^2+6bc \\ \hline a^2+ab+3ac-2b^2+6bc. \end{array}$$

47. If the expressions are not arranged according to powers, ascending or descending, of some common letter, a rearrangement will be found convenient.

Example. Find the product of $2a^2+4b^2-3ab$ and $3ab-5a^2+4b^2$.

$$\begin{array}{l} 2a^2-3ab+4b^2 \\ -5a^2+3ab+4b^2 \\ \hline -10a^4+15a^3b-20a^2b^2 \\ \qquad\quad +6a^3b-9a^2b^2+12ab^3 \\ \qquad\qquad\quad 8a^2b^2-12ab^3+16b^4 \\ \hline -10a^4+21a^3b-21a^2b^2 \qquad +16b^4 \end{array}$$

The rearrangement is not *necessary*, but convenient, because it makes the collection of like terms more easy.

EXAMPLES V.e

Multiply together

1. $x^2-3x-2,\ 2x-1.$
2. $4a^2-a-2,\ 2a+3.$
3. $2y^2-3y+1,\ 3y-1.$
4. $3x^2+4x+5,\ 4x-5.$
5. $2a^2-3a-6,\ a-2.$
6. $5b^2-2b+3,\ -2b-3.$
7. $3x^2-2x+7, 2x-7.$
8. $5c^2-4c+3,\ -2c+1.$
9. $x^2+x-2,\ x^2-x+2.$
10. $x^2-2x+5,\ x^2-2x+5.$
11. $2a^2-3a-6,\ a^2-a+2.$
12. $2k^2-3k-1,\ 3k^2-k-1.$
13. $a+b-c,\ a-b+c.$
14. $a-2b-3c,\ a-2b+3c.$
15. $x^2-xy+y^2, x^2+xy+y^2.$
16. $a^2-2ax+2x^2,\ a^2+2ax+2x^2.$
17. $a^2-b^2-3c^2,\ -a^2-b^2-3c^2.$
18. $x^3-3x^2-x,\ x^2-3x+1.$
19. $a^3-6a+5,\ a^3+6a-5.$
20. $2y^4-4y^2+1,\ 2y^4-4y^2-1.$
21. $5m^2+3-4m,\ 5-4m+3m^2.$
22. $8a^3-2a^2-3a,\ 3a^2+1-5a.$
23. $2x+2x^3-3x^2,\ 3x+2+2x^2.$
24. $a^3+b^3-a^2b^2,\ a^2b^2-a^3+b^3.$
25. $a^3+x^3+3ax^2+3a^2x,\ a^3+3ax^2-x^3-3a^2x.$

26. $5p^4 - p^3 + 4p^2 - 2p + 3,\ p^2 - 2p + 3.$

27. $m^5 - 2m^4 + 3m^3 - 4m^2,\ 4m^6 - 3m^5 + 2m^4.$

28. $a^4 + 1 + 6a^2 - 4a^3 - 4a,\ a^3 - 1 + 3a - 3a^2.$

29. $a^2 + b^2 + c^2 + ab + ac - bc,\ a - b - c.$

30. $x^4 + 6x^2y^2 + y^4 - 4x^3y - 4xy^3,\ -x^4 - y^4 - 6x^2y^2 - 4xy^3 - 4x^3y.$

48. Although the result of multiplying together two binomial factors, such as $x+8$ and $x-7$, can always be obtained by the methods already explained, it is of the atmost importance that the student should soon learn to write down the product rapidly *by inspection.*

This is done by observing in what way the coefficients of the terms in the product arise, and noticing that they result from the combination of the numerical coefficients in the two binomials which are multiplied together; thus

$$(x+8)(x+7) = x^2 + 8x + 7x + 56$$
$$= x^2 + 15x + 56.$$
$$(x-8)(x-7) = x^2 - 8x - 7x + 56$$
$$= x^2 - 15x + 56.$$
$$(x+8)(x-7) = x^2 + 8x - 7x - 56$$
$$= x^2 + x - 56.$$
$$(x-8)(x+7) = x^2 - 8x + 7x - 56$$
$$= x^2 - x - 56.$$

In each of these results we notice that:

1. The product consists of three terms.
2. The first term is the product of the first terms of the two binomial expressions.
3. The third term is the product of the second terms of the two binomial expressions.
4. The middle term has for its coefficient the sum of the numerical quantities (taken with their proper signs) in the second terms of the two binomial expressions.

The intermediate step in the work may be omitted, and the products written down at once, as in the following examples:

$$(x+2)(x+3) = x^2 + 5x + 6.$$
$$(x-3)(x+4) = x^2 + x - 12.$$
$$(x+6)(x-9) = x^2 - 3x - 54.$$
$$(x-4y)(x-10y) = x^2 - 14xy + 40y^2.$$
$$(x-6y)(x+4y) = x^2 - 2xy - 24y^2.$$

By an easy extension of these principles we may write down the product of *any* two binomials.

Thus $(2x+3y)(x-y)=2x^2+3xy-2xy-3y^2$

$$=2x^2+xy-3y^2.$$

$$(3x-4y)(2x+y)=6x^2-8xy+3xy-4y^2$$

$$=6x^2-5xy-4y^2.$$

$$(x+4)(x-4)=x^2+4x-4x-16$$

$$=x^2-16.$$

$$(2x+5y)(2x-5y)=4x^2+10xy-10xy-25y^2$$

$$=4x^2-25y^2.$$

EXAMPLES V.f

Write down the values of the following products:

1. $(a+3)(a-2)$.

2. $(a-7)(a-6)$.

3. $(x-4)(x+5)$.

4. $(b-6)(b+4)$.

5. $(y-7)(y-1)$.

6. $(a-1)(a-9)$.

7. $(c-5)(c+4)$.

8. $(x-9)(x-3)$.

9. $(y-4)(y+7)$.

10. $(a-3)(a+3)$.

11. $(x-5)(x-8)$.

12. $(a+7)(a-7)$.

13. $(k-6)(k-6)$.

14. $(a-5)(a+5)$.

15. $(c+7)(c+7)$.

16. $(p+9)(p-10)$.

17. $(z+5)(z-8)$.

18. $(x-9)(x+9)$.

19. $(x-3a)(x+2a)$.

20. $(a-2b)(a+2b)$.

21. $(x-4y)(x-4y)$.

22. $(a+4c)(a+4c)$.

23. $(c-5d)(c-5d)$.

24. $(p-2q)(p+2q)$.

25. $(2x-3)(3x+2)$.

26. $(3x-1)(2x+1)$.

27. $(5x-2)(5x+2)$.

28. $(3x+2a)(3x-2a)$.

29. $(6x+a)(6x-2a)$.

30. $(7x+3y)(7x-y)$.

CHAPTER VI

DIVISION

49. THE object of division is to find out the quantity, called the **quotient**, by which the **divisor** must be multiplied so as to produce the **dividend**.

Division is thus the inverse of multiplication.

The above statement may be briefly written

quotient × divisor = dividend,

or dividend ÷ divisor = quotient.

It is sometimes better to express this last result as a fraction, thus

$$\frac{\text{dividend}}{\text{divisor}} = \text{quotient}.$$

Example 1. Since the product of 4 and x is $4x$, it follows that when $4x$ is divided by x the quotient is 4,

or otherwise, $4x \div x = 4$.

Example 2. Divide $27a^5$ by $9a^3$.

$$\text{The quotient} = \frac{27a^5}{9a^3} = \frac{27aaaaa}{9aaa} = 3aa = 3a^2.$$

We remove from the divisor and dividend and factors common to both, just as in arithmetic.

Therefore, $27a^5 \div 9a^3 = 3a^2$.

Example 3. Divide $35a^3b^2c^3$ by $7ab^2c^2$.

$$\text{The quotient} = \frac{35aaa \cdot bb \cdot ccc}{7a \cdot bb \cdot cc} = 5aa \cdot c = 5a^2c.$$

In each of these cases it should be noticed that the index of any letter in the quotient is the difference of the indices of that letter in the dividend and divisor.

50. It is easy to prove that *the rule of signs holds for division.*

Thus

$$ab \div a = \frac{ab}{a} = \frac{a \times b}{a} = b.$$

$$-ab \div a = \frac{-ab}{a} = \frac{a \times (-b)}{a} = -b.$$

$$ab \div (-a) = \frac{ab}{-a} = \frac{(-a) \times (-b)}{-a} = -b.$$

$$-ab \div (-a) = \frac{-ab}{-a} = \frac{(-a) \times b}{-a} = b.$$

Hence in division as well as multiplication
like signs produce +,
unlike signs produce –.

Rule. To divide one simple expression by another:

The index of each letter in the quotient is obtained by subtracting the index of that letter in the divisor from that in the dividend.

To the result so obtained prefix with its proper sign the quotient of the coefficient of the dividend by that of the divisor.

Example 1. Divide $84a^5x^3$ by $-12a^4x$.

The quotient $= (-7) \times a^{5-4}x^{3-1} = -7ax^2$.

Or at once mentally,

$$84a^5x^3 \div (-12a^4x) = -7ax^2.$$

Example 2. $-45a^6b^2x^4 \div (-9a^3bx^2) = 5a^3bx^2$.

Note. If we apply the rule to divide any power of a letter by the same power of the letter we are led to a curious conclusion.

Thus, by the rule

$$a^3 \div a^3 = a^{3-3} = a^0;$$

but also $a^3 \div a^3 = \dfrac{a^3}{a^3} = 1,$

$$\therefore \quad a^0 = 1.$$

This result will appear somewhat strange to the beginner, but its full significance is explained in the Theory of Indices.

[See *Elementary Algebra*, Chap-XXX Art. 238.]

Rule. *To divide a compound expression by a single factor, divide each term separately by that factor, and take the algebraic sum of the partial quotients so obtained.*

This follows at once from Art. 38.

Examples. $(9x - 12y + 3z) \div (-3) = -3x + 4y - z.$

$$(36a^3b^2 - 24a^2b^5 - 20a^4b^2) \div 4a^2b = 9ab - 6b^4 - 5a^2b.$$

EXAMPLES VI. a

Divide

1. $2x^3$ by x^2.
2. $6a^5$ by $3a$.
3. $5a^7$ by a^4.
4. $21b^7$ by $7b^3$.
5. x^3y^2 by $-xy$.
6. $-3xy^3$ by $3y$.
7. $4p^2q^3$ by $-2pq$.
8. $15m^3n$ by $-5m$.

9. $-l^3m^2$ by $-lm$.
10. $-48x^9$ by $-6x^3$.
11. $35z^{11}$ by $-7z^5$.
12. $-7a^3b$ by $-7b$.
13. $-28p^5q$ by $28p^5$.
14. $-7x^8$ by $-x^7$.
15. $24xyz^3$ by $-3z^2$.
16. $-12b^2c^5$ by $6b^2c^5$.
17. $-9k^{11}$ by $-k^{11}$.
18. $2k^3l^5$ by $-kl$.
19. $-45a^4b^3c^{15}$ by $9a^2b^3c^{10}$.
20. $-x^3y^4z^5$ by $-x^3yz^5$.
21. $-168a^2b^2cx^2$ by $-7abx^2$.
22. $-35a^6b^6x^7$ by $-7a^2b^4x^7$.
23. $3x^2-2x$ by x.
24. $5a^3b-7ab^3$ by ab.
25. $48p^2q-24pq^2$ by $8pq$.
26. $-15x^5+25x^4$ by $-5x^3$.
27. $x^2-xy-xz$ by $-x$.
28. $10a^3-5a^2b+a$ by $-a$.
29. $4x^3+36ax^2-16x$ by $-4x$.
30. $3a^3-9a^2b-6ab^2$ by $-3a$.

51. To divide one compound expression by another:

Rule. 1. *Arrange divisor and dividend in ascending or descending powers of some common letter.*

2. *Divide the term on the left of the dividend by the term on the left of the divisor, and put the result in the quotient.*

3. *Multiply the WHOLE divisor by this quotient, and put the product under the dividend.*

4. *Subtract and bring down from the dividend as many terms as may be necessary.*

Repeat these operations till all the terms from the dividend are brought down.

Example 1. Divide $x^2+11x+30$ by $x+6$.

Arrange the work thus:

$$x+6)x^2+11x+30($$

divide x^2, the first term of the dividend, by x, the first term of the divisor; the quotient is x. Multiply the *whole* divisor by x, and put the product x^2+6x under the dividend.

We then have

$$x+6)x^2+11x+30(x$$
$$\underline{x^2+6x}$$

by subtraction, $\quad 5x+30$

On repeating the process above explained, we find that the next term in the quotient is + 5.

The entire operation is more compactly written as follows:

$$x+6)x^2+11x+30(x+5$$
$$\underline{x^2+6x}$$
$$5x+30$$
$$\underline{5x+30}$$

The reason for the rule is this : the dividend is separated into as many parts as may be convenient, and the complete quotient is found by taking the sum of all the partial quotients. By the above process $x^2+11x+30$ is separated into two parts, namely, x^2+6x, and $5x+30$, and each of these is divided by $x+6$; thus we obtain the partial quotients $+x$ and $+5$.

Example 2. Divide $24x^2-65xy+21y^2$ by $8x-3y$.

$$8x-3y)24x^2-65xy+21y^2(3x-7y$$
$$\underline{24x^2-9xy}$$
$$-56xy+21y^2$$
$$\underline{-56xy+21y^2}$$

Divide $24x^2$ by $8x$, this gives $3x$, the first term of the quotient. Multiply the whole divisor by $3x$, and place the result under the dividend. By subtraction we obtain $-56xy+21y^2$. Divide the first term of this by $8x$, and so obtain $-7y$, the second term of the quotient.

Example 3. Divide $16a^3-46a^2+39a-9$ by $8a-3$.

$$8a-3)16a^3-46a^2+39a-9(2a^2-5a+3$$
$$\underline{16a^3-6a^2}$$
$$-40a^2+39a$$
$$\underline{-40a^2+15a}$$
$$24a-9$$
$$\underline{24a-9}$$

Thus the quotient is $2a^2-5a+3$.

EXAMPLES VI. b

Divide

1. a^2+2a+1 by $a+1$.

2. b^2+3b+2 by $b+2$.

3. x^2+4x+3 by $x+1$.

4. y^2+5y+6 by $y+3$.

5. x^2+5x-6 by $x-1$.

6. x^2+2x-8 by $x-2$.

7. $p^2+3p-40$ by $p+8$.

8. $q^2-4q-32$ by $q+4$.

9. $a^2 + 5a - 50$ by $a + 10$.

10. $m^2 + 7m - 78$ by $m - 6$.

11. $x^2 + ax - 30a^2$ by $x + 6a$.

12. $a^2 + 9ab - 36b^2$ by $a + 12b$.

13. $-x^2 + 18x - 45$ by $x - 15$.

14. $x^2 - 42x + 441$ by $x - 21$.

15. $2x^2 - 13x - 24$ by $2x + 3$.

16. $5x^2 + 16x + 3$ by $x + 3$.

17. $6x^2 + 5x - 21$ by $2x - 3$.

18. $12a^2 + ax - 6x^2$ by $3a - 2x$.

19. $-5x^2 + xy + 6y^2$ by $-x - y$.

20. $6a^2 - ac - 35c^2$ by $2a - 5c$.

21. $12p^2 - 74pq + 12q^2$ by $2p - 12q$.

22. $4m^2 - 49n^2$ by $2m + 7n$.

23. $12a^2 - 31ab + 20b^2$ by $4a - 5b$.

24. $-25x^2 + 49y^2$ by $-5x + 7y$.

25. $21p^2 + 11pq - 40q^2$ by $3p + 5q$.

26. $8x^3 + 8x^2 + 4x + 1$ by $2x + 1$.

27. $-2x^3 + 13x^2 - 17x + 10$ by $-x + 5$.

28. $x^3 + ax^2 - 3a^2x - 6a^3$ by $x - 2a$.

29. $6x^3y - x^2y^2 - 7xy^3 + 12y^4$ by $2x + 3y$.

30. $8x^3 - 12x^2 - 14x + 21$ by $2x - 3$.

52. The process of Art. 51 is applicable to cases in which the divisor consists of more than two terms.

Example 1. Divide $a^4 - 2a^3 - 7a^2 + 8a + 12$ by $a^2 - a - 6$.

$$a^2 - a - 6)a^4 - 2a^3 - 7a^2 + 8a + 12(a^2 - a - 2$$
$$\underline{a^4 - a^3 - 6a^2}$$
$$-a^3 - a^2 + 8a$$
$$\underline{-a^3 + a^2 + 6a}$$
$$-2a^2 + 2a + 12$$
$$\underline{-2a^2 + 2a + 12}$$

Example 2. Divide $4x^3 - 5x^2 + 6x^5 - 15 - x^4 - x$ by $3 + 2x^2 - x$.

First arrange each of the expressions in descending powers of x.

$$2x^2 - x + 3)6x^5 - x^4 + 4x^3 - 5x^2 - x - 15(3x^3 + x^2 - 2x - 5$$
$$\underline{6x^5 - 3x^4 + 9x^3}$$
$$2x^4 - 5x^3 - 5x^2$$
$$\underline{2x^4 - x^3 + 3x^2}$$
$$-4x^3 - 8x^2 - x$$
$$\underline{-4x^3 + 2x^2 - 6x}$$
$$-10x^2 + 5x - 15$$
$$\underline{-10x^2 + 5x - 15}$$

Example 3. Divide $23x^2 - 2x^4 - 4x^3 + 12 + x^5 - 31x$ by $x^3 - 7x + 5$.

$$x^3 - 7x + 5)x^5 - 2x^4 - 4x^3 + 23x^2 - 31x + 12(x^2 - 2x + 3$$
$$\underline{x^5 \qquad - 7x^3 + 5x^2}$$
$$-2x^4 + 3x^3 + 18x^2 - 31x$$
$$\underline{-2x^4 \qquad + 14x^2 - 10x}$$
$$3x^3 + 4x^2 - 21x + 12$$
$$\underline{3x^3 \qquad - 21x + 15}$$
$$+ 4x^2 \qquad - 3$$

Now $4x^2$ is not divisible by x^3, so that the division cannot be carried on any further, thus the quotient is $x^2 - 2x + 3$, and there is a remainder $4x^2 - 3$.

In all cases where the division is not exact, the work should be carried on until the highest power in the remainder is lower than that in the divisor.

53. Occasionally it may be found convenient to arrange the expressions in *ascending* powers of some common letter.

Example. Divide $2a^3 + 10 - 16a - 39a^2 + 15a^4$ by $2 - 4a - 5a^2$.

$$2 - 4a - 5a^2)10 - 16a - 39a^2 + 2a^3 + 15a^4(5 + 2a - 3a^2$$
$$\underline{10 - 20a - 25a^2}$$
$$4a - 14a^2 + 2a^3$$
$$\underline{4a - 8a^2 - 10a^3}$$
$$-6a^2 + 12a^3 + 15a^4$$
$$\underline{-6a^2 + 12a^3 + 15a^4}$$

EXAMPLES VI. c

Divide

1. $a^3 - 6a^2 + 11a - 6$ by $a^2 - 4a + 3$.
2. $x^3 - 4x^2 + x + 6$ by $x^2 - x - 2$.
3. $y^3 + y^2 - 9y + 12$ by $y^2 - 3y + 3$.
4. $21m^3 \quad m^2 + m - 1$ by $7m^2 + 2m + 1$.
5. $6a^3 - 5a^2 - 9a - 2$ by $2a^2 - 3a - 1$.
6. $6k^3 - k^2 - 14k + 3$ by $3k^2 + 4k - 1$.
7. $6x^3 + 11x^2 - 39x - 65$ by $3x^2 + 13x + 13$.
8. $12x^2 - 8ax^2 - 27a^2x + 18a^2$ by $6x^2 - 13ax + 6a^2$.

9. $16x^3 + 14x^2y - 129xy^2 - 15y^3$ by $8x^2 + 27xy + 3y^2$.
10. $21c^3 - 5c^2d - 3cd^2 - 2d^3$ by $7c^2 + 3cd + d^2$.
11. $3x^4 - 10x^3 + 12x^2 - 11x + 6$ by $3x^2 - x + 3$.
12. $30a^4 + 11a^3 - 82a^2 - 12a + 48$ by $3a^2 + 2a - 4$.
13. $x^3 - x^2 - 8x - 13$ by $x^2 + 3x + 3$.
14. $a + 3a^3 + 6 - 10a^2$ by $a^2 - 4a + 3$.
15. $21m^3 - 27m - 26m^2 + 20$ by $3m + 7m^2 - 4$.
16. $18x^3 + 24a^3 - 40a^2x - 9ax^2$ by $9x^2 + 7a^2 - 18ax$.
17. $3y^4 - 4y^3 + 10y^2 + 3y - 2$ by $y^3 - y^2 + 3y + 2$.
18. $5a^3 + 1 + 10a^4 - 4a^2$ by $5a^3 - 2a + 1$.
19. $12x^4 + 5x^3 - 33x^2 - 3x + 16$ by $4x^2 - x - 5$.
20. $p^4 - 6p^3 + 13p^2 - 10p + 7$ by $p^2 - 3p + 2$.
21. $28x^4 + 69x + 2 - 71x^3 - 35x^2$ by $4x^2 + 6 - 13x$.
22. $5a^5 - 7a^4 - 9a^3 - 11a^2 - 38a + 40$ by $-5a^2 + 17a - 10$.
23. $x^3 - 8a^3$ by $x^2 + 2ax + 4a^2$.
24. $y^4 + 9y^2 + 81$ by $y^2 - 3y + 9$.
25. $x^4 + 4y^4$ by $x^2 + 2xy + 2y^2$.
26. $9a^4 - 4a^2 + 4$ by $3a^2 - 4a + 2$.
27. $a^8 + 64$ by $a^4 - 4a^2 + 8$.
28. $16x^4 + 36x^2 + 81$ by $4x^2 + 6x + 9$.
29. $4m^5 - 29m - 36 + 8m^2 - 7m^3 + 6m^4$ by $m^3 - 2m^2 + 3m - 4$.
30. $15x^4 + 22 - 32x^3 - 30x + 50x^2$ by $3 - 4x + 5x^2$.
31. $3a^2 + 8ab + 4b^2 + 10ac + 8bc + 3c^2$ by $a + 2b + 3c$.
32. $9x^2 - 4y^2 + 4yz - z^2$ by $-3x + 2y - z$.
33. $4c^2 - 12c - d^2 + 9$ by $2c + d - 3$.
34. $9p^2 - 16q^2 + 30p + 25$ by $-3p - 4q - 5$.
35. $x^5 - x^4y + x^3y^2 - x^3 + x^2 - y^3$ by $x^3 - x - y$.
36. $x^5 + x^4y - x^3y^2 + x^3 - 2xy^2$ by $x^2 + xy - y^2$.
37. $a^3b^3 + ab - 9 - b^4 + 3b^3 + 3b - a^4 - 3a^3 - 3a$ by $3 - b + a^3$.
38. $x^8 + 1$ by $x^3 + x^2 + x + 1$.
39. $2a^6 + 2$ by $a^3 + 2a^2 + 2a + 1$.
40. $x^9 - 6x^4 - 8x^3 - 1$ by $x^3 - 2x - 1$.

CHAPTER VII

REMOVAL AND INSERTION OF BRACKETS

54. QUANTITIES are sometimes enclosed within brackets to indicate that they must all be operated upon in the same way. Thus in the expression $2a - 3b - (4a - 2b)$ the brackets indicate that the expression $4a - 2b$ *treated as a whole* has to be subtracted from $2a - 3b$.

It will be convenient here to quote the rules for removing brackets which have already been given in Arts. 24 and 25.

When an expression within brackets is preceded by the sign +, the brackets can be removed without making any change in the expression.

When an expression within brackets is preceded by the sign –, the brackets may be removed if the sign of every term within the brackets be changed.

Example. Simplify, by removing brackets, the expression

$$(2a - 3b) - (3a + 4b) - (b - 2a).$$

The expression $= 2a - 3b - 3a - 4b - b + 2a$

$= a - 8b$, by collecting like terms.

55. Sometimes it is convenient to enclose within brackets part of an expression already enclosed within brackets. For this purpose it is usual to employ brackets of different forms. The brackets in common use are (), {}, [].

56. When there are two or more pairs of brackets to be removed, it is generally best to begin with the innermost pair. In dealing with each pair in succession we apply the rules quoted above.

Example. Simplify, by removing brackets, the expression

$$a - 2b - [4a - 6b - \{3a - c + (2a - 4b + c)\}].$$

Removing the brackets one by one,

the expression $= a - 2b - [4a - 6b - \{3a - c + 2a - 4b + c\}]$.

$= a - 2b - [4a - 6b - 3a + c - 2a + 4b - c]$

$= a - 2b - 4a + 6b + 3a - c + 2a - 4b + c$

$= 2a$, by collecting like terms.

Note. At first the beginner will find it best not to collect terms until all the brackets have been removed.

EXAMPLES VII. a

Simplify by removing brackets and collecting like terms:

1. $a + 2b + (2a - 3b)$.

2. $a + 2b - (2a - 3b)$.

3. $2a - 3b - (2a + 2b)$.

4. $a - 2 - (4 - 3a)$.

5. $(x - 3y) + (2x - 4y) - (x - 8y)$.

6. $a + 2b - 3c - (b - a - 4c)$.

7. $(x - 3y + 2z) - (z - 4y + 2x)$.

8. $4x - (2y + 2x) - (3x - 5y)$.

9. $2a + (b - 3a) - (4a - 8b) - (6b - 5a)$.

10. $m - (n - p) - (2m - 2p + 3n) - (n - m + 2p)$.

11. $a - b + c - (a + c - b) - (a + b + c) - (b + c - a)$.

12. $5x - (7y + 3x) - (2y + 7x) - (3x + 8y)$.

13. $(p - q) - (q - 2p) + (2p - q) - (p - 2q)$.

14. $2x^2 - (3y^2 - x^2) - (x^2 - 4y^2)$.

15. $(m^2 - 2n^2) - (2n^2 - 3m^2) - (3m^2 - 4n^2)$.

16. $(x - 2a) - (x - 2b) - \{2a - x - (2b + x)\}$.

17. $(a + 3b) - (b - 3a) - \{a + 2b - (2a - b)\}$.

18. $p^2 - 2q^2 - (q^2 + 2p^2) - \{p^2 + 3q^2 - (2p^2 - q^2)\}$.

19. $x - [y + \{x - (y - x)\}]$.

20. $(a - b) - \{a - b - (a + b) - (a - b)\}$.

21. $p - [p - (q + p) - \{p - (2p - q)\}]$.

22. $3x - y - [x - (2y - z) - \{2x - (y - z)\}]$.

23. $3a^2 - [6a^2 - \{8b^2 - (9c^2 - 2a^2)\}]$.

24. $[3a - \{2a - (a - b)\}] - [4a - \{3a - (2a - b)\}]$.

57. A coefficient placed before any bracket indicates that every term of the expression within the bracket is to be multiplied by that coefficient; but when there are two or more brackets to be considered, a prefixed coefficient must be used as a multiplier only when its own bracket is being removed.

Examples

1. $2x + 3(x - 4) = 2x + 3x - 12 = 5x - 12$.
2. $7x - 2(x - 4) = 7x - 2x + 8 = 5x + 8$.
3. Simplify $5a - 4[10a + 3\{x - a - 2(a + x)\}]$.

The expression

$$= 5a - 4\,[10a + 3\{(x - a - 2a - 2x)\}]$$
$$= 5a - 4\,[10a + 3\{- x - 3a\}]$$
$$= 5a - 4\,[10a - 3x - 9a] = 5a - 4\,[a - 3x]$$
$$= 5a - 4a + 12x = a + 12x.$$

On removing the innermost bracket each term is multiplied by -2. Then before multiplying by 3, the expression within its bracket is simplified. The other steps will be easily seen.

58. Sometimes a line called a **vinculum** is drawn over the symbols to be connected; thus $a - \overline{b + c}$ is used with the same meaning as $a - (b + c)$, and hence $a - \overline{b + c} = a - b - c$.

Note. The line between the numerator and denominator of a fraction is a kind of vinculum. Thus $\frac{x-5}{3}$ is equivalent to $\frac{1}{3}(x-5)$.

Example. Find the value of

$$84 - 7[-11x - 4\{-17x + 3(8 - \overline{9 + 5x})\}]$$

$$\begin{aligned}
\text{The expression } &= 84 - 7[-11x - 4\{-17x + 3(8 - \overline{9 - 5x})\}].\\
&= 84 - 7[-11x - 4\{-17x + 3(5x - 1)\}]\\
&= 84 - 7[-11x - 4\{-17x + 15x - 3\}]\\
&= 84 - 7[-11x - 4\{-2x - 3\}]\\
&= 84 - 7[-11x + 8x + 12]\\
&= 84 - 7[-3x + 12]\\
&= 84 + 21x - 84 = 21x.
\end{aligned}$$

When the beginner has had a little practice the number of steps may be considerably diminished.

Insertion of Brackets

59. The rules for insertion of brackets are the converse of those given on page 12, and may be easily deduced from them.

For the following equivalents have been established in Arts. 24 and 25:

$$a + b - c = a + (b - c),$$
$$a - b - c = a - (b + c),$$
$$a - b + c = a - (b - c).$$

From these results the rules follow.

Rule. 1. *Any part of an expression may be enclosed within brackets and the sign + prefixed, the sign of every term within the brackets remaining unaltered.*

Examples. $a - b + c - d - e = a - b + (c - d - e)$.

$$x^2 - ax + bx - ab = (x^2 - ax) + (bx - ab).$$

Rule. 2. *Any part of an expression may be enclosed within brackets and the sign − prefixed, provided the sign of every term within the brackets be changed.*

Examples. $a - b + c - d - e = a - (b - c) - (d + e)$.

$$xy - ax - by + ab = (xy - by) - (ax - ab).$$

60. The terms of an expression can be bracketed in various ways.

Example. The expression $ax - bx + cx - ay + by - c$

may be written

$$(ax - bx) + (cx - ay) + (by - cy),$$

or $$(ax - bx + cx) - (ay - by + cy),$$

or $$(ax - ay) - (bx - by) + (cx - cy).$$

61. When every term of an expression is divisible by a common factor, the expression may be simplified by dividing each term by this factor, and enclosing the quotient within brackets, the common factor being placed outside as a coefficient.

Thus $3x - 21 = 3(x - 7)$;

and $x^2 - 2ax + 4a^2 = x^2 - 2a(x - 2a)$.

EXAMPLES VII. b

Simplify by removing brackets:

1. $3(x - 2y) - 2(x - 4y)$.

2. $x - 3(y - x) - 4(x - 2y)$.

3. $16 - 3(2x - 3) - (2x + 3)$.

4. $4(x + 3) - 2(7 + x) + 2$.

5. $8(x - 3) - (6 - 2x) - 2(x + 2) + 5(5 - x)$.

6. $2x - 5(3x - 7 + y) + 4(2x + 3y - 8) - 7y$.

7. $2x - 5\{3x - 7(4x - 9)\}$.

8. $x^3 + 3(x^2y + xy^2) + y^3 - x^3 - 3(x^2y - xy^2) - y^3$.

9. $4x - 3\{x - (1 - y) + 2(1 - x)\}$.

10. $x - (y - z)[x - y - z - 2(y + z)]$.

11. $a^2 - [x^2 - \{x^2 - (z^2 - \overline{x^2 - y^2}) - 2y^2\} + y^2]$.

12. $5x + 4(y - 2z) - 4\{x + 2(y - z)\}$.

13. $a + \{-2b + 3(c - \overline{d - e})\}$.

14. $\{a^2 - (b^2 - c^2)\} - [2a^2 - \{a^2 - (b^2 - c^2)\} - 2(b^2 - c^2)]$.

15. $3p - \{5q - [6q + 2(10q - p)]\}$.

16. $3x - 2[2x - \{2(x - y) - y\} - y]$.

17. $3(5 - 6x) - 5[x - 5\{1 - 3(x - 5)\}]$.

18. $12 - [6a - (7 - \overline{a - 5}) - \{5a + (3 - \overline{2 - a})\}]$.

19. $b^2 - \{a^2 + ab - (a^2 + b^2)\} - [a^2 - \{3ab - (b^2 - a^2)\}]$.

20. $2[4x - \{2y + (2x - y) - (x + y)\}] - 2(-x - \overline{y - x})$.

21. $20(2 - x) + 3(x - 7) - 2[x + 9 - 3\{9 - 4(2 - x)\}]$.

22. $-4(a+y)+24(b-x)-2[x+y+a-3\{y+a-4(b+x)\}]$.

23. Multiply

$$2x-3y-4(x-2y)+5\{3x-2(x-y)\}$$

by $$4x-(y-x)-3\{2y-3(x+y)\}.$$

In each of the following expressions bracket the powers of x, so that the signs before the brackets may be (1) positive, (2) negative.

24. $ax^4+2x^3-cx^2+2x^2-bx^3-x^4$.

25. $ax^2+a^2x^3-bx^2-5x^2-cx^3$.

MISCELLANEOUS EXAMPLES II

1. Find the sum of $a-2b+c$, $3b-(a-c)$, $3a-b+3c$.
2. Subtract $1-x^2$ from 1, and add the result to $2y-x^2$.
3. Simplify $a+2b-3c+(b-3a+2c)-(3b-2a-2c)$.
4. Find the continued product of $3x^2y$, $2xy^2$, $-7xy^3$, $-5x^4y^5$.
5. What quantity must be added to $p+q$ to make $2q$? And what must be added to p^2-3pq to make $p^2+2pq+q^2$?
6. Divide $1-6x^4+5x^3$ by $1-x+3x^2$.
7. Multiply $3b^2+2a^2-5ab$ by $2a+3b$.
8. When $x=2$, find the value of $1-x+x^2-\dfrac{x^3}{1+x}$.
9. Find the algebraic sum of $3ax$, $-2xz$, $9ax$, $-7xz$, $4ax$, $-4xz$.
10. Simplify $9a-(2b-c)+2d-(5a+3b)+4c-2d$, and find its value when $a=7, b=-3, c=-4$.
11. Subtract ax^2-4 from nothing, and add the difference to the sum of $2x^3-5x$ and unity.
12. Multiply $3x^2y-4xy^3z+2x^3y^2z^3$ by $-6x^2y^2z^3$ and divide the result by $3xy^2z^2$.
13. Simplify by removing brackets $5[x-4\{x-3(2x-\overline{3x+2})\}]$.
14. Simplify $2x^2-(2xy-3y^2)+4y^2+(5xy-2x^2)+x^2-(2xy+6y^2)$.
15. Find the product of $2x-7y$ and $3x+8y$, and multiply the result by $x+2y$.
16. Find the sum of $3a+2b$, $-5c-2d$, $3e+5f$, $b-a+2d$, $-2a-3b+5c-2f$.
17. Divide $x^4-4x^3-18x^2-11x+2$ by x^2-7x+1.
18. If $a=-1, b=2, c=0, d=1$, find the value of $ad+ac-a^2-cd+c^2-a+2c+a^2b+2a^3$.

19. Simplify $3[1-2\{1-4(1-3x)\}]$, and find what quantity must be added to it to produce $3-8x$.

20. Divide the sum of $10x^2-7x(1+x^2)$ and $3(x^4+x^2+2)$ by $3(x^2+1)-(x+1)$.

21. Simplify $5x^4-8x^3-(2x^2-7)-(x^4+5)+(3x^3-x)$, and subtract the result from $4x^4-x+2$.

22. If $a=0,\ b=1,\ c=3,\ d=-2,\ e=2$; find the value of (1) $3c^b-d^e$; (2) $(c+a)(c-a)+b^2$; (3) e^c+a^b.

23. Find the product of $7x^2-y(x-2y)$ and $x(7x+y)-2y^2$.

24. Subtract $(a^3+4)+(a^2-2)$ from $(a^3+4)(a^2-2)$.

25. Express by means of symbols

(1) b's excess over c is greater than a by 7.

(2) Three times the sum of a and $2b$ is less by 5 than the product of b and c.

26. Simplify $3a^2-(4a-b^2)-\{2a^2-(3b-a^2)-\overline{2b-3a}\}-\{5b-7a-(c^2-b^2)\}$.

27. Find the continued product of x^2+xy+y^2, x^2-xy+y^2, $x^4-x^2y^2+y^4$.

28. Divide $4a^2-9b^2-4ac+c^2$ by $2a-3b-c$.

29. If $a=3, b=-2, c=0, d=2$, find the value of

(1) $c(a+b)+b(a+c)+a(c-b)$; (2) a^a+d^d.

30. From a rod $a+b$ centimetres long $b-c$ centimetres are cut off; how much remains?

31. A boy buys a marbles, wins b, and loses c; how many has he then?

32. Simplify $2a-\{5a-[8a-(2b+a)]\}$, and find the value of $(a-b)[a^2+b(a+b)]$ when $a=1, b=2$.

33. Divide $1-5x^4+4x^5$ by x^2-2x+1.

34. Multiply the sum of $3x^2-5xy$ and $2xy-y^2$ by the excess of $3x^2+y^2$ over $2y^2+3xy$.

35. Express in algebraical symbols

(1) Three times x diminished by the sum of y and twice z.

(2) Seven times a taken from three times b is equal to five times the product of c and d.

(3) The sum of m and n multiplied by their difference is equal to the difference of the squares of m and n.

36. If $a=2,\quad b=1,\quad c=0,\quad d=-1,$ find the value of $(d-b)(c-b)+(ac-bd)^2+(c^2-d)(2c-b)$.

CHAPTER VIII

REVISION OF ELEMENTARY RULES

[If preferred, this chapter may be postponed until the chapters on Simple Equations and Problems have been read.]

Substitutions

62. DEFINITION. The **square root** of any proposed expression is that quantity whose square, or second power, is equal to the given expression. Thus the square root of 81 is 9, because $9^2 = 81$.

The square root of a is denoted by $\sqrt[2]{a}$, or more simply $\sqrt{a}$.

Similarly the **cube, fourth, fifth** & c., **root** of any expression is that quantity whose third, fourth, fifth, & c., power is equal to the given expression.

The roots are denoted by the symbols $\sqrt[3]{\ }$, $\sqrt[4]{\ }$, $\sqrt[5]{\ }$ & c.

Examples. $\sqrt[3]{27} = 3$; because $3^3 = 27$.

$\sqrt[5]{32} = 2$; because $2^5 = 32$.

The root symbol $\sqrt{\ }$ is also called the **radical sign.**

Example 1. Find the value of $5\sqrt{(6a^3b^4c)}$, when $a = 3, b = 1, c = 8$.

$$\begin{aligned}5\sqrt{(6a^3b^4c)} &= 5\times\sqrt{(6\times 3^3\times 1^4\times 8)}\\ &= 5\times\sqrt{(6\times 27\times 8)}\\ &= 5\times\sqrt{(3\times 27)\times(2\times 8)}\\ &= 5\times 9\times 4 = 180.\end{aligned}$$

Note. An expression of the form $\sqrt{(6a^3b^4c)}$ is often written $\sqrt{6a^3b^4c}$, the line above being used as a vinculum indicating the square root of the expression *taken as a whole.*

Example 2. If $a = -4, b = -3, c = -1, f = 0, x = 4$, find the value of

$$7\sqrt[3]{(a^2cx)} - 3\sqrt{b^4c^2} + 5\sqrt{(f^7x)}.$$

$$\begin{aligned}\text{The expression } &= 7\sqrt[3]{(-4)^2(-1)4} - 3\sqrt{(-3)^4(-1)^2} + 0\\ &= 7\sqrt[3]{(-64)} - 3\sqrt{81}\\ &= 7\times(-4) - 3\times 9 = -55.\end{aligned}$$

EXAMPLES VIII. a

If $a = 4, b = 1, c = 6, d = 0$, find the value of

1. $\sqrt{b^4}$.
2. $\sqrt{9ab}$.
3. $\sqrt{6b^3c}$.
4. $\sqrt{9a^3b^2}$.
5. $\sqrt{4b^4c^2}$.
6. $\sqrt{6a^4b^3c}$.
7. $a\sqrt[3]{9ac}$.
8. $3b\sqrt[3]{3a^2c^2}$.
9. $\sqrt{a^3b^3} - \sqrt{9c^2}$.
10. $3\sqrt{a^3cd^2} - d\sqrt[3]{2a^2b} + \sqrt{6ac}$.

If $a = -3, b = 2, c = -1, x = -4, y = 0$, find the value of

11. $\sqrt{a^2cx}$.
12. $\sqrt{3ac^3}$.
13. $\sqrt{6abx}$.
14. $5\sqrt{c^3x}$.
15. $\sqrt{3ab^2c^2x}$.
16. $\sqrt[3]{a^3c^2}$.
17. $\sqrt[3]{bc^3x}$.
18. $\sqrt[3]{3a^2b^3c}$.
19. $\sqrt{3ac} - \sqrt{cx} + \sqrt{b^2cx}$.
20. $\sqrt{c^2y} + \sqrt{2a^2b} - \sqrt{9a^2}$.
21. If $x = 100, y = 81, z = 16$, find the value of $\sqrt{\frac{x}{4}} - \sqrt[4]{y} + \sqrt[3]{4z}$.
22. If $a = -6, b = 2, c = -1, x = -4, y = 0$, find the value of $2\sqrt{a^2cx} - 2\sqrt{a^2b^4x^3y^6} + \sqrt{8a^2b}$.

Fractional Coefficients and Indices

63. Fractional Coefficients. The rules which have been already explained in the case of integral coefficients are still applicable when the coefficients are fractional.

Example 1. Find the sum of $\frac{2}{3}x^2 + \frac{1}{3}xy - \frac{1}{4}y^2$, $-x^2 - \frac{2}{3}xy + 2y^2$, $\frac{2}{3}x^2 - xy - \frac{5}{4}y^2$.

$$\begin{array}{l} \frac{2}{3}x^2 + \frac{1}{3}xy - \frac{1}{4}y^2 \\ -x^2 - \frac{2}{3}xy + 2y^2 \\ \frac{2}{3}x^2 - xy - \frac{5}{4}y^2 \\ \hline \frac{1}{3}x^2 - \frac{4}{3}xy + \frac{1}{2}y^2 \end{array}$$

Here each column is added up separately; and the fractional coefficients combined by the rules of arithmetic.

Example 2. Divide $\frac{1}{4}x^3+\frac{1}{72}xy^2+\frac{1}{12}y^3$ by $\frac{1}{2}x+\frac{1}{3}y$.

$$
\begin{array}{l}
\frac{1}{2}x+\frac{1}{3}y\Big)\ \frac{1}{4}x^3+\frac{1}{72}xy^2+\frac{1}{12}y^3\ \Big(\frac{1}{2}x^2-\frac{1}{3}xy+\frac{1}{4}y^2 \\
\qquad\quad \frac{1}{4}x^3+\frac{1}{6}x^2y \\
\hline
\qquad\qquad -\frac{1}{6}x^2y+\frac{1}{72}xy^2 \\
\qquad\qquad -\frac{1}{6}x^2y-\frac{1}{9}xy^2 \\
\hline
\qquad\qquad\qquad\quad \frac{1}{8}xy^2+\frac{1}{12}y^3 \\
\qquad\qquad\qquad\quad \frac{1}{8}xy^2+\frac{1}{12}y^3 \\
\hline
\end{array}
$$

64. Fractional Indices. In all the examples hitherto explained the indices have been integers, but expressions involving fractional and negative indices such as $a^{2/3}$, $x^{-1/2}$, $3x^{3/4}+x^{1/4}-2$, $a^{-2}-4a^{-1}x-3x^2$ may be dealt with by the same rules. For a complete discussion of the theory of Indices the student is referred to the *Elementary Algebra*, Chap. xxx. It will be sufficient here to point out that the rules for combination of indices in multiplication and division given in Chapters V and VI are universally true.

Example 1. $x^{2/3}\times x^{3/4}=x^{2/3+3/4}=x^{\frac{17}{12}}$.

Example 2. $a^{-4}\times a^4=a^{-4+4}=a^0=1$. [See Note, Art. 50.]

Example 3. $2a^{\frac{1}{2}}b^{-1}\times 3a^{-\frac{1}{2}}b^{1/4}=6a^{\frac{1}{2}-\frac{1}{2}}b^{-1+\frac{1}{4}}=6a^0b^{-\frac{3}{4}}=6b^{-\frac{3}{4}}$.

Example 4. $3x^2y^{3/4}\div x^3y^{1/2}=3x^{2-3}y^{\frac{3}{4}-\frac{1}{2}}=3x^{-1}y^{\frac{1}{4}}$.

Example 5. $a^{-2}b^{1/3}\div a^2b^{-1/2}=a^{-2-3}b^{\frac{1}{3}+\frac{1}{2}}=a^{-4}b^{\frac{5}{6}}$.

It will be seen from these illustrations that the rules for combining indices in multiplication and division may be concisely expressed by the two statements,

(1) $a^m\times a^n=a^{m+n}$, (2) $a^m\div a^n=a^{m-n}$;

where m and n may have any values positive or negative, integral or fractional.

65. We shall now give some examples involving compound expressions.

Example 1. Multiply $x^{\frac{2}{3}} - 3x^{\frac{1}{3}} + 4$ by $2x^{\frac{1}{3}} - 1$.

$$\begin{array}{l} x^{\frac{2}{3}} - 3x^{\frac{1}{3}} + 4 \\ 2x^{\frac{1}{3}} - 1 \\ \hline 2x - 6x^{2/3} + 8x^{1/3} \\ \quad - x^{\frac{2}{3}} + 3x^{\frac{1}{3}} - 4 \\ \hline 2x - 7x^{\frac{2}{3}} + 11x^{\frac{1}{3}} - 4 \end{array}$$

Example 2. Multiply $c^x + 2c^{-x} - 7$ by $5 - 3c^{-x} + 2c^x$.

$$\begin{array}{l} c^x - 7 + 2c^{-x} \\ 2c^x + 5 - 3c^{-x} \\ \hline 2c^{2x} - 14c^x + 4 \\ \qquad + 5c^x - 35 + 10c^{-x} \\ \qquad\qquad - 3 + 21c^{-x} - 6c^{-2x} \\ \hline 2c^{2x} - 9c^x - 34 + 31c^{-x} - 6c^{-2x} \end{array}$$

Here the expressions have been arranged in descending powers of c, and it should be noticed that in this arrangement the numerical terms -7 and $+5$ stand between the terms involving c^x and c^{-x}.

Example 3. Divide

$24x^{\frac{1}{4}} - 16x^{-\frac{3}{4}} + x^{\frac{7}{4}} - 16x^{-\frac{1}{4}} - 5x^{\frac{5}{4}}$ by $8x^{-\frac{1}{4}} - 2x^{\frac{3}{4}} + x^{\frac{5}{4}} - 4x^{\frac{1}{4}}$.

Arrange divisor and dividend in descending powers of x.

$$x^{\frac{5}{4}} - 2x^{\frac{3}{4}} - 4x^{\frac{1}{4}} + 8x^{-\frac{1}{4}} \Big) \; x^{\frac{7}{4}} - 5x^{\frac{5}{4}} + 24x^{\frac{1}{4}} - 16x^{-\frac{1}{4}} - 16x^{-\frac{3}{4}} \Big(x^{\frac{1}{2}} - 3 - 2x^{-\frac{1}{2}}$$

$$\begin{array}{l} x^{\frac{7}{4}} - 2x^{\frac{5}{4}} - 4x^{\frac{3}{4}} + 8x^{\frac{1}{4}} \\ \hline - 3x^{\frac{5}{4}} + 4x^{\frac{3}{4}} + 16x^{\frac{1}{4}} - 16x^{-\frac{1}{4}} \\ - 3x^{\frac{5}{4}} + 6x^{\frac{3}{4}} + 12x^{\frac{1}{4}} - 24x^{-\frac{1}{4}} \\ \hline - 2x^{\frac{3}{4}} + 4x^{\frac{1}{4}} + 8x^{-\frac{1}{4}} - 16x^{-\frac{3}{4}} \\ - 2x^{\frac{3}{4}} + 4x^{\frac{1}{4}} + 8x^{-\frac{1}{4}} - 16x^{-\frac{3}{4}} \\ \hline \end{array}$$

EXAMPLES VIII. b

1. Find the sum of $-\frac{1}{3}m-\frac{1}{4}n, -\frac{2}{3}m+\frac{3}{4}n, -2m-n.$

2. Add together $\frac{2}{3}a-\frac{1}{6}b+\frac{1}{4}c, \frac{1}{2}a-\frac{1}{2}b,$

$\frac{1}{6}a+\frac{1}{12}b+\frac{1}{4}c, \frac{-1}{3}a+\frac{7}{12}b-\frac{1}{2}c.$

3. From $a+\frac{1}{2}b-\frac{1}{3}c$ take $\frac{1}{3}a-b+\frac{1}{2}c.$

4. Subtract $\frac{1}{4}a^2+\frac{1}{3}ab-\frac{1}{4}b^2$ from $\frac{1}{2}a^2-\frac{1}{3}ab+\frac{1}{4}b^2.$

5. Multiply $\frac{1}{3}x^2+\frac{1}{2}y^2$ by $\frac{1}{2}x-\frac{1}{3}y.$

6. Find the product of $\frac{1}{2}x^2-\frac{1}{3}x+\frac{1}{4}$ and $\frac{1}{2}x+\frac{1}{3}.$

7. Divide $\frac{2}{9}x^3-\frac{3}{4}y^3$ by $\frac{1}{3}x-\frac{1}{2}y.$

8. Divide $a^3-2a^2b+\frac{11}{9}ab^2-\frac{2}{9}b^3$ by $a^2-\frac{5}{3}ab+\frac{2}{3}b^2.$

9. Simplify $\frac{1}{4}(2x-3y)-\frac{1}{3}(3x+2y)+\frac{1}{12}(7x-5y).$

10. Find the sum of $\frac{1}{4}y^3-\frac{1}{12}y^2+\frac{3}{7}y-\frac{1}{3}, \frac{1}{2}y^2+\frac{1}{6}+\frac{1}{14}y,$

$-\frac{1}{6}y^2-\frac{1}{4}y+\frac{5}{12}.$

11. Find the product of $\frac{1}{2}x-\frac{1}{3}y+\frac{1}{3}(z-\frac{1}{2}y)$ and $\frac{1}{3}(x-z)-\frac{1}{2}(y-\frac{1}{3}x).$

12. Simplify by removing brackets $8\left(\frac{a}{4}-\frac{b}{2}\right)+5\left\{2a-3\left(a-\frac{b}{3}\right)\right\}.$

13. Divide $\frac{1}{3}x^3-\frac{17}{36}x^2+\frac{1}{3}x-\frac{1}{8}$ by $\frac{2}{3}x-\frac{1}{2}.$

14. Subtract $\frac{1}{12}(7x-9y)$ from $\frac{1}{3}(x-3y)-\frac{1}{2}(y-2x).$

15. Add together $\left(x-\frac{1}{2}y\right)\left(\frac{1}{3}x+y\right)$ and $\left(2x-\frac{1}{3}y\right)\left(\frac{1}{2}x-y\right).$

16. Multiply $\frac{2}{3}a^3-\frac{4}{5}a^2x+\frac{1}{2}x^3$ by $\frac{3}{5}a-2x.$

17. Divide $36a^2+\frac{1}{9}b^2+\frac{1}{4}-4ab-6a+\frac{1}{3}b$ by $6a-\frac{1}{3}b-\frac{1}{2}.$

18. Simplify $6\left\{x-\frac{3}{2}\left(y-\frac{4}{3}\right)\right\}\left\{\frac{1}{2}(2x-y)+2(y-1)\right\}.$

19. Multiply $\frac{3}{2}a^2 - \frac{1}{2}ab + b^2$ by $a^2 + \frac{1}{3}ab - \frac{2}{3}b^2$, and verify the result when $a = 1, b = 2$.

20. Multiply $x - x^{\frac{1}{2}}y^{\frac{1}{2}} + y$ by $x^{\frac{1}{2}} - y^{\frac{1}{2}}$.

21. Divide $x^{\frac{4}{3}} + x^{\frac{2}{3}}y^{\frac{1}{2}} + y$ by $x^{\frac{2}{3}} - x^{\frac{1}{3}}y^{\frac{1}{4}} + y^{\frac{1}{2}}$.

22. Find the product of $x^{\frac{1}{4}}y + y^{\frac{2}{3}}$ and $x^{\frac{1}{3}} - y^{\frac{1}{8}}$.

23. Multiply $a^{\frac{3}{2}} - x^{\frac{3}{2}}$ by $a^{\frac{2}{3}} + x^{\frac{2}{3}}$.

24. Divide $c^{-3} - 8c^{-1} - 3$ by $c^{-1} - 3$.

25. Divide $4x^{\frac{2}{3}}y^{-2} - 12x^{\frac{1}{3}}y^{-1} + 25 - 24x^{-\frac{1}{3}}y + 16x^{-\frac{2}{3}}y^2$

by $2x^{\frac{1}{3}}y^{-1} - 3 + 4x^{1/3}y$.

26. Find the value of $(ax^{-2} + a^{-1}x)(ax^{-2} - 3a^{-1}x)$.

27. Find the square of $a^{\frac{1}{4}} - 1 - a^{-\frac{1}{4}}$.

28. Find the continued product of $3a^{-2}b^{-1}x$, $a^{x\frac{1}{3}} - b^{\frac{2}{3}}$, and $ax^{2/3} + b$.

29. Divide $x - y$ by $x^{\frac{5}{6}}y^{\frac{1}{4}} + x^{\frac{1}{2}}y^{\frac{7}{12}} + x^{\frac{1}{6}}y^{\frac{11}{12}}$.

30. Multiply $a^2 + 2a^{-2} - 7$ by $5 + a^2 - 2a^{-2}$.

31. Find the value of $(3x^ay^{-a} - x^{-a}y^a)(x^ay - x^{-a}y^{-1})$.

Important Cases in Division

66. The following example in division is worthy of notice.

Example. Divide $a^3 + b^3 + c^3 - 3abc$ by $a + b + c$.

$$a + b + c)a^3 - 3abc + b^3 + c^3(a^2 - ab - ac + b^2 - bc + c^2$$

$$\underline{a^3 + a^2b + a^2c}$$

$$- a^2b - a^2c - 3abc$$

$$\underline{-a^2b - ab^2 - abc}$$

$$- a^2c + ab^2 - 2abc$$

$$\underline{- a^2c \qquad - abc - ac^2}$$

$$ab^2 - abc + ac^2 + b^3$$

$$\underline{ab^2 + b^3 + b^2c}$$

$$- abc + ac^2 - b^2c$$

$$\underline{- abc - b^2c - bc^2}$$

$$ac^2 + bc^2 + c^3$$

$$\underline{ac^2 + bc^2 + c^3}$$

Here the work is arranged in descending powers of a, and the other letters are taken alphabetically; thus in the first remainder a^2b precedes a^2c, and a^2c precedes $3abc$. A similar arrangement will be observed throughout the work.

67. The following examples in division may be easily verified; they are of great importance and should be carefully noticed.

$$\text{I.}\begin{cases}\dfrac{x^2-y^2}{x-y}=x+y,\\[2mm] \dfrac{x^3-y^3}{x-y}=x^2+xy+y^2,\\[2mm] \dfrac{x^4-y^4}{x-y}=x^3+x^2y+xy^2+y^3,\end{cases}$$

and so on; the divisor being $x - y$, the terms in the quotient *all positive* and the index in the dividend *either odd or even*.

$$\text{II.}\begin{cases}\dfrac{x^3+y^3}{x+y}=x^2-xy+y^2,\\[2mm] \dfrac{x^5+y^5}{x+y}=x^4-x^3y+x^2y^2-xy^3+y^4,\\[2mm] \dfrac{x^7+y^7}{x+y}=x^6-x^5y+x^4y^2-x^3y^3+x^2y^4-xy^5+y^6,\end{cases}$$

and so on; the divisor being $x + y$, the terms in the quotient *alternately positive and negative*, and the index in the dividend *always odd*.

$$\text{III.}\begin{cases}\dfrac{x^2-y^2}{x+y}=x-y,\\[2mm] \dfrac{x^4-y^4}{x+y}=x^3-x^2y+xy^2-y^3,\\[2mm] \dfrac{x^6-y^6}{x+y}=x^5-x^4y+x^3y^2-x^2y^3+xy^4-y^5,\end{cases}$$

and so on; the divisor being $x + y$, the terms in the quotient *alternately positive and negative*, and the index in the dividend *always even*.

IV. The expressions $x^2 + y^2, x^4 + y^4, x^6 + y^6, \ldots$ (where the index is *even*, and the terms *both positive*) are *never* exactly divisible by $x + y$ or by $x - y$.

All these different cases may be more concisely stated as follows:

(1) $x^n - y^n$ is divisible by $x - y$ if n be *any* whole number.

(2) $x^n + y^n$ is divisible by $x + y$ if n be any *odd* whole number.

(3) $x^n - y^n$ is divisible by $x + y$ if n be any *even* whole number.

(4) $x^n + y^n$ is never divisible by $x + y$ or by $x - y$, when n is an *even* whole number.

Dimension and Degree

68. Each of the letters composing a term is called a **dimension** of the term and the number of letters involved is called the **degree** of the term. Thus the product abc is said to be *of three dimensions*, or *of the third degree*; and ax^4 is said to be *of five dimensions* or *of the fifth degree*.

A numerical coefficient is not counted. Thus $8a^2b^5$ and a^2b^5 are each of *seven* dimensions.

69. The **degree of an expression** is the degree of the term of highest dimensions contained in it; thus $a^4 - 8a^3 + 3a - 5$ is *an expression of the fourth degree*, and $a^2x - 7b^2x^3$ *is an expression of the fifth degree*. But it is sometimes useful to speak of the dimensions of an expression with regard to some one of the letters it involves. For instance, the expression $ax^3 - bx^2 + cx - d$ is said to be of *three dimensions in x*.

70. A compound expression is said to be **homogeneous** when all its terms are of the same dimensions. Thus $8a^6 - a^4b^2 + 9ab^5$ is a *homogeneous expression of six dimensions*.

It is useful to notice that the product of two homogeneous expressions is also homogeneous.

Thus by Art. 47,

$$(2a^2 - 3ab + 4b^2)(-5a^2 + 3ab + 4b^2)$$

$$= -10a^4 + 21a^3b - 21a^2b^2 + 16b^4.$$

Here, the product of two homogeneous expressions each of two dimensions is a homogeneous expression of four dimensions.

Also the quotient of one homogeneous expression by another homogeneous expression is itself homogeneous.

For instance, in the example of Art. 66 it may be noticed that the divisor is homogeneous of one dimension, the dividend is homogeneous of three dimensions, and the quotient is homogeneous of two dimensions.

EXAMPLES VIII. c

1. Divide $a^3 + 30ab - 125b^3 + 8$ by $a - 5b + 2$.
2. Divide $x^3 + y^3 - z^3 + 3xyz$ by $x + y - z$.
3. Divide $a^3 - b^3 + 1 + 3ab$ by $a - b + 1$.
4. Divide $18cd + 1 + 27c^3 - 8d^3$ by $1 + 3c - 2d$.

Without actual division write down the quotients in the following cases:

5. $\dfrac{x^3-1}{x-1}$.

6. $\dfrac{a^3+b^3}{a+b}$.

7. $\dfrac{x^4-a^4}{x-a}$.

8. $\dfrac{x^4-a^4}{x+a}$.

9. $\dfrac{1+a^3}{1+a}$.

10. $\dfrac{16-b^4}{2+b}$.

11. $\dfrac{a^5+b^5}{a+b}$.

12. $\dfrac{a^5-b^5}{a-b}$.

13. $\dfrac{x^3+27y^3}{x+3y}$.

14. $\dfrac{a^6-x^6}{a+x}$.

15. $\dfrac{c^7+1}{c+1}$.

16. $\dfrac{x^6+y^6}{x^2+y^2}$.

17. In the expression $2a^3b^2+3ab^4+3a^2b^2x-x^5+20a^2b^3-11a^4+7a^3b^2$, which terms are *like*, and which are *homogeneous*?

18. In each term of the expression $7a^3bc^2-ab^2c+12b^3c^4-b^5c$, introduce some power of a which will make the whole expression homogeneous of eight dimensions.

19. By considering the dimensions of the product, correct the following statement: $(3x^2-5xy+y^2)(8x^2-2xy-3y^2)$
$=24x^4-46x^2y+9x^2y^2+13xy^3-3y^3$, it being known that there is no mistake in the *coefficients*.

20. Write down the square of $3a^2-2ab-b^2$, having given that the coefficients of the terms taken in descending powers of a are 9, – 12, – 2, 4, 1.

21. Write down the value of the product of $3a^2b+5a^3-ab^2$ and $ab^2+5a^3-3a^2b$, having given that the coefficients of the terms when arranged in ascending powers of b are 25, 0, – 9, 6, – 1.

22. The quotient of $x^3-y^3-1-3xy$
by $x-y-1$ is $x^2+xy+x+y^2-y+1$.

Introduce the letter z into dividend, divisor and quotient so as to make them respectively homogeneous expressions of three, one and two dimensions.

CHAPTER IX

SIMPLE EQUATIONS

71. AN **equation** asserts that two expressions are equal, but we do not usually employ the word equation in so wide a sense.

Thus the statement $x + 3 + x + 4 = 2x + 7$, which is *always* true whatever value x may have, is called an **identical equation**, or briefly an **identity**.

The parts of an equation to the right and left of the sign of equality are called **members** or **sides** of the equation and are distinguished as the *right side* and *left side*.

72. Certain equations are only true for particular values of the symbols employed. Thus $3x = 6$ is only true when $x = 2$, and is called an **equation of condition**, or more usually an equation. Consequently, an *identity* is an equation which is always true whatever be the values of the symbols involved; whereas an *equation* (in the ordinary use of the word) is only true for particular values of the symbols. In the above example $3x = 6$, the value 2 is said to **satisfy** the equation. The object of the present chapter is to explain how to treat an equation of the simplest kind in order to discover the value which satisfies it.

73. The letter whose value it is required to find is called the **unknown quantity**. The process of finding its value is called **solving the equation**. The value so found is called the root or the **solution** of the equation.

74. An equation which involves the unknown quantity in the first degree is called a **simple equation**. It is usual to denote the unknown quantity by the letter x.

The process of solving a simple equation depends only upon the following **axioms**.

1. If to equals we add equals the sums are equal.
2. If from equals we take equals the remainders are equal.
3. If equals are multiplied by equals the products are equal.
4. If equals are divided by equals the quotients are equal.

75. Consider the equation $7x = 14$.

It is required to find what numerical value x must have consistent with this statement.

Dividing both sides by 7 we get

$$x = 2, \qquad \text{[Axiom 4].}$$

Similarly, if $\frac{x}{2} = -6$,

multiplying both sides by 2, we get

$$x = -12, \qquad \text{[Axiom 3].}$$

Again, in the equation $7x - 2x - x = 23 + 15 - 10$, by collecting terms, we have $4x = 28$.

$$\therefore \quad x = 7.$$

76. To solve $3x - 8 = x + 12$.

This case differs from the preceding in that the unknown quantity occurs on both sides of the equation. We can, however, transpose any term from one side to the other by simply *changing its sign*. This we proceed to show.

Subtract x from both sides of the equation, and we get

$$3x - x - 8 = 12, \qquad \text{[Axiom 2].}$$

Adding 8 to both sides, we have

$$3x - x = 12 + 8, \qquad \text{[Axiom 1].}$$

Thus we see that $+ x$ has been removed from one side, and appears as $- x$ on the other; and $- 8$ has been removed from one side and appears as $+ 8$ on the other.

It is evident that similar steps may be employed in all cases. Hence we may enunciate the following rule.

Rule. *Any term may be transposed from one side of the equation to the other by changing its sign.*

It appears from this that *we may change the sign of every term in an equation*; for this is equivalent to transposing all the terms, and then making the right and left hand members change places.

Example. Take the equation $-3x - 12 = x - 24$.

Transposing, $\quad -x + 24 = 3x + 12$,

or $\quad 3x + 12 = -x + 24$,

which is the original equation with the sign of every term changed.

77. To solve $\frac{x}{2} - 3 = \frac{x}{4} + \frac{x}{5}$.

Here it will be convenient to begin by clearing the equation of *fractional* coefficients. This can always be done by multiplying both sides of the equation by the least common multiple of the denominators. [Axiom 3].

Thus, multiplying by 20,

$$10x - 60 = 5x + 4x;$$

transposing, $10x - 5x - 4x = 60;$

$$\therefore \quad x = 60.$$

78. We can now give a general rule for solving any simple equation with one unknown quantity.

Rule. *First, if necessary, clear of fractions; then transpose all the terms containing the unknown quantity to one side of the equation, and the known quantities to the other. Collect the terms on each side; divide both sides by the coefficient of the unknown quantity, and the value required is obtained.*

Example 1. Solve $5(x - 3) - 7(6 - x) + 3 = 24 - 3(8 - x)$.

Removing brackets,

$$5x - 15 - 42 + 7x + 3 = 24 - 24 + 3x;$$

transposing, $5x + 7x - 3x = 24 - 24 + 15 + 42 - 3;$

$$\therefore \quad 9x = 54;$$

$$\therefore \quad x = 6.$$

Example 2. Solve $(x + 1)(2x - 1) - 5x = (2x - 3)(x - 5) + 47$.

Forming the products, we have

$$2x^2 + x - 1 - 5x = 2x^2 - 13x + 15 + 47.$$

Erasing the term $2x^2$ on each side and transposing,

$$x - 5x + 13x = 15 + 47 + 1;$$

$$\therefore \quad 9x = 63;$$

$$\therefore \quad x = 7.$$

79. It is extremely useful for the beginner to acquire the habit of **verifying**, that is, proving the truth of his results, the habit of applying such tests tends to make the student self-reliant and confident in his own accuracy.

In the case of simple equations we have only to shew that when we substitute the value of x in the two sides of the equation we obtain the same result.

Example To shew that $x = 7$ *satisfies* the equation.

$$(x+1)(2x-1)-5x=(2x-3)(x-5)+47.$$

When $x = 7$, the left side $(x+1)(2x-1)-5x$

$$=(7+1)(14-1)-35=(8\times 13)-35=69.$$

The right side $(2x-3)(x-5)+47$

$$=(14-3)(7-5)+47=(11\times 2)+47=69,$$

Thus, since these two results are the same, $x = 7$ satisfies the equation.

EXAMPLES IX. a

Write down the solutions of the following equations:

1. $7x = 21.$ **2.** $3x = 15.$

3. $9x = 18.$ **4.** $5x = 5.$

5. $12x = 132.$ **6.** $33 = 11x.$

7. $4x = -12.$ **8.** $-10 = -5x.$

9. $4x = 18.$ **10.** $12x = 42.$

11. $30 = -6x.$ **12.** $4x = 0.$

13. $6x = 26.$ **14.** $0 = 11x.$

15. $1 = 11x.$ **16.** $3x = -27.$

17. $0 = -2x.$ **18.** $6x = 3.$

19. $5 = 15x.$ **20.** $-24 = -8x.$

Solve the following equations:

21. $6x + 3 = 15.$ **22.** $5x - 7 = 28.$

23. $13 = 7 + 2x.$ **24.** $15 = 37 - 11x.$

25. $4x - 7 = 11.$ **26.** $7x = 18 - 2x.$

27. $3x - 18 = 7 - 2x.$ **28.** $4x = 13 - 2x - 10.$

29. $3x = 7 - 2x + 8.$ **30.** $0 = 11 - 2x + 7 - 10x.$

31. $8x - 3 - 5x - 5 = 7x.$ **32.** $7x - 13 = 12 - 5x - 5.$

33. $5x - 17 + 3x - 5 = 6x - 7 - 8x + 115.$

34. $7x - 21 - 4x + 13 + 2x = 41 - 5x - 7 + 6x.$

35. $15 - 7x - 9x - 28 + 14x - 17 = 21 - 3x + 13 - 9x + 8x.$

36. $5x - 6x + 30 - 7x = 2x + 10 - 7x + 5x - 20.$

37. $5(x - 3) = 4(x - 2).$

38. $11(5 - 4x) = 7(5 - 6x).$

39. $3-7(x-1)=5-4x$.

40. $5-4(x-3)=x-2(x-1)$.

41. $8(x-3)-2(3-x)=2(x+2)-5(5-x)$.

42. $4(5-x)-2(x-3)=x-4-3(x+2)$.

43. $\frac{1}{2}x+\frac{1}{3}x=x-3$.

44. $\frac{1}{2}x-\frac{1}{3}x=\frac{1}{4}x+\frac{1}{2}$.

45. $x-\frac{x}{4}-\frac{1}{2}=3+\frac{x}{4}$.

46. $\frac{1}{2}x-\frac{3}{4}x-1\frac{1}{3}=\frac{1}{6}+2$.

47. $(x+3)(2x-3)-6x=(x-4)(2x+4)+12$.

48. $(x+2)(x+3)+(x-3)(x-2)-2x(x+1)=0$.

49. $(2x+1)(2x+6)-7(x-2)=4(x+1)(x-1)-9x$.

50. $(3x+1)^2+6+18(x+1)^2=9x(3x-2)+65$.

51. Shew that $x=5$ satisfies the equation

$5x-6(x-4)=2(x+5)+5(x-4)-6$.

52. Shew that $x=15$ is the solution of the equation

$7(25-x)-2x-15=2(3x-25)-x$.

53. Verify that $x=3$ satisfies the equation

$2(x+1)(x+3)+8=(2x+1)(x+5)$.

54. Shew that $x=4$ satisfies the equation $(3x+1)(2x-7)=6(x-3)^2+7$.

80. We shall now give some equations of greater difficulty.

Example 1. Solve $5x-(4x-7)(3x-5)=6-3(4x-9)(x-1)$.

Simplifying, we have

$$5x-(12x^2-41x+35)=6-3(4x^2-13x+9);$$

and by removing brackets

$$5x-12x^2+41x-35=6-12x^2+39x-27.$$

Erase the term $-12x^2$ on each side and transpose;

thus $5x+41x-39x=6-27+35$;

$$\therefore \quad 7x=14,$$

$$\therefore \quad x=2.$$

Note. Since the – sign before a bracket affects every term within it, in the first line of work we do not remove the brackets until we have formed the products.

Example 2. Solve $4-\frac{x-9}{8}=\frac{x}{22}-\frac{1}{2}$.

Multiply by 88, the least common multiple of the denominators;

$$352-11(x-9)=4x-44;$$

removing brackets, $352-11x+99=4x-44$;

transposing, $-11x-4x=-44-352-99$;

collecting terms and changing signs, $15x=495$;

$$\therefore \qquad x=33.$$

Note. In this equation $-\frac{x-9}{8}$ is regarded as a single term with the minus sign before it. In fact it is equivalent to $-\frac{1}{8}(x-9)$, the *vinculum* or line between the numerator and denominator having the same effect as a bracket. [Art. 58.]

In certain cases it will be found more convenient not to multiply throughout by the L.C.M. of the denominators, but to clear of fractions in two or more steps.

Example 3. Solve $\frac{x-4}{3}+\frac{2x-3}{35}=\frac{5x-32}{9}-\frac{x+9}{28}$.

Multiplying throughout by 9, we have

$$3x-12+\frac{18x-27}{35}=5x-32-\frac{9x+81}{28};$$

transposing, $\frac{18x-27}{35}+\frac{9x+81}{28}=2x-20$.

Now clear of fractions by multiplying by $5\times7\times4$ or 140;

$$\therefore \qquad 72x-108+45x+405=280x-2800;$$

$$\therefore \qquad 2800-108+405=280x-72x-45x;$$

$$\therefore \qquad 3097=163x;$$

$$\therefore \qquad x=19.$$

81. To solve equations whose coefficients are decimals, we may express the decimals as vulgar fractions, and proceed as before; but it is often found more simple to work entirely in decimals.

Example. Solve $.375x-1.875=.12x+1.185$.

Transposing, $.375x-.12x=1.185+1.1875$;

collecting terms, $(.375-.12)x=3.06$;

that is, $.255x=3.06$;

$$\therefore \qquad x=\frac{3.06}{.255}=12.$$

EXAMPLES IX. b

Solve the equations:

1. $(x+15)(x-3)-(x-3)^2=30-15(x-1).$

2. $15-3x=(2x+1)(2x-1)-(2x-1)(2x+3).$

3. $21-x(2x+1)+2(x-4)(x+2)=0.$

4. $3(x+5)-3(2x-1)=32-4(x-5)^2+4x^2.$

5. $3x^2-7x-(x+2)(x-2)=(x+1)(x-1)+(x-3)(x+3).$

6. $(x-6)(2x-9)-(11-2x)(7-x)=5x-4-7(x-2).$

7. $\frac{x-1}{5}+\frac{x-9}{2}=3.$

8. $\frac{x}{6}+\frac{x-8}{4}=1+\frac{x-6}{3}.$

9. $\frac{x+8}{3}=2+\frac{x-6}{7}.$

10. $\frac{6x-2}{9}+\frac{3x+5}{18}=\frac{1}{3}.$

Solve the equations:

11. $\frac{10x+1}{5}-1=5x-2.$

12. $x+3+\frac{x-2}{5}=7+2x.$

13. $\frac{x-6}{4}-\frac{x-4}{6}=1-\frac{x}{10}.$

14. $\frac{x+12}{6}-x=6\frac{1}{2}-\frac{x}{12}.$

15. $\frac{x+5}{6}-\frac{x+1}{9}=\frac{x+3}{4}.$

16. $\frac{11-6x}{5}-\frac{9-7x}{2}=\frac{5(x-1)}{6}.$

17. $\frac{47-6x}{5}-(x-6)=\frac{4(x-7)}{15}.$

18. $\frac{4-5x}{6}-\frac{1-2x}{3}=\frac{13}{42}.$

19. $\frac{3x-1}{10}-\frac{x-1}{4}=\frac{2x-31}{3}.$

20. $\frac{1-2x}{7}-\frac{2-3x}{8}=1\frac{1}{2}+\frac{x}{4}.$

21. $\frac{3}{4}(x-1)-\frac{5}{3}(x-4)=\frac{8}{5}(x-6)+\frac{5}{12}$.

22. $\frac{3}{5}(x-4)-\frac{1}{3}(2x-9)=\frac{1}{4}(x-1)-2$.

23. $\frac{1}{6}(x+4)-\frac{1}{2}(x-3)=\frac{1}{2}(3x-5)-\frac{1}{4}(x-6)-\frac{1}{5}(x-2)$.

24. $\frac{1}{7}(3-8x)-\frac{1}{5}(7-2x)+\frac{x-1}{5}=2-x-\frac{1}{5}(1-6x)$.

25. $\frac{1}{3}(x+4)-\frac{1}{9}(20-x)=\frac{1}{18}(5x-1)-\frac{1}{6}(5x-13)+8$.

26. $\frac{x+1}{2}-\frac{5x+9}{28}=\frac{x+6}{21}+5-\frac{x-12}{3}$.

27. $5-\frac{10x+1}{27}-\frac{x}{8}=\frac{13x+4}{18}-\frac{5(x-4)}{4}$.

28. $\frac{3x}{4}-\frac{x-7}{51}-(x-3)-\frac{6}{17}(x+10)+\frac{2x+5}{4}=0$.

29. $\frac{x+4}{39}-\frac{1}{5}(1-x)=2-\frac{3}{26}(6-5x)-\frac{1}{5}(x+4)$.

30. $\frac{3}{11}+\frac{1}{44}x=\frac{1}{2}\left(\frac{4}{11}-\frac{x}{33}\right)-\frac{5}{66}+\frac{1}{3}\left(1-\frac{x}{22}\right)$.

31. $.7x-3.35=6.4-3.2x$.

32. $.5x+.25+.1+1.25=.4x$.

33. $3.25x-.75x=9+1.5x$.

34. $.2x-.01x+.005x=11.7$.

35. $.5x-.6x=.75x-11$.

36. $.4x-.83x=.7-.3$.

37. Find the value of x which makes the two expressions $(3x-1)(4x-11)$ and $6(2x-1)(x-3)$ equal.

38. What value of x will make the expression $77x-3(2x-1)(4x-2)$ equal to $337-8(3x-1)(x+1)$?

CHAPTER X

SYMBOLICAL EXPRESSION

82. In solving algebraical problems the chief difficulty of the beginner is to express the conditions of the question by means of symbols. A question proposed in algebraical symbols will frequently be found puzzling, when a similar arithmetical question would present no difficulty.

Thus, the answer to the question "find a number greater than x by a" may not be self-evident to the beginner, who would of course readily answer an analogous arithmetical question, "find a number greater than 50 by 6." The process of addition which gives the answer in the second case supplies the necessary hint; and, just as the number which is greater than 50 by 6 is $50 + 6$, so the number which is greater than x by a is $x + a$.

83. The following examples will perhaps be the best introduction to the subject of this chapter. After the first we leave to the student the choice of arithmetical instances, should he find them necessary.

Example 1. By how much does x exceed 17?

Take a numerical instance: " by how much does 27 exceed 17?"

The answer obviously is 10, which is equal to $27 - 17$.

Hence the excess of x over 17 is $x - 17$.

Similarly, the defect of x from 17 is $17 - x$.

Example 2. If x is one *part* of 45 the other part is $45 - x$.

Example 3. If x is one *factor* of 45 the other factor is $\frac{45}{x}$.

Example 4. How far can a man walk in a hours at the rate of 4 km per hour?

In 1 hour he walks 4 km.

In a hours he walks a times as far, that is, $4a$ km.

Example 5. If Rs. 20 is divided equally among y persons, the share of each is the total sum divided by the number of persons, or Rs. $\frac{20}{y}$.

Example 6. Out of a purse containing Rs. x and y paise a man spends z paise; express in paise the sum left.

Rs. $x = 100x$ paise,

$\therefore$ the sum left $= (100x + y - z)$ paise.

EXAMPLES X. a

1. By how much does x exceed 5?
2. By how much is y less than 15?
3. What must be added to a to make 7?
4. What must be added to 6 to make b?
5. By what must 5 be multiplied to make a?
6. What is the quotient when 3 is divided by a?
7. By what must $6x$ be divided to get 2?
8. By how much does $6x$ exceed $2x$?
9. The sum of two numbers is x and one of the numbers is 10; what is the other?
10. The sum of three numbers is 100; if one of them is 25 and another is x, what is the third?
11. The product of two factors is $4x$; if one of the factors is 4, what is the other?
12. The product of two numbers is p, and one of them is m; what is the other?
13. How many times is x contained in $2y$?
14. The difference of two numbers is 8, and the greater of them is a; what is the other?
15. The difference of two numbers is x, and the lesser of them is 6; what is the other?
16. What number is less than 30 by y?
17. The sum of 12 equal numbers is $48x$, what is the value of each number?
18. How many numbers each equal to y must be taken to make $15xy$?
19. If there are x numbers each equal to $2a$, what is their sum?
20. If there are 5 numbers each equal to x, what is their product?
21. If there are x numbers each equal to p, what is their product?
22. If there are n books each worth Rs. y, what is the total cost?
23. If n books of equal value cost Rs. x, what does each cost?
24. How many books each worth Rs. 2 can be bought for Rs. y ?
25. If apples are sold at x for a rupee, what will be the cost in paise of y apples?
26. What is the price in paise of n oranges at Rs. 2 a score?

27. If I spend n paise out of a sum of Rs. 5, how many paise have I left?
28. What is the daily wage in paise of a man who earns Rs. 90 in p weeks, working 6 days a week?
29. How many days must a man work in order to earn Rs. 50 at the rate of y paise a day?
30. If x persons combine to pay a bill of Rs. y, what is the share of each in paise?
31. How many paise must a man pay out of a sum of Rs. p so as to have $36x$ paise left?
32. How many persons must contribute equally to a fund consisting of Rs. x, so that the subscription of each may equal y paise?
33. How many hours will it take to travel x kilometres at 10 per hour?
34. How far can I walk in p hours at the rate of q km per hour?
35. If I can walk m km in n days, what is my rate per day?
36. How many days will it take to travel y km at x km per day?

84. We subjoin a few harder examples worked out in full.

Example 1. What is(1) the sum, (2) the product of three consecutive numbers of which the least is n?

The two numbers consecutive to n are $n + 1$ and $n + 2$;

$\therefore$ the sum $= n + (n + 1) + (n + 2)$

$= 3n + 3.$

And the product $= n(n + 1)(n + 2)$.

Example 2. A boy is x years old, and five years hence his age will be half that of his father: how old is the father now?

In five years the boy will be $x + 5$ years old; therefore his father will then be $2(x + 5)$, or $2x + 10$ years old; his present age must therefore be $2x + 10 - 5$ or $2x + 5$ years.

Example 3. A and B are playing for money; A begins with Rs. p and B with q paise. B wins Rs. x; express by an equation the fact that A now has three times as much as B.

What B has won A has lost;

$\therefore$ A has Rs. $(p - x)$ that is $100(p - x)$ paise.

B has q paise + x rupees, that is, $(q + 100x)$ paise.

Thus the required equation is $100(p - x) = 3(q + 100x)$.

Example 4. A man travels a km by coach and b km by train; if the coach goes at the rate of 7 km per hour, and the train at the rate of 25 km per hour, how long does the journey take?

The coach travels 7 km in 1 hour;

$\therefore$ .... 1 .... $\frac{1}{7}$ hour;

that is, ... a .... $\frac{a}{7}$ hours.

Similarly, the train travels b km in $\frac{b}{25}$ hours.

$\therefore$ the whole time occupied is $\frac{a}{7}+\frac{b}{25}$ hours.

Example 5. How many men will be required to do in p hours what q men do in np hours?

np hours is the time occupied by q men;

$\therefore$ 1 hour .... $q \times np$ men;

that is, p hours .... $\frac{q \times np}{p}$ men.

Therefore the required number of men is qn.

EXAMPLES X. b

1. Write down three consecutive numbers of which a is the least.
2. Write down four consecutive numbers of which b is the greatest.
3. Write down five consecutive numbers of which c is the middle one.
4. What is the next odd number after $2n - 1$?
5. What is the even number next before $2n$?
6. Write down the product of three odd numbers of which the middle one is $2x + 1$.
7. How old is a man who will be x years old in 15 years?
8. How old was a man x years ago if his present age is n years?
9. In $2x$ years a man will be y years old, what is his present age?
10. How old is a man who in x years will be twice as old as his son now aged 20 years?
11. In 5 years a boy will be x years old; what is the present age of his father if he is twice as old as his son?
12. A has Rs. m and B has n paise; after A has won 75 paise from B, each has the same amount. Express this in algebraical symbols.

13. A has Rs. 25 and B has Rs. 13; after B has won Rs. x from A he then has four times as much as A. Express this in algebraical symbols.
14. How many km can a man walk in 30 minutes if he walks 1 km in x minutes?
15. How many km can a man walk in 50 minutes if he walks x km in y minutes?
16. How long will it take a man to walk p km if he walks 15 km in q hours?
17. How far can a pigeon fly in x hours at the rate of 2 km in 7 minutes?
18. A man travels x km by boat and y km by train, how long will the journey take if the train goes 30 km and the boat 10 km in an hour?
19. If x men do a work in $5x$ hours, how many men will be required to do the same work in y hours?
20. How long will it take p men to mow q ares of corn, if each man mows r ares a day?
21. Write down a number which, when divided by a, gives a quotient b and remainder c.
22. What is the remainder if x divided by y gives a quotient z ?
23. What is the quotient if when m is divided by n there is a remainder r?
24. If a bill is shared equally among n persons and each pays 90 paise, how many rupees does the bill amount to?
25. A man has Rs. x in his purse, he pays away Rs. $y \cdot 25$ paise and receives z paise; express in paise the sum he has left.
26. How many rupees does a man save in a year, if he earns Rs. x in a week and spends y paise in a calendar month?
27. What is the total cost of $6x$ nuts and $4x$ plums, when x plums cost one rupee and plums are three times as expensive as nuts?
28. If on an average there are x words in a line, and y lines in a page, how many pages will be required for a book which contains z words?

CHAPTER XI

PROBLEMS LEADING TO SIMPLE EQUATIONS

85. The principles of the last chapter may now be employed to solve various problems.

The method of procedure is as follows:

Represent the unknown quantity by a symbol x, and express in symbolical language the conditions of the question; we thus obtain a simple equation which can be solved by the methods already given in Chapter IX.

Example I. Find two numbers whose sum is 28, and whose difference is 4.

Let x be the smaller number, then $x + 4$ is the greater.

Their sum is $x + (x + 4)$, which is to be equal to 28,

Hence $x + x + 4 = 28$;

$$2x = 24;$$

$$\therefore \quad x = 12,$$

and $\quad x + 4 = 16,$

so that the numbers are 12 and 16.

The beginner is advised to test his solution by finding whether it satisfies the data of the question or not.

Example II. Divide Rs. 47 between A, B, C, so that A may have Rs. 10 more than B, and B Rs. 8 more than C.

Let x represent the *number* of rupees that C has; then B has $x + 8$ rupees, and A has $x + 8 + 10$ rupees.

Hence $x + (x + 8) + (x + 8 + 10) = 47$;

$$x + x + 8 + x + 8 + 10 = 47,$$

$$3x = 21;$$

$$\therefore \quad x = 7;$$

so that C has Rs. 7, B Rs. 15, A Rs. 25.

EXAMPLES XI. a

1. Six times a number increased by 11 is equal to 65; find it.
2. Find a number which when multiplied by 11 and then diminished by 18 is equal to 15.
3. If 3 be added to a number, and the sum multiplied by 12, the result is 84; find the number.
4. One number exceeds another by 3, and their sum is 27; find them.
5. Find two numbers whose sum is 30, and such that one of them is greater than the other by 8.
6. Find two numbers which differ by 10, so that one is three times the other.
7. Find two numbers whose sum is 19, such that one shall exceed twice the other by 1.
8. Find two numbers whose sum shall be 26 and their difference 8.
9. Divide Rs. 100 between A and B so that B may have Rs. 30 more than A.
10. Divide Rs. 66 between A, B, and C so that B may have Rs. 8 more than A, and C Rs. 14 more than B.
11. A, B, and C have Rs. 72 between them; C has twice as much as B, and B has Rs. 4 less than A; find the share of each.
12. How must a sum of 73 rupees be divided between A, B, and C, so that B may have 8 rupees less than A and 4 rupees more than C ?

Example III. Divide 60 into two parts, so that three times the greater may exceed 100 by as much as 8 times the less falls short of 200.

Let x be the greater part, then $60 - x$ is the less.

Three times the greater part is $3x$, and its excess over 100 is $3x - 100$.

Eight times the less is $8(60 - x)$, and its defect from 200 is $200 - 8(60 - x)$.

Whence the symbolical statement of the questions is

$$3x - 100 = 200 - 8(60 - x);$$

$$3x - 100 = 200 - 480 + 8x,$$

$$480 - 100 - 200 = 8x - 3x,$$

$$5x = 180;$$

$$\therefore \quad x = 36, \text{ the greater part,}$$

$$\text{and} \quad 60 - x = 24, \text{ the less.}$$

Example IV. *A* is 4 years older than *B*, and half *A*'s age exceeds one-sixth of *B*'s age by 8 years; find their ages.

Let x be the *number* of years in *B*'s age, then *A*'s age is $x + 4$ years.

One-half of *A*'s age is represented by $\frac{1}{2}(x + 4)$ years, and one-sixth of *B*'s age by $\frac{1}{6}x$ years.

Hence $\frac{1}{2}(x + 4) - \frac{1}{6}x = 8;$

multiplying by 6, $3x + 12 - x = 48;$

$$\therefore \qquad 2x = 36;$$

$$\therefore \qquad x = 18.$$

Thus *B*'s age is 18 years, and *A*'s age is 22 years.

13. Divide 75 into two parts, so that three times one part may be double of the other.

14. Divide 122 into two parts, such that one may be as much above 72 as twice the other is below 60.

15. A certain number is doubled and then increased by 5, and the result is less by 1 than three times the number; find it.

16. How much must be added to 28 so that the resulting number may be 8 times the added part?

17. Find the number whose double exceeds its half by 9.

18. What is the number whose seventh part exceeds its eighth part by 1?

19. Divide 48 into two parts, so that one part may be three-fifths of the other.

20. If *A*, *B*, and *C* have Rs. 76 between them, and *A*'s money is double of *B*'s and *C*'s one-sixth of *B*'s, what is the share of each?

21. Divide Rs. 511 between *A*, *B*, and *C*, so that *B*'s share will be one-third of *A*'s, and *C*'s share three-fourths of *A*'s and *B*'s together.

22. *B* is 16 years younger than *A*, and one-half *B*'s age is equal to one-third of *A*'s; how old are they?

23. *A* is 8 years younger than *B*, and 24 years older than *C*; one-sixth of *A*'s age, one-half of *B*'s, and one-third of *C*'s together amount to 38 years; find their ages.

24. Find two consecutive numbers whose product exceeds the square of the smaller by 7. [See Art. 84. Ex. 1.]

25. The difference between the squares of two consecutive numbers is 31; find the numbers.

86. We shall now give examples of somewhat greater difficulty.

Example I. *A* has Rs. 9·54 and *B* has Rs. 4·32; after *B* has won from *A* a certain sum, *A* has then five-sixths of what *B* has ; how much did *B* win?

Suppose that *B* wins x paise, *A* has then $954 - x$ paise, and *B* has $432 + x$ paise.

Hence $$954 - x = \frac{5}{6}(432 + x);$$

$$954 - x = 360 + \frac{5}{6}x;$$

$$\frac{11}{6}x = 594;$$

$$\therefore \quad x = 324.$$

Therefore B wins 324 paise, or Rs. 3·24.

Example II. *A* is twice as old as *B*, ten years ago he was four times as old; what are their present ages?

Let *B*'s age be x years, then *A*'s age is $2x$ years.

10 years ago their ages were respectively $x - 10$ and $2x - 10$ years ; thus we have

$$2x - 10 = 4(x - 10);$$

$$2x - 10 = 4x - 40,$$

$$2x = 30;$$

$$\therefore \quad x = 15,$$

so that *B* is 15 years old, *A* 30 years.

EXAMPLES XI. b

1. *A* has Rs. 12 and *B* has Rs. 8; after *B* has lost a certain sum to *A* his money is only three-sevenths of *A*'s; how much did *A* win?
2. *A* and *B* begin to play each with Rs. 15; if they play till *B*'s money is four-elevenths of *A*'s, what does *B* lose?
3. *A* and *B* have Rs. 28 between them; *A* gives Rs. 3 to *B* and then finds he has six times as much money as *B*; how much had each at first?
4. *A* had three times as much money as *B*; after giving Rs. 3 to *B* he had only twice as much; what had each at first?
5. A father is four times as old as his son; in 16 years he will only be twice as old; find their ages.
6. *A* is 20 years older than *B*, and 5 years ago *A* was twice as old as *B*; find their ages.
7. How old is a man whose age 10 years ago was three-eighths of what it will be in 15 years?

8. A is twice as old as B; 5 years ago he was three times as old; what are their present ages?

9. A father is 24 years older than his son; in 7 years the son's age will be two-fifths of his father's age; what are their present ages?

Example III. A person spent Rs. 345 in buying geese and ducks; if each goose cost Rs. 5, and each duck Rs. 2·50, and if the total number of birds bought was 108, how many of each did he buy?

In questions of this kind it is of essential importance to have all quantities expressed in the same denomination; in the present instance it will be convenient to express the money in paise.

Let x be the number of geese, then $180 - x$ is the number of ducks.

Since each goose costs 500 paise, x geese cost $500x$ paise.

And since each duck costs Rs. 2·50, $108 - x$ ducks cost $250(108 - x)$ paise.

Therefore the amount spent is $500x + 250(108 - x)$ paise.

But the question states that the amount is also Rs. 345, that is, 34500 paise.

Hence $\quad 500x + 250(108 - x) = 34500;$

$$10x + 5(108 - x) = 690,$$

$$10x - 5x = 150,$$

$\therefore \quad x = 30$, the number of geese,

and $\quad 108 - x = 78$, the number of ducks.

Note. In all these examples it should be noticed that the unknown quantity x represents a *number* of rupees, paise, ducks, years, etc.; and the student must be careful to avoid beginning a solution with a supposition of the kind, "let $x = A$'s share" or "let x = the ducks," or any statement so vague and inexact.

87. It will sometimes be found easier not to put x equal to the quantity directly required, but to some other quantity, involved in the question; by this means the equation is often simplified.

Example IV. A woman spends Re. 1·26 in buying eggs, and finds that 9 of them cost as much over 75 paise as 16 cost under Re. 1·50; how many eggs did she buy?

Let x be the price of an egg in paise; then 9 eggs cost $9x$ paise, and 16 eggs cost 16 cost paise;

$\therefore \quad 9x - 75 = 150 - 16x,$

$$25x = 225;$$

$\therefore \quad x = 9.$

Thus the price of an egg is 9 paise, and the number of eggs

$$= 126 \div 9 = 14.$$

10. A sum of Rs. 35·80 is divided between 50 men and women, the men each receiving 74 paise and the women 70 paise; find the number of each sex.

11. The price of 13 metres of cloth is as much less than Rs. 15 as the price of 27 metres exceeds Rs. 29; find the price per metre.

12. 50 kg of tea, worth Rs. 111, is made up of two sorts, part worth Rs. 3 per kg and the rest worth Re. 1·50 per kg; how much is there of each sort?

13. A man is hired for 60 days on condition that for each day he works he shall receive Rs. 5·50, but for each day that he is idle he shall pay Re. 1·25 for his board: at the end he received Rs. 73·50; how many days had he worked?

14. A sum of Rs. 25·07 is made up of 32 coins, which are either rupees or paise; how many are there of each?

15. A sum of Rs. 76·50 was paid in 50, 25, and 10 paise coins; the number of ten-paise coins used was four times the number of twenty-five paise coins and ten times the number of fifty-paise coins; how many were there of each?

16. A person buys coffee and tea at Rs. 3·75 and Rs. 3·50 per kg respectively; he spends Rs. 87, and in all gets 24 kg; how much of each did he buy?

17. A man sold a horse for a sum of money which was greater by Rs. 494 than half the price he paid for it, and gained thereby Rs. 150; what did he pay for the horse?

18. Two boys have 240 marbles between them; one arranges his in heaps of 6 each, the other in heaps of 9 each. There are 36 heaps altogether; how many marbles has each?

19. A man's age is four times the combined ages of his two sons, one of whom is three times as old as the other; in 24 years their combined ages will be 12 years less than their father's age; find their respective ages.

20. A sum of money is divided between three persons, A, B, and C, in such a way that A and B have Rs. 42 between them, B and C have Rs. 45, and C and A have Rs. 53; what is the share of each?

21. A person bought a number of oranges for Rs. 2·70, and finds that 12 of them cost as much over 30 paise as 16 of them cost under Re. 1·80; how many oranges were bought?

22. By buying eggs at 15 for 72 paise and selling them at a dozen for 90 paise a man gained Rs. 9·72; find the number of eggs.

23. I bought a certain number of apples at four for 6 paise, and three-fifths of that number at three for 6 paise; by selling them at sixteen for 30 paise I gained 24 paise; how many apples did I buy?

24. If 8 kg of tea and 24 kg of sugar cost Rs. 39·20, and if 3 kg of tea cost as much as 40 kg of sugar, find the price of each per kg.
25. Four dozen bottles of port plus three dozen bottles of sherry cost Rs. 193; if a bottle of port cost 90 paise more than a bottle of sherry, find the price of each per dozen.
26. A sum of Rs. 29.30 is divided among 23 boys and girls; if a boy receives Re. 1·30 and a girl Re. 1·18, find the number of each.
27. *A* and *B* begin to play with equal sums, when *B* has lost Rs. 3·72 he has one-half of what *A* has; how much had each at first?
28. Divide Rs. 13·26 between *A*, *B*, and *C*, so that *B*'s share is twice *A*'s and *A*'s one-third of *C*'s.
29. Two boys have Rs. 3·72 and Rs. 4·50 respectively; how much must the first give to the second in order that the latter may have twice as much as the former?
30. If 6 kg of coffee cost as much as 5 kg of tea, find the cost of each when 11 kg of coffee and 7 kg of tea can be bought for Rs. 48·50.
31. A bag of flour weighs 52 kg 500 gm and a bag of wheat weighs 43 kg 250 gm; if 590 kg is the weight of 13 bags, how many bags are there of flour and wheat respectively?
32. Two pieces of iron weigh 27 kg 250 gm and 36 kg 500 gm; what weight must be taken from the smaller and added to the larger in order that the weight of the first may then be two-thirds of the second?
33. A load of 21 tonnes 843 kg is carried in 20 carts and wagons; if a cart carries 824 kg 750 gm and a wagon 1 tonne 206 kg 750 gm; find the number of carts and wagons respectively.
34. One-fourth of a field belongs to *A*, one-third to *B*, and one-tenth to *C*; the remainder, which consists of 2 hectares 16 ares 60 centiares belongs to *D*; find the size of the field.
35. Two plots of land contain 71 ares 68 centiares, and are together worth Rs. 2630; if the first is worth Rs. 40 an are, and second Rs. 30 an are, find the size of each.

CHAPTER XII

ELEMENTARY FRACTIONS

Highest Common Factor of Simple Expressions

88. DEFINITION. The **highest common factor** of two or more algebraical expressions is the expression of highest dimensions [Art. 68] which divides each of them without remainder.

The abbreviation H.C.F. is sometimes used instead of the words *highest common factor*.

89. In the case of *simple expressions* the highest common factor can be written down by inspection.

Example 1. The highest common factor of a^4, a^3, a^2, a^6 is a^2.

Example 2. The highest common factor of $a^3b^4, a^2b^5c^2, a^4b^7c$ is a^2b^4; for a^2 is the highest power of a that will divide a^3, a^2, a^4; b^4 is the highest power of b that will divide b^4, b^5, b^7; and c is not a *common* factor.

90. If the expressions have numerical coefficients, find by Arithmetic their greatest common measure, and prefix it as a coefficient to the algebraical highest common factor.

Example. The highest common factor of $21a^4x^3y, 35a^2x^4y, 28a^3xy$ is $7a^2xy$; for it consists of the product of

(1) the greatest common measure of the numerical coefficients;

(2) the highest power of each letter which divides every one of the given expressions.

EXAMPLES XII.a

Find the highest common factor of

1. $3ab^2, 2ab^3$.

2. $x^3y^2, 4x^2y^5$.

3. $bc^5, 5b^3c$.

4. $4x^5, 2xy^2z^3$.

5. a^2b^2c, a^3bc^5.

6. $3a^2b, 9abc$.

7. $6x^2y^2z, 2xy$.

8. $15y^3, 5xy^6z^2$.

9. $12a^3bc^2, 18ab^2c^3$.

10. $7x^3y^5z^4, 21x^2yz^3$.

11. $8ax, 6a^2y, 10ab^2x^2$.

12. $a^2x^3y, b^3xy^4, cx^4y^2$.

13. $14bc^2, 63ba^2, 56b^2c$.

14. $15x^2y, 60x^5y^2z^3, 25x^3z^4$.

15. $17xy^2z, 51xyz^2, 34x^2yz$.

16. $77a^3b^5c^2, 33a^2b^3c^5, ab^2c^6$.

Lowest Common Multiple of Simple Expressions

91. DEFINITION. The **lowest common multiple** of two or more algebraical expressions is the expression of lowest dimensions which is divisible by each of them without remainder.

The abbreviation L.C.M. is sometimes used instead of the words *lowest common multiple.*

92. In the case of *simple expressions* the lowest common multiple can be written down by inspection.

Example 1. The lowest common multiple of a^4, a^3, a^2, a^6 is a^6.

Example 2. The lowest common multiple of a^3b^4, ab^5, a^2b^7 is a^3b^7; for a^3 is the lowest power of a that is divisible by each of the quantities a^3, a, a^2; and b^7 is the lowest power of b that is divisible by each of the quantities b^4, b^5, b^7.

93. If the expressions have numerical coefficients, find by Arithmetic their least common multiple, and prefix it as a coefficient to the algebraical lowest common multiple.

Example. The lowest common multiple of $21a^4x^3y, 35a^2x^4y, 28a^3xy$ is $420a^4x^4y$; for it consists of the product of

(1) the least common multiple of the numerical coefficients;

(2) the lowest power of each letter which is divisible by every power of that letter occurring in the given expressions.

EXAMPLES XII. b

Find the lowest common multiple of

1. $xyz, 3y^3$.

2. a^2b^4, abc.

3. $2x^3y, 3xy^2z$.

4. $4a^2, 3abx^4$.

5. $4a^4bc^3, 5ab^2$.

6. $2ab, 4xy$.

7. mn, nl, lm.

8. $xy^2, 3yz^2, 2zx^2$.

9. $2xy, 3yz, 4zx$.

10. $p^2qr, q^3p^2r, 7pq$.

11. $15x^2y, 25xyz^3$.

12. $9ab^3, 21a^2c$.

13. $27a^3, 81b^3, 18a^2b^5$.

14. $5ax^6, 6cy, 7a^2x^3c^5z$.

15. $15a^2b^3, 20ax^2y, 30x^3$.

16. $72p^2q^3r^4, 108p^3q^2r$.

Find both the highest common factor and the lowest common multiple of

17. $2ab^2, 3a^2b^3, 4a^4b$.

18. $15x^3y^2, 5x^2yz^5$.

19. $2a^4, 8a^2b^3c^7$.

20. $57ax^2y, 76xy^2z^7$.

21. $32a^4b^3c, 48a^7bc^5$.

22. $51m^2p^2, pn, 34mnp^4$.

23. $49a^4, 56b^4c, 21ac^3$.

24. $66a^2b^3cx^4, 55ab^5xy^3z, 121x^2yz^7$.

Elementary Fractions

94. DEFINITION. If a quantity x be divided into b equal parts, and a of these parts be taken, the result is called *the fraction* $\frac{a}{b}$ *of* x. If x be the unit, the fraction $\frac{a}{b}$ of x is called simply "the fraction $\frac{a}{b}$"; So that *the fraction* $\frac{a}{b}$ *represents a equal parts, b of which make up the unit.*

95. In this chapter we propose to deal only with the easier kinds of fractions, where the numerator and denominator are simple expressions.

Their reduction and simplification will be performed by the usual arithmetical rules. For the proofs of these rules the reader is referred to the *Elementary Algebra for Schools*, Chapter XIX and XXI.

Rule. *To reduce a fraction to its lowest terms; divide numerator and denominator by every factor which is common to them both, that is, by their highest common factor.*

Dividing numerator and denominator of a fraction by a common factor is called *cancelling* that factor.

Examples. (1) $\frac{6a^2c}{9ac^2} = \frac{2a}{3c}$.

(2) $\frac{7x^2yz}{28x^3yz^2} = \frac{1}{4xz}$. (3) $\frac{35a^5b^3c}{7ab^2c} = \frac{5a^4b}{1} = 5a^4b$.

EXAMPLES XII.c

Reduce to lowest terms:

1. $\frac{2a}{4ab}$.
2. $\frac{3a^2}{9ab}$.
3. $\frac{2bc^2}{6b^2c}$.
4. $\frac{2abc}{8a^2bc^2}$.
5. $\frac{xy^2z^3}{x^3y^4z}$.
6. $\frac{12mn}{15lm}$.
7. $\frac{14xy^3}{21x^2z^3}$.
8. $\frac{9a^3b}{12ab^3c}$.
9. $\frac{15a^2b^2c^3}{18abc^2}$.
10. $\frac{5a^3y^2z^4}{15ay^4z}$.
11. $\frac{10xy^3}{24x^3y}$.
12. $\frac{3m^2n^3p^2}{15mn^2p}$.
13. $\frac{15k^2p^3m^4}{25k^3pm^2}$.
14. $\frac{27a^4b^3x^2}{45a^3b^4x^4}$.
15. $\frac{56a^3c^4z^2}{77ac^2z^3}$.
16. $\frac{42x^2y^2z^2}{210x^3y^2z}$.

Multiplication and Division of Fractions

96. **Rule.** *To multiply algebraical fractions: as in Arithmetic, multiply together all the numerators for a new numerator, and all the denominators for a new denominator.*

Example 1. $\dfrac{2a}{3b} \times \dfrac{5x^2}{2a^2b} \times \dfrac{3b^2}{2x} = \dfrac{2a \times 5x^2 \times 3b^2}{3b \times 2a^2b \times 2x} = \dfrac{5x}{2a}$,

by cancelling like factors in numerator and denominator.

Example 2. $\dfrac{3a^2b}{5c^2} \times \dfrac{7bc}{3a^3} \times \dfrac{5ac}{7b^2} = 1$,

all the factors cancelling each other.

97. **Rule.** *To divide one fraction by another: invert the divisor and proceed as in multiplication.*

Example. $\dfrac{7a^3}{4x^3y^2} \times \dfrac{6c^3x}{5ab^2} \div \dfrac{28a^2c^2}{15b^2xy^2} = \dfrac{7a^3}{4x^3y^2} \times \dfrac{6c^3x}{5ab^2} \times \dfrac{15b^2xy^2}{28a^2c^2} = \dfrac{9c}{8x}$,

all the other factors cancelling each other.

EXAMPLES XII.d

Simplify the following expressions:

1. $\dfrac{xy}{ab} \times \dfrac{a^2b^3}{xy^2}$.

2. $\dfrac{ab}{2cd^3} \times \dfrac{4c^2d}{ab^3}$.

3. $\dfrac{2ax^2}{3y^3z} \times \dfrac{yz^3}{4a^2x}$.

4. $\dfrac{6a^2x^3}{7ab^2} \times \dfrac{14b^2c}{12ax}$.

5. $\dfrac{3ab^2}{5b^3c} \times \dfrac{15b^2c^2}{9a^2b}$.

6. $\dfrac{7c^2}{5bc^2} \times \dfrac{25c^2}{14bc}$.

7. $\dfrac{a^2m}{b^2y} \times \dfrac{2cd^2}{3ab} \times \dfrac{9my}{4m^2}$.

8. $\dfrac{4a^2b}{9xy} \times \dfrac{3p^2q^2}{8a^2b^2} \div \dfrac{pq}{x^2y^2}$.

9. $\dfrac{2a^3p^2}{5ax^4} \times \dfrac{10b^2}{4x^2} \div \dfrac{b^2p^2}{3x^6}$.

10. $\dfrac{y^2z^3}{zx^3} \times \dfrac{17y}{x^2z^2} \div \dfrac{34y^3}{x^5y}$.

11. $\dfrac{8a^2z^2}{2by} \times \dfrac{9ax^2}{5a^2z} \times \dfrac{x^3y^2}{2h^2y}$.

12. $\dfrac{15b^2}{40c} \times \dfrac{14d^3}{abc} \div \dfrac{81d^3}{27c^2}$.

Reduction to a Common Denominator

98. In order to find the sum or difference of any fractions, we must, as in Arithmetic, first reduce them to a common denominator; and it is most convenient to take the lowest common multiple of the denominators of the given fractions.

Example. Express with lowest common denominator the fractions

$$\frac{a}{3xy}, \frac{b}{6xyz}, \frac{c}{2yz}.$$

The lowest common multiple of the denominators is $6xyz$. Multiplying the numerator of each fraction by the factor which is required to make its denominator $6xyz$, we have the equivalent fractions

$$\frac{2az}{6xyz}, \frac{b}{6xyz}, \frac{3cx}{6xyz}.$$

Note. The Same Result Would Clearly Be Obtained By Dividing The Lowest common denominator by each of the denominators in turn, and multiplying the corresponding numerators by the respective quotients.

EXAMPLES XII. e

Express as equivalent fractions with common denominator:

1. $\frac{x}{2a}, \frac{2x}{a}$.
2. $\frac{y}{b}, \frac{2y}{3b}$.
3. $\frac{3a}{2c}, \frac{4a}{5c}$.
4. $\frac{x}{2y}, a$.
5. $\frac{m}{4n}, \frac{3m}{5n}$.
6. $\frac{x}{3y}, \frac{2a}{x}$.
7. $\frac{a}{b}, \frac{2a}{b^2}$.
8. $\frac{x}{3y}, \frac{3x}{y^2}$.
9. $\frac{a}{b}, \frac{x}{y}, 1$.
10. $\frac{a}{b}, \frac{b}{a}, 2a$.
11. $3, \frac{a}{2b}, \frac{b}{2a}$.
12. $\frac{1}{bc}, \frac{1}{ca}, \frac{1}{ab}$.
13. $\frac{a}{2xy}, \frac{b}{3yz}, \frac{c}{zx}$.
14. $\frac{m}{n}, \frac{n}{m}, \frac{p}{q}$.

Addition and Subtraction of Fractions

99. Rule. *To add or subtract fractions: express all the fractions with their lowest common denominator; form the algebraical sum of the numerators, and retain the common denominator.*

Example 1. Simplify $\frac{5x}{3} + \frac{3}{4}x - \frac{7x}{6}$.

The least common denominator is 12.

The expression $= \frac{20x + 9x - 14x}{12} = \frac{15x}{12} = \frac{5x}{4}$.

Example 2. Simplify $\frac{3ab}{5x} - \frac{ab}{2x} - \frac{ab}{10x}$.

The expression $= \frac{6ab - 5ab - ab}{10x} = \frac{0}{10x} = 0$.

Example 3. Simplify $\dfrac{2x}{a^2c^2} - \dfrac{y}{3ca^3}$.

The expression $= \dfrac{6ax - cy}{3a^3c^2}$, and admits of no further simplification.

Note. The beginner must be careful to distinguish between **erasing equal terms with different signs**, as in Example 2, and **cancelling equal factors** in the course of multiplication, or in reducing fractions to lowest terms. Moreover, in simplifying fractions he must remember that a factor can only be removed from numerator and denominator when it divides each *taken as a whole.*

Thus in $\dfrac{6ax - cy}{3a^3c^2}$, c cannot be cancelled because it only divides cy and not the *whole* numerator. Similarly, a cannot be cancelled because it only divides $6ax$ and not the whole numerator. The fraction is therefore in its simplest form.

When no denominator is expressed the denominator 1 may be understood.

Example 4. $3x - \dfrac{a^2}{4y} = \dfrac{3x}{1} - \dfrac{a^2}{4y} = \dfrac{12xy - a^2}{4y}$.

If a fraction is not in its lowest terms **it should be simplified** before combining it with other fractions.

Example 5. $\dfrac{ax}{2} - \dfrac{x^2y}{3xy} = \dfrac{ax}{2} - \dfrac{x}{3} = \dfrac{3ax - 2x}{6}$.

EXAMPLES XII.f

Simplify the following expressions:

1. $\dfrac{a}{2} + \dfrac{a}{3}$.
2. $\dfrac{b}{3} + \dfrac{b}{4}$.
3. $\dfrac{x}{4} - \dfrac{x}{5}$.
4. $\dfrac{2y}{3} + \dfrac{y}{6}$.
5. $\dfrac{a}{5} - \dfrac{b}{6}$.
6. $\dfrac{m}{8} - \dfrac{2n}{20}$.
7. $\dfrac{p}{7} + \dfrac{q}{21}$.
8. $\dfrac{5a}{12} - \dfrac{b}{4}$.
9. $\dfrac{a}{x} + \dfrac{b}{y}$.
10. $\dfrac{x}{y} - \dfrac{a}{b}$.
11. $\dfrac{2a}{3} + \dfrac{4a}{9b}$.
12. $\dfrac{ab}{3} - \dfrac{x^2y}{6xy}$.
13. $\dfrac{a}{4} - \dfrac{a}{8} + \dfrac{a}{12}$.
14. $\dfrac{2x}{3} - \dfrac{x}{6} + \dfrac{9x}{12}$.
15. $\dfrac{a}{xy} + \dfrac{2a}{yz} - \dfrac{3a}{zx}$.
16. $\dfrac{xy}{5x} - \dfrac{2y}{3} + \dfrac{4y}{8}$.
17. $2 + \dfrac{a}{b} - \dfrac{b^2}{ab}$.
18. $\dfrac{a}{p^2} + \dfrac{b}{pq} - \dfrac{c}{q^2}$.
19. $a - \dfrac{x^3}{a^2}$.
20. $\dfrac{m}{2} - \dfrac{n^3}{m^2}$.
21. $\dfrac{a^3}{ab^2} - 3$.
22. $k^4 - \dfrac{p^6}{k^2}$.
23. $\dfrac{d^2x}{dy^2} - 2\dfrac{dx}{dy} + \dfrac{xy}{2y^2}$.
24. $\dfrac{a^3}{3a^2b} - \dfrac{a^3}{ab^2} + \dfrac{ac}{6bc}$.

CHAPTER XIII

SIMULTANEOUS EQUATIONS

100. CONSIDER the equation $2x + 5y = 23$, which contains *two* unknown quantities.

By transposition we get

$$5y = 23 - 2x;$$

that is, $$y = \frac{23 - 2x}{5} \qquad \ldots(1).$$

From this it appears that for every value we choose to give to x there will be one corresponding value of y. Thus we shall be able to find as many pairs of values as we please which satisfy the given equation.

For instance, if $x = 1$, then from (1) we obtain $y = \frac{21}{5}$.

Again, if $x = -2$, then $y = \frac{27}{5}$; and so on.

But if also we have a second equation of the same kind,

such as $$3x + 4y = 24,$$

we have from this $$y = \frac{24 - 3x}{4} \qquad \ldots(2)$$

If now we seek values of x and y which satisfy *both* equations, the values of y in (1) and (2) must be identical.

Therefore $$\frac{23 - 2x}{5} = \frac{24 - 3x}{4}.$$

Multiplying up, $$92 - 8x = 120 - 15x;$$

$$\therefore \quad 7x = 28;$$

$$\therefore \quad x = 4.$$

Substituting this value in the first equation, we have

$$8 + 5y = 23;$$

$$\therefore \quad 5y = 15;$$

$$\therefore \quad \left.\begin{aligned} y &= 3, \\ \text{and} \quad x &= 4. \end{aligned}\right\}$$

Thus, if both equations are to be satisfied by the *same* values of x and y, there is only one solution possible.

101. DEFINITION. When two or more equations are satisfied by the same values of the unknown quantities, they are called **simultaneous equations.**

We proceed to explain the different methods for solving simultaneous equations. In the present chapter we shall confine our attention to the simpler cases in which the unknown quantities are involved in the first degree.

102. In the example already worked we have used the method of solution which best illustrates the meaning of the term *simultaneous equation*, but in practice it will be found that this is rarely the readiest mode of solution. It must be borne in mind that since the two equations are simultaneously true, *any* equation formed by combining them will be satisfied by the values of x and y which satisfy the original equations. Our object will always be to obtain an equation which involves *one only* of the unknown quantities.

103. The process by which we get rid of either of the unknown quantities is called **elimination**, and it should be effected in different ways according to the nature of the equations proposed.

Example 1. Solve

$$3x + 7y = 27 \qquad \text{...(1)},$$

$$5x + 2y = 16 \qquad \text{...(2)}.$$

To eliminate x we multiply (1) by 5 and (2) by 3, so as to make the coefficients of x in both equations equal. This gives

$$15x + 35y = 135,$$

$$15x + 6y = 48;$$

subtracting, $\quad 29y = 87;$

$\therefore \quad y = 3.$

To find x, substitute this value of y in *either* of the given equations,

Thus from (1), $3x + 21 = 27;$

$$\therefore \quad \left.\begin{array}{l} x = 2, \\ y = 3. \end{array}\right\}$$

and

Note. When one of the unknowns has been found, it is immaterial which of the equations we use to complete the solution. Thus, in the present example, if we substitute 3 for y in (2), we have

$$5x + 6 = 16;$$

$\therefore \quad x = 2, \qquad$ as before.

Example 2. Solve

$$7x + 2y = 47 \qquad \ldots(1),$$

$$5x - 4y = 1 \qquad \ldots(2).$$

Here it will be more convenient to eliminate y.

Multiplying (1) by 2, $14x + 4y = 94$,

and from (2) $5x - 4y = 1$;

adding, $19x = 95$;

$\therefore$ $x = 5$.

Substitute this value in (1),

$\therefore$ $35 + 2y = 47$;

$\therefore$ and $\left.\begin{matrix} y = 6, \\ x = 5. \end{matrix}\right\}$

Note. *Add* when the coefficients of one unknown are equal and *unlike* in sign; *subtract* when the coefficients are equal and *like* in sign.

Example 3. Solve

$$2x = 5y + 1 \qquad \ldots(1),$$

$$24 - 7x = 3y \qquad \ldots(2).$$

Here we can eliminate x by substituting in (2) its value obtained from (1). Thus

$$24 - \frac{7}{2}(5y + 1) = 3y;$$

$\therefore$ $48 - 35y - 7 = 6y$;

$\therefore$ $41 = 41y$;

$\therefore$ and from (1) $\left.\begin{matrix} y = 1, \\ x = 3. \end{matrix}\right\}$

104. Any one of the methods given above will be found sufficient; but there are certain arithmetical artifices which will sometimes shorten the work.

Example. Solve

$$28x - 23y = 22 \qquad \ldots(1),$$

$$63x - 55y = 17 \qquad \ldots(2).$$

Noticing that 28 and 63 contain a common factor 7, we shall make the coefficients of x in the two equations equal to the *least common multiple* of 28 and 63 if we multiply (1) by 9 and (2) by 4.

Thus $252x - 207y = 198$;

$252x - 220y = 68$;

subtracting, $13y = 130$;

that is $y = 10$,

and therefore from (1), $x = 9$.

EXAMPLES XIII. a

Solve the equations:

1. $x + y = 19, x - y = 7.$
2. $x + y = 23, x - y = 5.$
3. $x + y = 11, x - y = -9.$
4. $x + y = 24, x - y = 0.$
5. $x - y = 6, x + y = 0.$
6. $x - y = 25, x + y = 13.$
7. $3x + 5y = 50, 4x + 3y = 41.$
8. $x + 5y = 18, 3x + 2y = 41.$
9. $4x + y = 10, 5x + 7y = 47.$
10. $7x - 6y = 25, 5x + 4y = 51.$
11. $5x + 4y = 7, 4x + 5y = 2.$
12. $3x - 7y = 1, 4x + y = 53.$
13. $7x + 5y = 45, 2x - 3y = 4.$
14. $4x + 5y = 4, 5x - 3y = 79.$
15. $11x - 7y = 43, 2x - 3y = 13.$
16. $4x - 3y = 0, 7x - 4y = 36.$
17. $2x + 3y = 22, 5x + 2y = 0.$
18. $7x + 3y = 65, 7x - 8y = 32.$
19. $13x - y = 14, 2x - 7y = 9.$
20. $9x - 8y = 14, 15x - 14y = 20.$
21. $14x + 13y = 35, 21x + 19y = 56.$
22. $5x = 7y - 21, 21x - 9y = 75.$
23. $55x = 33y, 10x = 7y - 15.$
24. $5x - 7y = 11, 18x = 12y.$
25. $13x - 9y = 46, 11x - 12y = 17.$
26. $6x - 5y = 11, 28x + 21y = 7.$
27. $11y - 11x = 66, 7x + 8y = 3.$
28. $6y - 5x = 11, 4x = 7y - 22.$
29. $3x + 10 = 5y, 7y = 4x + 13.$
30. $4y = 47 + 3x, 5x = 30 - 15y.$
31. $11x + 13y = 7, 13x + 11y = 17.$
32. $13x - 17y = 11, 29x - 39y = 17.$
33. $19x + 17y = 7, 41x + 37y = 17.$

105. We add a few cases in which, before proceeding to solve, it will be necessary to simplify the equations.

Example. Solve

$$5(x + 2y) - (3x + 11y) = 14 \quad ...(1),$$

$$7x - 9y - 3(x - 4y) = 38 \quad ...(2).$$

From (1), $5x + 10y - 3x - 11y = 14;$

$\therefore \quad 2x - y = 14 \quad ...(3).$

From (2), $7x - 9y - 3x + 12y = 38;$

$\therefore \quad 4x + 3y = 38 \quad ...(4).$

From (3), $6x - 3y = 42.$

By addition, $10x = 80$; hence $x = 8$.

From (3) we obtain $y = 2$.

106. Sometimes the value of the second unknown is more easily found by elimination than by substituting the value of the unknown already found.

Example. Solve

$$3x - \frac{y-5}{7} = \frac{4x-3}{2} \quad \text{...(1)},$$

$$\frac{3y+4}{5} - \frac{1}{3}(2x-5) = y \quad \text{...(2)}.$$

Clear of fractions. Thus

from (1), $42x - 2y + 10 = 28x - 21$;

$\therefore \quad 14x - 2y = -31 \quad$ ...(3).

From (2), $9y + 12 - 10x + 25 = 15y$;

$\therefore \quad 10x + 6y = 37 \quad$ ...(4).

Eliminating y from (3) and (4), we find that

$$x = -\frac{14}{13}.$$

Eliminating x from (3) and (4), we find that

$$y = \frac{207}{26}.$$

107. Simultaneous equations may often be conveniently solved by considering $\frac{1}{x}$ and $\frac{1}{y}$ as the unknown quantities.

Example. Solve $\quad \frac{8}{x} - \frac{9}{y} = 1 \quad$ ...(1),

$$\frac{10}{x} + \frac{6}{y} = 7 \quad \text{...(2)}.$$

Multiply (1) by 2 and (2) by 3; thus

$$\frac{16}{x} - \frac{18}{y} = 2,$$

$$\frac{30}{x} + \frac{18}{y} = 21;$$

adding, $\quad \frac{46}{x} = 23;$

multiplying up, $46 = 23x$;

$\therefore \quad x = 2;$

and by substituting in (1), $y = 3$.

EXAMPLE XIII. b

Solve the equations:

1. $2x - y = 4, \frac{x}{2} + \frac{y}{4} = 5.$

2. $4x - y = 1, \frac{x}{2} + \frac{3y}{7} = 4.$

3. $x + 2y = 13, \frac{2x}{3} - \frac{y}{5} = 1.$

4. $\frac{3x}{10} + y = 1, x + 3y = 2.$

5. $x - \frac{2y}{3} = 0, 4x - 3y = 1.$

6. $\frac{3x}{5} - y = 7, 4x + 5y = 0.$

7. $5x = 4y, \frac{4x}{3} - \frac{3y}{5} = 7.$

8. $x - y = 0, \frac{5}{3}x - \frac{9}{2}y = 2\frac{5}{6}.$

9. $x + y = -2, \frac{x}{4} + \frac{y}{6} = 0.$

10. $\frac{1}{2}(x + 3) = 0, \frac{1}{6}x - y = 4\frac{1}{2}.$

11. $\frac{3}{5}x - 2y = 20, \frac{1}{2}(y + 8) = 2.$

12. $\frac{1}{3}x - \frac{1}{2}y = 0, 3x = 2y$

13. $3(x - y) + 2(x + y) = 15, 3(x + y) + 2(x - y) = 25.$

14. $3(x + y - 5) = 2(y - x), 3(x - y - 7) + 2(x + y - 2) = 0.$

15. $4(2x - y - 6) = 3(3x - 2y - 5), 2(x - y + 1) + 4x = 3y + 4.$

16. $7(2x - y) + 5(3y - 4x) + 30 = 0. 5(y - x + 3) = 6(y - 2x).$

17. $\frac{x + 4}{5} = \frac{y - 4}{7} = 2x + y + 4.$

18. $\frac{x - 12}{4} = \frac{y + 18}{3} = \frac{2x + 3y}{2}.$

19. $\frac{8}{x} + \frac{9}{y} = 7, \frac{6}{x} - \frac{1}{y} = 2\frac{2}{3}.$

20. $\frac{3}{x} + \frac{5}{y} = 37, \frac{7}{x} - \frac{3}{y} = 13.$

21. $\frac{10}{x} - \frac{3}{y} = 8, \frac{3}{x} + \frac{2}{y} = -3\frac{2}{5}.$

108. In order to solve simultaneous equations which contain two unknown quantities we have seen that we must have two equations. Similarly, we find that in order to solve simultaneous equations which contain three unknown quantities we must have three equations.

Rule. *Eliminate one of the unknowns from any pair of the equations, and then eliminate the same unknown from another pair. Two equations involving two unknowns are thus obtained, which may be solved by the rules already given. The remaining unknown is then found by substituting in any one of the given equations.*

Example. Solve

$$7x + 5y - 7z = -8 \qquad \ldots(1),$$

$$4x + 2y - 3z = 0 \qquad \ldots(2),$$

$$5x - 4y + 4z = 35 \qquad \ldots(3).$$

Choose y as the unknown to be eliminated.

Multiply (2) by 5, $20x + 10y - 15z = 0$;

Multiply (1) by 2, $14x + 10y - 14z = -16$;

by subtraction, $6x - z = 16 \qquad \ldots(4).$

Multiply (2) by 2, $8x + 4y - 6z = 0$;

from (3), $5x - 4y + 4z = 35$;

by addition, $13x - 2z = 35.$

Multiply (4) by 2, $12x - 2z = 32$;

by subtraction, $x = 3.$

From (4) we find $z = 2,$

and from (2), $y = -3.$

109. Some modification of the foregoing rule may often be used with advantage.

Example. Solve $\frac{x}{2} - 1 = \frac{y}{6} + 1 = \frac{z}{7} + 2,$

$$\frac{y}{3} + \frac{z}{2} = 13.$$

From the equation $\frac{x}{2} - 1 = \frac{y}{6} + 1,$

we have $3x - y = 12 \qquad \ldots(1).$

Also from the equation $\frac{x}{2} - 1 = \frac{z}{7} + 2,$

we have $7x - 2z = 42 \qquad \ldots(2).$

And from the equation $\frac{y}{3} + \frac{z}{2} = 13,$

we have $2y + 3z = 78 \qquad \ldots(3).$

Eliminating z from (2) and (3), we have

$$21x + 4y = 282;$$

and from (1) $12x - 4y = 48;$

Whence $x = 10$, $y = 18$.

Also by substitution in (2) we obtain $z = 14$.

EXAMPLES XIII.c

Solve the equations:

1. $3x-2y+z=4, \quad 2x+3y-z=3, \quad x+y+z=8.$
2. $3x+4y-6z=16, \quad 4x+y-z=24, \quad x-3y-2z=1.$
3. $x+2y+3z=32, \quad 4x-5y+6z=27, \quad 7x+8y-9z=14.$
4. $x-y+z=5, \quad 6x+3y+2z=84, \quad 3x+4y-5z=13.$
5. $7x-4y-3z=0, \quad 5x-3y+2z=12, \quad 3x+2y-5z=0.$
6. $4x+3y-z=9, \quad 9x-y+5z=16, \quad x+4y-3z=2.$
7. $3y-6z-5x=4, \quad 2z-3x-y=8, \quad x-2y+2z+2=0.$
8. $3y+2z+5x=21, 8x-3z+y=3, \quad 2z+2x-3y=39.$
9. $\frac{1}{2}x+y+\frac{1}{2}z=\frac{1}{2}, \quad x+2y+\frac{1}{3}z=\frac{1}{3}, \quad x+y-9z=1.$
10. $\frac{1}{2}x-\frac{1}{4}y=5-\frac{1}{6}z, \quad \frac{1}{6}x-\frac{1}{3}y=3-\frac{1}{6}z, \quad 2y+7=\frac{1}{4}(z-x).$
11. $\frac{1}{3}x+\frac{1}{4}(y+z)=1\frac{2}{3}, \quad 4x+\frac{1}{2}(z-y)=11, \quad \frac{1}{3}(z-4x)=y.$
12. $2x-\frac{1}{5}(z-2y)=2, \quad \frac{1}{3}(x+y)=\frac{1}{7}(3-z), \quad x=4y+3z.$
13. $\frac{7+y-2z}{3}=y-x=x-z=z-3.$
14. $\frac{x}{3}-\frac{y}{2}=y+\frac{z}{2}=x+y+z+2=0.$
15. $\frac{2x-y-z}{2}=\frac{2y-z-x}{3}=\frac{2z-x-y}{4}=x-y-z-6.$
16. $\frac{x}{2}+y=1, \frac{y}{3}-z=3, z+2y+3x+8=0.$

CHAPTER XIV

PROBLEMS LEADING TO SIMULTANEOUS EQUATIONS

110. IN the Examples discussed in the last chapter we have seen that it is essential to have as many equations as there are unknown quantities to determine. Consequently, in the solution of problems which give rise to simultaneous equations, it will always be necessary that the statement of the question should contain as many independent conditions as there are quantities to be determined.

Example 1. Find two numbers whose difference is 11, and one-fifth of whose sum is 9.

Let x be the greater number, y the less;

then $\qquad x - y = 11 \qquad$ ...**(1)**.

Also $\qquad \dfrac{x+y}{5} = 9$.

or $\qquad x + y = 45 \qquad$ ...**(2)**.

By addition $2x = 56$; and by subtraction $2y = 34$.

The numbers are therefore 28 and 17.

Example 2. If 15 kg of tea and 17 kg of coffee together cost Rs. 134.50, and 25 kg of tea and 13 kg of coffee together cost Rs. 170.50; find the price of each kg.

Suppose a kg of tea to cost x rupees,

and .... coffee .... y ....

Then from the question we have

$$15x + 17y = 134.50 \qquad \text{... (1)},$$

$$25x + 13y = 170.50 \qquad \text{... (2)}.$$

Multiplying (1) by 5 and (2) by 3, we have

$$75x + 85y = 672.50,$$

$$75x + 39y = 511.50.$$

Subtracting, $\qquad 46y = 161, \; y = 3.50$.

And from (1), $\quad 15x + 59.50 = 134.50$;

whence $\qquad 15x = 75$;

$\therefore \qquad x = 5$.

$\therefore$ the cost of a kg of tea is Rs. 5,

and the cost of a kg of coffee is Rs. 3.50.

Example 3. In a bag containing black and white balls, half the number of white is equal to a third of the number of black; and twice the whole number of balls exceeds three times the number of black balls by four. How many balls did the bag contain?

Let x be the number of white balls, and y the number of black balls; then the bag contains $x + y$ balls.

We have the following equations:

$$\frac{x}{2} = \frac{y}{3} \qquad \text{... (1),}$$

$$2(x + y) = 3y + 4 \qquad \text{... (2).}$$

Substituting from (1) in 2, we obtain

$$\frac{4y}{2} + 2y = 3y + 4;$$

whence $y = 12$:

and from (1), $x = 8$.

Thus there are 8 white and 12 black balls.

111. In a problem involving the digits of a number the student should carefully notice the way in which the value of a number is algebraically expressed in terms of its digits.

Consider a number of three digits such as 435; its value is $4 \times 100 + 3 \times 10 + 5$. Similarly, a number whose digits beginning from the left are x, y, z

$$= x \text{ hundreds} + y \text{ tens} + z \text{ units}$$

$$= 100x + 10y + z.$$

Example. A certain number of two digits is three times the sum of its digits, and if 45 be added to it the digits will be reversed; find the number.

Let x be the digit in the tens' place, y the digit in the units' place; then the number will be represented by $10x + y$, and the number formed by reversing the digits will be represented by $10y + x$.

Hence we have the two equations

$$10x + y = 3(x + y) \qquad \text{... (1),}$$

and $$10x + y + 45 = 10y + x \qquad \text{... (2).}$$

From (1), $7x = 2y$;

from (2), $y - x = 5$.

From these equations we obtain $x = 2$, $y = 7$.

Thus the number is 27.

EXAMPLES XIV

1. Find two numbers whose sum is 54, and whose difference is 12.
2. The sum of two numbers is 97 and their difference is 51; find the numbers.
3. One-fifth of the difference of two numbers is 3, and one-third of their sum is 17; find the numbers.
4. One-sixth of the sum of two numbers is 14, and half their difference is 13; find the numbers.
5. Four sheep and seven cows are worth Rs. 1703, while three cows and five sheep are worth Rs. 858. What is the value of each animal ?
6. A farmer bought 7 horses and 9 cows for Rs. 4290. He could have bought 10 horses and 5 cows for the same money; find the price of each animal.
7. Twice A's age exceeds three times B's age by 2 years; if the sum of their ages is 61 years, how old are they?
8. Half A's age exceeds a quarter of B's age by 1 year, and three-quarters of B's age exceeds A's by 11 years; find the age of each.
9. In eight hours C walks 3 kilometres more than D does in 6 hours, and in seven hours D walks 9 kilometres more than C does in six hours; how many kilometres does each walk in an hour?
10. In nine hours a coach travels one kilometre more than a train does in two hours, but in three hours the train travels 2 kilometres more than the coach does in thirteen hours; find the rate of each per hour.
11. A bill of Rs. 14.75 is paid with fifty paise and twenty-five paise coins, and three times the number of fifty paise coins exceeds twice the number of twenty-five paise coins by 8; how many of each are used ?
12. A bill of Rs. 2.84 is paid with ten paise and two paise coins, and five times the number of two paise coins exceeds seven times the number of ten paise coins by 6; how many of each are used ?
13. Forty-six tonnes of goods are to be carried in carts and wagons and it is found that this will require 10 wagons and 14 carts, or else 13 wagons and 9 cartes; how many tonnes can each wagon and each cart carry?
14. A sum of Rs. 89.90 is given to 17 boys and 15 girls; the same amount could have been given to 13 boys and 20 girls; find how much each boy and each girl receives.
15. A certain number of two digits is seven times the sum of the digits, and if 36 be taken from the number the digits will be reversed; find the number.

16. A certain number of two digits is four times the sum of the digits, and if 27 be added to the number the digits will be reversed; find the number.
17. A certain number between 10 and 100 is six times the sum of the digits, and the number exceeds the number formed by reversing the digits by 9; find the number.
18. The digits of a number between 10 and 100 are equal to each other, and the number exceeds 5 times the sum of the digits by 8; find the number.
19. A man has Rs. 100 in 10 paise, 5 paise and 2 paise coins; the number of the coins is 1550, and their weight is 6 kilograms 3 hectograms. If a 10 paise coin weighs 5 gm, a 5 paise coin 3.5 gm and a 2 paise coin 3 gm, find how many of each kind of the coins he has.
20. A man has Rs. 21 in 50 paise, 25 paise and 5 paise coins. He has in all 70 coins. If he changed the 5 paise pieces for 2 paise, and half the 25 paise for 10 paise pieces, he would then have 115 coins. How many of each had he at first?
21. Divide Rs. 100 between 3 men, 5 women, 4 boys, and 3 girls, so that each man shall have as much as a woman and a girl, each woman as much as a boy and a girl, and each boy half as much as a man and a girl.
22. If 17 kg of sugar and 4 kg of coffee cost Rs. 15.30, and 8 kg of sugar and 2 kg of coffee cost Rs. 7.50, find the cost per kg of sugar and coffee.
23. The value of a number of coins consisting of rupees and 25 paise pieces amounts to Rs. 35.25; the number of 25 paise pieces exceeds five times the number of rupees by 6. Find the number of each.
24. A sum of Rs. 51.50 is divided amongst 11 men and 16 women ; the same sum could have been divided amongst 8 men and 21 women. Find how much each man and woman receives.
25. If 4 bags together with 2 boxes weigh 9 kg 250 gm, and 3 bags with 16 boxes weigh 40 kg 650 gm, find the weight of each bag and box.
26. A man pays a rent of Rs. 3140 for two farms; for one he pays at the rate of Rs. 20 per are, and for the other at the rate of Rs. 25 per are; if the rate of payment for the two farms had been interchanged, his rent would have amounted to Rs. 2928.50. Find the size of each farm.
27. Two articles *A* and *B* are sold for Re. 1 and 50 paise per kilogram respectively; a person spends Rs. 67.75 in buying such articles. If he had bought half as much again of *A* and one-third as much again of *B*, he would have spent Rs. 99. What weight of each did he buy ?

CHAPTER XV

INVOLUTION

112. DEFINITION. **Involution** is the general name for multiplying an expression by itself so as to find its second, third, fourth, or any other power.

Involution may always be effected by actual multiplication. Here, however, we shall give some rules for writing down at once

(1) any power of a simple expression;

(2) the square and cube of any binomial;

(3) the square of any multinomial.

113. It is evident from the Rule of Signs that

(1) no *even* power of *any* quantity can be *negative*;

(2) any *odd* power of a quantity will have *the same sign* as the quantity itself.

Note. It is especially worthy of remark that the *Square* of every expression, whether positive or negative, is *positive*.

114. From definition we have, by the rules of multiplication,

$$(a^2)^3 = a^2 \cdot a^2 \cdot a^2 = a^{2+2+2} = a^6.$$

$$(-x^3)^2 = (-x^3)(-x^3) = x^{3+3} = x^6.$$

$$(-a^5)^3 = (-a^5)(-a^5)(-a^5) = -a^{5+5+5} = -a^{15}.$$

$$(-3a^3)^4 = (-3)^4(a^3)^4 = 81a^{12}.$$

Hence we obtain a rule for raising a simple expression to any proposed power.

Rule. (1) *Raise the coefficient to the required power by Arithmetic, and prefix the proper sign found by the Rule of Signs.*

(2) *Multiply the index of every factor of the expression by the exponent of the power required.*

Examples $(-2x^2)^5 = -32x^{10}.$

$$(-3ab^3)^6 = 729a^{a}b^{18}.$$

$$\left(\frac{2ab^3}{3x^2y}\right)^4 = \frac{16a^4b^{12}}{81x^8y^4}.$$

It will be seen that in the last case the numerator and the denominator are operated upon separately.

EXAMPLES XV. a

Write down the square of each of the following expressions:

1. a^2b.
2. $3ac^3$.
3. $5xy^2$.
4. $6b^3c^2$.
5. $4a^2bc^3$.
6. $-3x^2y^5$.
7. $-2a^2b^3c$.
8. $-3dx^4$.
9. $\frac{a^2c}{bd^3}$.
10. $\frac{2xz^3}{y^2}$.
11. $\frac{3a^3}{4b^2}$.
12. $-\frac{5}{7xy^2}$.
13. $-\frac{8p^2q^5}{3}$.
14. $\frac{m^2n^6}{9xy^4}$.
15. $-\frac{1}{4x^2yz^3}$.
16. $-\frac{3pq^2r^3}{5a^2x}$.

Write down the cube of each of the following expressions:

17. $2x$.
18. $3ab^2$.
19. $4x^3$.
20. $-3a^2b$.
21. $-4x^3y^2$.
22. $-b^2cd^3$.
23. $-6y^4$.
24. $-4p^3q^5$.
25. $\frac{1}{p^4r^3}$.
26. $-\frac{2}{ab^2c^3}$.
27. $-\frac{3x^3}{4yz^3}$.
28. $-\frac{2}{3}x^3$.

Write down the value of each of the following expressions:

29. $(ab^2)^4$.
30. $(-x^2y)^5$.
31. $(-2m^2n^3)^6$.
32. $(-x^3y^2)^7$.
33. $\left(\frac{1}{3a^2}\right)^5$.
34. $\left(-\frac{2a^3x}{3by^2}\right)^4$.
35. $\left(-\frac{a^3}{3}\right)^7$.
36. $\left(-\frac{2}{3}a^2\right)^6$.

115. By multiplication we have

$$(a+b)^2 = (a+b)(a+b)$$
$$= a^2 + 2ab + b^2 \quad \text{... (1).}$$
$$(a-b)^2 = (a-b)(a-b)$$
$$= a^2 - 2ab + b^2 \quad \text{... (2).}$$

These formulae may be enunciated verbally as follows:

Rule 1. *The square of the sum of two quantities is equal to the sum of their squares increased by twice their product.*

Rule 2. *The square of the difference of two quantities is equal to the sum of their squares diminished by twice their product.*

Example 1. $(x + 2y)^2 = x^2 + 2 \cdot x \cdot 2y + (2y)^2$

$= x^2 + 4xy + 4y^2.$

Example 2. $(2a^3 - 3b^2)^2 = (2a^3)^2 - 2 \cdot 2a^3 \cdot 3b^2 + (3b^2)^2$

$= 4a^6 - 12a^3b^2 + 9b^4.$

116. By repeated applications of the rules of the preceding article we may obtain the square of an expression which contains more than two terms.

Thus $(a + b + c)^2 = \{(a + b) + c\}^2$

$= (a + b)^2 + 2(a + b)c + c^2$

$= a^2 + b^2 + c^2 + 2ab + 2ac + 2bc.$

In the same way we may prove

$$(a - b + c)^2 = a^2 + b^2 + c^2 - 2ab + 2ac - 2bc.$$

$$(a + b + c + d)^2 = a^2 + b^2 + c^2 + d^2 + 2ab + 2ac + 2ad + 2bc + 2bd + 2cd.$$

In each of these instances we observe that the square consists of

(1) the sum of the squares of the several terms of the given expression;

(2) twice the sum of the products two and two of the several terms, taken with their proper signs; that is, in each product the sign is + or – according as the quantities composing it have like or unlike signs.

Note. *The square terms are always positive.*

The same laws hold whatever be the number of terms in the expression to be squared.

Rule. *To find the square of any multinomial : to the sum of the squares of the several terms add twice the product (with the proper sign) of each term into each of the terms that follow it.*

Example 1. $(x - 2y - 3z)^2 = x^2 + 4y^2 + 9z^2 - 2 \cdot x \cdot 2y - 2 \cdot x \cdot 3z + 2 \cdot 2y \cdot 3z$

$= x^2 + 4y^2 + 9z^2 - 4xy - 6xz + 12yz.$

Example 2. $(1 + 2x - 3x^2)^2 = 1 + 4x^2 + 9x^4 + 2 \cdot 1 \cdot 2x - 2 \cdot 1 \cdot 3x^2 - 2 \cdot 2x \cdot 3x^2$

$= 1 + 4x^2 + 9x^4 + 4x - 6x^2 - 12x^3 = 1 + 4x - 2x^2 - 12x^3 + 9x,$

by collecting like terms and rearranging.

Exercise XV. b

Write down the square of each of the following expressions :

1. $x + 2y$.
2. $x - 2y$.
3. $a + 3b$.
4. $2a - 3b$.
5. $3a + b$.
6. $x - 5y$.
7. $2m + 7n$.
8. $9 - x$.
9. $2 - ab$.
10. $abc + 1$.
11. $ab - cd$.
12. $2ab + xy$.
13. $1 - x^2$.
14. $3 + 2pq$.
15. $x^2 - 3x$.
16. $2a + ab$.
17. $a + b - c$.
18. $a - b - c$.
19. $2a + b + c$.
20. $2x - y - z$.
21. $x + 3y - 2z$.
22. $x^2 + x + 1$.
23. $3x + 2p - q$.
24. $1 - 2x - 3x^2$.
25. $2 - 3x + x^2$.
26. $x + y + a - b$.
27. $m - n + p - q$.
28. $2a + 3b + x - 2y$.

117. By actual multiplications we have

$$(a+b)^3 = (a+b)(a+b)(a+b) = a^3 + 3a^2b + 3ab^2 + b^3.$$

Also $$(a-b)^3 = a^3 - 3a^2b + 3ab^2 - b^3.$$

By observing the law of formation of the terms in these results we can write down the cube of any binomial.

Example 1. $(2x + y)^3 = (2x)^3 + 3(2x)^2y + 3(2x)y^2 + y^3$

$$= 8x^3 + 12x^2y + 6xy^2 + y^3.$$

Example 2. $(3x - 2a^2)^3 = (3x)^3 - 3(3x)^2(2a^2) + 3(3x)(2a^2)^2 - (2a^2)^3$

$$= 27x^3 - 54x^2a^2 + 36xa^4 - 8a^6.$$

Exercise XV. c

Write down the cube of each of the following expressions:

1. $p + q$.
2. $m - n$.
3. $a - 2b$.
4. $2c + d$.
5. $x + 3y$.
6. $x + yz$.
7. $2xy - 1$.
8. $5a + 2$.
9. $x^2 - 1$.
10. $2x^2 + y^2$.
11. $2a^3 - 3b^3$.
12. $4y^2 - 3$.

CHAPTER XVI
EVOLUTIONS

118. DEFINITION. The **root** of any proposed expression is that quantity which being multiplied by itself the requisite number of times produces the given expression.

The operation of finding the root is called **Evolution**: it is the reverse of Involution.

119. By the Rule of Signs we see that

(1) any *even* root of a *positive* quantity may be either *positive or negative*;

(2) *no negative* quantity can have an *even* root;

(3) every *odd* root of a quantity has the same sign as the quantity itself.

Note. It is especially worthy of remark that every positive quantity has two square roots equal in magnitude, but opposite in sign.

Example. $\sqrt{9a^2x^6} = \pm\, 3ax^2$.

In the present chapter, however, we shall confine our attention to the positive root.

Examples. $\sqrt{a^6b^4} = a^3b^2$, because $(a^3b^2)^2 = a^6b^4$.

$\sqrt[3]{-x^9} = -x^3$, because $(-x^3)^3 = -x^9$.

$\sqrt[5]{c^{20}} = c^4$, because $(c^4)^5 = c^{20}$.

$\sqrt[4]{81x^{12}} = 3x^3$, because $(3x^3)^4 = 81x^{12}$.

120. From the foregoing examples we may deduce a general rule for extracting any proposed root of a simple expression:

Rule. (1) *Find the root of the coefficient by Arithmetic, and prefix the proper sign.*

(2) *Divide the exponent of every factor of the expression by the index of the proposed root.*

Examples. $\sqrt[3]{-64x^6} = -4x^3$.

$\sqrt[4]{16a^8} = 2a^2$.

$\sqrt{\dfrac{81x^{10}}{25c^4}} = \dfrac{9x^5}{5c^2}$.

EXAMPLES XVI. a

Write down the square root of each of the following expressions:

1. $9x^4y^2$. **2.** $25a^6b^4$.

3. $49c^2d^6$. **4.** $a^6b^2c^{16}$.

5. $36x^6y^{36}$. **6.** $16x^8$.

7. $x^4y^6z^2$. **8.** $9p^6q^{12}$.

9. $\dfrac{4x^6}{16a^4}$. **10.** $\dfrac{a^{36}}{36}$.

11. $\dfrac{16x^{64}}{25}$. **12.** $\dfrac{144}{a^{12}}$.

Write down the cube root of each of the following expressions:

13. x^6y^9. **14.** $-a^6b^3$.

15. $8x^{27}$. **16.** $-27x^9$.

17. $-\dfrac{b^{27}}{27}$. **18.** $\dfrac{8a^9b^{12}}{y^{15}}$.

19. $\dfrac{125a^9x^{21}}{27c^6}$. **20.** $-\dfrac{64a^{27}b^3}{x^9}$.

Write down the value of each of the following expressions:

21. $\sqrt[4]{x^4y^{12}}$. **22.** $\sqrt[6]{a^{21}x^{18}}$.

23. $\sqrt[5]{-x^{20}y^{80}}$. **24.** $\sqrt[6]{64a^{42}}$.

25. $\sqrt[7]{a^{21}b^{14}}$. **26.** $\sqrt[9]{p^9q^{27}}$.

27. $\sqrt[7]{-x^{35}y^{58}}$. **28.** $\sqrt[4]{81x^4y^{12}}$.

29. $\sqrt[5]{32a^5b^{10}c^{25}}$.

121. By the formulae in Art. 115 we are able to write down the square of any binomial.

Thus $(2x+3y)^2 = 4x^2 + 12xy + 9y^2$.

Conversely, by observing the form of the terms of an expression, it may sometimes be recognised as a complete square, and its square root written down at once.

Example 1. Find the square root of $25x^2 - 40xy + 16y^2$.

$$\text{The expression} = (5x)^2 - 2.20xy + (4y)^2$$
$$= (5x)^2 - 2(5x)(4y) + (4y)^2 = (5x-4y)^2.$$

Thus the required square root is $5x - 4y$.

Example 2. Find the square root of $\frac{64a^2}{9b^2} + 4 + \frac{32a}{3b}$.

$$\text{The expression} = \left(\frac{8a}{3b}\right)^2 + (2)^2 + 2\left(\frac{16a}{3b}\right)$$

$$= \left(\frac{8a}{3b}\right)^2 + 2\left(\frac{8a}{3b}\right)(2) + (2)^2 = \left(\frac{8a}{3b} + 2\right)^2.$$

Thus the required square roots is $\frac{8a}{3b} + 2$.

122. When the square root cannot be easily determined by inspection we must have recourse to the rule explained in the next article, which is quite general, and applicable to all cases. *But the student is advised, here and elsewhere, to employ methods of inspection in preference to rules.*

123. *To find the square root of a compound expression.*

Since, the square of $a + b$ is $a^2 + 2ab + b^2$, we have to discover a process by which a and b, the terms of the root, can be found when $a^2 + 2ab + b^2$ is given.

The first term, a, is the square root of a^2.

Arrange the terms according to powers of one letter a.

The first term is a^2, and its square root is a. Set this down as the first term of the required root. Subtract a^2 from the given expression and the remainder is $2ab + b^2$ or $(2a + b) \times b$.

Now the first term $2ab$ of the remainder is the product of $2a$ and b. Thus to obtain b we divide the first term of the remainder by the double of the term already found ; if we add this new term to $2a$ we obtain the complete divisor $2a + b$.

The work may be arranged as follows:

$$
\begin{array}{r|l}
 & a^2 + 2ab + b^2 \; (a + b) \\
 & a^2 \\
\hline
2a + b & 2ab + b^2 \\
 & 2ab + b^2 \\
\hline
\end{array}
$$

Example. Find the square root of $9x^2 - 42xy + 49y^2$

$$
\begin{array}{r|l}
 & 9x^2 - 42xy + 49y^2 \; (3x - 7y \\
 & 9x^2 \\
\hline
6x - 7y & -42xy + 49y^2 \\
 & -42xy + 49y^2 \\
\hline
\end{array}
$$

Explanation. The square root of $9x^2$ is $3x$, and this is the first term of the root.

By doubling this we obtain $6x$, which is the first term of the divisor. Divide $-42xy$, the first term of the remainder, by $6x$ and we get $-7y$, the new term in the root, which has to be annexed both to the root and divisor. Next multiply the complete divisor by $-7y$ and subtract the result from the first remainder. There is now no remainder and the root has been found.

124. The rule can be extended so as to find the square root of any multinomial. The first two terms of the root will be obtained as before. When we have brought down *the second remainder*, the first part of the new divisor is obtained by doubling the terms of the root already found. We then divide the first term of the remainder by the first term of the new divisor, and set down the result as the next term in the root and in the divisor. We next multiply the complete divisor by the last term of the root and subtract the product from the last remainder. If there is now no remainder the root has been found; if there is a remainder we continue the process.

Example. Find the square root of

$$25x^2a^2 - 12xa^3 + 16x^4 + 4a^4 - 24x^3a.$$

Rearrange in descending powers of x.

$$\begin{array}{l|l}
 & 16x^4 - 24x^3a + 25x^2a^2 - 12xa^3 + 4a^4 \,(4x^2 - 3xa + 2a^2) \\
 & 16x^4 \\
8x^2 - 3ax & -24x^3a + 25x^2a^2 \\
 & -24x^3a + 9x^2a^2 \\
8x^2 - 6xa + 2a^2 & 16x^2a^2 - 12xa^3 + 4a^4 \\
 & 16x^2a^2 - 12xa^3 + 4a^4
\end{array}$$

Explanation. When we have obtained two terms in the root, $4x^2 - 3xa$, we have a remainder $16x^2a^2 - 12xa^3 + 4a^4$.

Double the terms of the root already found and place the result, $8x^2 - 6xa$, as the first part of the divisor. Divide $16x^2a^2$, the first term of the remainder, by $8x^2$, the first term of the divisor; we get $+2a^2$ which we annex both to the root and divisor. Now multiply the complete divisor by $2a^2$ and subtract. There is no remainder and the root is found.

125. Sometimes the following method may be used.

Example 7. Find by inspection the square root of

$$4a^2 + b^2 + c^2 + 4ab - 4ac - 2bc.$$

Arrange the terms in descending powers of a, and let the other letters be arranged alphabetically; then

the expression $= 4a^2 + 4ab - 4ac + b^2 - 2bc + c^2$

$$= 4a^2 + 4a(b - c) + (b - c)^2$$

$$= (2a)^2 + 2.2a(b - c) + (b - c)^2;$$

whence the square root is $2a + (b - c)$. [Art. 121.]

EXAMPLES XVI. b

By inspection or otherwise, find the square root of each of the following expressions:

1. $a^2 - 8a + 16.$
2. $x^2 + 14x + 49.$
3. $64 + 48x + 9x^2.$
4. $25 - 30m + 9m^2.$
5. $36n^4 - 84n^2 + 49.$
6. $81 + 144y^3 + 64y^6.$
7. $x^6 - 6x^3y^4z^4 + 9y^8z^8.$
8. $4a^2b^4 - 12ab^2c^5 + 9c^{10}.$
9. $\frac{1}{4}x^2 - 3xy^3 + 9y^6.$
10. $\frac{9a^2}{b^2} + \frac{24ac}{bd} + \frac{16c^2}{d^2}.$
11. $\frac{9a^2}{25b^2} - 2 + \frac{25b^2}{9a^2}.$
12. $\frac{16x^4}{49y^2} + \frac{49y^4}{16x^2} + 2xy.$
13. $16x^4 - 32x^3 + 24x^2 - 8x + 1.$
14. $25 - 30a + 29a^2 - 12a^3 + 4a^4.$
15. $9a^8 - 12a^6 - 2a^4 + 4a^2 + 1.$
16. $25p^4 - 30p^3 + 121 - 101p^2 + 66p.$
17. $8x^3 + 1 + 4x^4 - 4x.$
18. $201a^2 - 108a^3 + 100 + 36a^4 - 180a.$
19. $a^2 + b^2 + c^2 + 2ab - 2ac - 2bc.$
20. $y^2z^2 + z^2x^2 + x^2y^2 - 2x^2yz + 2xy^2z - 2xyz^2.$
21. $a^4 - 2a^3 + \frac{3a^2}{2} - \frac{a}{2} + \frac{1}{16}.$
22. $\frac{a^2}{9} - \frac{4ax}{3} + \frac{x^4}{4} + 4x^2 + \frac{ax^2}{3} - 2x^3.$
23. $9m^4 + \frac{n^2}{4} + \frac{9}{16} + \frac{3n}{4} + \frac{9m^2}{2} + 3m^2n.$
24. $9x^4 + 144x^2 + 12ax^2 + 4a^2 - 72x^3 - 48ax.$
25. $x^8 - 4x^7 + 4x^6 + 6x^5 - 14x^4 + 4x^3 + 9x^2 - 6x + 1.$
26. $a^2 + 9b^2 + c^2 - 6ab + 6bc - 2ac.$
27. $\frac{m^4}{n^4} - 2\frac{m^3}{n^3} + 5\frac{m^2}{n^2} - 4\frac{m}{n} + 4.$
28. $\frac{9a^2}{b^2} - 5 + \frac{b^2}{a^2} - \frac{6a}{b} + \frac{2b}{a}.$

[If preferred, the remainder of this chapter may be postponed and taken at a later stage.]

126. *To find the cube root of a compound expression.*

Since the cube $a+b$ is $a^3 + 3a^2b + 3ab^2 + b^3$, we have to discover a process by which a and b, the terms of the root, can be found when $a^3 + 3a^2b + 3ab^2 + b^3$ is given.

The first term a is the cube root of a^3.

Arrange the terms according to powers of one letter a; then the first term is a^3, and its cube root a. Set this down as the first term of the required root. Subtract a^3 from the given expression and remainder is

$3a^2b + 3ab^2 + b^3$ or $(3a^2 + 3ab + b^2) \times b$.

Now the first term of the remainder is the product of $3a^2$ and b. Thus to obtain b we divide the first term of the remainder by three times the square of the term already found.

Having found b we can complete the divisor, which consists of the following three terms:

1. Three times the square of a, the terms of the root already found.
2. Three times the product of this first term a, and the new term b.
3. The square of b.

The work may be arranged as follows:

$$
\begin{array}{lrr|l}
 & & & a^3 + 3a^2b + 3ab^2 + b^3 (a+b) \\
 & & & a^3 \\
\hline
3(a)^2 = & 3a^2 & & 3a^2b + 3ab^2 + b^3 \\
3 \times a \times b = & & + 3ab & \\
(b)^2 = & & + b^2 & \\
\hline
 & & 3a^2 + 3ab + b^2 & 3a^2b + 3ab^2 + b^3 \\
\hline
\end{array}
$$

Example 1. Find the cube root of $8x^3 - 36x^2y + 54xy^2 - 27y^3$

$$
\begin{array}{lrr|l}
 & & & 8x^3 - 36x^2y + 54xy^2 - 27y^3 (2x - 3y) \\
 & & & 8x^3 \\
\hline
3(2x)^2 & = 12x^3 & & -36x^2y + 54xy^2 - 27y^3 \\
3 \times 2x \times (-3y) = & & -18xy & \\
(-3y)^2 & = & + 9y^2 & \\
\hline
 & & 12x^2 - 18xy^2 - 27y^3 & -36x^2y + 54xy^2 - 27y^3 \\
\hline
\end{array}
$$

Example 2. Find the cube root of $8x^6 - 48x^5 + 60x^4 + 80x^3 - 90x^2 - 108x - 27$

$$8x^6 - 48x^5 + 60x^4 + 80x^3 - 90x^2 - 108x - 27(2x^2 - 4x - 3)$$

$$8x^6$$

$$3 \times (2x^2)^2 = 12x^4 \qquad -48x^5 + 60x^4 + 80x^3$$

$$3 \times (2x^2) \times (-4x) = -24x^3$$

$$(-4x)^2 = +16x^2$$

$$12x^4 - 24x^3 + 16x^2 \qquad -48x^5 + 96x^4 - 64x^3$$

$$3 \times (2x^2 - 4x)^2 = 12x^4 - 48x^3 + 48x^2 \qquad -36x^4 + 144x^3 - 90x^2 - 108x - 27$$

$$3 \times (2x^2 - 4x) \times (-3) = -18x^2 + 36x$$

$$(-3)^2 = +9$$

$$12x^4 - 48x^3 + 30x^2 + 36x + 9 \qquad -36x^4 + 144x^3 - 90x^2 - 108x - 27$$

Explanation. When we have obtained two terms in the roots, $2x^2 - 4x$, we have a remainder

$$-36x^4 + 144x^3 - 90x^2 - 108x - 27.$$

Take 3 times the square of the root already found and place the result, $12x^4 - 48x^3 + 48x^2$, as the first part of the new divisor. Divide $-36x^4$, the first term of the remainder, by $12x^4$, the first terms of the divisor; this gives -3 a new term of the root. To complete the divisor we take 3 times the product of $2x^2 - 4x$ and -3, and also the square of -3. Now multiply the complete divisor by -3 and subtract; there is no remainder and the root is found.

EXAMPLES XVI. c

Find the cube root of each of the following expressions:

1. $a^3 + 12a^2 + 48a + 64.$

2. $8x^3 + 12x^2 + 6x + 1.$

3. $64x^3 - 144x^2 + 108x - 27.$

4. $8p^6 - 36p^4 + 54p^2 - 27.$

5. $m^3 - 18m^2 + 108m - 216.$

6. $x^6 + 6x^4y^2 + 12x^2y^4 + 8y^6.$

7. $1 - 3c + 6c^2 - 7c^3 + 6c^4 - 3c^5 + c^6.$

8. $8 + 36m + 66m^2 + 63m^3 + 33m^4 + 9m^5 + m^6.$

9. $216 - 108k + 342k^2 - 109k^3 + 171k^4 - 27k^5 + 27k^6.$

10. $48y^5 + 108y + 60y^4 - 90y^2 - 27 + 8y^6 - 80y^3.$

11. $64 + 192k + 240k^2 + 160k^3 + 60k^4 + 12k^5 + k^6.$

12. $x^3 - 6x^2y - 3x^2z + 12xy^2 + 12xyz - 8y^3 - 12y^2z - 6yz^2 - z^3.$

[For additional examples see *Elementary Algebra*, pp. 109, 110.]

127. The ordinary rules for extracting square and cube roots in Arithmetic are based upon the algebraical methods explained in the present chapter. The following examples is given to illustrate the arithmetical process.

Example. Find the cube root of 614125.

Since 614125 lies between 512000 and 729000, that is, between $(80)^3$ and $(90)^3$, its cube root lies between 80 and 90 and therefore consists of two figures.

$$\begin{array}{rr|l}
 & & \quad a+b \\
 & & 614125\ (80+5=85) \\
 & & 512000 \\ \cline{3-3}
3a^2 = 3\times(80)^2 = & 19200 & 102125 \\
3\times a\times b = 3\times 80\times 5 = & 1200 & \\
b^2 = \quad 5\times 5 = & 25 & \\ \cline{2-2}
 & 20425 & 102125 \\ \cline{3-3}
\end{array}$$

In Arithmetic the ciphers are usually omitted, and there are other modification of the algebraical rules. Some reference to these will be found in Chap. XXIX of the *Elementary Algebra*.

CHAPTER XVII

RESOLUTION INTO FACTORS

128. DEFINITION. When an algebraical expression is the product of two or more expressions each of these latter quantities is called a **factors** of it, and the determination of these quantities is called the **resolution** of the expression into its factors.

In this chapter we shall explain the principal rules by which the resolution of expressions into their component factors may be effected.

129. When each of the terms which compose an expression is divisible by a common factor, the expression may be simplified by dividing each term separately by this factor, and enclosing the quotient within brackets; the common factor being placed outside as a coefficient.

Example 1. The terms of the expression $3a^2 - 6ab$ have a common factor $3a$:

$$\therefore \quad 3a^2 - 6ab = 3a(a - 2b).$$

Example 2. $5a^2bx^3 - 15abx^2 - 20b^3x^2 = 5bx^2\,(a^2x - 3a - 4b^2)$.

EXAMPLES XVII. a

Resolve into factors:

1. $x^2 + ax$.

2. $2a^2 - 3a$.

3. $a^3 - a^2$.

4. $a^3 - a^2b$.

5. $3m^2 - 6mn$.

6. $p^2 + 2p^2q$.

7. $x^5 - 5x^2$.

8. $y^2 + xy$.

9. $5a^2 - 25a^2b$.

10. $12x + 48x^2y$.

11. $10c^3 - 25c^4d$.

12. $27 - 162x$.

13. $x^2y^2z^2 + 3xy$.

14. $17x^2 - 51x$.

15. $2a^3 - a^2 + a$.

16. $3x^3 + 6a^2x^2 - 3a^3x$.

17. $7p^2 - 7p^3 + 14p^4$.

18. $4b^5 + 6a^2b^3 - 2b^2$.

19. $x^3y^3 - x^2y^2 + 2xy$.

20. $26a^3b^5 + 39a^4b^2$.

130. An expression may be resolved into factors if the terms can be arranged in groups which have a compound factor common.

Example 1. Resolve into factors $x^2 - ax + bx - ab$.

Noticing that the first two terms contain a common factor x, and the last two terms a common factor b, we enclose the first two terms in one bracket, and the last two another. Thus,

$$\begin{aligned} x^2 - ax + bx - ab &= (x^2 - ax) + (bx - ab) \\ &= x(x-a) + b(x-a) \\ &= (x-a) \text{ taken } x \text{ times } \textit{plus } (x-a) \text{ taken } b \text{ times} \\ &= (x-a) \text{ taken } (x+b) \text{ times} \\ &= (x-a)(x+b). \end{aligned}$$

Example 2. Resolve into factors $6x^2 - 9ax + 4bx - 6ab$.

$$\begin{aligned} 6x^2 - 9ax + 4bx - 6ab &= (6x^2 - 9ax)) + 4bx - 6ab) \\ &= 3x(2x - 3a) + 2b(2x - 3a) \\ &= (2x - 3a)(3x + 2b). \end{aligned}$$

Example 3. Resolve into factors $12a^2 + bx^2 - 4ab - 3ax^2$.

$$\begin{aligned} 12a^2 + bx^2 - 4ab - 3ax^2 &= (12a^2 - 4ab) - (3ax^2 - bx^2) \\ &= 4a(3a - b) - x^2(3a - b) \\ &= (3a - b)(4a - x^2). \end{aligned}$$

EXAMPLES XVII. b

Resolve into factors:

1. $x^2 + xy + xz + yz$.

2. $x^2 - xz + xy - yz$.

3. $a^2 + 2a + ab + 2b$.

4. $a^2 + ac + 4a + 4c$.

5. $2a + 2x + ax + x^2$.

6. $3q - 3p + pq - p^2$.

7. $am - bm - an + bn$.

8. $ab - by - ay + y^2$.

9. $pq + qr - pr - r^2$.

10. $2mx + nx + 2my + ny$.

11. $ax - 2ay - bx + 2by$.

12. $2a^2 + 3ab - 2ac - 3bc$.

13. $ac^2 + b + bc^2 + a$.

14. $ac^2 - 2a - bc^2 + 2b$.

15. $a^3 - a^2 + a - 1$.

16. $2x^3 + 3 + 2x + 3x^2$.

17. $a^2x - aby + 2ax - 2by$.

18. $axy + bcxy - az - bcz$.

131. Before proceeding to the next case of resolution into factors the student is advised to refer to Chap. V, Art. 48. Attention has there been drawn to the way in which, in forming the product of two binomials, the coefficients of the differnet terms combine so as to give a trinomial result.

Thus

$$(x+5)(x+3) = x^2 + 8x + 15 \quad ...(1),$$

$$(x-5)(x-3) = x^2 - 8x + 15 \quad ...(2),$$

$$(x+5)(x-3) = x^2 + 2x - 15 \quad ...(3),$$

$$(x-5)(x+3) = x^2 - 2x - 15 \quad ...(4),$$

We now propose to consider the converse problem: namely, the resolution of a trinomial expression, similar to those which occur on the right-hand side of the above identities, into its component binominal factors.

By examining the above results, we notice that:

1. The first term of both the factors is x.
2. The product of the second terms of the two factors is equal to the third term of the trinomial; e.g. in (2) above we see that 15 is the product of -5 and -3; and in (3) we see that -15 is the product of $+5$ and -3.
3. The algebraic sum of the second terms of the two factors is equal to the coefficient of x in the trinomial; e.g. in (4) the sum of -5 and $+3$ gives -2, the coefficient of x in the trinomial.

The application of these laws will be easily understood from the following examples.

Example 1. Resolve into factors $x^2 + 11x + 24$.

The second terms of the factors must be such that their product is $+24$ and their sum $+11$. It is clear that they must be $+8$ and $+3$.

$$\therefore \quad x^2 + 11x + 24 = (x+8)(x+3).$$

Example 2. Resolve into factors $x^2 - 10x + 24$.

The second terms of the factors must be such that their product is $+24$, and their sum -10. Hence they must *both* be *negative*, and it is easy to see that must be -6 and -4.

$$\therefore \quad x^2 - 10x + 24 = (x-6)(x-4).$$

Example 3. $x^2 - 18x + 81 = (x-9)(x-9) = (x-9)^2$.

Example 4. $x^4 = 10x^2 + 25 = (x^2+5)(x^2+5) = (x^2+5)^2$.

Example 5. Resolve into factors $x^2 - 11ax + 10a^2$.

The second terms of the factors must be such that their product is $+10a^2$, and their sum $-11a$. Hence they must be $-10a$ and $-a$.

$$\therefore \quad x^2 - 11ax + 10a^2 = (x-10a)(x-a).$$

Note. In examples of this kind the student should always verify his results, by forming the product (*mentally*, as explained in Chap. V) of the factors he has chosen.

EXAMPLES XVII. c

Resolve into factors:

1. $x^2 + 3x + 2$.
2. $y^2 + 5y + 6$.
3. $y^2 + 7y + 12$.
4. $a^2 - 3a + 2$.
5. $a^2 - 6a + 8$.
6. $b^2 - 5b + 6$.
7. $b^2 + 13b + 42$.
8. $b^2 - 13b + 40$.
9. $z^2 - 13z + 36$.
10. $x^2 - 15x + 56$.
11. $x^2 - 15x + 54$.
12. $z^2 + 15z + 44$.
13. $b^2 - 12b + 36$.
14. $a^2 + 15a + 56$.
15. $a^2 - 12a + 27$.
16. $x^2 + 9x + 20$.
17. $x^2 - 10x + 9$.
18. $x^2 - 16x + 64$.
19. $y^2 - 23y + 102$.
20. $y^2 - 24y + 95$.
21. $y^2 + 54y + 729$.
22. $a^2 + 10ab + 21b^2$.
23. $a^2 + 12ab + 11b^2$.
24. $a^2 - 23ab + 132b^2$.
25. $m^4 + 8m^2 + 7$.
26. $m^4 + 9m^2n^2 + 14n^4$.
27. $6 - 5x + x^2$.
28. $54 - 15a + a^2$.
29. $13 + 14y + y^2$.
30. $216 - 35a + a^2$.

132. Next consider a case where the third term of the trinomial is negative.

Example 1. Resolve into factors $x^2 + 2x - 35$.

The second terms of the factors must be such that their product is -35, and their *algebraical sum* $+2$. Hence they must have *opposite* signs, and the greater of them must be *positive* in order to give its sign to their sum.

The required terms are therefore $+7$ and -5.

$\therefore \qquad x^2 + 2x - 35 = (x + 7)(x - 5).$

Example 2. Resolve into factors $x^2 - 3x - 54$.

The second terms of the factors must be such that their product is -54, and their *algebraical sum* -3. Hence they must have *opposite* signs, and the greater of them must be *negative* in order to give its sign to their sum.

The required terms are therefore -9 and $+6$.

$\therefore \qquad x^2 - 3x - 54 = (x - 9)(x + 6).$

Remembering that in these cases the numerical quantities *must have opposite signs*, if preferred, the following method may be adopted.

Example 3. Resolve into factors $x^2y^2 + 23xy - 420$.

Find two numbers whose product is 420, and whose *difference* is 23. These are 35 and 12; hence inserting the signs so that the positive may predominate, we have

$$x^2y^2 + 23xy - 420 = (xy + 35)(xy - 12).$$

EXAMPLES XVII. d

Resolve into factors:

1. $x^2 + x - 2$.
2. $x^2 - x - 6$.
3. $x^2 - x - 20$.
4. $y^2 + 4y - 12$.
5. $y^2 + 4y - 21$.
6. $y^2 - 5y - 36$.
7. $a^2 + 8a - 33$.
8. $a^2 - 13a - 30$.
9. $a^2 + a - 132$.
10. $b^2 - 12b - 45$.
11. $b^2 + 14b - 51$.
12. $b^2 + 10b - 39$.
13. $m^2 - m - 56$.
14. $m^2 - 5m - 84$.
15. $m^2 + m - 56$.
16. $p^2 - 8p - 65$.
17. $p^2 + 3p - 108$.
18. $p^2 + p - 110$.
19. $x^2 + 2x - 48$.
20. $x^2 - 7x - 120$.
21. $x^2 - x - 132$.
22. $y^4 + 13y^2 - 48$.
23. $y^2 + 4xy - 96x^2$.
24. $y^2 + 7xy - 98x^2$.
25. $a^4 + a^2b^2 - 72b^4$.
26. $a^2 + ab - 240b^2$.
27. $14 - 5a - a^2$.
28. $35 - 2b - b^2$.
29. $96 - 4b - b^2$.
30. $72 + b - b^2$.

133. We proceed now to the resolution into factors of trinomial expressions when the coefficient of the highest power is not unity.

Again, referring to Chap. V, Art. 48, we may write down the following results:

$$(3x + 2)(x + 4) = 3x^2 + 14x + 8 \quad ...(1),$$

$$(3x - 2)(x - 4) = 3x^2 - 14x + 8 \quad ...(2),$$

$$(3x + 2)(x - 4) = 3x^2 - 10x - 8 \quad ...(3),$$

$$(3x - 2)(x + 4) = 3x^2 + 10x - 8 \quad ...(4).$$

The converse problem presents more difficulty than the cases we have yet considered.

Before endeavouring to give a general method of procedure it will be worth while to examine in detail two of the identities given above.

Consider the result $3x^2 - 14x + 8 = (3x - 2)(x - 4)$.

The first term $3x^2$ is the product of $3x$ and x.

The third term $+ 8$ .... -2 and -4.

The middle term $-14x$ is the result of adding together the two products $3x \times -4$ and $x \times -2$.

Again, consider the result $3x^2 - 10x - 8 = (3x + 2)(x - 4)$.

The first term $3x^2$ is the product of $3x$ and x.

The third term -8 .... $+2$ and -4.

The middle term $-10x$ is the result of the adding together the two products $3x \times -4$ and $x \times 2$; and its sign is negative because the greater of these two products is negative.

134. The beginner will frequently find that it is not easy to select the proper factors at the first trial. Practice alone will enable him to detect at a glance whether any pair he has chosen will combine so as to give the correct coefficients of the expression to be resolved.

Example. Resolve into factors $7x^2 - 19x - 6$.

Write down $(7x \quad 3)(x \quad 2)$ for a first trial, noticing that 3 and 2 must have opposite signs. These factors give $7x^2$ and -6 for the first and third terms. But since $7 \times 2 - 3 \times 1 = 11$, the combination fails to give the correct coefficient of the middle term.

Next try $(7x \quad 2)(x \quad 3)$.

Since $7 \times 3 - 2 \times 1 = 19$, these factors will be correct if we insert the signs so that the negative shall predominate.

Thus $7x^2 - 19x - 6 = (7x + 2)(x - 3)$.

[Verify by mental multiplication.]

135. In actual work it will not be necessary to put down all these steps at length. The student will soon find that the different cases may be rapidly reviewed, and the unsuitable combinations rejected at once.

It is especially important to pay attention to the two following hints:

1. If the third term of the trinomial is positive, then the second terms of its factors have both the same sign, and this sign is the same as that of the middle term of the trinomial.
2. If the third term of the trinomial is negative, then the second terms of its factors have opposite signs.

Example 1. Resolve into factors

$$14x^2 + 29x - 15 \quad \ldots(1),$$

$$14x^2 - 29x - 15 \quad \ldots(2).$$

In each case we may write down $(7x \quad 3)(2x \quad 5)$ as a first trial, noticing that 3 and 5 must have opposite signs.

And since $7 \times 5 - 3 \times 2 = 29$, we have only now to insert the proper signs in each factor.

In (1) the positive sign must predominate,

in (2) the negative......

Therefore $14x^2 + 29x - 15 = (7x - 3)(2x + 5)$.

$$14x^2 - 29x - 15 = (7x + 3)(2x - 5).$$

Example 2. Resolve into factors $5x^2 + 17x + 6$ ...(1),

$$5x^2 - 17x + 6 \quad \ldots(2).$$

In (1) we notice that the factors which give 6 are both positive.

In (2) .... negative.

And therefore for (1) we may write

$$(5x + \ )(x + \ ).$$

(2) ... $(5x - \ )(x - \ )$.

And, since $5 \times 3 + 1 \times 2 = 17$, we see that

$$5x^2 + 17x + 6 = (5x + 2)(x + 3).$$

$$5x^2 - 17x + 6 = (5x - 2)(x - 3).$$

Note. In each expression the third term 6 also admits of factors 6 and 1; but this is one of the cases referred to above which the student would reject at once as unsuitable.

EXAMPLES XVII. e

Resolve into factors:

1. $2a^2 + 3a + 1$.

2. $3a^2 + 4a + 1$.

3. $4a^2 + 5a + 1$.

4. $2a^2 + 5a + 2$.

5. $3a^2 + 10a + 3$.

6. $2a^2 + 7a + 3$.

7. $5a^2 + 7a + 2$.

8. $2a^2 + 9a + 10$.

9. $2a^2 + 7a + 6$.

10. $2x^2 + 9x + 4$

11. $2x^2 + 5x - 3$.

12. $3x^2 + 5x - 2$.

13. $3y^2 + y - 2$.

14. $3y^2 - 7y - 6$.

15. $2y^2 + 9y - 5$.

16. $2b^2 - 5b - 3$.

17. $6b^2 + 7b - 3$.

18. $2b^2 + b - 15$.

19. $4m^2 + 5m - 6$.

20. $4m^2 - 4m - 3$.

21. $6m^2 - 7m - 3$.

22. $4x^2 - 8xy - 5y^2$.

23. $6x^2 - 7xy + 2y^2$.

24. $6x^2 - 13xy + 2y^2$.

25. $12a^2 - 17ab + 6b^2$.

26. $6a^2 - 5ab - 6b^2$.

27. $6a^2 + 35ab - 6b^2$.

28. $2 - 3y - 2y^2$.

29. $3 + 23y - 8y^2$.

30. $8 + 18y - 5y^2$.

31. $4 + 17x - 15x^2$.

32. $6 - 13a + 6a^2$.

33. $28 - 31b - 5b^2$.

136. By multiplying $a + b$ by $a - b$ we obtain the identity

$$(a + b)(a - b) = a^2 - b^2,$$

a result which may be verbally expressed as follows:

The product of the sum and the difference of any two quantities is equal to the difference of their squares.

Conversely, *the difference of the squares of any two quantities is equal to the product of the sum and the difference of the two quantities.*

Thus any expression which is the difference of two squares may at once be resolved into factors.

Example. Resolve into factors $25x^2 - 16y^2$.

$$25x^2 - 16y^2 = (5x)^2 - (4y)^2.$$

Therefore the first factor is the sum of $5x$ and $4y$, and the second factor is the difference of $5x$ and $4y$.

$$\therefore \quad 25x^2 - 16y^2 = (5x + 4y)(5x - 4y).$$

The intermediate steps may usually be omitted.

Example. $1 - 49c^6 = (1 + 7c^3)(1 - 7c^3)$.

The difference of the squares of two numerical quantities is sometimes conveniently found by the aid of the formula

$$a^2 - b^2 = (a + b)(a - b).$$

Example. $(329)^2 - (171)^2 = (329 + 171)(329 - 171)$

$$= 500 \times 158$$

$$= 79000.$$

EXAMPLES XVII. f

Resolve into factors:

1. $a^2 - 9$.
2. $a^2 - 49$.
3. $a^2 - 81$.
4. $a^2 - 100$.
5. $x^2 - 25$.
6. $x^2 - 144$.
7. $64 - x^2$.
8. $81 - 4x^2$.
9. $4y^2 - 1$.
10. $y^2 - 9a^2$.
11. $4y^2 - 25$.
12. $9y^2 - 49x^2$.
13. $4m^2 - 81$.
14. $36a^2 - 1$.
15. $k^2 - 64l^2$.
16. $9a^2 - 25b^2$.
17. $121 - 16y^2$.
18. $121 - 36x^2$.
19. $25 - c^1$.
20. $a^2b^2 - x^2y^2$.
21. $49a^4 - 100b^2$.
22. $64x^2 - 49z^2$.
23. $4p^2q^2 - 81$.
24. $a^4b^4c^2 - 9$.
25. $x^6 - 4a^4$.
26. $x^4 - 25z^4$.
27. $a^{10} - p^2q^4$.
28. $16a^{16} - 9b^6$.
29. $25x^{12} - 4$.
30. $a^6b^8c^4 - 9x^2$.

Find by factors the value of

31. $(39)^2 - (31)^2$.
32. $(51)^2 - (49)^2$.
33. $(1001)^2 - 1$.
34. $(82)^2 - (18)^2$.
35. $(275)^2 - (225)^2$.
36. $(936)^2 - (64)^2$.

137. If we divide $a^3 + b^3$ by $a + b$ the quotient is $a^2 - ab + b^2$; and if we divide $a^3 - b^3$ by $a - b$ the quotient is $a^2 + ab + b^2$.

We have therefore the following identities:

$$a^3 + b^3 = (a+b)(a^2 - ab + b^2); \quad a^3 - b^3 = (a-b)(a^2 + ab + b^2).$$

These results are very important, and enable us to resolve into factors any expression which can be written as the sum or the difference of two cubes.

Example 1. $8x^3 - 27y^3 = (2x)^3 - (3y)^3 = (2x - 3y)(4x^2 + 6xy + 9y^2)$.

Note. The middle term $6xy$ is the *product* of $2x$ and $3y$.

Example 2. $64a^3 + 1 = (4a)^3 + (1)^3 = (4a + 1)(16a^2 - 4a + 1)$

We may usually omit the intermediate step and write down the factors at once.

Examples. $343a^6 - 27x^3 = (7a^2 - 3x)(49a^4 + 21a^2x + 9x^2)$.

$8x^9 + 729 = (2x^3 + 9)(4x^6 - 18x^3 + 81)$.

EXAMPLES XVII. g

Resolve into factors:

1. $a^3 - b^3$.
2. $a^3 + b^3$.
3. $1 + x^3$.
4. $1 - y^3$.
5. $8x^3 + 1$.
6. $x^3 - 8z^3$.
7. $a^3 + 27b^3$.
8. $x^3y^3 - 1$.
9. $1 - 8a^3$.
10. $b^3 - 8$.
11. $27 + x^3$.
12. $64 - p^3$.
13. $125a^3 + 1$.
14. $216 - b^3$.
15. $x^3y^3 + 343$.
16. $1000x^3 + 1$.
17. $512a^3 - 1$.
18. $a^3b^3c^3 - 27$.
19. $8x^3 - 343$.
20. $x^3 + 216y^3$.
21. $x^6 - 27z^3$.
22. $m^3 - 1000n^6$.
23. $a^3 - 729b^3$.
24. $125a^6 + 512b^3$.

138. We shall now give some harder applications of the foregoing rules, followed by a miscellaneous exercise in which all the processes of this chapter will be illustrated.

Example 1. Resolve into factors $(a + 2b)^2 - 16x^2$.

The sum of $a + 2b$ and $4x$ is $a + 2b + 4x$,

and their difference is $a + 2b - 4x$.

$$\therefore \quad (a + 2b)^2 - 16x^2 = (a + 2b + 4x) \quad (a + 2b - 4x).$$

If the factors contain like terms they should be collected so as to give the result in its simplest form.

Example 2. $(3x + 7y)^2 - (2x - 3y)^2$

$$= \{(3x + 7y) + (2x - 3y)\} \quad \{(3x + 7y) - (2x - 3y)\}$$
$$= (3x + 7y + 2x - 3y)(3x + 7y - 2x + 3y)$$
$$= (5x + 4y)(x + 10y).$$

139. By suitably grouping together the terms, compound expressions can often be expressed as the difference of two squares, and so be resolved into factors.

Example 1. Resolve into factors $9a^2 - c^2 + 4cx - 4x^2$.

$$9a^2 - c^2 + 4cx - 4x^2 = 9a^2 - (c^2 - 4cx + 4x^2)$$
$$= (3a)^2 - (c - 2x)^2$$
$$= (3a + c - 2x)(3a - c + 2x).$$

Example 2. Resolve into factors $2bd - a^2 - c^2 + b^2 + d^2 + 2ac$.

Here the terms $2bd$ and $2ac$ suggest the proper preliminary arrangement of the expression. Thus

$$\begin{aligned}&2bd - a^2 - c^2 + b^2 + d^2 + 2ac\\&= b^2 + 2bd + d^2 - a^2 + 2ac - c^2\\&= b^2 + 2bd + d^2 - (a^2 - 2ac + c^2)\\&= (b + d)^2 - (a - c)^2 = (b + d + a - c)(b + d - a + c).\end{aligned}$$

140. The following case is important

Example. Resolve into factors $x^4 + x^2y^2 + y^4$.

$$\begin{aligned}x^4 + x^2y^2 + y^4 &= (x^4 + 2x^2y^2 + y^4) - x^2y^2\\&= (x^2 + y^2)^2 - (xy)^2\\&= (x^2 + y^2 + xy)(x^2 + y^2 - xy)\\&= (x^2 + xy + y^2)(x^2 - xy + y^2).\end{aligned}$$

141. Sometimes an expression may be resolved into more than two factors.

Example 1. Resolve into factors $16a^4 - 81b^4$.

$$\begin{aligned}16a^4 - 81b^4 &= (4a^2 + 9b^2)(4a^2 - 9b^2)\\&= (4a^2 + 9b^2)(2a + 3b)(2a - 3b).\end{aligned}$$

Example 2. Resolve into factors $x^6 - y^6$.

$$\begin{aligned}x^6 - y^6 &= (x^3 + y^3)(x^3 - y^3)\\&= (x + y)(x^2 - xy + y^2)(x - y)(x^2 + xy + y^2).\end{aligned}$$

Note. When an expression can be arranged either as the difference of two squares, or as the difference of two cubes, each of the methods explained in Arts. 136, 137 will be applicable. It will, however, be found simplest to first use the rule for resolving into factors the difference of two squares.

142. In all cases where an expression to be resolved contains a simple factor common to each of its terms, this should be first taken outside a bracket as explained in Art. 129.

Example. resolve into factors $28x^4y + 64x^3y - 60x^2y$.

$$\begin{aligned}28x^4y + 64x^3y - 60x^2y &= 4x^2y(7x^2 + 16x - 15)\\&= 4x^2y(7x - 5)(x + 3).\end{aligned}$$

EXAMPLES XVII. h

Resolve into two or more factors:

1. $(x+y)^2 - z^2$. **2.** $(x-y)^2 - z^2$.

3. $(a+2b)^2 - c^2$. **4.** $(a+3c)^2 - 1$.

5. $(2x-1)^2 - a^2$. **6.** $a^2 - (b+c)^2$.

7. $4a^2 - (b-1)^2$. **8.** $9 - (a+x)^2$.

9. $(2a-3b)^2 - c^2$. **10.** $(18x+y)^2 - (17x-y^2)$.

11. $(6a+3)^2 - (5a-4)^2$. **12.** $4a^2 - (2a-3b)^2$.

13. $x^2 - (2b-3c)^2$. **14.** $(x+y)^2 - (m-n)^2$.

15. $(3x+2y)^2 - (2x-3y)^2$. **16.** $a^2 - 2ax + x^2 - 4b^2$.

17. $x^2 + a^2 + 2ax - z^2$. **18.** $1 - a^2 - 2ab - b^2$.

19. $12xy + 25 - 4x^2 - 9y^2$. **20.** $c^2 - a^2 - b^2 + 2ab$.

21. $x^2 - 2x + 1 - m^2 - 4mn - 4n^2$.

22. $x^4 + y^4 - z^4 - a^4 + 2x^2y^2 - 2a^2z^2$.

23. $(m+n+p)^2 - (m-n+p)^2$. **24.** $a^4 + a^2 + 1$.

25. $a^4b^4 - 16$. **26.** $256x^4 - 81y^4$.

27. $16a^4b^2 - b^6$. **28.** $64m^7 - mn^6$.

29. $x^4 - x^4y^4$. **30.** $a^2b^5 - 81a^2b$.

31. $400a^2x - x^3$. **32.** $1 - 729y^6$.

33. $216b^6 + a^3b^3$. **34.** $250z^3 + 2$.

35. $1029 - 3x^3$. **36.** $ax^3 - ax^2 - 240ax$.

37. $acx^2 + bcx - adx - bd$. **38.** $m^4 + 4m^2n^2p^2 + 4n^4p^4$.

39. $8x^2y^3 - x^5$. **40.** $6x^3y^2 + 15x^2y^2 - 36xy^2$.

41. $2m^8n^4 - 7m^4n^6 - 4n^8$. **42.** $98x^4 - 7x^2y^2 - y^4$.

43. $a^2b^2 - a^2 - b^2 + 1$. **44.** $x^3 - 2x^2 - x + 2$.

45. $(a+b)^3 + 1$. **46.** $a^2x^3 - 8a^2y^3 - 4b^2x^3 + 32b^2y^3$.

47. $2p - 3q + 4p^2 - 9q^2$. **48.** $119 + 10m - m^2$.

49. $24a^2b^2 - 30ab^3 - 36b^4$. **50.** $240x^2 + x^6y^4 - x^{10}y^8$.

51. $x^4 + 4x^2 + 16$. **52.** $x^4 + y^4 - 7x^2y^2$.

53. $a^4 - 18a^2b^2 + b^4$. **54.** $x^8 + x^4 + 1$.

[For additionl exampls see *Elementary Algebra*, pages 125, 174, 216, 217.]

CONVERSE USE OF FACTORS

143. The actual processes of multiplication and division can often be partially or wholly avoided by a skilful use of factors.

It should be observed that the formulae which the student has seen exemplified in this chapter are just as useful in their converse as in their direct application. Thus the formula for resolving into factors the difference of two squares is equally useful as enabling us to write down at once the product of the sum and the difference of two quantities.

Example 1. Multiply $2a + 3b - c$ by $2a - 3b + c$.

These expressions may be arranged thus:

$$2a + (3b - c) \text{ and } 2a - (3b - c).$$

Hence the product $= \{2a + (3b - c)\}\{(2a - (3b - c)\}$

$$= (2a)^2 - (3b - c)^2$$

$$= 4a^2 - (9b^2 - 6bc + c^2)$$

$$= 4a^2 - 9b^2 + 6bc - c^2.$$

Example 2. Find the product of

$$x + 2,\ x - 2,\ x^2 - 2x + 4,\ x^2 + 2x + 4.$$

Taking the first factor with the third, and the second with the fourth,

the product $= \{(x + 2)(x^2 - 2x + 4)\}\{(x - 2)(x^2 + 2x + 4)\}$

$$= (x^3 + 8)(x^3 - 8)$$

$$= x^6 - 64.$$

Example 3. Divide the product of $2x^2 + x - 6$ and $6x^2 - 5x + 1$ by $3x^2 + 5x - 2$.

Denoting the division by means of a fraction,

the required quotient $= \dfrac{(2x^2 + x - 6)(6x^2 - 5x + 1)}{3x^2 + 5x - 2}$

$$= \frac{(2x - 3)(x + 2)(3x - 1)(2x - 1)}{(3x - 1)(x + 2)}$$

$$= (2x - 3)(2x - 1),$$

by cancelling factors which are common to numerator and denominator.

Example 4. Prove the identity

$$17(5x + 3a)^2 - 2(40x + 27a)(5x + 3a) = 25x^2 - 9a^2.$$

Since each term of the first expression contains the factor $5x + 3a$, the first side

$$= (5x + 3a)\{17(5x + 3a) - 2(40x + 27a)\}$$
$$= (5x + 3a)(85x + 51a - 80x - 54a)$$
$$= (5x + 3a)(5x - 3a)$$
$$= 25x^2 - 9a^2.$$

EXAMPLES XVII. k

Employ factors to obtain the product of

1. $a - b + c, a - b - c$.

2. $2x - y + z, 2x + y + z$.

3. $1 + 2x - x^2, 1 - 2x - x^2$.

4. $c^2 + 3c + 2, c^2 - 3c - 2$.

5. $a + b - c + d, a + b + c - d$.

6. $p - q + x - y, p - q - x + y$.

7. $a^3 - 4a^2b + 8ab^2 - 8b^3, a^3 + 4a^2b + 8ab^2 + 8b^3$.

Find the continued product of

8. $(a - b)^2, (a + b)^2, (a^2 + b^2)^2$.

9. $(1 - x)^3, (1 + x)^3, (1 + x^2)^3$.

10. $a^2 - 4a + 3, a^2 - a - 2, a^2 + 5a + 6$.

11. $3 - y, 3 + y, 9 - 3y + y^2, 9 + 3y + y^2$.

12. $1 + c + c^2, 1 - c + c^2, 1 - c^2 + c^4$.

13. Divide $a^3(a + 2)(a^2 - a - 56)$ by $a^2 + 7a$.

14. Divide the product of $x^2 + x - 2$ and $x^2 + 4x + 3$ by $x^2 + 5x + 6$.

15. Divide $3x^2(x + 4)(x^2 - 9)$ by $x^2 + x - 12$.

16. Divide the product of $2a^2 + 11a - 21$ and $3a^2 - 20a - 7$ by $a^2 - 49$.

17. Divide $(2a^2 - a - 3)(3a^2 - a - 2)$ by $6a^2 - 5a - 6$.

18. Divide $x^6 - 7x^3 - 8$ by $(x + 1)(x^2 + 2x + 4)$.

Prove the following identities:

19. $(a + b)^3 - (a - b)^2(a + b) = 4ab(a + b)$.

20. $c^4 - d^4 - (c - d)^3(c + d) = 2cd(c^2 - d^2)$.

21. $(m - n)(m + n)^3 - m^4 + n^4 = 2mn(m^2 - n^2)$.

22. $(x + y)^4 - 3xy(x + y)^2 = (x + y)(x^3 + y^3)$.

23. $3ab(a - b)^2 + (a - b)^4 = (a - b)(a^3 - b^3)$.

[For additional examples see *Elementary Algebra* pages 220, 221.]

MISCELLANEOUS EXAMPLES III

1. Find the product of $10x^2-12-3x$ and $2x-4+3x^2$.

2. If $a=1, b=-1, c=2, d=0$, find the value of

$$\frac{a^2-b^2}{a^2+b^2}+\frac{b^2-cd}{2b^2+cd}+\frac{c^3-b^3}{3abc}.$$

3. Simplify $2\,[4x-\{2y+(2x-y)-(x+y)\}]$.

4. Solve the equations:

(1) $\frac{x-3}{5}-\frac{2-x}{3}=\frac{1-2x}{15}$; (2) $3x-4y=25$, $5x+2y=7$.

5. Write down the square of $2x^3-x+5$.

6. Find the H. C. F. and L. C. M. of $3a^2b^3c, 12a^4b^2c^3, 15a^3b^3c$.

7. Divide a^4+4b^4 by $a^2-2ab+2b^2$.

8. Find in rupees the price of $5k$ articles at $80a$ paise each.

9. Find the square root of $x^4-8x^3+24x^2-32x+16$.

10. If $a=5, b=3, c=1$, find the value of $\frac{(a-b)^2}{a+b}+\frac{(b-c)^2}{b+c}+\frac{(a-c)^2}{a+c}$.

11. Solve $\frac{5}{3}(7x+5)-7\frac{2}{3}=13-\frac{4}{3}\left(x-\frac{1}{2}\right)$.

12. A is twice as old as B; twenty years ago he was three times as old. Find their ages.

13. Simplify $(1-2x)-\{3-(4-5x)\}+\{(6-(7-8x)\}$.

14. The product of two expressions is $6x^4+5x^3y+6x^2y^2+5xy^3+6y^4$, and one of them is $2x^2+3xy+2y^2$; find the other.

15. How old is a boy who $2x$ years ago was half as old as his father now aged 40?

16. Find the lowest common multiple of $2a^2, 3ab, 5a^3bc, 6ab^2c, 7a^2b$.

17. Find the factors of

(1) $x^2-xy-72y^2$.

(2) $6x^2-13x+6$.

18. Find two numbers which differ by 11, and such that one third of the greater exceeds one-fourth of the less by 7.

19. If $a=1, b=-1, c=2, d=0$, find the value of

$$\frac{a+b}{a-b}+\frac{c+d}{c-d}+\frac{ad-bc}{bd+ac}-\frac{c^2-d^2}{a^2+b^2}.$$

20. Simplify $\frac{3}{2}x - y - \left\{2x - \frac{1}{2}y - 7 - \left(\frac{x}{2} - 4\right) + \left(2 - \frac{1}{2}x\right)\right\}$

21. Solve the equations:

(1) $(3x - 8)(3x + 2) - (4x - 11)(2x + 1) = (x - 3)(x + 7)$;

(2) $\frac{x - y}{2} + \frac{x + y}{3} = \frac{25}{6}$, $x + y - 5 = \frac{2}{3}(y - x)$.

22. A train which travels at the rate of p kilometers per hour takes q hours between two stations; what will be the rate of a train which takes r hours?

23. Find the sum of $\frac{3}{4}a - \frac{1}{3}x$, $1 - \frac{a}{2}$, $\frac{2}{3}x - \left(2a - \frac{1}{2}\right)$, $\frac{1}{3}x - \frac{1}{4}a$.

24. Resolve into factors

(1) $12x^2 + ax - 20a^2$;

(2) $a^2 - 16 - 6ax + 9x^2$.

25. Solve

(1) $x + 1 + 2(x + 3) = 4(x + 5)$;

(2) $4x + 9y = 12$, $6x - 3y = 7$.

26. Find the value of $\frac{-x + \sqrt{3 - 2x^2}}{x(1 + 3x) - x^3}$, when $x = -\frac{1}{3}$.

27. Find the quotient when the product of $b^3 + c^3$ and $b^3 - c^3$ is divided by $b^3 - b^2c + 2bc^2 - c^3$.

28. *A*, *B*, and *C* have Rs. 168 between them; *A*'s share is greater than *B*'s by Rs. 8, and *C*'s share is three - fourths of *A*'s. Find the share of each.

29. Find the square root of $9x^6 - 12x^5 + 22x^4 + x^2 + 12x + 4$.

30. Simplify by removing brackets $a^2 - [(b - c)^2 - \{c^2 - (a - b)^2\}]$.

CHAPTER XVIII

HIGHEST COMMON FACTOR

144. DEFINITION. The **highest common factor** of two or more algebraical expressions is the *expression of highest dimensions* which divides each of them without remainder.

Note. The term *greatest common measure* is sometimes used instead of *highest common factor*, but this usage is incorrect, for in Algebra our object is to find the factor of *highest dimensions* which is common to two or more expressions, and we are not concerned with the *numerical* values of the expression or their divisors. The term *greatest common measure* ought to be confined solely to arithmetical quantities, for it can easily be shewn by trial that the algebraical highest common factor is not always the greatest common measure.
[See *Elementary Algebra*, Art. 145.]

145. We have already explained how to write down by inspection the highest common factor of two or more *simple* expressions. [See Chap. XII.] An analogous method will enable us readily to find the highest common factor of *compound* expressions which are given as the product of factors, or which can be easily resolved into factors.

Example 1. Find the highest common factor of

$$4cx^3 \text{ and } 2cx^3 + 4c^2x^2.$$

It will be easy to pick out the common factors if the expressions are arranged as follows:

$$4cx^3 = 4cx^3,$$

$$2cx^3 + 4c^2x^2 = 2cx^2(x + 2c);$$

therefore the H.C.F. is $2cx^2$.

Example 2. Find the highest common factor of

$$3a^2 + 9ab, a^3 - 9ab^2, a^3 + 6a^2b + 9ab^2.$$

Resolving each expression into its factors, we have

$$3a^2 + 9ab = 3a(a + 3b).$$

$$a^3 - 9ab^2 = a(a + 3b)(a - 3b),$$

$$a^3 + 6a^2b + 9ab^2 = a(a + 3b)(a + 3b);$$

therefore the H.C.F. is $a(a + 3b)$.

146. When there are two or more expressions containing different powers of the same *compound* factor, the student should be careful to notice that the highest common factor must contain the highest power of the compound factor which is common to all the given expressions.

Example 1. The highest common factor of

$$x(a-x)^2,\ a(a-x)^3,\ \text{and } 2ax(a-x)^5 \text{ is } (a-x)^2.$$

Example 2. Find the highest common factor of

$$ax^2+2a^2x+a^3,\ 2ax^2-4a^2x-6a^3,\ 3(ax+a^2)^2.$$

Resolving the expressions into factors, we have

$$ax^2+2a^2x+a^3 = a(x^2+2ax+a^2) = a(x+a)^2 \quad \ldots(1),$$

$$2ax^2-4a^2x-6a^3 = 2a(x^2-2ax-3a^2)$$

$$= 2a(x+a)(x-3a) \quad \ldots(2),$$

$$3(ax+a^2)^2 = 3\{a(x+a)\}^2 = 3a^2(x+a)^2 \quad \ldots(3).$$

Therefore from (1), (2), (3), by inspection, the highest common factor is $a(x+a)$.

EXAMPLES XVIII. a

Find the highest common factor of

1. $x^3-y^2,\ x^2-xy.$
2. $3(a-b)^3,\ a^2-2ab+b^2.$
3. $3a^3-2a^2b,\ 3a^2-2ab.$
4. $9a^2-4b^2,\ 6a^2+4ab.$
5. $c^4-cd^3,\ c^4-c^2d^2.$
6. $x^6-x^4y^2,\ x^3y^2+x^2y^3.$
7. $a^2x^3(a-x)^3,\ 2a^2x^2(a-x)^2.$
8. $2x^2-8x+8,\ (x-2)^3.$
9. $ax+x,\ a^4x+ax.$
10. $x^2y^2-y^4,\ xy^2+y^3,\ xy-y^2.$
11. $x^3+xy^2,\ x^2+xy,\ x^2y+xy^2.$
12. $x^3y^3-y^6,\ y^2(xy-y^2)^2.$
13. $(a^2-ax)^2,\ (ax-x^2)^3.$
14. $(abc-bc^2)^2,\ (a^2c-ac^2)^2.$
15. $x^3-x^2-42x,\ x^4-49x^2.$
16. $(x^3-5x^2)^2,\ x^5-8x^4+15x^3.$
17. $a^3-36a,\ a^3+2a^2-48a.$
18. $3a^2+7a-6,\ 2a^2+7a+3.$
19. $2x^2-9x+4,\ 3x^2-7x-20.$
20. $3c^4+5c^3-12c^2,\ 6c^5+7c^4-20c^3.$
21. $4m^4-9m^2,\ 6m^3-5m^2-6m,\ 6m^4+5m^3-6m^2.$
22. $3a^4x^3-8a^3x^3+4a^2x^3,\ 3a^5x^2-11a^4x^2+6a^3x^2,$
    $3a^4x^3+16a^3x^3-12a^2x^3.$

147. The highest common factor should always be determined by inspection when possible, but it will sometimes happen that expressions cannot be readily resolved into factors. To find the highest common factor in such cases, we adopt a method analogous to that used in Arithmetic for finding the greatest common measure of two or more numbers.

148. We shall now work out examples illustrative of the algebraical process of finding the highest common factor; for the proof of the rules the reader may consult the *Elementary Algebra*, Art. 146, 147. We may here conveniently *enunciate* two principles, which the student should bear in mind in reading the examples which follow.

I. *If an expression contain a certain factor, any multiple of the expression is divisible by that factor.*

II. *If two expressions have a common factor, it will divide their sum and their difference; and also the sum and the difference of any multiples of them.*

Example. Find the highest common factor of

$$4x^3 - 3x^2 - 24x - 9$$

and $$8x^3 - 2x^2 - 53x - 39.$$

x	$4x^3 - 3x^2 - 24x - 9$		
	$4x^3 - 5x^2 - 21x$	$8x^3 - 2x^2 - 53x - 39$	2
$2x$	$2x^2 - 3x - 9$	$8x^3 - 6x^2 - 48x - 18$	
	$2x^2 - 6x$	$4x^2 - 5x - 21$	2
	$3x - 9$	$4x^2 - 6x - 18$	
3	$3x - 9$	$x - 3$	

Therefore the H.C.F. is $x - 3$.

Explanation. First arrange the given expressions according to descending or ascending powers of x. The expressions so arranged having their first terms of the same order, we take for divisor that whose highest power has the smaller coefficient. Arrange the work in parallel columns as above. When the first remainder $4x^2 - 5x - 21$ is made the divisor we put the quotient x to the *left* of the dividend. Again, when the second remainder $2x^2 - 3x - 9$ is in turn made the divisor, the quotient 2 is placed to the *right*; and so on. As in Arithmetic, the last divisor $x - 3$ is the highest common factor required.

149. This method is only useful to determine the *compound* factor of the highest common factor. Simple factors of the given expressions must be first removed from them, and the highest common factor of these, if any, must be observed and multiplied into the *compound* factor given by the rule.

Example. Find the highest common factor of

$$24x^4 - 2x^3 - 60x^2 - 32x$$

and $$18x^4 - 6x^3 - 39x^2 - 18x.$$

We have $24x^4 - 2x^3 - 60x^2 - 32x = 2x \quad (12x^3 - x^2 - 30x - 16)$,

and $18x^4 - 6x^3 - 39x^2 - 18x = 3x \quad (6x^3 - 2x^2 - 13x - 6)$.

Also $2x$ and $3x$ have the common factor x. Removing the simple factors $2x$ and $3x$, and *reserving* their common factor x, we continue as in Art. 148.

$$\begin{array}{r|r|r|l}
2x & 6x^3 - 2x^2 - 13x - 6 & 12x^3 - x^2 - 30x - 16 & 2 \\
 & 6x^3 - 8x^2 - 8x & 12x^3 - 4x^2 - 26x - 12 & \\
\hline
2 & 6x^2 - 5x - 6 & 3x^2 - 4x - 4 & x \\
 & 6x^2 - 8x - 8 & 3x^2 + 2x & \\
\hline
 & 3x + 2 & -6x - 4 & -2 \\
 & & -6x - 4 & \\
\hline
\end{array}$$

Therefore the H.C.F. is $x\,(3x + 2)$.

150. So far the process of Arithmetic has been found exactly applicable to the algebraical expressions we have considered. But in many cases certain modifications of the arithmetical method will be found necessary. These will be more clearly understood if it is remembered that, at every stage of the work, the remainder must contain as a factor of itself the highest common factor we are seeking. [See Art. 148, I and II.]

Example 1. Find the highest common factor of

$3x^3 - 13x^2 + 23x - 21$

and $6x^3 + x^2 - 44x + 21$.

$$\begin{array}{r|r|l}
3x^3 - 13x^2 + 23x - 21 & 6x^3 + x^2 - 44x + 21 & 2 \\
 & 6x^3 - 26x^2 + 46x - 42 & \\
\hline
 & 27x^2 - 90x + 63 & \\
\end{array}$$

Here on making $27x^2 - 90x + 63$ a divisor, we find that it is not contained in $3x^3 - 13x^2 + 23x - 21$ with an *integral* quotient.

But noticing that $27x^2 - 90x + 63$ may be written in the form $9\,(3x^2 - 10x + 7)$, and also bearing in mind that every remainder in the course of the work contains the H.C.F., we conclude that the H.C.F. we are seeking is contained in $9\,(3x^2 - 10x + 7)$.

But the two original expressions have no *simple* factors, therefore their H.C.F. can have none. We may therefore *reject* the factor 9 and go on with divisor $3x^2 - 10x + 7$.

Resuming the work, we have

$$
\begin{array}{r|l|l|l}
x & 3x^3-13x^2+23x-21 & 3x^2-10x+7 & x \\
 & \underline{3x^3-10x^2+7x} & \underline{3x^2-7x} & \\
-1 & \quad -3x^2+16x-21 & \quad -3x+7 & -1 \\
 & \quad \underline{-3x^2+10x-7} & \quad \underline{-3x+7} & \\
 & \quad 2)\ \underline{6x-14} & & \\
 & \qquad 3x-7 & &
\end{array}
$$

Therefore the highest common factor is $3x-7$.

The factor 2 has been removed on the same grounds as the factor 9 above.

151. Sometimes the process is more convenient when the expressions are arranged in ascending powers.

Example. Find the highest common factor of

$$3-4a-16a^2-9a^3 \qquad \ldots(1),$$

and

$$4-7a-19a^2-8a^3 \qquad \ldots(2).$$

As the expressions stand we cannot begin to divide one by the other without using a fractional quotient. The difficulty may be obviated by *introducing* a suitable factor, just as in the last case we found it useful to remove a factor when we could no longer proceed with the division in the ordinary way. The given expressions have no common *simple* factor, hence their H.C.F. cannot be affected if we multiply either of them by any simple factor.

Multiply (1) by 4 and use (2) as a divisor:

$$
\begin{array}{r|c|}
 & 4-7a-19a^2-8a^3 \\
 & \underline{\qquad 5 \qquad\qquad\qquad} \\
4 & 20-35a-95a^2-40a^3 \\
 & \underline{20-28a-48a^2} \\
 & -7a-47a^2-40a^3 \\
 & \underline{-5 \qquad\qquad\qquad} \\
7a & 35a+235a^2+200a^3 \\
 & \underline{35a-49a^2-84a^2} \\
 & 284a^2\ \underline{|284a^2+284a^3} \\
 & 1+a.
\end{array}
$$

$$
\begin{array}{l|l}
12-16a-64a^2-36a^3 & 3 \\
12-21a-57a^2-24a^3 & \\
\hline
a\,|\,5a-7a^2-12a^3 & \\
\quad 5-7a-12a^2 & 5 \\
\quad 5+5a & \\
\quad -12a-12a^2 & -12a \\
\quad -12a-12a^2 & \\
\end{array}
$$

Therefore the H.C.F. is $1 + a$. After the first division the factor a is removed as explained in Art. 150; then the factor 5 is introduced because the first term of $4-7a-19a^2-8a^3$ is not divisible by the first term of $5-7a-12a^2$. At the next stage a factor -5 is introduced, and finally the factor $284a^2$ is removed.

152. From the last two examples it appears that we may multiply or divide either of the given expressions, or any of the remainders which occur in the course of the work, by any factor which does not divide both of the given expressions.

EXAMPLES XVIII. b

Find the highest common factor of

1. $2x^3+3x^2+x+6,\ 2x^3+x^2+2x+3.$

2. $2y^3-9y^2+9y-7,\ y^3-5y^2+5y-4.$

3. $2x^3+8x^2-5x-20,\ a^3+a^2-10a+8.$

4. $a^3+3a^2-16a+12,\ a^3+a^2-10a+8.$

5. $6x^3-x^2-7x-2,\ 2x^3-7x^2+x+6.$

6. $q^3-3q+2,\ q^3-5q^2+7q-3.$

7. $a^4+a^3-2a^2+a-3,\ 5a^3+3a^2-17a+6.$

8. $3y^4-3y^3-15y^2-9y,\ 4y^5-16y^4-44y^3-24y^2.$

9. $15x^4-15x^3+10x^2-10x,\ 30x^5+120x^4+20x^3+80x^2.$

10. $2m^4+7m^3+10m^2+35m,\ 4m^4+14m^3-4m^2-6m+28.$

11. $3x^4-9x^3+12x^2-12x,\ 6x^3-6x^2-15x+6.$

12. $2a^5-4a^4-6a,\ a^5+a^4-3a^3-3a^2.$

13. $x^3+4x^2-2x-15,\ x^3-21x-36.$

14. $9a^4+2a^2x^2+x^4,\ 3a^4-8a^3x+5a^2x^2-2ax^3.$

15. $2-3a+5a^2-2a^3,\ 2-5a+8a^2-3a^3.$

16. $3x^2-5x^3-15x^4-4x^5,\ 6x-7x^2-29x^3-12x^4.$

[For additional examples see *Elementary Algebra*, p. 133.]

CHAPTER XIX

FRACTIONS

153. THE principles explained in Chapter XVIII may now be applied to the reduction and simplification of fractions. For the proofs of the rules in the present chapter the reader is referred to the *Elementary Algebra*, Chapter XIX.

Reduction to Lowest Terms

154. Rule. *The value of a fraction is not altered if we multiply or divide the numerator and denominator by the same quantity.*

[*Elementary Algebra*, Art. 150.]

An algebraical fraction may therefore be reduced to an equivalent fraction by dividing numerator and denominator by any common factor; if this factor be the highest common factor, the resulting fraction is said to be in its *lowest terms*.

Example 1. Reduce to lowest terms $\dfrac{24\,a^3c^2x^2}{18a^3x^2 - 12a^2x^3}$.

$$\text{The expression} = \frac{24a^3c^3x^2}{6a^2x^2\,(3a - 2x)} = \frac{4ac^2}{3a - 2x}.$$

Example 2. Reduce to lowest terms $\dfrac{6x^2 - 8xy}{9xy - 12y^2}$.

$$\text{The expression} = \frac{2x\,(3x - 4y)}{3y\,(3x - 4y)} = \frac{2x}{3y}.$$

Note. The beginner should be careful not to begin cancelling until he has expressed both numerator and denominator in the most convenient form, by resolution into factors where necessary.

EXAMPLES XIX. a

Reduce to lowest terms:

1. $\dfrac{3x^2}{6x^2 - 3xy}$.

2. $\dfrac{a^2 - 2a}{4a^3 - 8a^2}$.

3. $\dfrac{3ab + b^2}{6a^2b^2 + 2ab^2}$.

4. $\dfrac{5x^2yz^2}{5x^2y + 10x^2z}$.

5. $\dfrac{9x^2 - y^2}{6x^2y - 2xy^2}$.

6. $\dfrac{2x^2y^2 - 8}{3x^2y + 6x}$.

7. $\dfrac{x^2+4x}{x^2+x-12}$.

8. $\dfrac{7a^2x-7a^2c}{5cx^2-10c^2x+5c^3}$.

9. $\dfrac{x^2+x-30}{5x^2+30x}$.

10. $\dfrac{(2a+b)^2}{4a^3-ab^2}$.

11. $\dfrac{a^3+b^3}{a^2-ab-2b^2}$.

12. $\dfrac{2c^2+5cd-3d^2}{c^2+6cd+9d^2}$.

13. $\dfrac{x^2-4x-21}{3x^2+10x+3}$.

14. $\dfrac{x^2-2x-15}{3x^2-12x-15}$.

15. $\dfrac{2x^2+x-3}{2x^2+11x+12}$.

16. $\dfrac{3a^3-24}{4a^2+4a-24}$.

17. $\dfrac{4x^3-25xy^2}{2x^2+xy-15y^2}$.

18. $\dfrac{18a^3+6a^2x+2ax^2}{27a^3-x^3}$.

155. When the factors of the numerator and denominator cannot be determined by inspection, the fraction may be reduced to its lowest terms by dividing both numerator and denominator by the highest common factor, which may be found by the rules given in Chap. XVIII.

Example. Reduce to lowest terms $\dfrac{3x^3-13x^2+23x-21}{15x^3-38x^2-2x+21}$.

The H.C.F. of numerator and denominator is $3x-7$.

Dividing numerator and denominator is $3x-7$, we obtain as respective quotients x^2-2x+3 and $5x^2-x-3$.

Thus $\dfrac{3x^3-13x^2+23x-21}{15x^3-38x^2-2x+21}=\dfrac{(3x-7)(x^2-2x+3)}{(3x-7)(5x^2-x-3)}=\dfrac{x^2-2x+3}{5x^2-x-3}$.

156. If either numerator or denominator can readily be resolved into factors we may use the following method:

Example. Reduce to lowest terms $\dfrac{x^3+3x^2-4x}{7x^3-18x^2+6x+5}$.

The numerator $= x(x^2+3x-4) = x(x+4)(x-1)$.

Of these factors the only one which can be a common divisor is $x-1$. Hence, arranging the denominator so as to shew $x-1$ as a factor,

the fraction $=\dfrac{x(x+4)(x-1)}{7x^2(x-1)-11x(x-1)-5(x-1)}$

$=\dfrac{x(x+4)(x-1)}{(x-1)(7x^2-11x-5)}=\dfrac{x(x+4)}{7x^2-11x-5}$.

EXAMPLES XIX . b

Reduce to lowest terms:

1. $\dfrac{x^3 - x^2 + 2x - 2}{3x^4 + 7x^2 + 2}$.

2. $\dfrac{a^3 + a + 2}{a^3 - 4a^2 + 5a - 6}$.

3. $\dfrac{y^3 - 2y^2 - 2y - 3}{3y^3 + 4y^2 + 4y + 1}$.

4. $\dfrac{m^3 - m^2 - 2m}{m^3 - m^2 - m - 2}$.

5. $\dfrac{a^3 - 2ab^2 + 21b^3}{a^3 - 4a^2b - 21ab^2}$.

6. $\dfrac{9x^3 - a^2x - 2a^3}{3x^3 - 10ax^2 - 7a^2x - 4a^3}$.

7. $\dfrac{5x^3 - 4x^2 - 1}{2x^3 - 3x^2 + 1}$.

8. $\dfrac{c^3 + 2c^2d - 12cd^2 - 9d^3}{2c^3 + 6c^2d - 28cd^2 - 24d^3}$.

9. $\dfrac{x^4 - 21x + 8}{8x^4 - 21x^3 + 1}$.

10. $\dfrac{y^5 + 6y^4 + 2y^3 - 9y^2}{y^4 + 7y^3 + 3y^2 - 11y}$.

11. $\dfrac{1 - x^2 + 6x^3}{2 - x + 9x^3}$.

12. $\dfrac{2 - 5x - 4x^2 + 3x^3}{4 + 4x + 9x^2 + 4x^3 - 5x^4}$.

[For additional examples see *Elementary Algebra*, p. 139.]

Multiplication and Division of Fractions

157. Rule. *To multiply together two or more fractions: multiply the numerators for a new numerator, and the denominators for a new denominator.* [*Elementary Algebra*, Art. 157.]

Thus $$\frac{a}{b} \times \frac{c}{d} = \frac{ac}{bd}.$$

Similarly, $$\frac{a}{b} \times \frac{c}{d} \times \frac{e}{f} = \frac{ace}{bdf};$$

and so for any number of fractions. In practice the application of this rule is modified by removing in the course of the work factors which are common to numerator and denominator.

Example. Simplify $\dfrac{2a^2 + 3a}{4a^3} \times \dfrac{4a^2 - 6a}{12a + 18}$.

$$\text{The expression } = \frac{a(2a+3)}{4a^3} \times \frac{2a(2a-3)}{6(2a+3)}, = \frac{2a-3}{12a},$$

by cancelling those factors which are common to both numerator and denominator.

158. Rule. *To divide one fraction by another: invert the divisor, and proceed as in multiplication.* [*Elementary Algebra*, Art. 158.]

Thus $$\frac{a}{b} \div \frac{c}{d} = \frac{a}{b} \times \frac{d}{c} = \frac{ad}{bc}.$$

Example. Simplify $\dfrac{6x^2 - ax - 2a^2}{ax - a^2} \times \dfrac{x - a}{9x^2 - 4a^2} \div \dfrac{2x + a}{3ax + 2a^2}$.

$$\text{The expression} = \frac{6x^2 - ax - 2a^2}{ax - a^2} \times \frac{x - a}{9x^2 - 4a^2} \times \frac{3ax + 2a^2}{2x + a}$$

$$= \frac{(3x - 2a)(2x + a)}{a(x - a)} \times \frac{x - a}{(3x + 2a)(3x - 2a)} \times \frac{a(3x + 2a)}{2x + a} = 1.$$

since all the factors cancel each other.

EXAMPLES XIX.c

Simplify

1. $\dfrac{x^2 - 1}{x^2 + 3x} \times \dfrac{2x^3 + 6x^2}{x^2 + x}$.

2. $\dfrac{ab + 2}{4a^2 - 12ab} \times \dfrac{a^2b - 3ab^2}{a^2b^2 - 4}$.

3. $\dfrac{2c^2 + 3cd}{4c^2 - 9d^2} \div \dfrac{c + d}{2cd - 3d^2}$.

4. $\dfrac{5y - 10y^2}{12y^2 + 6y^3} \div \dfrac{1 - 2y}{2y + y^2}$.

5. $\dfrac{x^2 - 4}{x^2 + 4x + 4} \div \dfrac{x - 2}{x + 2}$.

6. $\dfrac{b^2 - 5b}{3b - 4a} \times \dfrac{9b^2 - 16a^2}{b^2 - 25}$.

7. $\dfrac{x^2 + 9x + 20}{x^2 + 5x + 4} \div \dfrac{x^2 + 7x + 10}{x^2 + 3x + 2}$.

8. $\dfrac{y^2 - y - 12}{y^2 - 16} \times \dfrac{y^2 - 2y - 24}{y^2 + 6y + 9}$.

9. $\dfrac{a^3 + 27}{a^2 + 9a + 14} \div \dfrac{a^2 - 4a - 21}{a^2 - 49}$.

10. $\dfrac{2a^2 - 3a - 2}{a^2 - a - 6} \times \dfrac{3a^2 - 8a - 3}{3a^2 - 5a - 2}$.

11. $\dfrac{b^3 + 125}{5b^2 + 24b - 5} \times \dfrac{25b^2 - 1}{b^3 - 5b^2 + 25b}$.

12. $\dfrac{3m^2 - m - 2}{3m^2 + 8m + 4} \div \dfrac{4m^2 + m - 5}{m + 2}$.

13. $\dfrac{2p^2 + 4p}{p^2 - 9} \times \dfrac{p^2 - 5p + 6}{p^2 - 5p} \times \dfrac{p^2 - 2p - 15}{p^2 - 4}$.

14. $\dfrac{64a^2b^2 - 1}{x^2 - x - 56} \times \dfrac{x^2 - 49}{8a^3b - a^2} \div \dfrac{x - 7}{a^2x - 8a^2}$.

15. $\dfrac{4x^2 + 4x - 15}{x^2 + 2x - 48} \times \dfrac{x + 8}{2x^2 - 15x + 18} \div \dfrac{2x^2 + 5x}{(x - 6)^2}$.

16. $\dfrac{a^2 + 8ab - 9b^2}{a^2 + 6ab - 27b^2} \times \dfrac{a^2 - 7ab + 12b^2}{a^3 - b^3} \times \dfrac{a^3 + a^2b + ab^2}{a^2 - 3ab - 4b^2}$.

17. $\dfrac{ax^2 - 16a^3}{x^2 - ax - 30a^2} \times \dfrac{x^2 + ax - 20a^2}{ax^2 + 9a^2x + 20a^3} \div \dfrac{x^2 - 8ax + 16a^2}{x^2 + 8ax + 15a^2}$.

18. $\dfrac{(a - b)^2 - c^2}{a^2 - ab + ac} \times \dfrac{a^2 + ab + ac}{(a - c)^2 - b^2} \times \dfrac{(a + b)^2 - c^2}{(a + b + c)^2}$.

[For additional examples see *Elementary Algebra*, page 142.]

CHAPTER XX

LOWEST COMMON MULTIPLE

159. DEFINITION. The **lowest common multiple** of two or more algebraical expressions is *the expression of lowest dimensions* which is divisible by each of them without remainder.

The lowest common multiple of compound expressions which are given as the product of factors, or which can be easily resolved into factors, can be readily found by inspection.

Example 1. The lowest common multiple of $6x^2(a-x)^2, 8a^3(a-x)^3$ and $12ax(a-x)^5$ is $24a^3x^2(a-x)^5$.

For it consists of the product of

(1) the L. C. M. of the numerical coefficients;

(2) the lowest power of each factor which is divisible by every power of that factor occurring in the given expressions.

Example 2. Find the lowest common multiple of

$$3a^2 + 9ab, 2a^3 - 18ab^2, a^3 + 6a^2b + 9ab^2.$$

Resolving each expression into its factors, we have

$$3a^2 + 9ab = 3a(a+3b),$$

$$2a^3 + 18ab^2 = 2a(a+3b)(a-3b),$$

$$a^3 + 6a^2b + 9ab^2 = a(a+3b)(a+3b)$$

$$= a(a+3b)^2.$$

Therefore the L.C.M. is $6a(a+3b)^2(a-3b)$.

Example 3. Find the lowest common multiple of

$$(yz^2 - xyz)^2, y^2(xz^2 - x^3), z^4 + 2xz^3 + x^2z^2.$$

Resolving each expression into its factors, we have

$$(yz^2 - xyz)^2 = \{yz(z-x)\}^2 = y^2z^2(z-x)^2,$$

$$y^2(xz^2 - x^3) = y^2x(z^2 - x^2) = xy^2(z-x)(z+x),$$

$$z^4 + 2xz^3 + x^2z^2 = z^2(z^2 + 2xz + x^2) = z^2(z+x)^2.$$

Therefore the L.C.M. is $xy^2z^2(z+x)^2(z-x)^2$.

EXAMPLES XX. a

Find the lowest common multiple of

1. $a^2, a^3 - a^2$.
2. $x^2, x^2 - 3x^3$.
3. $4m^2, 6m^3 - 8m^2$.
4. $6x^2, x^4 + 3x^2$.
5. $b^2 + b, b^3 - b$.
6. $x^2 - 4, x^3 + 8$.
7. $9a^2b - b, 6a^2 + 2a$.
8. $k^2 - k + 1, k^3 - 1$.
9. $m^2 - 5m + 6, m^2 + 5m - 14$.
10. $y^2 + 3y^3, y^3 - 9y^5$.
11. $x^2 - 9x + 14, x^2 + 4x - 12$.
12. $x^3 + 27y^3, x^2 + xy - 6y^2$.
13. $b^2 + 9b + 20, b^2 + b - 20$.
14. $c^2 - 3cx - 18x^2, c^2 - 8cx + 12x^2$.
15. $a^2 - 4a - 5, a^2 - 8a + 15, a^3 - 2a^2 - 3a$.
16. $2x^2 - 4xy - 16y^2, x^2 - 6xy + 8y^2, 3x^2 - 12y^2$.
17. $3x^3 - 12a^2x, 4x^2 + 16ax + 16a^2$.
18. $a^5c - a^3c^3, (a^2c + ac^2)^2$.
19. $(a^2x - 2ax^2)^2, (2ax - 4x^2)^2$.
20. $(2a - a^2)^3, 4a^2 - 4a^3 + a^4$.
21. $2x^2 - x - 3, (2x - 3)^2, 4x^2 - 9$.
22. $2x^2 - 7x - 4, 6x^2 - 7x - 5, x^3 - 8x^2 + 16x$.
23. $10x^2y^2(x^3 - y^3), 15y^4(x - y)^3, 12x^3y(x - y)(x^2 - y^2)$.
24. $2x^2 + x - 6, 7x^2 + 11x - 6, (7x^2 - 3x)^2$.
25. $6a^3 - 7a^2x - 3ax^2, 10a^2x - 11ax^2 - 6x^3, 10a^2 - 21ax - 10x^2$.

160. When the given expressions are such that their factors cannot be determined by inspection, they must be resolved by finding the highest common factor.

Example 4. Find the lowest common multiple of

$$2x^4 + x^3 - 20x^2 - 7x + 24 \text{ and } 2x^4 + 3x^3 - 13x^2 - 7x + 15.$$

The highest common factor is $x^2 + 2x - 3$.

By division, we obtain

$$2x^4 + x^3 - 20x^2 - 7x + 24 = (x^2 + 2x - 3)(2x^2 - 3x - 8).$$

$$2x^4 + 3x^3 - 13x^2 - 7x + 15 = (x^2 + 2x - 3)(2x^2 - x - 5).$$

Therefore, the L.C.M. is $(x^2 + 2x - 3)(2x^2 - 3x - 8)(2x^2 - x - 5)$.

EXAMPLES XX. b

Find the lowest common multiple of

1. $x^3 - 2x^2 - 13x - 10$ and $x^3 - x^2 - 10x - 8$.
2. $y^3 + 3y^2 - 3y - 9$ and $y^3 + 3y^2 - 8y - 24$.
3. $m^3 + 3m^2 - m - 3$ and $m^3 + 6m^2 + 11m + 6$.
4. $2x^4 - 2x^3 + x^2 + 3x - 6$ and $4x^4 - 2x^3 + 3x - 9$.
5. Find the highest common factor and the lowest common multiple of $(x - x^2)^3, (x^2 - x^3)^2, x^3 - x^4$.
6. Find the lowest common multiple of $(a^4 - a^2x^2)^2, (a^2 + ax)^3, (ax - x^2)^2$.
7. Find the highest common factor and lowest common multiple of $6x^2 + 5x - 6$ and $6x^2 + x - 12$; and show that the product of the H.C.F. and L.C.M. is equal to the product of the two given expressions.
8. Find the highest common factor and the lowest common multiple of $a^2 + 5ab + 6b^2, a^2 - 4b^2, a^3 - 3ab^2 + 2b^3$.
9. Find the lowest common multiple of $1 - x^2 - x^4 + x^5$ and $1 + 2x + x^2 - x^4 - x^5$.
10. Find the highest common factor of $(a^3 - 4ab^2)^2, (a^3 + 2a^2b)^3, (a^2x + 2abx)^2$.
11. Find the highest common factor and the lowest common multiple of $(3a^2 - 2ax)^2, 2a^2x(9a^2 - 4x^2), 6a^3x - 13a^2x^2 + 6ax^3$.
12. Find the lowest common multiple of $x^3 + x^2y + xy^2, x^3y - y^4, x^5y + x^3y^3 + xy^5$.

[For additional examples see *Elementary Algebra*, page 146.]

CHAPTER XXI

ADDITION AND SUBTRACTION OF FRACTIONS

161. To find the algebraical sum of a number of fractions we must, as in Arithmetic, first reduce them to a common denominator. For this purpose, it is usually the most convenient to take the *lowest* common denominator.

Rule. *To reduce fractions to their lowest common denominator, find the* L.C.M. *of the given denominators, and take it for the common denominator; divide it by the denominator of the first fraction, and multiply the numerator of this fraction by the quotient so obtained; and do the same with all the other given fractions.*

Example. Express with lowest common denominator

$$\frac{5x}{2a(x-a)} \text{ and } \frac{4a}{3x(x^2-a^2)}.$$

The lowest common denominator is $6ax(x-a)(x+a)$.

We must therefore multiply the numerators by $3x(x+a)$ and $2a$, respectively.

Hence the equivalent fractions are

$$\frac{15x^2(x+a)}{6ax(x-a)(x+a)} \text{ and } \frac{8a^2}{6ax(x-a)(x+a)}.$$

162. We may now enunciate the rule for the addition or subtraction of fractions.

Rule. *To add or subtract fractions: reduce them to the lowest common denominator; find the algebraical sum of the numerators and retain the common denominator.*

Thus $$\frac{a}{b}+\frac{c}{d}=\frac{ad+bc}{bd},$$

and $$\frac{a}{b}-\frac{c}{d}=\frac{ad-bc}{bd}.$$

[*See Elementary Algebra*, Art. 165]

163. We begin with examples in further illustration of those already discussed in Chapter XII.

Example 1. Find the value of $\frac{2x+a}{3a}+\frac{5x^2-4ax}{9a^2}$.

The lowest common denominator is $9a^2$.

Therefore the expression $=\frac{3a(2x+a)+5x^2-4ax}{9a^2}$

$$=\frac{6ax+3a^2+5x^2-4ax}{9a^2}=\frac{3a^2+2ax+5x^2}{9a^2}.$$

Example 2. Find the value of $\frac{x-2y}{xy}+\frac{3y-a}{ay}-\frac{3x-2a}{ax}$.

The lowest common denominator is axy.

Thus the expression $=\frac{a(x-2y)+x(3y-a)-y(3x-2a)}{axy}$

$$=\frac{ax-2ay+3xy-ax-3xy+2ay}{axy}$$

$$=0.$$

Since the terms in the numerator destroy each other.

Note. To ensure accuracy the beginner is recommended to use brackets as in the first line of work above.

EXAMPLES XXI. a

Find the value of

1. $\frac{a-2}{3}+\frac{a-1}{2}+\frac{a+5}{6}$.

2. $\frac{3x-1}{4}+\frac{x+3}{6}+\frac{2x-1}{3}$.

3. $\frac{2b-1}{5}+\frac{b-3}{2}-\frac{7b+3}{10}$.

4. $\frac{2m-5}{9}-\frac{m+3}{6}+\frac{m-5}{12}$.

5. $\frac{2x-1}{5}+\frac{3x-1}{7}-\frac{x-2}{35}$.

6. $\frac{2x-5}{x}-\frac{x-4}{x}-\frac{x^2-4x}{3x^2}$.

7. $\frac{y-z}{yz}+\frac{z-x}{zx}+\frac{x-y}{xy}$.

8. $\frac{a+x}{2a}+\frac{a+2x}{3a}-\frac{x-5a}{6a}$.

9. $\frac{2a^2-5a}{a}-\frac{a^3+3a^2}{a^2}+\frac{9a^3-a^4}{a^3}$.

10. $\frac{x-y}{y}+\frac{x+y}{x}-\frac{6xy-4x^2}{3xy}$.

11. $\frac{a^3-2b^3-c^3}{5b^3}-\frac{3a^3-3c^3}{15b^3}$.

12. $\frac{ab-bc}{2bc}-\frac{a}{3c}-\frac{2a^2-ab}{2ab}$.

13. $\frac{2ay-xy+4x}{2xy}-1-\frac{a}{2x}$.

14. $\frac{a^2-ab}{a^2b}-\frac{b-c}{bc}-\frac{2c^2-ac}{c^2a}$.

164. We shall now consider the addition and subtraction of fractions whose denominators are compound expressions. *The lowest common multiple of the denominators should always be written down by inspection when possible.*

Example 1. Simplify $\frac{2x-3a}{x-2a} - \frac{2x-a}{x-a}$.

The lowest common denominator is $(x-2a)(x-a)$.

Hence, multiplying the numerators by $(x-a)$ and $(x-2a)$ respectively, we have

$$\text{the expression} = \frac{(2x-3a)(x-a)-(2x-a)(x-2a)}{(x-2a)(x-a)}$$

$$= \frac{2x^2-5ax+3a^2-(2x^2-5ax+2a^2)}{(x-2a)(x-a)}$$

$$= \frac{2x^2-5ax+3a^2-2x^2+5ax-2a^2}{(x-2a)(x-a)} = \frac{a^2}{(x-2a)(x-a)}.$$

Note. In finding the value of such an expression as $-(2x-a)(x-2a)$, the beginner should first express the product in brackets and then remove the brackets, as we have done. After a little practice he will be able to take both steps together.

Example 2. Find the value of $\frac{3x+2}{x^2-16} + \frac{x-5}{(x+4)^2}$.

The lowest common denominator is $(x-4)(x+4)^2$.

$$\text{Hence the expression} = \frac{(3x+2)(x+4)+(x-5)(x-4)}{(x-4)(x+4)^2}$$

$$= \frac{3x^2+14x+8+x^2-9x+20}{(x-4)(x+4)^2} = \frac{4x^2+5x+28}{(x-4)(x+4)^2}.$$

165. If a fraction is not in its lowest terms, it should be simplified before it is combined with other fractions.

Example. Simplify $\frac{x^2+5xy-4y^2}{x^2-16y^2} - \frac{xy-3y^2}{x^2+xy-12y^2}$

$$\text{The expression} = \frac{x^2+5xy-4y^2}{x^2-16y^2} - \frac{y(x-3y)}{(x+4y)(x-3y)}$$

$$= \frac{x^2+5xy-4y^2}{x^2-16y^2} - \frac{y}{x+4y} = \frac{x^2+5xy-4y^2-y(x-4y)}{x^2-16y^2}$$

$$= \frac{x^2+5xy-4y^2-xy+4y^2}{x^2-16y^2} = \frac{x^2+4xy}{x^2-16y^2} = \frac{x(x+4y)}{(x+4y)(x-4y)} = \frac{x}{x-4y}.$$

EXAMPLES XXI. b

Find the value of

1. $\frac{1}{a-2}+\frac{1}{a-3}$.

2. $\frac{1}{x-4}-\frac{1}{x-2}$.

3. $\frac{1}{b-2}-\frac{1}{b+2}$.

4. $\frac{a}{x-a}-\frac{b}{x-b}$.

5. $\frac{a-x}{a+x}+\frac{a+x}{a-x}$.

6. $\frac{a+3}{a-3}-\frac{a-3}{a+3}$.

7. $\frac{x}{x-1}-\frac{x^2}{x^2-1}$.

8. $\frac{3a}{a^2-4}-\frac{1}{a+2}$.

9. $\frac{x^2}{x^2-4y^2}+\frac{x-2y}{x+2y}$.

10. $\frac{1}{a(a-b)}+\frac{1}{a(a+b)}$.

11. $\frac{3a}{2x(x-a)}-\frac{2a}{3x(x+a)}$.

12. $\frac{5}{x-2}-\frac{4x}{(x-2)(x+1)}$.

13. $\frac{1}{y^2-2y-3}+\frac{3(y+2)}{y^2-y-6}$.

14. $\frac{1}{1-a}+\frac{a}{(1-a)^2}$.

15. $\frac{3}{x+y}-\frac{2x}{(x+y)^2}$.

16. $\frac{3b}{(b+1)^2}-\frac{2}{b+1}$.

17. $\frac{2x+y}{x^2-y^2}-\frac{2x-y}{(x+y)^2}$.

18. $\frac{b+c}{b^2-2bc+c^2}-\frac{b-2c}{b^2-c^2}$.

19. $\frac{x}{xy-y^2}-\frac{xy}{x^3-x^2y}$.

20. $\frac{a^2+2a}{a^2+a-2}-\frac{a}{a+1}$.

21. $\frac{4a^2-b^2}{2ab-b^2}-\frac{4a}{2a+b}$.

22. $\frac{x^2}{x^3+1}-\frac{1}{x+1}$.

23. $\frac{2b-4}{b^3+8}+\frac{1}{b+2}$.

24. $\frac{x^2-2y^2}{x^2+xy+y^2}+\frac{x^2y^3-2y^4}{x^3y-y^4}$.

25. $\frac{1}{a^2-6a+9}-\frac{1}{a^2-5a+6}$.

26. $\frac{1}{a^2-3a+2}+\frac{1}{a^2+3a-10}$.

27. $x+2-\frac{x-2}{x-1}$.

28. $4+\frac{a-6}{2+a}-2a$.

29. $\frac{1}{x^2}+\frac{x^2}{x+1}-\frac{1}{x}$.

30. $\frac{1}{x}-\frac{2}{x-2}+\frac{1}{x-4}$.

31. $\frac{3}{a+2}-\frac{1}{a-2}-\frac{2}{a+6}$.

166. The following examples furnish additional practice in the simplification of fractions.

Example. Simplify $\dfrac{4}{3b+3} - \dfrac{2}{5b-5} + \dfrac{7b+5}{b^2-1}$.

$$\text{The expression} = \frac{4}{3(b+1)} - \frac{2}{5(b-1)} + \frac{7b+5}{b^2-1}$$
$$= \frac{20(b-1) - 6(b+1) + 15(7b+5)}{15(b^2-1)}$$
$$= \frac{119b+49}{15(b^2-1)} = \frac{7(17b+7)}{15(b^2-1)}.$$

167. Sometimes the work will be simplified by combining two of the fractions together, instead of finding the lowest common multiple of all the denominators at once.

Example. Simplify $\dfrac{3}{8(a-x)} - \dfrac{1}{8(a+x)} - \dfrac{a-2x}{4(a^2+x^2)}$.

Taking the first two fractions together,

$$\text{the expression} = \frac{3(a+x)-(a-x)}{8(a^2-x^2)} - \frac{a-2x}{4(a^2+x^2)}$$
$$= \frac{a+2x}{4(a^2-x^2)} - \frac{a-2x}{4(a^2+x^2)}$$
$$= \frac{(a+2x)(a^2+x^2)-(a-2x)(a^2-x^2)}{4(a^4-x^4)}$$
$$= \frac{a^3+2a^2x+ax^2+2x^3-(a^3-2a^2x-ax^3+2x^3)}{4(a^4-x^4)}$$
$$= \frac{4a^2x+2ax^2}{4(a^4-x^4)} = \frac{ax(2a+x)}{2(a^4-x^4)}.$$

EXAMPLES XXI. c

Find the value of

1. $\dfrac{6}{2x-1} - \dfrac{3}{2x+1} - \dfrac{2-3x}{4x^2-1}$.

2. $\dfrac{1}{2a+3c} - \dfrac{1}{2a-3c} + \dfrac{6c}{4a^2-9c^2}$.

3. $\dfrac{1+2a}{3-3a} - \dfrac{3a^2+2a}{2-2a^2} + 1$.

4. $\dfrac{2x}{9-6x} + \dfrac{5}{6+4x} - \dfrac{4x^2-9x}{27-12x^2}$.

5. $\dfrac{1}{x-a} + \dfrac{2a}{(x-a)^2} + \dfrac{a^2}{(x-a)^3}$.

6. $\dfrac{2}{(a+1)^2} - \dfrac{a-3}{(a+1)^4} + \dfrac{2}{(a+1)^3}$.

7. $\dfrac{a^3}{(a-b)^3}-\dfrac{a}{a-b}-\dfrac{ab}{(a-b)^2}$.

8. $\dfrac{1}{x+3}-\dfrac{1}{x}+\dfrac{1}{x+1}$.

9. $\dfrac{1}{2y^2-y-3}-\dfrac{1}{2y^2+y-1}$.

10. $\dfrac{5}{4+3x-x^2}-\dfrac{2}{3+4x+x^2}$.

11. $\dfrac{1}{z(z-1)}+\dfrac{1}{z(z+1)}-\dfrac{2}{z^2-1}$.

12. $\dfrac{2}{(x-2)^2}-\dfrac{x}{x^2+4}+\dfrac{1}{x-2}$.

13. $\dfrac{2}{3-a}-\dfrac{3}{(2+a)(3-a)(1+2a)}+\dfrac{1}{(3-a)(1+2a)}$.

14. $\dfrac{y-2}{(y-3)(y-4)}-\dfrac{2(y-3)}{(y-2)(y-4)}+\dfrac{y-4}{(y-2)(y-3)}$.

15. $\dfrac{1}{1-x}-\dfrac{2+x}{(1-x)(2-x)}+\dfrac{2+3x+3x^2}{(1-x)(2-x)(3+x)}$.

16. $\dfrac{2}{x^2-5xy+6y^2}-\dfrac{3}{x^2-xy-6y^2}+\dfrac{1}{x^2-4y^2}$.

17. $\dfrac{5a}{6(a^2-1)}-\dfrac{a+3}{2(a^2+2a-3)}+\dfrac{a+1}{3a^2+6a+3}$.

18. $\dfrac{x-5}{x^2-4x-5}+\dfrac{2x}{x^2+2x}-\dfrac{3x-6}{x^2+x-6}$.

19. $\dfrac{a}{a-b}-\dfrac{b^2}{a^2+ab+b^2}-\dfrac{a^3+b^3}{a^3-b^3}$.

20. $\dfrac{3(6-x)}{x^3+27}+\dfrac{x-3}{x^2-3x+9}-\dfrac{1}{x+3}$.

21. $\dfrac{1}{(x-y)^2}-\dfrac{1}{x^2+2xy+y^2}-\dfrac{4xy}{x^4-2x^2y^2+y^4}$.

22. $\dfrac{x}{(x-a)^2}-\dfrac{a}{x^2-a^2}-\dfrac{ax}{(x-a)^3}$.

23. $\dfrac{1}{2-x}+\dfrac{1}{2+x}-\dfrac{3}{4+x^2}$.

24. $\dfrac{x}{4(1+x)}-\dfrac{x}{4(1-x)}+\dfrac{3}{2(1+x^2)}$.

25. $\dfrac{3}{2m-4}-\dfrac{3}{2m+4}-\dfrac{2}{3m^2+12}$.

26. $\dfrac{2a-6}{a^2-6a+9}-\dfrac{2a-3}{a^2-a-6}$.

27. $\dfrac{a}{a-b}-\dfrac{b}{a+b}-\dfrac{b^2}{a^2+b^2}$.

28. $\dfrac{x-3}{x-4}-\dfrac{x-1}{x-2}-\dfrac{1}{(x-2)^2}$.

29. $\dfrac{x-3}{x-6}-\dfrac{x-6}{x-3}+\dfrac{x-3}{x}-\dfrac{x}{x-3}$.

30. $\dfrac{1}{a-6}-\dfrac{1}{3(a-2)}+\dfrac{1}{3(a+2)}-\dfrac{1}{a+6}$.

168. To find a meaning for the fraction, $\frac{-a}{-b}$, we define it as the quotient resulting from the division of $-a$ by $-b$; and this is obtained by dividing a by b, and, by the rule of signs, prefixing +.

Therefore $$\frac{-a}{-b} = +\frac{a}{b} = \frac{a}{b} \qquad ...(1)$$

Again, $\frac{-a}{b}$ is the quotient resulting from the division of $-a$ by b; and this is obtained by dividing a, by b and by the rule of signs, prefixing –.

Therefore $$\frac{-a}{b} = -\frac{a}{b} \qquad ...(2)$$

Likewise $\frac{a}{-b}$ is the quotient resulting from the division of a by $-b$; and this is obtained by dividing a by b, and by the rule of signs, prefixing –.

Therefore $$\frac{a}{-b} = -\frac{a}{b}. \qquad ...(3)$$

These results may be enunciated as follows :

(1) *If the signs of both numerator and denominator of a fraction be changed, the sign of the whole fraction will be unchanged.*

(2) *If the sign of the numerator alone be changed, the sign of the whole fraction will be changed.*

(3) *If the sign of the denominator alone be changed, the sign of the whole fraction will be changed.*

Example 1. $\frac{b-a}{y-x} = \frac{-(b-a)}{-(y-x)} = \frac{-b+a}{-y+x} = \frac{a-b}{x-y}.$

Example 2. $\frac{x-x^2}{2y} = -\frac{-x+x^2}{2y} = \frac{x^2-x}{2y}.$

Example 3. $\frac{3x}{4-x^2} = -\frac{3x}{-4+x^2} = -\frac{3x}{x^2-4}.$

Example 4. Simplify $\frac{a}{x+a} + \frac{2x}{x-a} + \frac{a(3x-a)}{a^2-x^2}.$

Here it is evident that the lowest common denominator of the first two fractions is $x^2 - a^2$, therefore it will be convenient to alter the sign of the denominator in the third fraction.

Thus the expression $= \frac{a}{x+a} + \frac{2x}{x-a} - \frac{a(3x-a)}{a^2-x^2}$

$$= \frac{a(x-a) + 2x(x+a) - a(3x-a)}{x^2-a^2}$$

$$= \frac{ax - a^2 + 2x^2 + 2ax - 3ax + a^2}{x^2-a^2} = \frac{2x^2}{x^2-a^2}.$$

Example 5. Simplify $\dfrac{1}{(a-b)(a-c)}+\dfrac{1}{(b-c)(b-a)}+\dfrac{1}{(c-a)(c-b)}$.

Here in finding the L.C.M. of the denominators it must be observed that there are not *six* different compound factors to be considered; for three of them differ from the other three only in sign.

Thus $(a-c)=-(c-a),\ (b-a)=-(a-b),\ (c-b)=-(b-c)$.

Hence, replacing the second factor in each denominator by its equivalent, we may write the expression in the form

$$-\frac{1}{(a-b)(c-a)}-\frac{1}{(b-c)(a-b)}-\frac{1}{(c-a)(b-c)}.$$

Now the L.C.M. is $(b-c)(c-a)(a-b)$;

and the expression $=\dfrac{-(b-c)-(c-a)-(a-b)}{(b-c)(c-a)(a-b)}$

$$=\frac{-b+c-c+a-a+b}{(b-c)(c-a)(a-b)}=0.$$

Note. In examples of this kind, it will be found convenient to arrange the expressions **cyclically**, that is, so that a is followed by b, b by c, and c by a.

169. If the sign of each of *two* factors in a product is changed, the sign of the product is unaltered; thus

$(a-x)(b-x)=\{-(x-a)\}\{-(x-b)\}=(x-a)(x-b)$.

Similarly, $(a-x)^2=(x-a)^2$.

In other words, in the simplification of fractions we may change the sign of each of *two* factors in a denominator without altering the sign of the fraction; thus

$$\frac{1}{(b-a)(c-b)}=\frac{1}{(a-b)(b-c)}.$$

170. The arrangement adopted in the following example is worthy of notice.

Example. Simplify $\dfrac{1}{a-x}-\dfrac{1}{a+x}-\dfrac{2x}{a^2+x^2}-\dfrac{4x^3}{a^4+x^4}$.

Here it should be evident that the first two denominators give L.C.M. a^2-x^2, which readily combines with a^2+x^2 to give L.C.M. a^4-x^4, which again combines with a^4+x^4 to give L.C.M. a^8-x^8. Hence it will be convenient to proceed as follows:

The expression $=\dfrac{a+x-(a-x)}{a^2-x^2}-\ldots\ldots-\ldots\ldots$

$$=\frac{2x}{a^2-x^2}-\frac{2x}{a^2+x^2}-\ldots\ldots=\frac{4x^3}{a^4-x^4}-\frac{4x^3}{a^4+x^4}=\frac{8x^7}{a^8-x^8}.$$

EXAMPLES XXI. d

Find the value of

1. $\frac{5}{1+2x}-\frac{3x}{1-2x}+\frac{4-13x}{4x^2-1}$.

2. $\frac{10}{9-a^2}-\frac{2}{3+a}+\frac{1}{a-3}$.

3. $\frac{5a}{6(a^2-1)}+\frac{1}{2(1-a)}+\frac{1}{3(a+1)}$.

4. $\frac{2y}{2y-3}-\frac{5}{6y+9}+\frac{12y+8}{27-12y^2}$.

5. $\frac{x+a}{x-a}-\frac{x-a}{x+a}+\frac{4ax}{a^2-x^2}$.

6. $\frac{3-2c}{3+2c}+\frac{2c+3}{2c-3}+\frac{12}{4c^2-9}$.

7. $\frac{a}{a-b}-\frac{b}{a+b}+\frac{b}{b-a}$.

8. $\frac{a}{a^2-b^2}+\frac{b}{a^2+b^2}+\frac{a}{b^2-a^2}$.

9. $\frac{a}{x^2-x}+\frac{a}{x-x^3}-\frac{a}{x^2-1}$.

10. $\frac{x^6-x^3y^3}{y^6-x^6}+\frac{x^3y^3}{x^3y^3-y^6}$.

11. $\frac{1}{(y-2)(y-3)}+\frac{2}{(y-1)(3-y)}+\frac{1}{(y-1)(y-2)}$.

12. $\frac{a}{(x-a)(a-b)}-\frac{b}{(x-b)(a-b)}+\frac{x}{(a-x)(b-x)}$.

13. $\frac{2}{x-1}+\frac{3}{(1-x)^2}-\frac{1}{2x-1}$.

14. $\frac{1}{a-b}-\frac{a}{(a-b)^2}-\frac{ab}{(b-a)^3}$.

15. $\frac{a}{(a-b)}+\frac{c}{(x-a)}-\frac{b+c}{(b-a)(b-x)}$.

16. $\frac{x-z}{(x-y)(a-x)}-\frac{y-z}{(y-x)(y-a)}$.

17. $\frac{a+b}{b}-\frac{2a}{a+b}+\frac{a^3-a^2b}{b(b^2-a^2)}$.

18. $\frac{a^2-ab}{b^2-ab}-\frac{a^2-b^2}{ab-a^2}+\frac{a}{b}$.

19. $\frac{1}{a+x}+\frac{1}{a-2x}-\frac{1}{x-a}+\frac{1}{2x+a}$.

20. $\frac{3}{a-x}-\frac{1}{3x+a}+\frac{3}{x-a}+\frac{1}{a-3x}$.

21. $\frac{x}{(x-y)(x-z)}+\frac{y}{(y-z)(y-x)}+\frac{z}{(z-x)(z-y)}$.

22. $\frac{a}{(b-c)(b-a)}+\frac{b}{(c-a)(c-b)}+\frac{c}{(a-b)(a-c)}$.

23. $\frac{y-z}{(x-y)(x-z)}+\frac{z-x}{(y-z)(y-x)}+\frac{x-y}{(z-x)(z-y)}$.

24. $\frac{1+p}{(p-q)(p-r)}+\frac{1+q}{(q-r)(q-p)}+\frac{1+r}{(r-p)(r-q)}$.

25. $\frac{1}{4(x+a)}-\frac{1}{4(a-x)}+\frac{x}{2(x^2-a^2)}+\frac{x^3}{a^4-x^4}$.

26. $\frac{1}{2a^3(a+x)}-\frac{1}{2a^3(x-a)}+\frac{1}{a^2(a^2+x^2)}+\frac{2a^4}{x^8-a^8}$.

27. $\frac{a}{a^2-b^2}-\frac{b}{a^2+b^2}+\frac{a^3+b^3}{b^4-a^4}+\frac{ab}{(a+b)(a^2+b^2)}$.

CHAPTER XXII

MISCELLANEOUS FRACTIONS

171. DEFINITION. A fraction whose numerator and denominator are whole numbers is called a **Simple Fraction.**

A fraction of which the numerator or denominator is itself a fraction is called a **Complex Fraction.**

Thus $\dfrac{a}{\frac{b}{c}}, \dfrac{\frac{a}{b}}{x}, \dfrac{\frac{a}{b}}{\frac{c}{d}}$ are Complex Fractions.

In the last of these types the outside quantities, a and d, are sometimes referred to as the extremes, while the two middle quantities, b and c, are called the *means.*

Instead of using the horizontal line to separate numerator and denominator, it is sometimes convenient to write complex fractions in the forms

$$a\left|\frac{b}{c}, \quad \frac{a}{b}\right| x, \quad \frac{a}{b}\left|\frac{c}{d}\right..$$

Simplification of Complex Fractions

172. It is proved in the *Elementary Algebra*, Art. 176, that

$$\frac{\frac{a}{b}}{\frac{c}{d}} = \frac{a}{b} \div \frac{c}{d} = \frac{a}{b} \times \frac{d}{c} = \frac{ad}{bc}.$$

The student should notice the following particular cases, and should be able to write down the results readily

$$\frac{1}{\frac{a}{b}} = 1 \div \frac{a}{b} = 1 \times \frac{b}{a} = \frac{b}{a}.$$

$$\frac{a}{\frac{1}{b}} = a \div \frac{1}{b} = a \times b = ab.$$

173. The following examples illustrate the simplification of complex fractions.

Example 1. Simplify $\dfrac{x+\dfrac{a^2}{x}}{x-\dfrac{a^4}{x^3}}$.

$$\text{The expression} = \left(x+\frac{a^2}{x}\right) \div \left(x-\frac{a^4}{x^3}\right) = \frac{x^2+a^2}{x} \div \frac{x^4-a^4}{x^3}$$

$$= \frac{x^2+a^2}{x} \times \frac{x^2}{x^4-a^4} = \frac{x^2}{x^2-a^2}.$$

Example 2. Simplify $\dfrac{\dfrac{3}{a}+\dfrac{a}{3}-2}{\dfrac{a}{6}+\dfrac{1}{2}-\dfrac{3}{a}}$.

Here the reduction may be simply effected by multiplying the fractions above and below by $6a$, which is the L.C.M. of the denominators.

$$\text{Thus the expression} = \frac{18+2a^2-12a}{a^2+3a-18}$$

$$= \frac{2(a^2-6a+9)}{(a+6)(a-3)} = \frac{2(a-3)}{a+6}.$$

Example 3. Simplify $\dfrac{\dfrac{a^2+b^2}{a^2-b^2}-\dfrac{a^2-b^2}{a^2+b^2}}{\dfrac{a+b}{a-b}-\dfrac{a-b}{a+b}}$.

$$\text{The numerator} = \frac{(a^2+b^2)^2-(a^2-b^2)^2}{(a^2+b^2)(a^2-b^2)} = \frac{4a^2b^2}{(a^2+b^2)(a^2-b^2)};$$

$$\text{similarly, the denominator} = \frac{4ab}{(a+b)(a-b)}.$$

$$\text{Hence the fraction} = \frac{4a^2b^2}{(a^2+b^2)(a^2-b^2)} \div \frac{4ab}{(a+b)(a-b)}$$

$$= \frac{4a^2b^2}{(a^2+b^2)(a^2-b^2)} \times \frac{(a+b)(a-b)}{4ab} = \frac{ab}{a^2+b^2}.$$

Note. To ensure accuracy and neatness, when the numerator and denominator are somewhat complicated, the beginner is advised to simplify each separately as in the above example.

174. In the case of **Continued Fractions** we begin from the lowest fraction, and simplify step by step.

Example. Find the value of $\dfrac{1}{4-\dfrac{3}{2+\dfrac{x}{1-x}}}$.

The expression $= \dfrac{1}{4-\dfrac{3}{\dfrac{2-2x+x}{1-x}}} = \dfrac{1}{4-\dfrac{3(1-x)}{2-x}}$

$= \dfrac{1}{\dfrac{8-4x-3+3x}{2-x}} = \dfrac{1}{\dfrac{5-x}{2-x}} = \dfrac{2-x}{5-x}$.

EXAMPLES XXII.a

Find the value of

1. $\dfrac{1}{x+\dfrac{y}{z}}$.

2. $\dfrac{a}{b-\dfrac{c}{d}}$.

3. $\dfrac{1-a}{\dfrac{1}{a^2}-1}$.

4. $\dfrac{b}{\dfrac{1}{1-a}}$.

5. $\dfrac{\dfrac{a}{x}-\dfrac{x}{a}}{\dfrac{1}{x}-\dfrac{1}{a}}$.

6. $\dfrac{\dfrac{1}{x^2}-\dfrac{1}{y^2}}{\dfrac{y}{x}-\dfrac{x}{y}}$.

7. $\dfrac{a-\dfrac{b}{d}}{\dfrac{a}{b}-\dfrac{1}{d}}$.

8. $\dfrac{\dfrac{p}{q}-r}{\dfrac{1}{pq}-\dfrac{r}{p^2}}$.

9. $\dfrac{a+\dfrac{6}{a}-5}{1+\dfrac{8}{a^2}-\dfrac{6}{a}}$.

10. $\dfrac{y-3+\dfrac{y^2}{3}}{y-\dfrac{9}{y}+3}$.

11. $\dfrac{\dfrac{1}{n}-\dfrac{3}{n^2}-\dfrac{4}{n^3}}{n-\dfrac{16}{n}}$.

12. $\dfrac{x-2+\dfrac{6}{x+3}}{x-4+\dfrac{12}{x+3}}$.

13. $\dfrac{b-2-\dfrac{6}{b+3}}{b-4+\dfrac{6}{b+3}}$.

14. $\dfrac{\dfrac{a}{b^2}-\dfrac{b}{a^2}}{\dfrac{1}{a^2}+\dfrac{1}{ab}+\dfrac{1}{b^2}}$.

Find the value of

15. $\dfrac{\dfrac{c+d}{c-d}-\dfrac{c-d}{c+d}}{\dfrac{c+d}{c-d}+\dfrac{c-d}{c+d}}$.

16. $\dfrac{a-\dfrac{a-b}{1-ab}}{1-\dfrac{a(a-b)}{1-ab}}$.

17. $\dfrac{\dfrac{x+3}{7}-\dfrac{x+3}{x+4}}{\dfrac{x-3}{4}+\dfrac{x-3}{x-1}}$.

18. $1+\dfrac{1}{1+\dfrac{1}{a}}$.

19. $x+\dfrac{1}{x-\dfrac{1}{x}}$.

20. $2-\dfrac{3}{4-\dfrac{c}{d}}$.

21. $\dfrac{x}{1+\dfrac{x}{1-\dfrac{1}{x}}}$.

22. $\dfrac{1}{x+\dfrac{1}{x+\dfrac{2}{x}}}$.

23. $\dfrac{1}{1-\dfrac{1}{1-\dfrac{1}{y}}}$.

24. $\dfrac{1-x^2}{2-\dfrac{x}{1-\dfrac{1}{1+x}}}$.

25. $\dfrac{y}{1-\dfrac{1-y}{1-\dfrac{y^2}{2-y}}}$.

26. $\dfrac{a}{b-\dfrac{c}{d-\dfrac{e}{f}}}$.

27. $\dfrac{x^2-1}{2x^2-\dfrac{4x^2-1}{1+\dfrac{x}{x-1}}}$.

28. $\dfrac{3a-2c}{3a-2c-\dfrac{3a}{1-\dfrac{3(a-c)}{3a-2c}}}$.

175. Sometimes it is convenient to express a single fraction as a group of fractions.

Example. $\dfrac{5x^2y-10xy^2+15y^3}{10x^2y^2}=\dfrac{5x^2y}{10x^2y^2}-\dfrac{10xy^2}{10x^2y^2}+\dfrac{15y^3}{10x^2y^2}$

$$=\frac{1}{2y}-\frac{1}{x}+\frac{3y}{2x^2}.$$

176. Since a fraction represents the quotient of the numerator by the denominator, we may often express a fraction in an equivalent form, partly integral and partly fractional.

Example 1. $\dfrac{x+7}{x+2}=\dfrac{(x+2)+5}{x+2}=1+\dfrac{5}{x+2}$.

Example 2. $\frac{3x-2}{x+5} = \frac{3(a+5)-15-2}{x+5} = \frac{3(x+5)-17}{x+5} = 3 - \frac{17}{x+5}.$

Example 3. Shew that $\frac{2x^2-7x-1}{x-3} = 2x-1-\frac{4}{x-3}.$

By actual division,

$$
\begin{array}{r}
x-3)\,2x^2-7x-1\,(2x-1 \\
\underline{2x^3-6x} \\
-x-1 \\
\underline{-x+3} \\
-4
\end{array}
$$

Thus the quotient is $2x-1$, and the remainder is -4.

Therefore, $\frac{2x^2-7x-1}{x-3} = 2x-1-\frac{4}{x-3}.$

177. If the numerator be of lower dimensions than the denominator, we may still perform the division, and express the result in a form which is partly integral and partly fractional.

Example. Prove that $\frac{2x}{1+3x^2} = 2x-6x^3+18x^5-\frac{54x^7}{1+3x^3}.$

By division

$$
\begin{array}{r}
1+3x^2)\,2x \qquad (2x-6x^3+18x^5 \\
\underline{2x+6x^3} \\
-6x^3 \\
\underline{-6x^3-18x^5} \\
18x^5 \\
\underline{18x^5+54x^7} \\
-54x^7
\end{array}
$$

whence the result follows.

Here the division may be carried on to any number of terms in the quotient, and we can stop at any term we please by taking for our remainder the fraction whose numerator is the remainder last found, and whose denominator is the divisor.

Thus, if we carried on the quotient to four terms, we should have

$$\frac{2x}{1+3x^2} = 2x-6x^3+18x^5-54x^7+\frac{162x^9}{1+3x^2}.$$

The terms in the quotient may be fractional; thus if x^2 is divided by x^3-a^3, the first four terms of the quotient are $\frac{1}{x}+\frac{a^3}{x^4}+\frac{a^6}{x^7}+\frac{a^9}{x^{10}}$, and the remainder is $\frac{a^{12}}{x^{10}}$.

178. The following exercise contains miscellaneous examples which illustrate most of the processes connected with fractions.

EXAMPLES XXII. b

Simplify the following fractions:

1. $\dfrac{1-x^3}{1+2x+2x^2+x^3}$.

2. $\dfrac{12x^2+x-1}{1-8x+16x^2} \div \dfrac{1+6x+9x^2}{16x^2-1}$.

3. $\dfrac{a+b}{a-b}+\dfrac{4ab}{b^2-a^2}$.

4. $\dfrac{a+b}{a^2-ab-2b^2}-\dfrac{2a}{a^2-4b^2}$.

5. $\dfrac{x^3-1}{x-1}-\dfrac{x^4+x^2+1}{x^2+x+1}$.

6. $\dfrac{(x+y)^2}{x-y}-\dfrac{(x-y)^2}{x+y}$.

7. $\dfrac{abx^2-acx+bxy-cy}{ax^2+xy-ax-y}$.

8. $\dfrac{1}{x}\left(\dfrac{a}{a-x}-\dfrac{a}{a+3x}\right)-\dfrac{3}{a+3x}$.

9. $\dfrac{2}{x^2-6x+8}+\dfrac{3}{x^2-11x+28}+\dfrac{5}{x^2-9x+14}$.

10. $\dfrac{3a-\dfrac{1}{3a}}{3a+1}\times\dfrac{a}{3a-1}$.

11. $\dfrac{\dfrac{x^2+a^2}{x}-a}{a^3+x^3}+\dfrac{\dfrac{1}{x}}{x+a}$.

12. $\dfrac{1}{1-\dfrac{x}{x-1}}-\dfrac{1}{\dfrac{x}{x+1}-1}$.

13. $\dfrac{2x^2-\dfrac{7x^2-27}{x-1}}{3x^2-\dfrac{3(x^2-27x+54)}{1-x}}$.

14. $\dfrac{cd\,(a^2+b^2)+ab\,(c^2+d^2)}{cd\,(a^2-b^2)+ab\,(c^2-d^2)}$.

15. $\left(\dfrac{x}{1+x^2}\times\dfrac{1+x}{x^2}\right)-\dfrac{1}{x^2}$.

16. $\dfrac{1}{x^3-3ax^2+4a^3}-\dfrac{1}{x^3-ax^2-4a^2x+4a^3}$.

17. $\dfrac{\dfrac{a^2+4}{2}-a}{\dfrac{2}{a}-1}\times\dfrac{a^2-4}{a^3+8}$.

18. $\dfrac{\dfrac{2}{a^2}\left(4a^2-\dfrac{1}{9}\right)}{\dfrac{1}{a}+6}+\dfrac{1}{3}$.

19. $\dfrac{2x^3+x^2-3x}{35x^2+24x-35}\times\dfrac{5x^2-8x-21}{x^3+7x^2-8x}\div\dfrac{2x^2-3x-9}{7x^2+51x-40}$.

20. $\dfrac{q+r-p}{(p-q)(p-r)}+\dfrac{r+p-q}{(q-r)(q-p)}+\dfrac{p+q-r}{(r-p)(r-q)}$.

21. $\left\{\left(\dfrac{x+y}{x-y}+\dfrac{x-y}{x+y}\right)\div\left(\dfrac{x+y}{x-y}-\dfrac{x-y}{x+y}\right)\right\}-\dfrac{x^3+x^2y+xy^2+y^3}{2x^2y+2xy^2}$.

Simplify the following fractions

22. $\dfrac{a^2-(b-c)^2}{(c+a)^2-b^2}+\dfrac{b^2-(c-a)^2}{(a+b)^2-c^2}+\dfrac{c^2-(a-b)^2}{(b+c)^2-a^2}.$

23. $\left(\dfrac{x^2}{y}+\dfrac{y^2}{x}\right)\left(\dfrac{1}{y^2-x^2}\right)-\dfrac{y}{x^2+xy}+\dfrac{x}{xy-y^2}-\dfrac{1}{x+y}.$

24. $\dfrac{a^3-1}{a^2+a-6}\div\left[\dfrac{a^2-4a+3}{a^2-4a+4}\div\left\{\dfrac{a^2-9}{a^4+a^2+1}\div\dfrac{a^2-a-2}{a^3+1}\right\}\right].$

25. $\left(\dfrac{1}{2a}+\dfrac{1}{2a-x}\right)\left(\dfrac{1}{3a}-\dfrac{1}{3a-x}\right)-\dfrac{x^2-4ax}{6a^2(x-2a)(x-3a)}.$

26. $\dfrac{1}{6a-6}-\dfrac{1}{6a+6}+\dfrac{1}{3a^2+3}-\dfrac{2a^2}{3a^4+3}.$

27. $\dfrac{4ab^2}{2a^4+32b^4}+\dfrac{1}{8a+16b}-\dfrac{a}{4a^2+16b^2}-\dfrac{1}{8(2b-a)}.$

28. $\dfrac{3b^2+b}{6b^2-1-b}+\dfrac{2b-7}{1-2b}+\dfrac{2b^2-3b}{4b^2-8b+3}+3.$

29. $\dfrac{1}{\left(1-\dfrac{y}{x}\right)\left(1-\dfrac{z}{x}\right)}+\dfrac{1}{\left(1-\dfrac{z}{y}\right)\left(1-\dfrac{x}{y}\right)}+\dfrac{1}{\left(1-\dfrac{x}{z}\right)\left(1-\dfrac{y}{z}\right)}.$

30. $\dfrac{\dfrac{x^4+x^3y+x^2y^2}{(x^2-y^2)^3}\times\left(1+\dfrac{y}{x}\right)^2}{\left(1-\dfrac{y^3}{x^3}\right)\div\left(\dfrac{y}{x^2}+\dfrac{1}{x}\right)}.$ **31.** $\dfrac{m^2+\dfrac{1}{m^2}+1}{m^2-\dfrac{1}{m^4}}-\dfrac{m^3+m}{\dfrac{1}{m}-m^3}.$

32. $\left(\dfrac{ab}{ab-b^2}-\dfrac{ac}{ac-bc}\right)\left(\dfrac{1}{1-\dfrac{b}{a}}+\dfrac{1}{1-\dfrac{c}{b}}+\dfrac{1}{1-\dfrac{a}{c}}\right).$

33. $\left\{\dfrac{\dfrac{a-c}{1+ac}+c}{1-\dfrac{c(a-c)}{1+ac}}-\dfrac{a-\dfrac{a-c}{1-ac}}{1-\dfrac{a(a-c)}{1-ac}}\right\}\div\left(\dfrac{a}{c}-\dfrac{c}{a}\right).$

34. $\dfrac{\dfrac{1}{(3a+x)^2}}{\dfrac{1}{a}}+\dfrac{\dfrac{1}{3}}{x-3a}-\dfrac{1}{3(x+3a)}+\dfrac{\dfrac{1}{(x-3a)^2}}{a}.$

[For additional examples see *Elementary Algebra*, pp. 168-177.]

CHAPTER XXIII

HARDER EQUATIONS

179. Some of the equations in this chapter will serve as a useful exercise for revision of the methods already explained; but we also add others presenting more difficulty, the solution of which will often be facilitated by some special artifice.

The following examples worked in full will sufficiently illustrate the most useful methods.

Example 1. Solve $\dfrac{6x-3}{2x+7}=\dfrac{3x-2}{x+5}$.

Clearing of fractions, we have

$$(6x-3)(x+5)=(3x-2)(2x+7),$$

$$6x^2+27x-15=6x^2+17x-14;$$

$$\therefore \quad 10x=1;$$

$$\therefore \quad x=\frac{1}{10}.$$

Note. By a simple reduction many equations can be brought to the form in which the above equation is given. When this is the case, the necessary simplification is readily completed by multiplying up, or "multiplying across" , as it is sometimes called.

Example 2. Solve $\dfrac{8x+23}{20}-\dfrac{5x+2}{3x+4}=\dfrac{2x+3}{5}-1$.

Multiplying by 20, we have

$$8x+23-\frac{20(5x+2)}{3x+4}=8x+12-20.$$

By transposition, $31=\dfrac{20(5x+2)}{3x+4}$.

Multiplying across,

$$93x+124=20(5x+2),$$

$$84=7x;$$

$$\therefore \quad x=12.$$

180. When two or more fractions have the same denominator, they should be taken together and simplified.

Example 1. Solve $\frac{24-5x}{x-2}+\frac{8x-49}{4-x}=\frac{28}{x-2}-13.$

By transposition, we have

$$\frac{8x-49}{4-x}+13=\frac{28-(24-5x)}{x-2};$$

$$\therefore \quad \frac{3-5x}{4-x}=\frac{4+5x}{x-2}.$$

Multiplying across, we have

$$3x-5x^2-6+10x=16-4x+20x-5x^2;$$

that is, $$-3x=22;$$

$$\therefore \quad x=-\frac{22}{3}.$$

Example 2. Solve $\frac{x-8}{x-10}+\frac{x-4}{x-6}=\frac{x-5}{x-7}+\frac{x-7}{x-9}.$

This equation might be solved by at once clearing of fractions, but the work would be laborious. The solution will be much simplified by proceeding as follows.

The equation may be written in the form

$$\frac{(x-10)+2}{x-10}+\frac{(x-6)+2}{x-6}=\frac{(x-7)+2}{x-7}+\frac{(x-9)+2}{x-9};$$

whence we have $1+\frac{2}{x-10}+1+\frac{2}{x-6}=1+\frac{2}{x-7}+1+\frac{2}{x-9};$

which gives $$\frac{1}{x-10}+\frac{1}{x-6}=\frac{1}{x-7}+\frac{1}{x-9}.$$

Transposing, $$\frac{1}{x-10}-\frac{1}{x-7}=\frac{1}{x-9}-\frac{1}{x-6};$$

$$\therefore \quad \frac{3}{(x-10)(x-7)}=\frac{3}{(x-9)(x-6)}.$$

Hence, since the numerators are equal, the denominators must be equal;

that is, $$(x-10)(x-7)=(x-9)(x-6),$$
$$x^2-17x+70=x^2-15x+54;$$

$$\therefore \quad 16=2x;$$

$$\therefore \quad x=8.$$

EXAMPLES XXIII.a

Solve the following equations:

1. $\frac{3}{5x-9}=\frac{1}{4x-10}$.
2. $\frac{7}{6x-17}=\frac{3}{4x-13}$.
3. $\frac{7}{9}=\frac{3-4x}{4-5x}$.
4. $\frac{1}{6-5x}+\frac{4}{17x+3}=0$.
5. $\frac{5x-8}{x-4}=\frac{5x+14}{x+7}$.
6. $\frac{8x-1}{6x+2}=\frac{4x-3}{3x-1}$.
7. $\frac{22x-12}{8x-5}=2+\frac{3x+7}{4x+8}$.
8. $\frac{9x-22}{2x-5}-\frac{3x-5}{2x-7}=3$.
9. $\frac{8x-19}{4x-10}-\frac{1}{2}=\frac{3x-4}{2x+1}$.
10. $\frac{7x+2}{3(x-1)}=\frac{1}{3}+\frac{6x-1}{3x+1}$.
11. $\frac{x-5}{2}+\frac{2x-1}{3x+2}=\frac{5x-1}{10}-1\frac{2}{5}$.
12. $\frac{5x-17}{13-4x}+\frac{2x-11}{14}-\frac{23}{42}=\frac{3x-7}{21}$.
13. $x-\frac{4x-3}{7x+4}-\frac{1-9x}{6}=\frac{4x+3}{8}-\frac{1}{24}+2x$.
14. $\frac{3}{x+1}-\frac{2\frac{1}{3}}{x+2}=\frac{1}{x+3}-\frac{1}{3x+6}$.
15. $\frac{3\frac{1}{2}}{x-4}-\frac{18}{3x-18}=\frac{7}{4x-16}-\frac{4}{x-6}$.
16. $\frac{1}{x+6}+\frac{1}{3x+12}=\frac{3}{2x+10}-\frac{1}{6(x+4)}$.
17. $\frac{x-1}{x-2}-\frac{x-5}{x-6}=\frac{x-3}{x-4}-\frac{x-7}{x-8}$.
18. $\frac{1}{x-9}+\frac{1}{x-17}=\frac{1}{x-11}+\frac{1}{x-15}$.
19. $\frac{1}{2x-1}+\frac{1}{2x-7}=\frac{1}{2x-3}+\frac{1}{2x-5}$.
20. $\frac{x-1}{x-2}-\frac{x}{x-1}=\frac{x-4}{x-5}-\frac{x-3}{x-4}$.
21. $\frac{5x-64}{x-13}-\frac{4x-55}{x-14}=\frac{2x-11}{x-6}-\frac{x-6}{x-7}$.
22. $\frac{5x+29}{x+6}-\frac{2x+9}{x+5}=\frac{x-6}{x-5}+\frac{2x-11}{x-6}$.
23. $\frac{12x+1}{3x-1}+\frac{5}{1-9x^2}=\frac{11+12x}{1+3x}$.
24. $\frac{5x^2}{x^2-9}-\frac{x+3}{x-3}=5-\frac{x-3}{x+3}$.

[For additional examples see *Elementary Algebra*, p. 180.]

Literal Equations

181. In the equations we have discussed hitherto the coefficients have been numerical quantities. When equations involve *literal* coefficients, these are supposed to be known, and will appear in the solution.

Example 1. Solve $(x+a)(x+b)-c(a+c)=(x-c)(x+c)+ab$.

Multiplying out, we have

$$x^2+ax+bx+ab-ac-c^2=x^2-c^2+ab,$$

whence $$ax+bx=ac,$$

$$(a+b)x=ac;$$

$$\therefore \quad x=\frac{ac}{a+b}.$$

Example 2. Solve $\dfrac{a}{x-a}-\dfrac{b}{x-b}=\dfrac{a-b}{x-c}$.

Simplifying the left side, we have

$$\frac{a(x-b)-b(x-a)}{(x-a)(x-b)}=\frac{a-b}{x-c},$$

$$\frac{(a-b)x}{(x-a)(x-b)}=\frac{a-b}{x-c};$$

$$\therefore \quad \frac{x}{(x-a)(x-b)}=\frac{1}{x-c}.$$

Multiplying across, $$x^2-cx=x^2-ax-bx+ab,$$

$$ax+bx-cx=ab,$$

$$(a+b-c)x=ab;$$

$$\therefore \quad x=\frac{ab}{a+b-c}.$$

Example 3. Solve the simultaneous equations:

$$ax-by=c \qquad \text{... (1),}$$

$$px+qy=r \qquad \text{... (2).}$$

To eliminate y, multiply (1) by q and (2) by b;

thus $$aqx-bqy=cq,$$

$$bpx+bqy=br.$$

By addition, $$(aq+bp)x=cq+br;$$

$$\therefore \quad x=\frac{cq+br}{aq+bp}.$$

We might obtain y by substituting this value of x in *either* of the equations (1) or (2); but y is more conveniently found by eliminating x, as follows.

Multiplying (1) by p and (2) by a, we have

$$apx - bpy = cp,$$
$$apx + aqy = ar.$$

By subtraction, $(aq + bp)y = ar - cp$;

$$\therefore \quad y = \frac{ar - cp}{aq + bp}.$$

EXAMPLES XXIII. b

Solve the following equations:

1. $ax + b^2 = a^2 - bx.$
2. $x^2 - a^2 = (2a - x)^2.$
3. $a^2(a - x) + abx = b^2(x - b).$
4. $(b + 1)(x + a) = (b - 1)(x - a).$
5. $a(x + b) - b^2 = a^2 - b(a - x).$
6. $c^2x - d^3 = d^2x + c^3.$
7. $a(x - a) + b(x - b) + c(x - c) = 2(ab + bc + ca).$
8. $\frac{a^2}{x} - b = \frac{b^2}{x} + a.$
9. $\frac{x}{2a} = \frac{x}{b} + \frac{1}{b^2} - \frac{1}{4a^2}.$
10. $x + (x - a)(x - b) + a^2 + b^2 = b + x^2 - a(b - 1).$
11. $\frac{2x - a}{b} - \frac{3x - b}{a} = \frac{3a^2 - 8b^2}{ab}.$
12. $\frac{a - x}{a - b} - \frac{b - x}{a + b} = \frac{a^2 + b^2}{a^2 - b^2}.$
13. $\frac{ax - b}{c} + \frac{bx - c}{a} = \frac{a - cx}{b}.$
14. $\frac{x + a - b}{x + b + c} = \frac{x + b - c}{x + a + b}.$
15. $p(p - x) - \frac{p}{q}(x - q)^2 - p(p - q) + pq\left(\frac{x}{q} - 1\right)^2 = 0.$

Solve the following simultaneous equations:

16. $x - y = a + b, \; ax + by = 0.$
17. $cx - dy = c^2 + d^2, \; x + y = 2c.$
18. $ax = by, \; x - y = c.$
19. $\frac{x}{2} + \frac{y}{3} = a + b, \frac{x}{a} + \frac{y}{b} = 5.$
20. $\frac{a}{z} - \frac{b}{y} = 0, \; \frac{x}{a} + \frac{y}{b} = 2.$
21. $\frac{x + y}{x - y} = \frac{a}{b}, \; \frac{x - y}{a + b} = 2b.$
22. $\frac{x}{b} - \frac{y}{a} = \frac{a}{b} + \frac{b}{a}, a(a + x) = b(b - y).$
23. $\frac{x + y}{p} - \frac{x - y}{q} = 0, \; \frac{x - y}{2p} + \frac{x + y}{2q} = p^2 + q^2.$
24. $\frac{2x - b}{a} = \frac{2y + a}{b} = \frac{3x + y}{a + 2b}.$
25. $\frac{ax + by}{bx + ay} = \frac{1}{2} = \frac{a^2 - b^2}{bx + ay}.$

Irrational or Surd Equations

182. DEFINITION. If the root of a quantity cannot be exactly obtained the root is called a **surd**.

Thus $\sqrt{2}, \sqrt[3]{5}, \sqrt[5]{a^3}, \sqrt{a^2+b^2}$ are surds.

A surd is sometimes called an **irrational quantity**; and quantities which are not surds are, for the sake of distinction, termed **rational quantities**.

183. Sometimes equations are proposed in which the unknown quantity appears under the radical sign. For a fuller discussion of surd equations the student may consult the *Elementary Algebra*, Chap. XXXI. Here we shall only consider a few simple cases, which can generally be solved by the following method. Bring to one side of the equation a single radical term by itself: on squaring both sides this radical will disappear. By repeating this process any remaining radicals can in turn be removed.

Example 1. Solve $2\sqrt{x} - \sqrt{4x-11} = 1$.

Transposing, $2\sqrt{x} - 1 = \sqrt{4x-11}$.

Square both sides; then

$$4x - 4\sqrt{x} + 1 = 4x - 11,$$

$$4\sqrt{x} = 12,$$

$$\sqrt{x} = 3;$$

$$\therefore \quad x = 9.$$

Example 2. Solve $2 + \sqrt[3]{x-5} = 13$.

Transposing, $\sqrt[3]{x-5} = 11$.

Here we must *cube* both sides; thus $x - 5 = 1331$;

whence $x = 1336$.

Example 3. Solve $\dfrac{6\sqrt{x}-11}{3\sqrt{x}} = \dfrac{2\sqrt{x}+1}{\sqrt{x}+6}$.

Multiplying across, we have

$$(6\sqrt{x} - 11)(\sqrt{x} + 6) = 3\sqrt{x}\,(2\sqrt{x} + 1);$$

that is, $6x - 11\sqrt{x} + 36\sqrt{x} - 66 = 6x + 3\sqrt{x}$,

$$-11\sqrt{x} + 36\sqrt{x} - 3\sqrt{x} = 66,$$

$$22\sqrt{x} = 66,$$

$$\sqrt{x} = 3;$$

$$\therefore \quad x = 9.$$

EXAMPLES XXIII. c

Solve the equations:

1. $\sqrt{x-2}=1$.
2. $\sqrt{5-2x}=7$.
3. $\sqrt[3]{x-7}=2$.
4. $2\sqrt{x+1}=3$.
5. $3\sqrt[3]{1-2x}=-1$.
6. $\frac{1}{2}=\sqrt[3]{2x}$.
7. $\sqrt{1-5x}=3\sqrt{1-x}$.
8. $2\sqrt{5x-3}-7\sqrt{x}=0$.
9. $\sqrt{4x^2-11x-7}=2x-3$.
10. $3\sqrt{1-7x+4x^2}=5-6x$.
11. $1+\sqrt[3]{x^3-3x^2+7x-11}=x$.
12. $\sqrt{x-11}=\sqrt{x}-1$.
13. $\sqrt{4x+13}+2\sqrt{x}=13$.
14. $3+\sqrt{12x-33}=2\sqrt{3x}$.
15. $\dfrac{\sqrt{x}-1}{\sqrt{x}+3}=\dfrac{\sqrt{x}-3}{\sqrt{x}}$.
16. $\dfrac{\sqrt{x}+4}{3\sqrt{x}-8}=\dfrac{\sqrt{x}+5}{3\sqrt{x}-7}$.
17. $\dfrac{2\sqrt{x}-3}{\sqrt{x}-1}=\dfrac{2\sqrt{x}-\frac{1}{3}}{\sqrt{x}+\frac{2}{3}}$.
18. $\dfrac{2\sqrt{x}-7}{\sqrt{x}-\frac{14}{3}}=2+\dfrac{15}{4\sqrt{x}-13}$.
19. $\sqrt{1+4x}+2\sqrt{x}=\dfrac{3}{\sqrt{x}}$.
20. $\sqrt{x}+\sqrt{x-3}=\dfrac{1}{\sqrt{x-3}}$.
21. $\sqrt{4x+7}-\sqrt{x+1}=\sqrt{x-3}$.
22. $\sqrt{4x-3}-\sqrt{x+3}=\sqrt{x-4}$.

CHAPTER XXIV

HARDER PROBLEMS

184. In previous chapters we have given collections of problems which lead to simple equations. We add here a few examples of somewhat greater difficulty.

Example 1. If the numerator of a fraction is increased by 2 and the denominator by 1, it becomes equal to $\frac{5}{8}$; and, if the numerator and denominator are each diminished by 1, it becomes equal $\frac{1}{2}$ find the fraction.

Let x be the numerator of the fraction, y the denominator; then the fraction is $\frac{x}{y}$.

From the first supposition,

$$\frac{x+2}{y+1}=\frac{5}{8} \qquad ...(1)$$

from the second, $\frac{x-1}{y-1}=\frac{1}{2}$ ...(2)

From the first equation, $8x-5y=-11$, and from the second,

$$2x-y=1;$$

whence $x=8,\ y=15.$

Thus the fraction is $\frac{8}{15}$.

Example 2. At what time between 4 and 5 o'clock will the minute-hand of a watch be 13 minutes in advance of the hour-hand?

Let x denote the required number of minutes after 4 o'clock; then, as the minute-hand travels twelve times as fast as the hour-hand, the hour-hand will move over $\frac{x}{12}$ minute-divisions in x minutes.

At 4 o'clock the minute-hand is 20 divisions behind the hour-hand, and finally the minute-hand is 13 divisions in advance; therefore the minute-hand moves over 20 + 13, or 33 divisions more than the hour-hand.

Hence $x=\frac{x}{12}+33,\ \frac{11}{12}x=33;$

$$\therefore \qquad x=36.$$

Thus the time is 36 minutes past 4.

If the question be asked as follows: "At what *times* between 4 and 5 o'clock will there be 13 minutes between the two hands?" we must also take into consideration the case when the minute-hand is 13 divisions *behind* the hour-hand. In this case the minute-hand gains 20 – 13, or 7 divisions.

Hence $x=\frac{x}{12}+7$

which gives $x=7\frac{7}{11}$.

Therefore the *times* are $7\frac{7'}{11}$ past 4, and 36′ past 4.

Example 3. A grocer buys 15 kg of figs and 28 kg of currants for Rs. 52; by selling the figs at a loss of 10 per cent., and the currants at a gain of 30 per cent., he clears Rs. 6 on his outlay; how much per kg did he pay for each?

Let x, y denote the number of paise in the price of a kg of figs and currants respectively; then -the outlay is

$$15x+28y \text{ paise.}$$

Therefore $$15x+28y=5200 \qquad \ldots(1).$$

The loss upon the figs is $\frac{1}{10}\times 15\,x$ paise, and the gain upon the currants is $\frac{3}{10}\times 28y$ paise; therefore the total gain is

$$\frac{42y}{5}-\frac{3x}{2} \text{ paise;}$$

$$\frac{42y}{5}-\frac{3x}{2}=600;$$

that is, $$28y-5x=2000 \qquad \ldots(2).$$

From (1) and (2) we find that $x=160$, and $y=100$; that is, the figs cost Re. 1.60 per kg and the currants cost Re. 1 per kg.

Example 4. Two persons *A* and *B* start simultaneously from two places, c kilometres apart, and walk in the same direction. *A* travels at the rate of *p* kilometers per hour, and *B* at the rate of q kilometers; how far will *A* have walked before he overtakes *B*?

Suppose *A* has walked *x* km when *B* overtakes him; then *B* has walked $x-c$ km.

A walking at the rate of p km per hour will travel x km in $\frac{x}{p}$ hours; and *B* will travel $x-c$ km in $\frac{x-c}{q}$ hours; these two times being equal, we have

$$\frac{x}{p}=\frac{x-c}{q},$$

$$qx=px-pc;$$

whence $$x=\frac{pc}{p-q}.$$

Therefore A has travelled $\frac{pc}{p-q}$ kilometers.

Example 5. A train travelled a certain distance at a uniform speed. Had the speed been 3 kilometres per hour more, the journey would have occupied 2 hours less; and had the speed been 3 kilometres per hour less, the journey would have occupied 3 hours more. Find the distance.

Let the speed of the train be x kilometres per hour, and let the time occupied be y hours; then the distance traversed will be represented by xy kilometres.

On the first supposition the speed per hour is $x+3$ kilometres, and the time taken is $y-2$ hours. In this case the distance traversed will be represented by $(x+3)(y-2)$ kilometres.

On the second supposition the distance traversed will be represented by $(x-3)(y+3)$ kilometres.

All these expressions for the distance must be equal;

$$\therefore \quad xy=(x+3)(y-2)=(x-3)(y+3)$$

From these equations we have

$$xy=xy+3y-2x-6,$$

or $$3y-2x=6 \quad \ldots(1);$$

and $$xy=xy-3y+3x-9,$$

or $$3x-3y=9 \quad \ldots(2).$$

From (1) and (2) we obtain $x=15$, $y=12$.

Hence the distance is 180 kilometres.

EXAMPLES XXIV

1. If the numerator of a fraction is increased by 5 it reduces to $\frac{2}{3}$, and if the denominator is increased by 9 it reduces to $\frac{1}{3}$: find the fraction.

2. Find a fraction such that it reduces to $\frac{3}{5}$ if 7 be subtracted from its denominator, and reduces to $\frac{3}{8}$ on subtracting 3 from its numerator.

3. If unity is taken from the denominator of a fraction it reduces to $\frac{1}{2}$; if 3 is added to the numerator it reduces to $\frac{4}{7}$; required the fraction.

4. Find a fraction which becomes $\frac{3}{4}$ on adding 5 to the numerator and subtracting 1 from the denominate:, and reduces to $\frac{1}{3}$ on subtracting 4 from the numerator and adding 7 to the denominator.

5. If 9 is added to the numerator a certain fraction will be increased by $\frac{1}{3}$; if 6 is taken from the denominator the fraction reduces to $\frac{2}{3}$; required the fraction.

6. At what time between 9 and 10 o'clock are the hands of a watch together?

7. When are the hands of a clock 8 minutes apart between the hours of 5 and 6 ?

8. It what time between 10 and 11 o'clock is the hour-hand six minute: ahead of the minute-hand?

9. At what time between 1 and 2 o'clock are the hands of a watch in the same straight line?

10. When are the hands of a clock at right angles between the hours df 5 and 6?

11. At what times between 12 and 1 o'clock are the hands of a watch at right angles?

12. A person buys 20 metres of cloth and 25 metres of canvas for Rs. 22.50. By selling the cloth at a gain of 15 per cent. and the canvas at a gain of 20 per cent he clears Rs. 3.75: find the price of each per metre.

13. A dealer spends Rs. 6950 in buying horses at Rs. 250 each and cows at Rs. 200 each; through disease he loses 20 per cent, of the horses and 25 per cent, of the cows. By selling the animals at the price he gave for them he receives Rs. 5400: find how many of each kind he bought.

14. The population of a certain district, is 33000, of whom 835 can neither read nor write. These consist of 2 per cent, of all the males and 3 per cent, of all the females: find the number of males and females,

15. Two persons C and D start simultaneously from two places a kilometres apart, and walk to meet each other; if C walks p kilometres per hour, and D one kilometre per hour faster than C, how far will D have walked when they meet?

16. A can walk a kilometres per hour faster than B; supposing that he gives B a start of c kilometres, and that B walks n kilometres per hour, how far will A have walked when he overtakes B ?

17. *A, B, C* start from the same place at the rates of a, $a+4$, $a+2b$ kilometres per hour respectively. B starts n hours after *A*, how long after *B* must *C* start in order that they may overtake *A* at the same instant, and how far will they then have walked?

18. Find the distance between two towns when by increasing the speed 7 kilometres per hour a train can perform the journey in 1 hour less, and by reducing the speed 5 kilometres per hour can perform the journey in 1 hour more.

19. A person buys a certain quantity of land. If he had bought 7 hectares more each hectare would have cost Rs. 80 less, and if each hectare had cost Rs. 360 more he would have obtained 15 hectares less: how much did he pay for the land?

20. A can walk half a kilometre per hour faster than *B*, and three-quarters of a kilometre per hour faster than *C*. To walk a certain distance *C* takes three-quarters of an hour more than *B*, and two hours more than *A*: find their rates of walking per hour.

21. A person spends Rs. 15 in buying goods; if each kg had cost 25 paise more he would have got 5 kg less, but if each kg had cost 15 paise less he would have received 5 kg more: what weight did he buy?

22. Five silver coins weigh 125 gm and are worth Rs. 6. Ten bronze coins weigh 500 gm and are worth 80 paise. A number of silver and bronze coins which are worth Rs. 134 weigh 11 kg 250 gm: how many coins of each kind are there?

23. *A* and *B* are playing for money; in the first game *A* loses one half of his money, but in the second he wins one-quarter of what *B* then has. When they cease playing, *A* has won Rs. 6, and *B* has still Rs. 14.50 more than *A*; with what amounts did they begin?

24. The area of three fields is 5 hectares 16-ares; and the area of the largest and smallest fields exceeds by 30 areas twice the area of the middle field. If the smallest field had been twice as large, and the other two fields half their actual size, the total area would have been 40 area 20 centiares less than it is: find the area of each of the fields.

25. *A, B, C* each spend the same amount in buying different qualities of the same commodity. *B* pays 36 paise per kg less than *A* and obtains 750 gm more; *C* pays 60 paise per kg more than *A* and obtains one kg less: how much does each spend?

26. *B* pays Rs. 28 more rent for his garden than *A*; he has 75 ares more and pays Re. 1.75 per hectare more. Cpays Rs. 72.50 more than A; he has 6 hectares 25 ares more but pays 25 paise per hectare less: find the size of the gardens.

MISCELLANEOUS EXAMPLES IV

1. When $a=-3,\quad b=5,\quad c=-1,\quad d=0,$ find the value of $26c\sqrt[3]{a^3-c^2d+5bc-4ac+d^2}$.

2. Solve the equations:

(1) $\frac{1}{3}x-\frac{3}{4}y=8-2x,\ \frac{1}{2}y-3x=3-y;$

(2) $1=y+z=2(z+x)=3(x+y)$.

3. Simplify

(1) $\frac{a-x}{a+x}-\frac{4x^2}{a^2-x^2}+\frac{a-3x}{x-a};$

(2) $\frac{b^2-3b}{b^2-2b+4}\times\frac{b^2+b-30}{b^2+3b-18}\div\frac{b^2-3b^2-10b}{b^3+8}.$

4. Find the square root of $9-36x+60x^2-\frac{160}{3}x^3+\frac{80}{3}x^4-\frac{64}{9}x^5+\frac{64}{81}x^6$.

5. In a cricket match the extras in the first innings arc one-sixteenth of the score, and in the second innings the extras are one-twelfth of the score. The grand total is 296, of which 21 are extras: find the score in each innings.

6. Find the value of $\frac{a^2-x^2}{\frac{1}{a^2}-\frac{2}{ax}+\frac{1}{x^2}}\times\frac{\frac{1}{a^2x^2}}{a+x}.$

7. Find the value of $\frac{1}{3}(a+2)-3\left(1-\frac{1}{6}b\right)-\frac{2}{3}\left(2a-3b+\frac{3}{2}\right)+\frac{3}{2}b-4\left(\frac{1}{2}a-\frac{1}{3}\right).$

8. Resolve into factors

(1) $3a^2-20a-7;$ (2) $a^4b^2-b^4a^2.$

9. Reduce to lowest terms $\frac{4x^3+7x^2-x+2}{4x^3+5x^2-7x-2}.$

10. Solve the equations:

(1) $x-6-\frac{x-12}{3}=\frac{x-4}{2}+\frac{x-8}{4};$

(2) $x+y-z=0,\ x-y+z=4,\ 5x+y+z=20;$

(3) $\frac{ax+b}{c}+\frac{dx+e}{f}=1.$

11. Simplify $\dfrac{x+3}{x^2+5x+6}-\dfrac{x+2}{x^2-9x+14}+\dfrac{4}{x^2-10x+21}$.

12. A purse of rupees is divided amongst three persons, the first receiving half of them and one more, the second half of the remainder and one more, and the third six. Find the number of rupees the purse contained.

13. If $h=-1,\quad k=2,\quad l=0,\quad m=1,\quad n=-3,$ find the value of
$$\frac{h^3(m-l)-\sqrt{3hn}+hk}{m(l-h)-2hm^2+\sqrt[3]{4hk}}.$$

14. Find the L.C.M of
$$15(p^3+q^3),\ 5(p^2-pq+q^2),\ 4(p^2+pq+q^2),\ 6(p^2-q^2).$$

15. Find the square root of

(1) $\dfrac{4x^2}{9}+\dfrac{9}{4x^2}-2;$ (2) $1-6a+5a^2+12a^3+4a^4.$

16. Simplify $\dfrac{20x^2+27x+9}{15x^2+19x+6}+\dfrac{20x^2+27x+9}{12x^2+17x+6}.$

17. Solve the equations:

(1) $\dfrac{a(x-b)}{a-b}+\dfrac{b(x-a)}{b-a}=1;$ (2) $\dfrac{9}{x-4}+\dfrac{3}{x-8}=\dfrac{4}{x-9}+\dfrac{8}{x-3}.$

18. A sum of money is to be divided among a number of persons; if Rs. 8 is given to each there will be Rs. 3 short, and if Rs. 7.50 is given to each there will be Rs. 2 over: find the number of persons.

19. Resolve into factors:

(1) $2x^2-3ab+(a-6b)x;$

(2) $4x^2-4xy-15y^2.$

20. In the expression x^3-2x^2+3x-4 substitute $a-2$ for x, and arrange the result according to the descending powers of a.

21. Simplify

(1) $\dfrac{x}{1-\dfrac{1}{1+x}};$ (2) $\dfrac{x^2}{a+\dfrac{x^2}{a+\dfrac{x^2}{a}}}.$

22. Find the H.C.F. of $3x^3-11x^2+x+15$ and $5x^4-7x^3-20x^2-11x-3.$

23. Express in the simplest form

(1) $\dfrac{\dfrac{x}{y}-\dfrac{y}{x}}{\dfrac{x+y}{y}+\dfrac{y+x}{x}};$ (2) $\left(\dfrac{x^3-1}{x-1}+\dfrac{x^3+1}{x+1}\right)\div\left(\dfrac{1}{x-1}+\dfrac{1}{x+1}\right).$

24. A person possesses Rs. 5000 stock, some at 3 per cent,- four times as much at $3\frac{1}{2}$ per cent., and the rest at 4 per cent. find the amount of each kind of stock when his income is Rs. 176.

25. Simplify the expression $-3[(a+b)-\{(2a-3b)-(5a+7b-16c)-(-13a+2b-3c-5d)\}]$, and find its value when $a=1, b=2, c=3, d=4$.

26. Solve the following equations:

(1) $11y-x=10, 11x-101y=110$;

(2) $x+y-z=3, x+z-y=5, y+z-x=7$.

27. Express the following fractions in their simplest form:

(1) $\dfrac{32x^3-2x+12}{12x^5-x^4+4x^2}$; (2) $\dfrac{1}{x+\dfrac{1}{1+\dfrac{x+3}{2-x}}}$.

28. What value of a will make the product of $3-8a$ and $3a+4$ equal to the product of $6a+11$ and $3-4a$?

29. Find the L.C.M. of x^3-x^2-3x-9 and $x^3-2x^2-5x-12$.

30. A certain number of two digits is equal to seven times the sum of its digits: if the digit in the units' place be decreased by two and that in the tens' place by one, and if the number thus formed be divided by the sum of its digits, the quotient is 10. Find the number.

31. Find the value of $\dfrac{6x^2-5xy-6y^2}{2x^2+xy-y^2} \times \dfrac{3x^2-xy-4y^2}{2x^2-5xy+3y^2} \div \dfrac{9x^2-6xy-8y^2}{2x^2-3xy+y^2}$.

32. Resolve each of the following expressions into four factors:

(1) $4a^4-17a^2b^2+4b^4$; (2) x^8-256y^8.

33. Find the expression of highest dimensions which will divide and $24a^4b-2a^3b^2-9ab^4$ and $18a^6+a^4b^2-6a^3b^3$ without remainder.

34. Find the square root of

(1) $x(x+1)(x+2)(x+3)+1$;

(2) $(2a^2+13a+15)(a^2+4a-5)(2a^2+a-3)$.

35. Simplify $x-\dfrac{2x-6}{x^2-6x+9}-3+\dfrac{x^2+3x-4}{x^2+x-12}$.

36. A quantity of land, partly pasture and partly arable, is sold at the rate of Rs. 60 per are for the pasture and Rs. 40 per are for the arable, and the whole sum obtained is Rs. 10000. If the average price per are were Rs. 50, the sum obtained would be 10 per cent. higher; find how much of the land is pasture, and how much arable.

CHAPTER XXV

QUADRATIC EQUATIONS

185. DEFINITION. An equation which contains the square of the unknown quantity, but no higher power, is called a **quadratic equation,** or an **equation of the second degree.**

If the equation contains both the square and the first power of the unknown it is called an *adfected* quadratic; if it contains only the square of the unknown it is said to be a *pure* quadratic.

Thus $2x^2 - 5x = 3$ is an adfected quadratic,

and $5x^2 = 20$ is a pure quadratic.

186. A pure quadratic may be considered as a simple equation in which the *square* of the unknown quantity is to be found.

Example. Solve $\dfrac{9}{x^2 - 27} = \dfrac{25}{x^2 - 11}$.

Multiplying up, $9x^2 - 99 = 25x^2 - 675$;

$$\therefore \quad 16x^2 = 576;$$

$$\therefore \quad x^2 = 36;$$

and taking the square root of these equals, we have

$$x = \pm 6.$$

Note. We prefix the double sign to the number on the right-hand side for the reason given in Art. 119.

187. In extracting the square root of the two sides of the equation $x^2 = 36$, it might seem that we ought to prefix the double sign to the quantities on both sides, and write $\pm x = \pm 6$. But an examination of the various cases shews this to be unnecessary. For $\pm x = \pm 6$ gives the four cases:

$$+x = +6, \; +x = -6, \; -x = +6, \; -x = -6,$$

and these are all included in the two already given, namely, $x = +6$, $x = -6$. Hence, when we extract the square root of the two sides of an equation, it is sufficient to put the double sign before the square root of *one* side.

188. Solution by Completing the Square. The equation $x^2 = 36$ is an instance of the simplest form of quadratic equations. The equation $(x-3)^2 = 25$ may be solved in a similar way; for taking the square root of both sides, we have two *simple* equations,

$$x-3=\pm 5.$$

Taking the upper sign, $x-3=+5$, Whence $x=8$;
taking the lower sign, $x-3=-5$, Whence $x=-2$.
$\therefore$ the solution is $x=8$, or -2.

Now the given equation $(x-3)^2 = 25$
may be written $x^2 - 6x + (3)^2 = 25$,
or $\quad x^2 - 6x = 16$.

Hence, by retracing our steps, we learn that the equation

$$x^2 - 6x = 16$$

can be solved by first adding $(3)^2$ or 9 to each side, and then extracting the square root; and the reason why we add 9 to each side is that this quantity added to the left side makes it a *perfect square*.

Now whatever the quantity a may be,

$$x^2 + 2ax + a^2 = (x+a)^2,$$

and
$$x^2 - 2ax + a^2 = (x-a)^2;$$

so that if a trinomial is a perfect square, and *its highest power, x^2, has unity for its coefficient*, we must always have the term without x equal to the square of half the coefficient of x. If, therefore, the terms in x^2 and x are given, the square may be completed by adding the square of half the coefficient of x.

Example. Solve $x^2 + 14x = 32$.

The square of half 14 is $(7)^2$.

$\therefore \quad x^2 + 14x + (7)^2 = 32 + 49;$

that is, $\quad (x+7)^2 = 81;$

$\therefore \quad x + 7 = \pm 9;$

$\therefore \quad x = -7 + 9$, or $-7 - 9$;

$\therefore \quad x = 2$, or -16.

189. When an expression is a perfect square, the *square terms* are always *positive*. **Hence, before completing the square the coefficient of x^2 should be made equal to $+1$.**

Example 1. Solve $7x = x^2 - 8$.

Transpose *so as to have the terms involving x on one side, and the square term positive.*

Thus $x^2 - 7x = 8$.

Completing the square, $x^2 - 7x + \left(\frac{7}{2}\right) = 8 + \frac{49}{4}$.

that is, $\left(x - \frac{7}{2}\right)^2 = \frac{81}{4}$;

$\therefore \quad x - \frac{7}{2} = \pm\frac{9}{2}$;

$\therefore \quad x = \frac{7}{2} \pm \frac{9}{2}$;

$\therefore \quad x = 8$, or -1.

Example 2. Solve $4 - \frac{8}{3x+1} = \frac{3x^2+5}{3x+1}$

Clearing of fractions, $12x + 4 - 8 = 3x^2 + 5$;

bringing the terms involving x to one side, we obtain

$$3x^2 - 12x = -9.$$

Divide throughout by 3; then $x^2 - 4x = -3$;

$\therefore \quad x^2 - 4x + (2)^2 = 4 - 3$;

that is, $(x-2)^2 = 1$;

$\therefore \quad x - 2 = \pm 1$;

$\therefore \quad x = 3$, or 1.

EXAMPLES XXV.a

Solve the equations:

1. $7(x^2 - 7) = 6x^2$.

2. $(x+8)(x-8) = 17$.

3. $(7+x)(7-x) = 24$.

4. $\frac{x^2+8}{x^2+20} = \frac{1}{2}$.

5. $\frac{11}{3-x} = 4(x+3)$.

6. $\frac{x(3x+5)+21}{(3x-2)(2x+3)} = 1$.

7. $x^2 + 2x = 8$.

8. $x^2 + 6x = 40$.

9. $x^2 + 35 = 12x$.

10. $x^2 + x = 6$.

11. $x^2 - 156 = x$.

12. $11x + 12 = x^2$.

13. $x^2 + 4x = 32$.

14. $9x + 36 = x^2$.

15. $x^2+15x-34=0.$

Solve the equations :

16. $\frac{1}{3}(2x^2+7)-(6-x^2)=\frac{3}{7}(x^2+3)$. **17.** $\frac{x+5}{x--2}=\frac{x+37}{2x-1}$.

18. $\frac{x+3}{x+2}+\frac{x-2}{x-3}=\frac{5}{(x+2)(x-3)}$. **19.** $\frac{x^2-4x+115}{2x+2}=3x-5$.

20. $\frac{3x+1}{2}-\frac{4}{x-1}=x+2$.

190. We have shewn that the square may readily be completed when the coefficient of x^2 is unity. All cases may be reduced to this by dividing the equation throughout by the coefficient of x^2.

Example 1. Solve $32-3x^2=10x$.

Transposing, $3x^2+10x=32$.

Divide throughout by 3, so as to make the coefficient of x^2 unity.

Thus $$x^2+\frac{10}{3}x=\frac{32}{3}.$$

Completing the square,

$$x^2+\frac{10}{3}x+\left(\frac{5}{3}\right)^2=\frac{32}{3}+\frac{25}{9};$$

that is, $$\left(x+\frac{5}{3}\right)^2=\frac{121}{9};$$

$$\therefore \quad x+\frac{5}{3}=\pm\frac{11}{3};$$

$$\therefore \quad x=-\frac{5}{3}\pm\frac{11}{3}=2, \text{ or } -5\frac{1}{3}.$$

Example 2. Solve $5x^2+11x=12$.

Dividing by 5, $x^2+\frac{11}{5}x=\frac{12}{5}$.

Completing the square, $x^2+\frac{11}{5}x+\left(\frac{11}{10}\right)^2=\frac{12}{5}+\frac{121}{100}$,

that is, $$\left(+x\frac{11}{10}\right)^2=\frac{361}{100};$$

$$x+\frac{11}{10}=\pm\frac{19}{10};$$

$$\therefore \quad x=-\frac{1}{10}\pm\frac{19}{10}=\frac{4}{5}, \text{ or } -3.$$

191. We see then that the following steps are required for solving an adfected quadratic equation:

(1) *If necessary, simplify the equation so that the terms in* x^2 *and* x *are on one side of the equation, and the term without* x *on the other.*

(2) *Make the coefficient* x^2 *unity and positive by dividing throughout by the coefficient* x^2.

(3) *Add to each side of the equation that square of half the coefficient of* x.

(4) *Take the square root of each side.*

(5) *Solve the resulting simple equations.*

192. When the coefficients are literal the same method may be used.

Example. Solve $7(x+2a)^2+3a^2=5a(7x+23a)$.

Simplifying, $7x^2+28ax+28a^2+3a^2$
$$=35ax+115a^2;$$

that is, $$7x^2-7ax=84a^2,$$

or $$x^2-ax=12a^2.$$

Completing the square,
$$x^2-ax+\left(\frac{a}{2}\right)^2=12a^2+\frac{a^2}{4};$$

that is, $$\left(x-\frac{a}{2}\right)^2=\frac{49a^2}{4};$$

$$\therefore \quad x-\frac{a}{2}=\pm\frac{7a}{2};$$

$$\therefore \quad x=4a, \text{ or } -3a.$$

193. In all the instances considered hitherto the quadratic equations have had two roots. Sometimes, however, there is only one solution. Thus if $x^2-2x+1=0$, then $(x-1)^2=0$, whence $x=1$ is the only solution. Nevertheless, in this and similar cases we find it convenient to say that the quadratic has *two equal roots*.

EXAMPLES XXV.b

Solve the equations:

1. $3x^2+2x=21$.

2. $5x^2=8x+21$.

3. $6x^2-x-1=0$.

4. $3-11x=4x^2$.

5. $21x^2=2x+3$.

6. $10+23x+12x^2=0$.

7. $15x^2-6x=9$.

8. $4x^2-17x=15$.

9. $8x^2-19x-15=0$.

Solve the equations:

10. $10x^2+3x=1$.

11. $12x^2+7x=12$.

12. $20x^2-x-1=0$.

13. $x^2+2ax=15a^2$.

14. $2x^2-8a^2=15ax$.

15. $3x^2=k(2k-5x)$.

16. $11bx+20b^2=3x^2$.

17. $9x^2-143c^2=6cx$.

18. $2a^2x^2=ax+1$.

19. $(x-3)(x-2)=2(x^2-4)$.

20. $5(x+1)(3x+5)=3(3x^2+11x+10)$.

21. $3x^2+13+(x-1)(2x+1)=2x(2x+3)$.

22. $\frac{7x-3}{x+1}=\frac{3x}{2}$.

23. $\frac{2}{3x}=\frac{x-1}{2x-1}$.

24. $\frac{3x-1}{x+9}=\frac{2x-9}{x-4}$.

25. $\frac{6x-5}{x+5}=\frac{x}{3}-5$.

26. $\frac{x-4}{7x+1}+\frac{1}{2}=\frac{11}{2(3+2x)}$.

27. $3(2x+3)^2+2(2x+3)(2-x)=(x-2)^2$.

28. $(3x-7)^2-(2x-3)^2=(x-4)(3x+1)$.

[For additional examples see *Elementary Algebra*, p. 197.]

194. Solution by Formula. From the preceding examples it appears that after suitable reduction and transposition every quadratic equation can be written in the form

$$ax^2+bx+c=0$$

where *a*, *b*, *c* may have any numerical values whatever. If therefore we can solve this quadratic we can solve any.

Transposing, $ax^2+bx=-c$;

dividing by *a*, $x^2+\frac{b}{a}x=-\frac{c}{a}$.

Complete the square by adding to each side $\left(\frac{b}{2a}\right)^2$; thus

$$x^2+\frac{b}{a}+\left(\frac{b^2}{2a}\right)=\frac{b^2}{4a^2}-\frac{c}{a};$$

that is,
$$\left(x+\frac{b}{2a}\right)^2=\frac{b^2-4ac}{4a^2};$$

extracting the square root, $x+\frac{b}{2a}=\frac{\pm\sqrt{(b^2-4ac)}}{2a}$;

$$\therefore \qquad x=\frac{-b\pm\sqrt{(b^2-4ac)}}{2a}.$$

195. In the result $x=\dfrac{-b\pm\sqrt{(b^2-4ac)}}{2a}$,

it must be remembered that the expression $\sqrt{(b^2-4ac)}$ is the square root of the compound quantity b^2-4ac, *taken as a whole.* We cannot simplify the solution unless we know the numerical values of a, b, c. It may sometimes happen that these values do not make b^2-4ac a perfect square. In such a case the exact numerical solution of the equation cannot be determined.

Example. Solve $5x^2-13x-11=0$.

Here $a=5, b=-13, c=-11$; therefore by the formula we have

$$x=-\frac{(-13)\pm\sqrt{(-13)^2-4.5(-11)}}{2.5}$$

$$=\frac{13\pm\sqrt{169+220}}{10}=\frac{13\pm\sqrt{389}}{10}.$$

Since 389 has not an exact square root this result cannot be simplified; thus the two roots are

$$\frac{13+\sqrt{389}}{10},\ \frac{13-\sqrt{389}}{10}.$$

196. Solution by Factors. There is still one method of obtaining the solution of a quadratic which will sometimes be found shorter than either of the methods already given.

Consider the equation $x^2+\dfrac{7}{3}x=2$.

Clearing of fractions, $3x^2+7x-6=0$ ...(1);

by resolving the left-hand side into factors we have

$$(3x-2)(x+3)=0.$$

Now if *either* of the factors $3x-2$, $x+3$ be zero, their product is zero. Hence the quadratic equation is satisfied by either of the suppositions

$$3x-2=0, \text{ or } x+3=0.$$

Thus the roots are $\dfrac{2}{3}, -3$.

It appears from this that *when a quadratic equation has been simplified and brought to the form of equation* (1), its solution can always be readily obtained if the expression on the left-hand side can be resolved into factors. Each of these factors equated to zero gives a simple equation, and a corresponding root of the quadratic.

Example 1. Solve $2x^2 - ax + 2bx = ab$.

Transposing, *so as to have all the terms on one side of the equation*, we have

$$2x^2 - ax + 2bx - ab = 0.$$

Now $\quad 2x^2 - ax + 2bx - ab = x(2x - a) + b(2x - a)$

$$= (2x - a)(x + b).$$

Therefore $\quad (2x - a)(x + b) = 0;$

whence $\quad 2x - a = 0$ or $x + b = 0,$

$\therefore \quad x = \frac{a}{2}$, or $-b$.

Example 2. Solve $\quad 2(x^2 - 6) = 3(x - 4).$

We have $2x^2 - 12 = 3x - 12;$

that is, $\quad 2x^2 = 3x \quad \ldots(1).$

Transposing, $2x^2 - 3x = 0,$

$$x(2x - 3) = 0.$$

$\therefore \quad x = 0$, or $2x - 3 = 0.$

Thus the roots are $0, \frac{3}{2}$.

Note. In equation (1) above we might have divided both sides by x and obtained the simple equation $2x=3$, whence $x = \frac{3}{2}$, which is *one* of the solutions of the given equation. But the student must be particularly careful to notice that whenever an x is removed by division from every term of an equation it must not be neglected, since the equation is satisfied by $x=0$, which is therefore one of the roots.

197. Formation of Equations with given roots.

It is now easy to form an equation whose roots are known.

Example 1. Form the equation whose roots are 4 and -3.

Here $\quad x = 4$, or $x = -3;$

$\therefore$ Here $\quad x - 4 = 0$, or $x + 3 = 0;$

both of these statements are included in

$$(x - 4)(x + 3) = 0,$$

or $\quad x^2 - x - 12 = 0,$

which is the required equation.

Example 2. Form the equation whose roots are a and $-\frac{b}{3}$.

Here $x=a$, or $x=-\frac{b}{3}$;

$\therefore$ the equation is $(x-a)\left(x+\frac{b}{3}\right)=0$;

that is, $(x-a)(3x-b)=0$,

or $3x^2-3ax+bx-ab=0$.

[See *Elementary Algebra*, Chapter XXXVI.]

EXAMPLES XXV.c

Solve the formula the equations:

1. $x^2+2x-3=0$.
2. $x^2-2x-1=0$.
3. $x^2-3x=5$.
4. $3x^2-2x=1$.
5. $2x^2-9x=4$.
6. $3x^2+7x=6$.
7. $4x^2-14=3x$.
8. $6x^2-3-7x=0$.
9. $12x^2+10=23$.

Solve by resolution into factors:

10. $x^2-9x=90$.
11. $x^2-11x=152$.
12. $x^2-85=12x$.
13. $2x^2-3x=2$.
14. $3x^2+5x+2=0$.
15. $4x^2-14=x$.
16. $5x^2-11x+2=0$.
17. $x^2-a^2=0$.
18. $x^2-7ax=8a^2$.
19. $12x^2-23bx+10b^2=0$.
20. $3ax^2+2bx=7x$.
21. $24x^2+22cx=21c^2$.
22. $x^2-2x+4b=2bx$.

Solve the equations:

23. $2x(x+9)=(x+1)(5-x)$.
24. $(2x-1)^2-11=5x+(x-3)^2$.
25. $6(x-2)^2+13(1-x)(x-2)+6x^2=6(2x-1)$.
26. $\frac{3}{x-6}-\frac{4}{x-5}=1$.
27. $\frac{3}{2x-1}-\frac{2}{x+1}=\frac{2}{x}$.
28. $\frac{10}{x-4}-\frac{9}{x}=\frac{4}{x-5}$.
29. $\frac{x+3}{x-3}+\frac{4(x-6)}{x+6}=3$.

30. $3x = \frac{1}{x+1} + 2.$ **31.** $\frac{x}{3} - \frac{6}{x} = \frac{x^2-6}{3(x+4)}.$

32. $\frac{23}{x+4} + \frac{3x}{11} = \frac{1}{3}(x+5).$ **33.** $\frac{x+1}{x-3} - \frac{5}{x} = 6.$

Solve the equations :

34. $\frac{x+2}{x-1} - \frac{4-x}{2x} = 2\frac{1}{3}.$ **35.** $\frac{21x^3-16}{3x^2-4} - 7x = 5.$

36. $\frac{3x+1}{x+8} + \frac{x-8}{3x-1} = \frac{17}{12}.$ **37.** $\frac{1}{2(x-1)} + \frac{3}{x^2-1} = \frac{1}{4}.$

38. $\frac{a^2(x-b)}{a-b} - x^2 = \frac{b^2(a-x)}{b-a}.$ **39.** $(p-q)x + \frac{2q}{x} = (p+q).$

40. $\frac{b}{x-a} + \frac{a}{x-b} = 2.$ **41.** $(x-1)^2 = \left(\frac{b}{c} - \frac{c}{b}\right)^2 x.$

[For additional examples see *Elementary Algebra*, P. 201.]

198. Simultaneous Quadratic Equations. If from either of two equations which involve x and y the value of one of the unknowns can be expressed in terms of the other, then by substitution in the second equation we obtain a quadratic which may be solved by any one of the methods explained in this chapter.

Example. Solve the simultaneous equations

$$5x + 7y = 1,$$
$$4x^2 + 3xy - 2y^2 = 10.$$

From the first equation, $x = \frac{1-7y}{5}$, and therefore by substitution in the second equation, we have

$$\frac{4(1-7y)^2}{25} + \frac{3y(1-7y)}{5} - 2y^2 = 10;$$

whence $4 - 56y + 196y^2 + 15y - 105y^2 - 50y^2 = 250;$

that is, $$41y^2 - 41y - 246 = 0;$$

$\therefore$ $$y^2 - y - 6 = 0;$$

$\therefore$ $$(y-3)(y+2) = 0;$$

$\therefore$ $$y = 3, \text{ or } -2.$$

From the first equation, we see that if $y = 3$, then $x = -4$ and if $y = -2$, then $x = 3$.

199. In the case of **homogeneous equations** the most convenient method of solution is to substitute $y = mx$ in each of the given equations. By division we eliminate x and obtain a quadratic to determine the values of m.

Example. Solve the simultaneous equations

$$5x^2 + 3y^2 = 32, \; x^2 - xy + 2y^2 = 16.$$

Put $y = mx$ and substitute in each equation. Thus

$$x^2(5+3m^2) = 32 \qquad \ldots(1),$$

and

$$x^2(1-m+2m^2) = 16 \qquad \ldots(2).$$

By division, $\dfrac{5+3m^2}{1-m+2m^2} = \dfrac{32}{16} = 2;$

that is, $m^2 - 2m - 3 = 0;$

$\therefore$ $(m-3)(m+1) = 0;$

$\therefore$ $m = 3$, or -1.

(1) Take $m = 3$ and substitute in either (1) or (2).
From (1), $32x^2 = 32$; Hence $x = \pm 1$.

$\therefore$ $y = mx = 3x = \pm 3.$

(2) Take $m = -1$ and substitute in (1). Thus

$8x^2 = 32$; Hence $x = \pm 2$.

$\therefore$ $y = mx = -x = \mp 2.$

EXAMPLES XXV.d

Solve the simultaneous equations:

1. $x + 3y = 9,$ $xy = 6.$
2. $3x - 4y = 2,$ $xy = 2.$
3. $2x + y = 5,\; 5x^2 - xy = 2.$
4. $x - 2y = 3,\; x^2 + 4y^2 = 29.$
5. $3x + y = 9,\; 3xy - y^2 = 9.$
6. $2x - 5y = 1,\; x^2 - 8y^2 = 1.$
7. $\dfrac{x}{2} - y = 1,\; xy = 24.$
8. $\dfrac{3}{x} - \dfrac{1}{y} = 1,\; 10xy = 1.$
9. $x - \dfrac{y}{2} = 3,\; xy - y^2 = 4.$
10. $\dfrac{x}{2} - \dfrac{1}{y} = 2,\; \dfrac{3}{x} + \dfrac{y}{2} = 1.$
11. $\dfrac{x}{2} + \dfrac{y}{3} = 3,\; \dfrac{8}{x} - \dfrac{3}{y} = 1.$
12. $2x - \dfrac{9}{y} = 1,\; 3y - \dfrac{2}{x} = 8.$
13. $3x^2 + 7y^2 = 55,\; 2x^2 + 7xy = 60.$
14. $16xy - 3x^2 = 77,\; 7xy + 3y^2 = 110.$
15. $2x^2 + 5y^2 = 143,\; 8xy + 3y^2 = 195.$
16. $x^2 + 2xy + 2y^2 = 17,\; 3x^2 - 9xy - y^2 = 119.$
17. $21x^2 + 3xy - y^2 = 371,\; 5x^2 + 3xy + 5y^2 = 265.$

CHAPTER XXVI

PROBLEMS LEADING TO QUADRATIC EQUATIONS

200. WE shall now discuss some problems which give rise to quadratic equations.

Example. 1. A train travels 300 kilometres at a uniform speed; if the speed had been 5 kilometres per hour more, the journey would have taken two hours less: find the speed of the train.

Suppose the train travels at the speed of x kilometres per hour, then the time occupied is $\frac{300}{x}$ hours.

On the other supposition the time is $\frac{300}{x+5}$ hours;

$$\therefore \qquad \frac{300}{x+5} = \frac{300}{x} - 2;$$

Hence $\qquad x^2 + 5x - 750 = 0, \quad \text{or} \quad (x+30)(x-25) = 0,$

$$\therefore \qquad x = 25, \text{ or } -30.$$

Hence the train travels 25 kilometres per hour, the negative value being inadmissible.

[For an explanation of the meaning of the negative value see *Elementary Algebra*, p. 209.]

Example. 2. A man buys a number of articles for Rs. 10, and sells all but two for Rs. 10.80 at 10 paise a piece more than they cost; how many did he buy?

Let x be the number of articles bought; then the cost price of each is $\frac{1000}{x}$ paise, and the sale price is $\frac{1080}{x-2}$ paise.

$$\therefore \qquad \frac{1080}{x-2} - \frac{1000}{x} = 10;$$

that is, $$\frac{108}{x-2} - \frac{100}{x} = 1.$$

After simplification, $8x + 200 = x^2 - 2x$, or $x^2 - 10x - 200 = 0$;

that is, $\qquad (x-20)(x+10) = 0;$

$$\therefore \qquad x = 20, \text{ or } -10.$$

Thus the number required is 20.

Example. 3. A cistern can be filled by two pipes in $33\frac{1}{3}$ minutes; if the larger pipe takes 15 minutes less than the smaller to fill the cistern, find in what time it will be filled by each pipe singly.

Suppose that the two pipes running singly would fill the cistern in x and $x - 15$ minutes; then they will fill $\frac{1}{x}$ and $\frac{1}{x-15}$ of the cistern respectively in one minute, and therefore when running together they will fill $\left(\frac{1}{x}+\frac{1}{x-15}\right)$ of the cistern in one minute.

But they fill $\frac{1}{33\frac{1}{3}}$, or $\frac{3}{100}$ of the cistern in one minute.

Hence $\frac{1}{x}+\frac{1}{x-15}=\frac{3}{100}$.

$$100(2x-15)=3x(x-15),$$

$$3x^2-245x+1500=0,$$

$$(x-75)(3x-20)=0;$$

$$\therefore \qquad x=75, \text{ or } 6\frac{2}{3}.$$

Thus the smaller pipe takes 75 minutes, the larger 60 minutes.

The other solution $6\frac{2}{3}$ is inadmissible.

201. Sometimes it will be found convenient to use more than **one** unknown.

Example. Nine times the side of one square exceeds the perimeter of a second square by one metre, and six times the area of the second square exceeds twenty-nine times the area of the first by one square metre; find the length of a side of each square.

Let x metres and y metres represent the sides of the two squares; then the perimeter of the second square is $4y$ metres; thus

$$9x-4y=1.$$

The areas of the two squares are x^2 and y^2 square metres; thus

$$6y^2-29x^2=1.$$

From the first equation, $y=\frac{9x-1}{4}$.

By substitution in the second equation,

$$\frac{3(9x-1)^2}{8} - 29x^2 = 1;$$

that is, $11x^2 - 54x - 5 = 0,$

or $(x-5)(11x+1) = 0;$

Whence $x = 5$, the negative value being inadmissible.

Also, $y = \dfrac{9x-1}{4} = 11.$

Thus the lengths are 5 metres and 11 metres.

EXAMPLES XXVI

1. Find a number which is less than its square by 72.
2. Divide 16 into two parts such that the sum of their squares is 130.
3. Find two numbers differing by 5 such that the sum of their squares is equal to 233.
4. Find a number which when increased by 13 is 68 times the reciprocal of the number.
5. Find two numbers differing by 7 such that their product is 330.
6. The breadth of a rectangle is five metres shorter than the length, and the area is 374 square metres: find the sides.
7. One side of a rectangle is 7 metres longer than the other, and its diagonal is 13 metres: find the area.
8. Find two consecutive numbers the difference of whose reciprocals is $\dfrac{1}{306}$.
9. Find two consecutive even numbers the difference of whose reciprocals is $\dfrac{1}{480}$.
10. The difference of the reciprocals of two consecutive odd numbers is $\dfrac{2}{675}$; find them.
11. A farmer bought a certain number of sheep for Rs. 3150; through disease he lost 10, but by selling the remainder at Rs. 10 each more than he gave for them, he gainod Rs. 1190: how many did he buy?
12. By walking three-quarters of a kilometre more than his ordinary pace per hour, a man finds that he takes $1\frac{1}{2}$ hours less than usual to walk 11 kilometres: what is the ordinary rate?

13. A cistern can be filled by the larger of two pipes in 5 minutes less than by the smaller. When the taps are both running the cistern is filled in 6 minutes: find the time in which the cistern could be filled by each of the pipes.

14. A man buys a dozen eggs, and calculates that if they had been 20 paise per dozen cheaper he could have bought two more for a rupee: what is the price per dozen?

15. The large wheel of a carriage is 30 cm more in circumference than the small wheel, and makes 40 revolutions less in 1 km 320 m: find the circumference of each wheel.

16. A boy was sent out to buy a rupee's worth of oranges. He ate five, and in consequence his master had to pay at the rate of 20 paise per dozen more than the market price. How many oranges did the boy buy?

17. A lawn 45 metres long and 40 broad has a path of uniform width round it; if the area of the path is 450 square metres, find its width.

18. By selling one more apple for five paise than she formerly did, a woman finds that she gets five paise less per dozen: how much does she now get per dozen?

19. Four times the side of one square is less than the perimeter of a second square by 12 metres, and eleven times the area of the first is less than five times the area of the second by 9 square metres: find the length of a side of each square.

20. Find a number of two digits such that if it be divided by the sum of its digits the quotient is 7, and if 27 be subtracted from the number the order of the digits is reversed. [Art. 111.]

21. A person buys some $5\frac{1}{2}$ per cent. stock; if the price had been Rs. 5 less he would have received one per cent. more interest on his money: at what price did he buy the stock?

22. The area of each of two rectangles is 1008 square metres; the length of one is 8 metres more than that of the other, and the difference of their breadths is 3 metres: find their sides.

23. There are three numbers of which the second is greater than the first by 6 and less than the third by 9. If the product of all three is 280 times the greatest, find the numbers.

24. Find four consecutive integers such that the product of the two greatest is represented by a number which has the two least for its digits.

25. Two trains A and B start simultaneously from two stations P and Q which are 260 kilometres apart. A reaches Q in $3\frac{3}{7}$ hours, and B reaches P in $4\frac{2}{3}$ hours after they meet: find the speed of each train.

CHAPTER XXVII

RATIO AND PROPORTION

202. DEFINITION. **Ratio** is the relation which one quantity bears to another **of the same kind**, the comparison being made by considering what multiple, part, or parts, one quantity is of the other.

The ratio of A to B is usually written $A : B$. The quantities A and B are called the *terms* of the ratio. The first term is called the **antecedent**, the second term the **consequent.**

A ratio is said to be a ratio of *greater inequality*, of *less inequality*, or of *equality*, according as the antecedent is *greater than*, *less than*, or *equal to* the consequent.

203. To find what multiple or part A is of B we divide A by B; hence the ratio $A : B$ may be measured by the fraction $\frac{A}{B}$, and we shall usually find it convenient to adopt this notation.

In order to compare two quantities they must be expressed in terms of the same unit. Thus the ratio of £ 2 to 15*s*. is measured by the fraction $\frac{2 \times 20}{15}$ or $\frac{8}{3}$.

Note. A ratio expresses the *number* of times that one quantity contains another, and therefore *every ratio is an abstract quantity*.

Example. If $\frac{8x - 3y}{4y - 7x} = \frac{4}{13}$, find the ratio of x to y.

On multiplying across, we have $104x - 39y = 16y - 28x$;

$\therefore \quad 132x = 55y,$

whence $\quad \frac{x}{y} = \frac{55}{132} = \frac{5}{12}.$

204. Since by the laws of fractions $\frac{a}{b} = \frac{ma}{mb}$; it follows that the ratio $a : b$ is equal to the ratio $ma : mb$; that is, *the value of a ratio remains unaltered if the antecedent and the consequent are multiplied or divided by the same quantity.*

Example 1. Two numbers are in the ratio of 5 : 8. If 9 be added to each they are in the ratio of 8 : 11. Find the numbers.

Let the numbers be denoted by $5x$ and $8x$.

Then, $\quad \frac{5x + 9}{8x + 9} = \frac{8}{10};$

whence $\quad x = 3.$

Hence the numbers are 15 and 24.

Example 2. If $\frac{x}{y} = \frac{3}{4}$, find the value of $\frac{5x - 3y}{7x + 2y}$.

$$\text{The expression} = \frac{\frac{5x}{y} - 3}{\frac{7x}{y} + 2} = \frac{\frac{15}{4} - 3}{\frac{21}{4} + 2} = \frac{3}{29}.$$

Note. This example might also have been worked by substituting for x and y the values $3k$ and $4k$ respectively.

205. Two or more ratios may be compared by reducing their equivalent fractions to a common denominator.

Thus suppose $a:b$ and $x:y$ are two ratios. Now $\frac{a}{b} = \frac{ay}{by}$, and $\frac{x}{y} = \frac{bx}{by}$; hence the ratio $a:b$ is greater than, equal to, or less than the ratio $x:y$ according as ay is greater than, equal to, or less than bx.

206. DEFINITION. Ratios are **compounded** by multiplying together the fractions which denote them; or by multiplying together the antecedents for a new antecedent, and the consequents for a new consequent.

Example 3 Find the ratio compounded of the three ratios

$$2a : 3b,\ 6ab : 5c^2,\ c : a.$$

$$\text{The required ratio} = \frac{2a}{3b} \times \frac{6ab}{5c^2} \times \frac{c}{a} = \frac{4a}{5c}.$$

207. DEFINITION. When the ratio $a:b$ is compounded with itself the resulting ratio is $a^2 : b^2$, and is called the **duplicate ratio** of $a:b$. Similarly, $a^3 : b^3$ is called the **triplicate ratio** of $a:b$. Also $\sqrt{a} : \sqrt{b}$ is called the **subduplicate ratio** of $a:b$.

Examples.

(1) The duplicate ratio of $2a : 3b$ is $4a^2 : 9b^2$.

(2) The subduplicate ratio of $49 : 25$ is $7 : 5$.

(3) The triplicate ratio of $2x : 1$ is $8x^3 : 1$.

Example 4. Find the ratio compounded of the triplicate ratio of $2x$ to $3y^2$, and the subduplicate ratio of $81y^6 : 256x^4$.

$$\text{The required ratio} = \left(\frac{2x}{3y^2}\right)^3 \times \sqrt{\frac{81y^6}{256x^4}}$$

$$= \frac{8x^3}{27y^6} \times \frac{9y^3}{16x^2} = \frac{x}{6y^3}.$$

208. When two or more ratios are equal, many useful propositions may be proved by introducing a single symbol to denote each of the given ratios.

The following important theorem will illustrate this method of proof.

If $\frac{a}{b}=\frac{c}{d}=\frac{e}{f}$, *prove that* $\frac{la+mc+ne}{lb+md+nf}$ *is equal to each of the given ratios.*

Let $k=\frac{a}{b}=\frac{c}{d}=\frac{e}{f}$; then $a=bk$, $c=dk$, $e=fk$; and therefore $la=lbk$, $mc=mdk$, $ne=nfk$.

$\therefore \quad la+mc+ne=lbk+mdk+nfk=(lb+md+nf)\,k;$

$\therefore \quad \frac{la+mc+ne}{lb+md+nf}=k=\frac{a}{b}=\frac{c}{d}=\frac{e}{f}.$

This is true for all value of l, m, n; also the method is clearly applicable to any number of equal ratios.

As a particular case suppose that $l=m=n$; thus if $\frac{a}{b}=\frac{c}{d}=\frac{e}{f}=\ldots$, each of these ratios is equal to

$$\frac{a+c+e+\ldots\ldots}{b+d+f+\ldots\ldots};$$

a result of such frequent utility that the following verbal equivalent should be noticed:

When a series of fractions are equal, each of them is equal to the sum of all the numerators divided by the sum of all the denominators

Example 1. If $\frac{a}{b}=\frac{c}{d}=\frac{e}{f}$, prove that $\sqrt{\frac{2a^4b^2+3a^2e^2-5e^4f}{2b^6+3b^2f^2-5f^5}}=\frac{ac}{bd}$.

Let $k=\frac{a}{b}=\frac{c}{d}=\frac{e}{f}$; then $a=bk, c=dk, e=fk$.

$$\therefore \text{the first side}=\sqrt{\frac{2k^4b^6+3k^4b^2f^2-5k^4f^5}{2b^6+3b^2f^2-5f^5}}$$

$$=\sqrt{k^4}=k^2=\frac{a}{b}\times\frac{c}{d}=\frac{ac}{bd}.$$

Example 2. If $\frac{x}{cm-bn}=\frac{y}{cl-an}=\frac{z}{bl-am}$, show that $ax-by+cz=0$.

Denote each of the given ratios by k; then

$$x=(cm-bn)k,\ y=(cl-an)k,\ z=(bl-am)k;$$

$$\therefore \quad ax-by+cz=k\{a\,(cm-bn)-b(cl-an)+c\,(bl-am)\}$$
$$=k\times 0=0.$$

EXAMPLES XXVII. a

1. If $3(4x-5y)=2x-y$, find the ratio of $x:y$.

2. If $\dfrac{5a+3b}{4a+5b}=\dfrac{2}{3}$, find the ratio of $a:b$.

3. Two numbers are in the ratio of 5 to 7, and if 9 be added to each the resulting numbers are in the ratio of 4 to 5: what are the numbers?

4. What number must be taken from each term of the ratio $15:31$ that the ratio so obtained may be equal to $1:3$?

5. A has Rs. 8.25 and B has Rs. 16.75. How much must B give to A in order that the amounts they then possess shall be in the ratio of 9 to 16?

6. If $\dfrac{a}{b}=\dfrac{7}{6}$, find the value of $3a+5b:7b-5a$.

7. If $\dfrac{2x}{3y}=\dfrac{5}{4}$, find the ratio of $8x-7y$ to $y+8x$.

8. If $\dfrac{a}{b}=\dfrac{3}{5}$, and $\dfrac{c}{d}=\dfrac{7}{4}$, find the value of $\dfrac{4ad+bc}{2bc-ad}$.

9. If $\dfrac{a}{x}=\dfrac{1}{3}$, and $\dfrac{b}{y}=\dfrac{1}{4}$, find the value of $\dfrac{3ay-2bx}{5bx-3ay}$.

10. If $16a=25b$, find the duplicate ratio of a to b.

11. If $25x=9y$, find the subduplicate ratio of x to y. Find the ratio compounded of

12. The three ratios $3a^2b:4b^3c, 2c^2:8a^3, 16b^2c:6ac$.

13. The ratio $63a^2:12b^3$, and the duplicate ratio of $4b:7a$.

14. The duplicate ratio of $2x:3y$, and the ratio $27y^2:8x^3$.

15. The subduplicate ratio of $9:16c^2$ and the ratio $4c:2x$.

16. Find the triplicate ratio of $\sqrt[3]{(x+y)^2}:\sqrt[3]{(x^2-y^2)}$.

17. If $\dfrac{a}{b}=\dfrac{c}{d}=\dfrac{e}{f}$, prove that each of these ratios is equal to

(1) $\dfrac{5a-7c+3e}{5b-7d+3f}$; (2) $\sqrt{\dfrac{4a^2-5ace+6e^2f}{4b^2-5bde+6f^2}}$.

18. If $\dfrac{p}{q}=\dfrac{r}{s}=\dfrac{t}{u}$, prove that

(1) $\dfrac{p^2-pr+t^2}{q^2-qs+u^2}=\dfrac{pt}{qu}$; (2) $\dfrac{r^3-p^2tu}{s^3-q^2u^2}=\dfrac{prt}{qsu}$.

19. If $\dfrac{x}{b-c}=\dfrac{y}{c-a}=\dfrac{z}{a-b}$, prove that

(1) $x+y+z=0$; (2) $(b+c)x+(c+a)y+(a+b)z=0$.

20. If $\frac{a}{b}=\frac{c}{d}=\frac{e}{f}$, prove that each ratio is equal to

(1) $\sqrt[3]{\frac{4ac^2-3ce^3+2ace}{4bd^2-3cf^3+2bdf}}$; (2) $\sqrt[5]{\frac{6a^2c^2e-c^4ef+7ac^5}{6b^2d^2f-d^4f^2+7ad^5}}$.

21. If $\frac{x}{1}=\frac{y}{2}=\frac{z}{3}$, prove that $\sqrt{5x^2+8y^2+7z^2}=5y$.

22. The sides of a triangle are as $1:1\frac{1}{2}:1\frac{3}{4}$, and the perimeter is 221 metres: find the sides.

23. If $\frac{x}{lm-n^2}=\frac{y}{mn-l^2}=\frac{z}{nl-m^2}$, show that $lx+my+nz=0$, and $mx+y+lz=0$.

24. If $\frac{p}{bz-cy}=\frac{-q}{cx+az}=\frac{-r}{ay+bx}$, show that $ap+bq-cr=0$, and $xp-yq+zr=0$.

Proportion

209. DEFINITION. When two ratios are equal, the four quantities composing them are said to be **proportionals**. Thus if $\frac{a}{b}=\frac{c}{d}$, then a, b, c, d are proportionals. This is expressed by saying that a is to b as c is to d and the proportion is written

$$a:b::c:d,$$

or

$$a:b=c:d.$$

The terms a and d are called the *extremes*, b and c the *means*.

210. *If four quantities are in proportion, the product of the extremes is equal to the product of the means.*

Let a, b, c, d be the proportionals.

Then by definition $\frac{a}{b}=\frac{c}{d}$;

whence $ad=bc$

Hence if any three terms of a proportion are given, the fourth may be found. Thus if a, c, d are given, then $b=\frac{ad}{c}$.

Conversely, if there are any four quantities, a, b, c, d, such that $ad=bc$, then a, b, c, d are proportionals; a and b being the extremes, b and c the means; or *vice versa*.

Example 1. Find a fourth proportional to $6xy^2$, $9x^3y$, $4xy^3$.

Denote the required proportional by p; then

$$6xy^2:9x^3y=4xy^3:p;$$

$$\therefore \quad 6xy^2p=9x^3y\times 4xy^3;$$

whence $$p=6x^3y^2.$$

Example 2. Find the values of x which satisfy the proportion

$$3x + 13 : 7x - 8 = 2x + 7 : 5x - 8.$$

Since the product of the extremes is equal to that of the means,

we have $$(3x + 13)(5x - 8) = (7x - 8)(2x + 7);$$

on reduction, $$x^2 + 8x - 48 = 0;$$

whence $$x = 4, \text{ or } -12.$$

Example 3. Find x and y from the equations

$$2x - 25 : y - 7 = x + y : x + 2y - 23 = 3 : 2$$

From the equation $2x - 25 : y - 7 = 3 : 2$,

we have $$2(2x - 25) = 3(y - 7),$$

or $$4x - 3y = 29 \qquad \ldots (1)$$

From the equation $x + y : x + 2y - 23 = 3 : 2$,

we have $$2(x + y) = 3(x + 2y - 23),$$

or $$x + 4y = 69 \qquad \ldots (2)$$

Multiplying (2) by 4 and subtracting (1), we have

$$19y = 247, \text{ or } y = 13;$$

by substitution in (2), we find $x = 17$

211. DEFINITION.

211. DEFINITION. Quantities are said to be in **continued proportion** when the first is to the second, as the second is to the third, as the third to the fourth; and so on. Thus $a, b, c, d, \ldots$ are in continued proportion when

$$\frac{a}{b} = \frac{b}{c} = \frac{c}{d} = \ldots\ldots\ldots$$

If three quantities, a, b, c are in continued proportion, then

$$a : b = b : c;$$

$$\therefore \quad ac = b^2$$

In this case b is said to be a **mean proportional** between a and c; and c is said to be a **third proportional** to a and b.

Example 1. Find a mean proportional between $45x^3y$ and $245xy^5$.

Denote the mean proportional by p; then

$$45x^3y : p = p : 245xy^5;$$

$$\therefore \quad p^2 = 45x^3y \times 245xy^5 = 9 \times 5 \times 5 \times 49x^4y^6;$$

$$\therefore \quad p = \pm 3 \times 5 \times 7x^2y^3 = \pm 105x^2y^3.$$

Example 2. Find a third proportional to $3(a+b)^2$ and $6(a^2 - b^2)$.

Let x be the required third proportional; then

$$3(a+b)^2 : 6(a^2 - b^2) = 6(a^2 - b^2) : x$$

$$\therefore \quad 3x(a+b)^2 = 36(a^2 - b^2)^2 = 36(a+b)^2(a-b)^2$$

$$\therefore \quad x = 12(a-b)^2$$

212. *If three quantities are proportionals the first is to the third in the duplicate ratio of the first to the second.*

Let the three quantities be a, b, c; then $\frac{a}{b} = \frac{b}{c}$.

Now $$\frac{a}{c} = \frac{a}{b} \times \frac{b}{c} = \frac{a}{b} \times \frac{a}{b} = \frac{a^2}{b^2};$$

that is, $$a : c = a^2 : b^2.$$

213. *If $a : b = c : d$ and $e : f = g : h$, then will*

$$ae : bf = cg : dh$$

For $$\frac{a}{b} = \frac{c}{d} \text{ and } \frac{e}{f} = \frac{g}{h};$$

$$\therefore \quad \frac{ae}{bf} = \frac{cg}{dh}, \text{ or } ae : bf = cg : dh.$$

Thus two or more proportions may be compounded by multiplying together the corresponding terms.

COR. If $a : b = c : d$,
and $b : x = d : y$,
then $a : x = c : y$.
This is the theorem known as *ex* aquali in Geometry.

214. If four quantities, a, b, c, d form a proportion, many other proportions may be deduced by the properties of fractions. The results of these operations are very useful, and some of them are often quoted by the annexed names borrowed from Geometry.

(1) If $a : b = c : d$, then $b : a = d : c$. [*Invertendo.*]

For $\frac{a}{b} = \frac{c}{d}$; therefore $1 \div \frac{a}{b} = 1 \div \frac{c}{d}$;

that is, $\frac{b}{a} = \frac{d}{c}$; or $b : a = d : c$.

(2) If $a : b = c : d$, then $a : c = b : d$, [*Alternando.*]

For $ad = bc$; therefore $\frac{ad}{cd} = \frac{bc}{cd}$;

that is, $\frac{a}{c} = \frac{b}{d}$; or $a : c = b : d$.

(3) If $a : b = c : d$, then $a + b : b = c + d : d$. [*Componendo.*]

For $\frac{a}{b} = \frac{c}{d}$; therefore $\frac{a}{b} + 1 = \frac{c}{d} + 1$;

that is, $\frac{a+b}{b} = \frac{c+d}{d}$; or $a + b : b = c + d : d$.

(4) If $a:b=c:d$, then $a-b:b=c-d:d$. [*Dividendo*.]

For $\frac{a}{b}=\frac{c}{d}$; therefore $\frac{a}{b}-1=\frac{c}{d}-1$;

that is, $\frac{a-b}{b}=\frac{c-d}{d}$; or $a-b:b=c-d:d$.

(5) If $a:b=c:d$, then $a+b:a-b=c+d:c-d$.

For by (3), $\frac{a+b}{b}=\frac{c+d}{d}$;

and by (4), $\frac{a-b}{b}=\frac{c-d}{d}$;

$\therefore$ by division, $\frac{a+b}{a-b}=\frac{c+d}{c-d}$; or $a+b:a-b=c+d:c-d$.

Several other proportions may be proved in a similar way.

Example. If x, y, z be three proportionals, shew that

$$x+y:y+z=y:z.$$

Since $x:y=y:z$,

componendo, $x+y:y=y+z:z$;

alternando, $x+y:y+z=y:z$.

215. It may be useful to remind the student that in all the above cases a and b must be quantities of the same kind, and c and d must also be quantities of the same kind. This follows at once from Art. 203. Further, it should be noticed that *alternation* of the terms of a proportion cannot take place unless all the four quantities are of the same kind.

216. The results of Art. 214 are the algebraical equivalents of some of the propositions in the fifth book of Euclid, and the student is advised to make himself familiar with them in their verbal form. For example, *dividendo* may be quoted as follows:

When there are four proportionals, the excess of the first above the second is to the second, as the excess of the third above the fourth is to the fourth.

217. Some other easy deductions may be made from any given proportion. These follow directly from the properties of algebraical fractions, and may be left as an exercise for the student. For example, if

$$a:b=c:d,$$

we have $ma:mb=nc:nd$, $pa:qb=pc:qd$, $a^n:b^n=c^n:d^n$,

$$pa^n:qd^n=pc^n:qd^n.$$

218. Many results in Proportion can be established by the introduction of an auxiliary letter to denote the equal ratios which form the proportion.

Example 1. If $a : b = c : d$, shew that

$$pa + qb : ma - nb = pc + qd : mc - nd.$$

Let $k = \frac{a}{b} = \frac{c}{d}$; then $a = bk$, and $c = dk$;

$$\therefore \quad \frac{pa + qb}{ma - nb} = \frac{pbk + qb}{mbk - nb} = \frac{b(pk + q)}{b(mk - n)}$$

$$= \frac{pk + q}{mk - n} = \frac{pdk + qd}{mdk - nd}.$$

$$\therefore \quad \frac{pa + qb}{ma - nb} = \frac{pc + qd}{mc - nd},$$

or $pa + qb : ma - nb = pc + qd : mc - nd.$

Example 2. If $a : b = x : y$, shew that

$$pa^2 + qax + rx^2 : pb^2 + qby + ry^2 = a^2 + x^2 : b^2 + y^2.$$

Let $k = \frac{a}{b} = \frac{x}{y}$; then $a = bk$, $x = yk$;

$$\therefore \quad \frac{pa^2 + qax + rx^2}{pb^2 + qby + ry^2} = \frac{pb^2k^2 + qbyk^2 + ry^2k^2}{pb^2 + qby + ry^2} = k^2.$$

Again $\frac{a^2 + x^2}{b^2 + y^2} = \frac{b^2k^2 + y^2k^2}{b^2 + y^2} = k^2.$

$$\therefore \quad \frac{pa^2 + qax + rx^2}{pb^2 + qby + ry^2} = \frac{a^2 + x^2}{b^2 + y^2}.$$

EXAMPLES XXVII. b

Find a fourth proportional to

1. $p^2qr, pq^2, pr.$ **2.** $x^2, 3xy^2, xy.$

3. $6a^2b^3, 2ab^2, 3a^2b.$

Find a mean proportional between

4. $12ab^3, 3a^5b.$ **5.** $16x^5, 49x^3y^2.$

6. $27ab^2c^3, 75a^3b^2c.$

Find a third proportional to

7. $1, x^2.$ **8.** $2ab, 3bc.$

9. $(a+b)^2, a^3 + b^3.$

Solve the equations:

10. $3x-5:5x-11=2:3$.

11. $2x+1:x+5=6x-7:3x+5$.

12. $3x-2:x+2=5x-2:x+8$.

13. $x:y=3:4=x+y:3x+1$.

14. $x-2:y-1=73-y:5y-x=5:4$.

15. $5x-1:3y+16=y+1:x+y+2=3:5$.

If a, b, c be three proportionals, shew that

16. $a-b:b-c=b:c$.

17. $a+b:a-b=b+c:b-c$.

18. $a+b:b+c=a:b$.

If a: b = c : d, prove that

19. $a^6+c^6:b^6+d^6=a^3c^3:b^3d^3$.

20. $p(a+b)+qb:p(c+d)+qd=a:c$.

21. $a^2+c^2:b^2+d^2=\sqrt{a^4+c^4}:\sqrt{b^4+d^4}$.

22. $al+cm:bl+dm=ap+cq:bp+dq$.

23. $(3a+2c)(a-5c):(3b+2d)(b-5d)=a^2-ac+c^2:bd+d^2$.

24. $a^2+b^2:\dfrac{a^3}{a+b}=c^2+d^2:\dfrac{c^3}{c+d}$.

25. $\dfrac{a}{a-b}:\dfrac{a+b}{b}=\dfrac{c}{c-d}:\dfrac{c+d}{d}$.

If a, b, c be three proportionals, shew that

26. $ma+nb:mb+nc=ma-nb:mb-nc$.

27. $a^2+b^2:(a+b)^2=b^2+c^2:(b+c)^2$.

28. $\dfrac{a}{a-b}:\dfrac{a+b}{b}=\dfrac{b}{b-c}:\dfrac{b+c}{c}$.

Miscellaneous Propositions in Ratio and Proportion

219. If to each term of the ratio $8:3$ we add 4, a new ratio $12:7$ is obtained, and we see that it is less than the former because $\frac{12}{7}$ is clearly less than $\frac{8}{3}$.

This is a particular case of a more general proposition which we shall now prove.

220. *A ratio of greater inequality is diminished, and a ratio of less inequality is increased, by adding the same quantity to both its terms.*

Let $\frac{a}{b}$ be the ratio, and let $\frac{a+x}{b+x}$ be the new ratio formed by adding x to both its terms.

Now $$\frac{a}{b}-\frac{a+x}{b+x}=\frac{ax-bx}{b(b+x)}=\frac{x(a-b)}{b(b+x)};$$

and $a-b$ is positive or negative according as a is greater or less than b.

Hence if $a>b$, $\frac{a+x}{b+x}<\frac{a}{b}$; and if $a<b$, $\frac{a+x}{b+x}>\frac{a}{b}$,

which proves the proposition.

221. Both cases may be included in one statement which is easily remembered:

Any ratio is made more nearly equal to unity by adding the same quantity to each of its terms.

222. Similarly, it can be proved that *a ratio of greater inequality is increased, and a ratio of less inequality is diminished, by taking the same quantity from both its terms.*

Thus if we take the ratio $\frac{9}{5}$ and subtract 4 from each term, we get a new ratio $\frac{5}{1}$, which is clearly greater than $\frac{9}{5}$; again, if we take the ratio $\frac{7}{8}$ and subtract 5 from each term, we get a new ratio $\frac{2}{3}$, which is clearly less than $\frac{7}{8}$.

The general proof we leave as an exercise for the student.

223. In Art. 205 it has been shown how two or more ratios may be compared. In what follows, we shall suppose that the terms of all the ratios are positive.

Example. Find which of the two ratios $5x+2y:5x-2y$ and $2x+y:2x-y$ is the greater.

$$\frac{5x+2y}{5x-2y}-\frac{2x+y}{2x-y}=\frac{10x^2-xy-2y^2-(10x^2+xy-2y^2)}{(5x-2y)(2x-y)}$$

$$=-\frac{2xy}{(5x-2y)(2x-y)}.$$

Hence the second ratio is the greater.

Note. The terms $5x-2y$ and $2x-y$ are supposed to be positive. This condition is satisfied if $2x>y$.

224. If either, or both, of the terms of a ratio be a surd quantity, then no two integers can be found which will *exactly* measure their ratio. Thus the ratio $\sqrt{2}:1$ cannot be exactly expressed by any two integers.

225. DEFINITION If the ratio of any two quantities can be expressed exactly by the ratio of two integers the quantities are said to be **commensurable**; otherwise, they are said to be **incommensurable**.

Although we cannot find two integers which will exactly measure the ratio of two incommensurable quantities, we can always find two integers whose ratio differs from that required by a small quantity as we please.

Thus $\dfrac{\sqrt{5}}{4} = \dfrac{2.236068\ldots}{4} = .559017\ldots$

and therefore $\dfrac{\sqrt{5}}{4}$ is $> \dfrac{559017}{1000000}$ and $< \dfrac{559018}{1000000}$,

and it is evident that by carrying the decimals further, any degree of approximation may be arrived at.

A general proof of this statement will be found in the Higher Algebra [Art. 27]. We hence infer that any theorem in Ratio or Proportion established on the supposition that the terms are commensurable is also true when the terms of the Ratio or Proportion are incommensurable.

226. We shall conclude with a collection of miscellaneous examples.

Example 1. If $x:y = a:b$, shew that

$$\frac{x^3}{y} - \frac{y^3}{x} : \frac{a^3}{b} - \frac{b^3}{a} = xy:ab.$$

The product of the extremes $= ax^2 \cdot \dfrac{bx}{y} - by^2 \cdot \dfrac{ay}{x} = a^2x^2 - b^2y^2.$

The product of the means $= a^2x \cdot \dfrac{ay}{b} - b^2y \cdot \dfrac{bx}{a} = a^2x^2 - b^2y^2;$

which proves the proposition. [See Art. 210.]

Example 2. If x, y, z are three proportionals, shew that

$$(x + y + z)(x^2 - xy + y^2) = x(x^2 + y^2 + z^2).$$

The first side $= \dfrac{1}{x}(x^2 + xy + xz)(x^2 + xy + y^2)$

$= \dfrac{1}{x}(x^2 + xy + y^2)(x^2 - xy + y^2)$, since $xz = y^2$,

$= \dfrac{1}{x}(x^4 + x^2y^2 + y^4) = \dfrac{1}{x}(x^4 + x^2y^2 + x^2z^2)$

$= x(x^2 + y^2 + z^2).$

Example 3. If $b^2 + bx + x^2 : a^2 + ay + y^2 = b^2 - bx + x^2 : a^2 - ay + y^2$, prove that either $x : a = b : y$, or $x : b = y : a$.

We have, *alternando*, $\dfrac{b^2 + bx + x^2}{b^2 - bx + x^2} = \dfrac{a^2 + ay + y^2}{a^2 - ay + y^2}$.

Componendo and dividendo, $\dfrac{2bx}{2b^2 + 2x^2} = \dfrac{2ay}{2a^2 + 2y^2}$;

$$\therefore \quad bx(a^2 + y^2) = ay(b^2 + x^2), \quad bxa^2 + bxy^2 - ayb^2 - ayx^2 = 0,$$

$$by(xy - ab) - ax(xy - ab) = 0;$$

$$(by - ax)(xy - ab) = 0.$$

$\therefore$ either $by - ax = 0$; whence $x : b = y : a$,

or $xy - ab = 0$; whence $x : a = b : y$.

EXAMPLES XXVII. c

1. If x is positive, and less than each of the quantities a and b, find the condition that the ratio of $a - x$ to $b - x$ may be greater than the ratio of a to b.
2. Show that $a : b > a^2 + b^2 : 2ab$ if $a : b$ is a ratio of greater inequality.
3. If a and b be positive and $a > b$, shew that the ratio of $a + b$ to $a - b$ is greater than the ratio of $a^2 + b^2$ to $a^2 - b^2$.
4. Show that the ratio $x + y : x - y$ is increased by subtracting y from each term.
5. Find which of the two ratios $3x + 4y : 2x + 3y$ and $3x - 4y : 2x - 3y$ is the greater.
6. If $\dfrac{a}{b} = \dfrac{c}{d}$, show that

   (1) $\dfrac{2a + 3b}{3a - 7b} = \dfrac{2c + 3d}{3c - 7d}$ (2) $\dfrac{a^2 - c^2}{b^2 - d^2} = \dfrac{(a + 2c)(a + 3c)}{(b + 2d)(b + 3d)}$.
7. Find the ratio of x to y when $x^2 + 12y^2 = 7xy$.
8. Given that $3x + 10$ has to $9x + 4$ the duplicate ratio of 5 to 7, find x. If a, b, c, d are in proportion, show that
9. $a + c : a + b + c + d = a : a + b$. **10.** $(a - b) - (c - d) = \dfrac{(a - b)(b - d)}{b}$.
11. $\dfrac{a^3}{b} + \dfrac{b^3}{a} : \dfrac{c^3}{d} + \dfrac{d^3}{c} = ab : cd$.
12. Compound the ratios

    $\dfrac{x - y}{a + b} : \dfrac{x^3 - y^3}{a^2 - b^2}$ and $\dfrac{x^2 + xy + y^2}{a^2 - b^2} : \dfrac{x^2 - y^2}{(a + b)^2}$.

13. Find a fourth proportional to $x^2 + x - 2, x^2 - 1, x^2 - 4$.

If a, b, c be three proportionals, prove that

14. $(a^2 - b^2)(b^2 - c^2) = b^2(a - c)^2$.

15. $a^2 + b^2 : b(a + c) = a^2 - b^2 : b(a - c)$.

16. $a(a + b) : b(b - a) = b(b + c) : c(c - b)$

17. $(a + b + c)(b^2 - bc + c^2) = c(a^2 + b^2 + c^2)$.

18. If $a : b = c : d$ prove that

(1) $a + \frac{1}{b} + c + \frac{1}{d} : b + \frac{1}{c} + d + \frac{1}{a} = a : b$.

(2) $\left(\frac{1}{a} - \frac{1}{c}\right) - \left(\frac{1}{b} - \frac{1}{d}\right) = \frac{(a - b)(a - c)}{abc}$.

19. If $3a + 5b : 3a - 5b = 3c + 5d : 3c - 5a$, prove that $a : b = c : d$.

20. Two casks A and B were filled with wine and water, mixed in the cask A in the ratio of $5 : 6$, and in the cask B in the ratio of $2 : 5$. What quantity must be taken from each to form a mixture which shall contain 32 litres of water and 18 litres of wine?

21. Two numbers each consisting of the same two digits are in the ratio of $3 : 8$. Find the numbers.

22. If $a : x = y : b$, prove that $a^2 - ax + x^2 : ax + ab - xy$
$= y^2 - by + b^2 : by - ab + xy$.

23. If $p : q$ be in the duplicate ratio of $p - r : q - r$, prove that $r^2 = pq$.

24. If $\frac{x}{(b - c)(b + c - 2a)} = \frac{y}{(c - a)(c + a - 2b)} = \frac{z}{(a - b)(a + b - 2c)}$, show that $x + y + z = 0$.

25. If $a^2l^2 + b^2m^2 : c^2p^2 + d^2q^2 = a^2l^2 - b^2m^2 : c^2p^2 - d^2q^2$, show that aq, bp, cm, dl are in proportion.

26. If $p^2 + a^2 : q^2 + b^2 = ap : bq$, shew that p, q, a, b are in proportion.

27. If $au^2 + bv^2 : ax^2 + by^2 = au^2 - bv^2 : ax^2 + by^2$, show that x, y, u, v are proportionals.

28. In a certain examination the number of those who passed was three times the number of those who were rejected. If there had been 16 fewer candidates, and if 6 more had been rejected, the numbers of those who passed and of those who were rejected would have been as $2 : 1$. Find the number of candidates.

29. A and B have between them Rs. 10.50. They make a bet, each staking a sum proportional to the money he has. If A wins he will have double what B will then have; but if he loses, B will have three times what A will then have: what has each at first?

MISCELLANEOUS EXAMPLES V

[The following examples have been selected from the Entrance and Matriculation Papers of the Universities of Calcutta, Bombay, Madras, Allahabad. They are arranged progressively, and may be used from time to time to test the student's progress.]

1. Subtract $b\{a-(b+c)\}$ from the sum of $a\{(a-(c-b)\}$ and $c\{a-(b-c)\}$. **[MADRAS.]**

2. If $a=2, b=3, c=4$, find the value of $\frac{a-b+c}{a+b-c}+\frac{b-c+a}{b+c-a}+\frac{c-a+b}{c+a-b}$. **[BOMBAY.]**

3. Reduce to its simplest form $a^2+2d^2-(2e^2-b^2)-\{(d^2-e^2-c^2)+(d^2-e^2)\}$. **[BOMBAY.]**

4. Divide $x^4-24x^2+x^3-35x+57$ by x^2+2x-3. **[CALCUTTA.]**

5. Solve the equation $\frac{2x-3}{6}+\frac{3x-8}{11}=\frac{4x+15}{13}+\frac{1}{2}$. **[CALCUTTA.]**

6. Simplify $42\left\{\frac{4x-3y}{6}-\frac{1}{7}(3x-4y)\right\}-56\left\{\frac{1}{7}(3x-2y)-\frac{2x-3y}{8}\right\}$. **[ALLAHABAD.]**

7. Find the continued product of x^2-2y^2, $x^2-2xy+2y^2$, x^2+2y^2, $x^2+2xy+2y^2$. **[BOMBAY.]**

8. The sum of Rs. 49 was divided amongst 150 children, each girl receiving 50 paise and each boy 25 paise. How many boys were there? **[CALCUTTA.]**

9. Solve the equation $\frac{17-3x}{5}-\frac{4x+2}{3}=5-6x+\frac{7x+14}{3}$. **[BOMBAY.]**

10. Divide x^4-10x^2+9 by x^2-2x-3. **[CALCUTTA.]**

11. Remove brackets from $(c-a-b)-\{(b+c-a)-(a-b-c)-(c+a-b)\}$. **[MADRAS.]**

12. A post is a fourth of its length in the mud, a third of its length in the water, and 5 meters above the water: what is the length? **[CALCUTTA.]**

13. Solve the equations :

(1) $\frac{x-1}{3}-\frac{x-9}{2}+\frac{3x-2(x-2)}{7}=4\frac{1}{2}$.

(2) $5x+11y=146, 11x+5y=110$. **[CALCUTTA.]**

14. If $V=5a+4b-6c$, $X=7c-3a-9b$, $Y=20a+7b-5c$, $Z=13a-5b+9c$, calculate the value of $V-(X+Y)+Z$. **[MADRAS.]**

15. Find the square root of $4x^4+8ax^3+4a^2x^2+16b^2x^2+16ab^2x+16b^4$. **[CALCUTTA.]**

16. A number consists of two digits whose sum is 10. If 72 be subtracted from the number, the digits will be inverted : what is the number? **[BOMBAY.]**

17. Divide $a(a+b)(a+c)-b(b+c)(b+a)$ by $a+b+c$. **[MADRAS.]**

18. Resolve into factors $a^2+6ab+5b^2$; $a^2+5ab-6b^2$; $a^3-a^2b-ab^2+b^3$. **[BOMBAY.]**

19. Solve the equations:

(1) $\frac{2x-13}{9}-\frac{x-1}{11}=\frac{x}{8}+\frac{x}{7}-9$;

(2) $\frac{x+y}{2}+\frac{3x-5y}{4}=4, \frac{x}{14}+\frac{y}{18}=2.$ **[CALCUTTA.]**

20. Find the square root of $1+2x-x^3+\frac{1}{4}x^4$. **[MADRAS]**

21. One student said to another, "If you give me half your money I shall have 100 rupees." The other replied, "I shall have 100 rupees if you give me a third of your money." How much had each? **[BOMBAY.]**

22. Remove brackets form the expression $(x-a)(x-b)(x-c)-[bc(x-a)$ $-\{(a+b+c)x-a(b+c)\}x]$. **[ALLAHABAD.]**

23. Find the factor of highest dimensions which will divide $4x^3-8ax^2-20a^2x+24a^3$ and $6x^3+24ax^2+6a^2x-36a^3$. **[CALCUTTA.]**

24. Find the factors of each of the expressions $6x^2+5x-6$; $3x^2-10x-8$; $9x^4-82x^2y^2-9y^2$. **[BOMBAY.]**

25. Find the values of x, y, z in the following set of simultaneous equations:
$3y+x-2=0, 3z-4y=x+15, 2x+7z=7.$ **[CALCUTTA.]**

26. Reduce to its lowest terms $\frac{3x^3-27ax^2+78a^2x-72a^3}{2x^3+10ax^2-4a^2x-48a^3}$. **[CALCUTTA.]**

27. Divide $bc(c-b)+ca(a-c)+ab(b-a)$ by $(a-b)(a-c)$. **[MADRAS.]**

28. Find the square root of

(1) $\frac{x^4}{4}-\frac{2x^3}{3}-\frac{11x^2}{36}+x+\frac{9}{16}$;

(2) $(a^2+b^2)(a^2b^2+1)-2ab(a^2-1)(b^2-1)-4a^2b^2$. **[MADRAS.]**

29. Simplify $\frac{9a^2b^2}{16(x+y)}\div\left[\left\{\frac{3a(x-y)}{7(c+d)}\div\frac{4(c-d)}{21ab^2}\div\frac{c^2-d^2}{4(x^2-y^2)}\right\}\right]$. **[BOMBAY.]**

30. Solve the equations :

(1) $(6x+9)^2+(8x-7)^2=(10x+3)^2-71$;

(2) $.65x+\frac{.585x-.975}{.6}=\frac{1.56}{.2}-\frac{.39x-.78}{.9}$.

(3) $\left.\begin{aligned}\frac{x-2}{2}-\frac{x+y}{14}&=\frac{x-y-1}{8}-\frac{y+12}{4},\\ \frac{x+7}{3}+\frac{y-5}{10}&=1-x-\frac{5(y+1)}{7}.\end{aligned}\right\}$ **[CALCUTTA.]**

31. Find the lowest common multiple of $9x^4 - 28x^2 + 3$, $27x^4 - 12x^2 + 1$, $27x^4 + 6x^2 - 1$, $x^4 - 6x^2 + 9$. **[CALCUTTA.]**

32. What value of c makes $(x-2)^2 - (x-1)(x-3) = c$ an identity? **[BOMBAY.]**

33. Resolve into factors $(2a + 2b - ab)^2 - (b^2 - 4a)(a^2 - 4b)$. **[MADRAS.]**

34. Two persons started at the same time from A. One rode on horseback at the rate of $11\frac{1}{4}$ km an hour and arrived at B half-an-hour later than the other who travelled the same distance by train at the rate of 45 km an hour. Find the distance between A and B. **[CALCUTTA.]**

35. Find the value of $\dfrac{4a+6b}{a+b} + \dfrac{6a-4b}{a-b} - \dfrac{4a^2+6b^2}{a^2-b^2} + \dfrac{4b^2-6a^2}{a^2+b^2} + \dfrac{20b^4}{a^4-b^4}$. **[MADRAS.]**

36. Extract the square root of $x^6 + 10x^4 - 4x^5 - 20x^3 - 24x + 16 + 25x^2$. **[BOMBAY.]**

37. Simplify $\dfrac{1+\dfrac{a-b}{a+b}}{1-\dfrac{a-b}{a+b}} \div \dfrac{1+\dfrac{a^2-b^2}{a^2+b^2}}{1-\dfrac{a^2-b^2}{a^2+b^2}}$. **[CALCUTTA.]**

38. Solve the equations:

(1) $\dfrac{2x-9}{27} + \dfrac{x}{18} - \dfrac{x-3}{4} = 8\dfrac{1}{3} - x$;

(2) $1.2x - \dfrac{.18x - .05}{.5} = .4x + 8.9$;

(3) $\dfrac{x+6}{y} = \dfrac{3}{4}$, $\dfrac{x}{y-2} = \dfrac{1}{2}$. **[BOMBAY.]**

39. Resolve into factors:

(1) $b^3 - a^3 - (c^2 - ab)(b - a)$;

(2) $a(b^2 + c^2 - a^2) + b(a^2 + c^2 - b^2)$. **[MADRAS.]**

40. A person bought a picture at a certain price and paid the same price for the frame. If the frame had cost Rs. 15 less and the picture Rs. 10 more, the price of the frame would have been only half that of the picture. Find the cost of the picture. **[CALCUTTA.]**

41. Find the factor of lowest dimensions which is divisible by $1 + a + a^5$ and $1 + a^4 + a^5$. **[MADRAS.]**

42. Simplify the fractions:

(1) $\left(\dfrac{1}{m-n} - \dfrac{1}{m-s}\right) \div \left\{\dfrac{1}{(m-n)^2} - \dfrac{1}{(m-s)^2}\right\}$;

(2) $\left(\dfrac{x}{1-\dfrac{1}{x}}-x-\dfrac{1}{1-x}\right)\div\left(\dfrac{x}{1+\dfrac{1}{x}}+x-\dfrac{1}{1+x}\right).$ [CALCUTTA.]

43. Extract the square root of $\dfrac{x^2}{y^2}+\dfrac{y^2}{4x^2}-\dfrac{x}{y}+\dfrac{y}{2x}-\dfrac{3}{4}.$ [BOMBAY.]

44. If $x=b+c$, $y=c-a$, $z=a-b$, shew that

$$x^2+y^2+z^2-2xy-2xz+2yz=4b^2.$$ [CALCUTTA.]

45. Simplify the fraction $\left(y-\dfrac{a^2-xy}{y-x}\right)\left(x+\dfrac{a^2-xy}{y-x}\right)+\left(\dfrac{a^2-xy}{y-x}\right)^2.$ [ALLAHABAD.]

46. Solve the equations:

(1) $\dfrac{x+2\frac{1}{2}}{15}+\dfrac{x+3\frac{1}{3}}{25}=\dfrac{x+4\frac{1}{6}}{55}$;

(2) $\dfrac{1}{3}-\dfrac{7x-1}{6\frac{1}{2}-3x}=\dfrac{8\left(x-\frac{1}{2}\right)}{3(x-2)}$;

(3) $(x+7)(y-3)+7=(y+3)(x-1)+5,\ 5x-11y+35=0$ [CALCUTTA.]

47. From the sum of the square of $\dfrac{1}{a-b}$ and $\dfrac{1}{a+b}$ subtract the square of $\dfrac{2b}{a^2-b^2}$. [BOMBAY.]

48. A person being asked his age replied, "Ten years ago I was five times as old as my son, but twenty years hence I shall be only twice as old as he." What is his age? [MADRAS.]

49. Divide $(a-b)^2c^2+(a-b)c^3-(c^2-a^2)b^2+(c-a)b^3$ by $(a-b)c^2-(c-a)b^2$. [CALCUTTA.]

50. Find the highest factor common to the numerator and denominator of the fraction $\dfrac{x^4-15x^2+28x-12}{2x^3-15x+14}$, and reduce the expression to its lowest terms. [BOMBAY.]

51. Find the value of $24\left\{x-\dfrac{1}{2}(x-3)\right\}\left\{x-\dfrac{2}{3}(x+2)\right\}\left\{x-\dfrac{3}{4}\left(x-\dfrac{4}{3}\right)\right\}$ and subtract the result from $(x+2)(x-3)(x+4)$. [MADRAS.]

52. A and B walk at the rate of $5\frac{1}{4}$ and $6\frac{3}{4}$ kilometers per hour respectively. If A start $2\frac{1}{2}$ hours before B, how far will he have travelled before he is overtaken? [ALLAHABAD.]

53. Find the highest common factor of $7x^4 - 10ax^3 + 3a^2x^2 - 4a^3x + 4a^4$ and $8x^4 - 13ax^3 + 13ax^3 + 5a^2x^2 - 3a^3x + 3a^4$. [BOMBAY.]

54. Solve the equations:

(1) $\frac{2}{x} + \frac{3}{y} = 2, \frac{5}{x} + \frac{10}{y} = 5\frac{5}{6}$;

(2) $x - 2y + z = 0, 9x - 8y + 3z = 0, 2x + 3y + 5z = 36$;

(3) $\frac{x-2}{x-3} + \frac{x-3}{x-4} = \frac{x-1}{x-2} + \frac{x-4}{x-5}$. [CALCUTTA.]

55. Find the square root of

$$\frac{4x^2}{9y^2} - \frac{x}{z} - \frac{16x^2}{15yz} + \frac{9y^2}{16z^2} + \frac{6xy}{5z^2} + \frac{16x^2}{25z^2}.$$

[MADRAS.]

56. If $\frac{a}{b} = \frac{b}{c} = \frac{c}{d}$, prove that

(1) $\frac{a}{d} = \frac{a^3}{b^3}$;

(2) $(ab + bc + cd)^2 = (a^2 + b^2 + c^2)(b^2 + c^2 + d^2)$. [CALCUTTA.]

57. Divide $(4x^3 - 3a^2x)^2 + (4y^3 - 3a^2y)^2 - a^6$ by $x^2 + y^2 - a^2$. [BOMBAY.]

58. A letter-carrier has to go daily from P to Q in a prescribed time. If he goes two and a half kilometres per hour faster than his ordinary speed he arrives at Q half an hour before the time; but if he goes two and a half kilometres per hour slower he arrives an hour too late. Find his ordinary speed and the distance from P to Q. [MADRAS.]

59. If $s = a + b + c$, prove that

$$(as + bc)(bs + ca)(cs + ab) = (b + c)^2(c + a)^2(a + b)^2.$$

[ALLAHABAD.]

60. Solve the equations:

(1) $r(q + x) - pr = t(q + x) - pt$;

(2) $\frac{16x - 27\frac{4}{5}}{3x - 4} + \frac{77 - x}{3(x-1)} = 5 + \frac{23}{x-1}$. [MADRAS.]

61. The expression $ax - 3b$ is equal to 30 when x is 3, and to 42 when x is 7; what is its value when x is 4.3, and for what value of x is it equal to zero? [CALCUTTA.]

62. Simplify the fractions :

(1) $a+\left[\dfrac{b-a}{1+ab}\times\dfrac{a}{b}\div\left\{1-\dfrac{a(b-a)}{1+ba}\right\}\right]$;

(2) $\dfrac{3\frac{1}{4}-\frac{1}{3}(x-2)}{1\frac{1}{12}+\left(x-\frac{3}{2}\right)}$. **[BOMBAY.]**

63. Find the highest common factor of $x(6x^2-8y^2)-y(3x^2-4y^2)$ and $2xy(2y-x)+4x^3-2y^3$. **[CALCUTTA.]**

64. Extract the square root of

$$\frac{x^4}{y^4}+\frac{y^4}{x^4}-2\left(\frac{x^3}{y^3}+\frac{y^3}{x^3}\right)+3\left(\frac{x^2}{y^2}+\frac{y^2}{x^2}\right)-4\left(\frac{x}{y}+\frac{y}{x}\right)+5.$$

[MADRAS.]

65. A boy receives a fixed sum as pocket-money at the beginning of every week, and in each week he spends half of all that he had at its beginning. He had no money before the first pocket-money was given him, and at the end of the third week he had Rs. 3.50. What was his weekly allowance? **[BOMBAY.]**

66. If $a:b=c:d$, prove that $(a^2+c^2)(b^2+d^2)=(ab+cd)^2$. **[ALLAHABAD.]**

67. Solve the equations :

(1) $x-y-z=-15,\ y+x+2z=40,\ 4z-5x-6y=-110$;

(2) $\dfrac{a-x^2}{bx}-\dfrac{b-x}{c}=\dfrac{c-x}{b}-\dfrac{b-x^2}{cx}$;

(3) $.011x+\dfrac{.001x-.125}{.6}=\dfrac{5-x}{.03}-.145$;

(4) $16\left(\dfrac{a-x}{a+x}\right)^3=\dfrac{a+x}{a-x}$. **[CALCUTTA.]**

68. Simplify the expression: $\dfrac{a^4+b^4+ab(a^2+b^2)}{(a+b)^2}$

$-\dfrac{a^4+b^4-ab(a^2+b^2)}{(a-b)^2}+\dfrac{12a^2b^2}{(a+b)^2-(a-b)^2}$. **[MADRAS.]**

69. A person walks from A and B, a distance of 15 kilometres, in 2 hr. $17\frac{1}{2}$ min., and returns in 2 hr. 20 min. His rates of walking up-hill, down-hill, on the level, are 6, 7, $6\frac{1}{2}$ kilometres per hour respectively. What is the length of the level road between A and B ? **[BOMBAY.]**

70. If $\dfrac{a}{b}=\dfrac{c}{d}$, prove that $\dfrac{(a+c)^3}{(b+d)^3}=\dfrac{a(a-c)^2}{b(b-d)^2}$. **[CALCUTTA.]**

71. Extract the square root of
$(a^2 - c^2)^2 + (b^2 - d^2)^2 - 2(a^2 + c^2)(b^2 + d^2) + 4(a^2c^2 + b^2d^2)$. [CALCUTTA.]

72. Show that the expressions $\left(\frac{x}{a}\right)^2 + \left(\frac{z-x}{b}\right)^2$ and $\frac{z^2}{a^2+b^2} + \frac{a^2+b^2}{a^2b^2}\left(x - \frac{za^2}{a^2+b^2}\right)^2$ are identical. [BOMBAY.]

73. A man rides one-third of the distance from A to B at the rate of a kilometres per hour, and the remainder at the rate of $2b$ kilometres per hour. If he had travelled at a uniform rate of $3c$ kilometres per hour, he could have ridden from A to B and back again in the same time. Prove that $\frac{2}{c} = \frac{1}{a} + \frac{1}{b}$. [CALCUTTA.]

74. Find the continued product of $a + b + c, b + c - a, c + a - b, a + b - c$; and resolve $4a^2b^2 - (a^2 + b^2 - c^2)^2$ into four factors. [BOMBAY.]

75. Solve the equations:

(1) $\frac{x}{x-2} + \frac{9-x}{7-x} = \frac{x+1}{x-1} + \frac{8-x}{6-x}$;

(2) $\frac{m}{x} + \frac{n}{y} = a, \frac{n}{x} + \frac{m}{y} = b.$ [MADRAS.]

76. Find the quotient when $(ax + by)^3 + (ax - by)^3 - (ay - bx)^3 + (ay + bx)^3$ is divided by $(a + b)^2 x^2 - 3ab(x^2 - y^2)$. [CALCUTTA.]

77. A person walked out a certain distance at the rate of kilometres per hour, and then ran part of the way back at the rate of 14 kilometres per hour, walking the remaining distance in 7 minutes. He was out 35 minutes : how far did he run? [ALLAHABAD.]

78. Simplify the fractions:

(1) $\frac{a^2 + ac}{a^2c - c^3} - \frac{a^2 - c^2}{a^2c + 2ac^2 + c^3} - \frac{2c}{a^2 - c^2}$.

(2) $\frac{1}{abx} + \frac{1}{a(a-b)(x-a)} + \frac{1}{b(b-a)(x-b)} - \frac{1}{x(a-x)(b-x)}$.

[CALCUTTA.]

79. If $ap = bq = cr$, shew that $\frac{p^2}{qr} + \frac{q^2}{rp} + \frac{r^2}{pq} = \frac{bc}{a^2} + \frac{ca}{b^2} + \frac{ab}{c^2}$. [MADRAS.]

80. Solve the equations:

(1) $\frac{3x + 11}{26} - \frac{402 + x}{12} = 99 - \frac{371 - 6x}{2}$;

(2) $\frac{10x + 4}{21} + \frac{7 - 2x^2}{14(x-1)} = \frac{11 - 5x}{15} + \frac{4x - 3\frac{2}{5}}{6}$;

(3) $\left.\begin{aligned} 10x - \frac{5y+3}{4} &= 30 + \frac{12y+7x}{5}, \\ 16y + \frac{5x-2}{3} &= 26\frac{1}{2} - \frac{8y+1}{2}. \end{aligned}\right\}$ **[BOMBAY.]**

81. Extract the square root of

(1) $(ab + ac + bc)^2 - 4abc(a + c)$;

(2) $x^4 + 2(y + z)x^3 + (3y^2 + 2yz + 3z^2)x^2$
$+ 2(y^3 + y^2z + yz^2 + z^3)x + y^4 + 2y^2z^2 + z^4$. **[CALCUTTA.]**

82. Find the value of

$$\frac{(a+b)^2}{(x-a)(x+a+b)} - \frac{a+2b+x}{2(x-a)} + \frac{(a+b)x}{x^2+bx-a^2-ab} + \frac{1}{2}.$$ **[MADRAS.]**

83. A father's age is four times that of his eldest son and five times that of his youngest son; when the elder son has lived to three times his present age, the father's age will exceed twice that of his younger son by three years. Find their present ages. **[BOMBAY.]**

84. Find the quotient when $x(1 + y^2)(1 + z^2) + y(1 + z^2)(1 + x^2) + z(1 + x^2)(1 + y^2) + 4xyz$ is divided by $1 + yz + zx + xy$. **[CALCUTTA.]**

85. If $\frac{x}{(b-c)(b+c-2a)} = \frac{y}{(c-a)(c+a-2b)} = \frac{z}{(a-b)(a+b-2c)}$, find the value of $x + y + z$. **[CALCUTTA.]**

86. (1) $\frac{x-7}{x-3} + \frac{x-2}{x-9} + \frac{x-4}{x-1} = 3$;

(2) $\sqrt{\frac{x-a}{x-b}} + \frac{a}{x} = \sqrt{\frac{x-b}{x-a}} + \frac{b}{x}$;

(3) $(a^2 + b^2)(x - 1) = ab(2x - y)$; $4x = y + 2$. **[MADRAS.]**

87. Extract the square root of $\frac{x^3}{16} - \frac{x^2}{6} - \frac{x^{\frac{3}{2}}}{4} + \frac{x}{9} + \frac{x^{\frac{1}{2}}}{3} + \frac{1}{4}$, and the cube root of

$$8x^6 + 36x^5 + 66x^4 - 63x^3 + 33x^2 - 9x + 1.$$ **[BOMBAY.]**

88. Simplify $\frac{x^{3n}}{x^n - 1} - \frac{x^{2n}}{x^n + 1} - \frac{1}{x^n - 1} + \frac{1}{x^n + 1}$; and when $x\sqrt{n+1} = \sqrt{n-1}$, find the value of $\left(\frac{x}{x-1}\right)^2 + \left(\frac{x}{x+1}\right)^2$. **[CALCUTTA.]**

89. *A*, *B*, and *C* work together at building a wall for 10 days, after which *B* stops working and *A* and *C* together finish it in 5 days. Find the time in which each could build it separately, if *A* and *B* together can do as much in a day as *C* can do in three days, and 3 days, work of *B* is equal to 4 days' work of *C*. **[MADRAS.]**

90. If $a:b=c:d=e:f$, shew that each of these ratios is equal to $\sqrt[3]{a^3+c^3+e^3}:\sqrt[3]{b^3+d^3+f^3}$. **[CALCUTTA.]**

91. Solve the equations:

(1) $(a-x)(x-b)=ab-x^2$; (2) $\sqrt{x+5}+\sqrt{4x+9}=\sqrt{9x+28}$;

(3) $\frac{4}{x}-\frac{5}{y}=\frac{x+y}{xy}+\frac{57}{35}$, $xy=\frac{35}{34}(y-x)$. **[BOMBAY.]**

92. Simplify the fractions:

(1) $\frac{a^2}{x(a-x)}+\frac{x^2}{a(x-a)}-\frac{(a-x)^2}{ax}$;

(2) $\frac{(ac+bd)^3-(ad-bc)^3}{(a-b)(c-d)}+\frac{(ac+bd)^3+(ad+bc)^3}{(a+b)(c+d)}$. **[MADRAS.]**

93. If $x+y=2z$, show that $\frac{x}{x-z}+\frac{y}{y-z}=2$. **[BOMBAY.]**

94. Divide $\frac{a^3}{b^3}+\frac{b^3}{c^3}+\frac{c^3}{a^3}-3$ by $\frac{a}{b}+\frac{b}{c}+\frac{c}{a}$. **[MADRAS.]**

95. If $\frac{x}{b+c-a}=\frac{y}{c+a-b}=\frac{z}{a+b-c}$, find the value of $(b-c)x+(c-a)y+(a-b)z$. **[CALCUTTA.]**

96. Solve the equations:

(1) $ax+by=1=bx-\frac{b}{a}+ay-\frac{a}{b}$;

(2) $\frac{(x-a)(x+b)}{x-a+b}=\frac{x(x-c)-b(x+c)}{x-b-c}$. **[MADRAS.]**

97. Simplify the fraction: $\frac{2}{a+x}-\frac{1}{a-x}+\frac{3x}{a^2-x^2}+\frac{ax}{a^3+x^3}$. **[CALCUTTA.]**

98. Two passengers have between them 380 kg of luggage, and are charged for the excess above the weight allowed Rs. 3.75 and Rs. 7.25 respectively. If the luggage had all belonged to one of them he would have been charged Rs. 15. How much luggage is each passenger allowed to carry free of charge; and how much luggage had each passenger? **[CALCUTTA.]**

99. Shew that the expression $(a-b)^2(c+d)^2+4ab(c^2+d^2)-4cd(a^2+b^2)$ is an exact square. **[MADRAS.]**

100. Simplify the fractions:

(1) $\frac{1}{x(x-y)(x-z)}+\frac{1}{y(y-z)(y-x)}+\frac{1}{z(z-x)(z-y)}$,

(2) $\frac{\frac{a}{a-b}-\frac{a}{a+b}}{\frac{b}{a-b}-\frac{b}{a+b}}\times\frac{a^2}{a^2+b^2}\div\frac{\frac{a+b}{a-b}-\frac{a-b}{a+b}}{\frac{a+b}{a-b}+\frac{a-b}{a+b}}$ **[CALCUTTA.]**

101. Find the quotient of $a^{\frac{5}{2}} - a^{\frac{3}{2}}b + ab^{\frac{3}{2}} - 2a^{\frac{1}{2}}b^2 + b^{\frac{5}{2}}$ by $a^{\frac{3}{2}} - ab^{\frac{1}{2}} + a^{\frac{1}{2}}b - b^{\frac{3}{2}}$; and extract the square root of $a^3 - 2a^{\frac{3}{2}}b^{\frac{2}{3}} + 2a^{\frac{3}{2}}c^{\frac{3}{2}} - 2b^{\frac{2}{3}}C^{\frac{3}{2}} + b^{\frac{4}{3}} + c^3$. **[BOMBAY.]**

102. Solve the equations:

(1) $\sqrt{x+16} - \sqrt{x} = \frac{6}{\sqrt{x}}$; (2) $\sqrt{x^2 + 11x + 20} - \sqrt{x^2 + 5x - 1} = 3$;

(3) $\sqrt{\{4x^2 + 20x + 17 + \sqrt{16x^2 + 11x + 10}\}} + 2(x+2) = 0$. **[CALCUTTA.]**

103. A man rowing against a stream meets a log of wood which is being carried down by the current. He continues rowing in the same direction for a quarter of an hour longer, and then turns and rows down the stream, overtaking the log $\frac{3}{4}$ kilometres lower down than the point where he first met it. Find the rate at which the current flows. **[MADRAS.]**

104. Resolve into their simplest factors:

(1) $a^8 + a^4x^4 + x^8$; (2) $x^8 - 16a^8$. **[CALCUTTA.]**

105. Divide 127 into four parts, so that the first increased by 18, the second diminished by 5, the third multiplied by 6, and the fourth divided by $2\frac{1}{2}$, shall be all equal. **[BOMBAY.]**

106. Simplify the fraction $\frac{a^3}{(a-b)(a-c)} + \frac{b^3}{(b-c)(b-a)} + \frac{c^3}{(c-a)(c-b)}$. **[CALCUTTA.]**

107. Solve the equations:

(1) $\frac{a+\sqrt{x}}{(b-\sqrt{x})(c-\sqrt{x})} + \frac{b+\sqrt{x}}{(c-\sqrt{x})(a-\sqrt{x})} + \frac{c+\sqrt{x}}{(a-\sqrt{x})(b-\sqrt{x})} = 0$;

(2) $\sqrt[3]{1+x} + \sqrt[3]{1-x} = \sqrt[3]{2}$. **[CALCUTTA.]**

108. Reduce to its lowest terms $\frac{xy + 2x^2 - 3y^2 + 4yz + xz - z^2}{2x^2 - 9xz - 5xy + 4z^2 - 8yz - 12y^2}$. **[MADRAS.]**

109. If $x + \frac{1}{x} = p$, express $x^3 + \frac{1}{x^3}$ in terms of p. **[BOMBAY.]**

110. *A* challenged *B* to ride a bicycle race of 1040 metres. He first gave *B* a start of 120 metres, but lost by 5 seconds; he then gave *B* a start of 5 seconds and won by 40 metres. How long does each take to ride the distance? **[CALCUTTA.]**

ANSWERS

I. a. Page 3.

1. 10. **2.** 25. **3.** 6. **4.** 8.
5. 1. **6.** 4. **7.** 64. **8.** 1.
9. 27. **10.** 9. **11.** 1008. **12.** 1000.
13. 192. **14.** 320. **15.** 7. **16.** 24.
17. 84. **18.** 21. **19.** 320. **20.** 336.
21. 140. **22.** 1680. **23.** 245. **24.** 48.
25. 7. **26.** 768. **27.** 5000. **28.** 1512.
29. 6. **30.** 1. **31.** 3. **32.** 2.
33. $\frac{1}{7}$. **34.** 6. **35.** $\frac{1}{10}$. **36.** 32.
37. 9. **38.** 125. **39.** $\frac{1}{6}$. **40.** $7\frac{1}{2}$.

I. b. Page 4.

1. 60. **2.** 0. **3.** 350. **4.** 126.
5. 140. **6.** 12. **7.** 147. **8.** 0.
9. 49. **10.** 0. **11.** 0. **12.** 8000.
13. 216. **14.** 0. **15.** 648. **16.** $\frac{1}{3}$.
17. 2. **18.** 0. **19.** 0. **20.** 3.
21. 0. **22.** $\frac{1}{2}$. **23.** $1\frac{1}{4}$. **24.** 0.
25. $5\frac{1}{3}$. **26.** 0. **27.** $\frac{1}{2}$. **28.** $\frac{5}{16}$.
29. 0. **30.** $\frac{1}{5}$.

I. c. Page 6.

1. 8. **2.** 29. **3.** 4. **4.** 42.
5. 0. **6.** 0. **7.** 6. **8.** 9.
9. 0. **10.** 9. **11.** 1. **12.** 31.
13. 12. **14.** 31. **15.** 12. **16.** 0.
17. 31. **18.** 49. **19.** 1.

II. Page 9.

1. $16a$. **2.** $24x$. **3.** $39b$. **4.** $151c$.
5. $32p$. **6.** $40d$. **7.** $-26x$. **8.** $-40b$.
9. $-17y$. **10.** $-66c$. **11.** $-47y$. **12.** $-93m$.
13. $-s$. **14.** $7y$. **15.** 0. **16.** $3ab$.
17. $3xy$. **18.** pq. **19.** $-5abc$. **20.** $3xyz$.

21. a^2. 22. $-b^3$. 23. $-21a^3$. 24. $-16x^3$.
25. $11a^2b^2$. 26. $-9a^2x$. 27. $-12p^3q^2$. 28. $-5m^4n$.
29. $-43\,abcd$. 30. $-11pqx$.

III. a. Page 12.

1. $3a-6c$. 2. $6x$.
3. $3p+5q-2r$. 4. $34a+2b$.
5. $l+m+n$. 6. $5a-2d$.
7. $-a-2x+3y$. 8. $16x-7y$.
9. $4a$. 10. $8+2x-2z$.
11. $39a-5b+4c$. 12. x.
13. $3e+3f$. 14. $-10p+12q+7r$.
15. $11ab-5kl+5xy$. 16. $2ax+2cz$.
17. $4ax$. 18. $fg-st$.
19. $7cx-10s$. 20. $-2ab+8cd$.

III. b. Page 14.

1. xy. 2. x^2+x+1.
3. x^2+4x. 4. a^2b+b^3.
5. $10x^3+x^2-10x$. 6. $10x^5$.
7. $7m^3+3m^2-1$. 8. $3ax^3-cx+2d$.
9. $2py^2+qy-3r$. 10. $7y^3+10y^2$.
11. $-2a+8a^3$. 12. $4+y+2y^2$.
13. $8a^3x^2+x$. 14. $x^5-x^4y-y^5$.
15. $a^3-3abc+b^3+c^3$. 16. $-ap^5-bp^3+3cp+1$.
17. $3c^7+11c^6-7c^5$. 18. $4h^4+3h^3+5h-10$.
19. x^3+1. 20. z^2+3xz.

IV. Page 16.

1. $a+b+2c$. 2. $a-4b-2c$.
3. $-2x-5y+4z$. 4. $9x-15y-14z$.
5. $-m+4n-4p$. 6. $p-5q+2r$.
7. $-5a+10b+11c$. 8. $2b$.
9. $-x+8y+3z$. 10. $3x+4y-24z$.
11. $3x+8y-2z$. 12. $-2x+3y+8z$.
13. $4n+p$. 14. $-2p+5q-3r$.
15. $-2ab-cd+3ac$. 16. $-cd-ac-bd$.

17. $3xy - yz + 2zx$.

18. $2pq + 4qr - 8rs$.

19. $mn - 22np + 3pm$.

20. $x^2y + 5xy^2 - 4xyz$.

21. $2x^3 - 6x^2 + 2x$.

22. $-3x^3 + x$.

23. $a^3 - abc$.

24. $-12 + 9bc + 6b^2c^2$.

25. $3p^3 - 3p^2q + 10pq^2 - q^3$.

26. $2 + 2x - 2x^2 - x^3$.

27. $-1 + 3x^2y - 12xyz$.

28. $-17a^2x^2 + 13x^2 + 20$.

29. $p^3 - q^3 - 6pqr$.

30. $-x^3$.

31. $4 + 6x - 10x^2$.

32. $x^3 + 3x^2 + 5x + 7$.

33. $-7a^3 - 5a^2 + 12$.

34. $-x^4 + 3x^3 - 4x^2 + x - 10$.

35. $-5x + 7x^2 - 7x^3$.

36. $2x^2yz + 4y^2zx + 2xyz^2$.

37. $2a^5 + a^3x^2 - 7a^2x^3 - 3ax^4$.

38. $2 - 2x + x^2 - x^3 - 2x^4 + x^5$.

39. $-m^3 + 22m^2n - 16mn^2 + 2n^3$.

40. $1 - 3p^3 + 3pq^2 + 2q^3$.

Miscellaneous Examples. I. Page 18.

1. 18, 72.

2. $3ab - bc + 5ca$; $4ab - 2bc$.

3. $-2x - y$.

4. (1) $b + b^2$. (2) $a + b$.

5. $c^3 - 8c^2 - 8c + 1$.

6. (1) -6. (2) 10.

7. $2a^3 - 2a$.

8. $-2b^2 + b + 1$.

9. $2x^2 + 2x$.

10. $4a^2 + 3a - 19$.

11. $6 - 3x - 2x + 2x^3$.

12. $9a^2 + 2a$.

13. 72.

14. -33.

15. $x^3 + 2x^2 + 5$.

16. $-6p^4 - p^3 + 2p^2 + 2p + 11$.

17. $3x^3 - 2x^2 + 11x - 5$.

18. $2c$.

19. $2x^3 + 1$.

20. $7pq$.

21. $b^4 - 5b^3 - 2b^2 + 3b + 8$.

22. $7m^3 - 11m^2 - m - 7$.

23. $9x^5 + 10x^4y + x^3y^2 + x^2y^3 + xy^4$.

24. $-4 - 3x - 7x^2 + 4x^3$.

25. $7 + 2x - 2x^2$.

26. (1) 36. (2) 1.

27. $a^2 - 18a + 1$.

28. $x^3 - x^2 + 7$.

29. $2x + 3y - 8z$.

30. 0.

V. a. Page 22.

1. $35x$.

2. $6b$.

3. x^5.

4. $30x^3$.

5. $42c^7$.

6. $45y^7$.

7. $15m^8$.

8. $24a^{10}$.

9. $12xy$.

10. $30ab^2$.

11. $20c^2d^5$.

12. $15p^4q^5$.

13. $30a^2x^2$.

14. $12q^2r^2$.

15. a^2b^2.

16. $15a^2cd$.

17. a^7x^2. 18. $12x^3y^7$. 19. a^8b^9. 20. $3a^9b^3$.
21. $5a^6b^5$. 22. $42p^5r^{10}$. 23. $54x^8y^4$. 24. $105a^2b^3c^4$.
25. $42x^2y^3z^5$. 26. $60a^4b^3c^3d^2$.
27. $a^3bc - a^3c^2$. 28. $x^5y^3z^2 - x^2yz^3 + 4x^3y^2z^7$.
29. $15a^3b^2c^4 - 9ab^4c^4$. 30. $3a^5b^2 - 15a^4b^2 + 18a^4b$.
31. $3a^2x^2 - 6b^3x^2$. 32. $2a^3x^3y - a^2b^3xy^2 + 3a^2xy$.
33. $14p^4q - 2p^3q^2 + 2p^2$. 34. $4m^4n + 20m^3n^2 - 12m^2n^3$.
35. $3xy^3z - 9x^2yz^2 - 6yz$. 36. $2a^5bx - 6a^4bx^2$.

V. b. Page 24.

1. $-2a$. 2. $-12x$. 3. x^5. 4. $-15m^4$.
5. $-12q^3$. 6. $16y^6$. 7. $-9m^6$. 8. $-16x^8$.
9. $12xy$. 10. $-20a^2x$. 11. $12p^2q^5$. 12. $-12a^2b^2$.
13. $-6a^3b^3$. 14. $-abc^2$.
15. $-24a^2bc^3d$. 16. $36a^2b^2c^2$.
17. $-36a^5b$. 18. $-24pqst$. 19. $a^2b^2 - a^2bc + ab^2c$.
20. $3a^4x^3 + 4a^3x^4 - 5a^2x^5$. 21. $-a^5c^2 + a^4c^4 - a^3c^5$.
22. $abx^2y^2 - cdx^2y^2 + efx^2y^2$.

V. c. Page 24.

1. −6. 2. 5. 3. −1. 4. 1.
5. −12. 6. 81. 7. 2. 8. −2.
9. 0. 10. −2. 11. −3. 12. 32.
13. 0. 14. −4. 15. −1. 16. 9.
17. 1. 18. 8. 19. 4. 20. −72.
21. −7. 22. −21. 23. 2. 24. 0.
25. 6. 26. 10. 27. −9. 28. −9.
29. −2. 30. −50. 31. 7. 32. 20.

V. d. Page 27.

1. $a^2 + 12a + 35$. 2. $x^2 + x - 12$.
3. $a^2 - 13a + 42$. 4. $y^2 - 16$.
5. $x^2 + x - 72$. 6. $c^2 - 64$.
7. $k^2 - 25$. 8. $m^2 + 3m - 108$.
9. $x^2 - x - 132$. 10. $a^2 - 13a - 14$.
11. $p^2 - 100$. 12. $d^2 + 14d + 49$.
13. $-x^2 + 8x - 16$. 14. $y^2 - 9$.
15. $a^2 - 9a + 20$. 16. $-x^2 + 18x - 80$.

17. $k^2 + 3k - 28$.
18. $y^2 + 14y + 49$.
19. $6a^2 - 11a - 10$.
20. $2x^2 - 9x - 35$.
21. $6x^2 + x - 12$.
22. $3y^2 + 16y - 35$.
23. $35m^2 - 43m + 12$.
24. $14p^2 + 45p - 14$.
25. $2x^2 - 3ax - 9a^2$.
26. $6a^2 + 5ab - 6b^2$.
27. $25c^2 - 16d^2$.
28. $3a^2 - 4ax - 4x^2$.
29. $49b^2 - 7bc - 2c^2$.
30. $4a^2 - 25c^2$.
31. $12x^2 - 17xy - 5y^2$.
32. $4y^2 - 9z^2$.
33. $x^2y^2 - 4b^2$.
34. $4x^2 - 6ax + 6bx - 9ab$.
35. $6ax - 8ay + 9bx - 12by$.
36. $2mnxy - 2pxy + 3mnz - 3pz$.

V. e. Page 28.

1. $2x^3 - 7x^2 - x + 2$.
2. $8a^3 + 10a^2 - 7a - 6$.
3. $6y^3 - 11y^2 + 6y - 1$.
4. $12x^3 + x^2 - 25$.
5. $2a^3 - 7a^2 + 12$.
6. $-10b^3 - 11b^2 - 9$.
7. $6x^3 - 25x^2 + 28x - 49$.
8. $-10c^3 + 13c^2 - 10c + 3$.
9. $x^4 - x^2 + 4x - 4$.
10. $x^4 - 4x^3 + 14x^2 - 20x + 25$.
11. $2a^4 - 5a^3 + a^2 - 12$.
12. $6k^4 - 11k^3 - 2k^2 + 4k + 1$.
13. $a^2 - b^2 + 2bc - c^2$.
14. $a^2 - 4ab + 4b^2 - 9c^2$.
15. $x^4 + x^2y^2 + y^4$.
16. $a^4 + 4x^4$.
17. $-a^4 + b^4 + 6b^2c^2 + 9c^4$.
18. $x^5 - 6x^4 + 9x^3 - x$.
19. $a^6 - 36a^2 + 60a - 25$.
20. $4y^8 - 16y^6 + 16y^4 - 1$.
21. $15m^4 - 32m^3 + 50m^2 - 32m + 15$.
22. $24a^5 - 46a^4 + 9a^3 + 13a^2 - 3a$.
23. $4x^5 - x^3 + 4x$.
24. $-a^6 + 2a^5b^2 - a^4b^4 + b^6$.
25. $a^6 - 3a^4x^2 + 3a^2x^4 - x^6$.
26. $5p^6 - 11p^5 + 21p^4 - 13p^3 + 19p^2 - 12p + 9$.
27. $4m^{11} - 11m^{10} + 20m^9 - 29m^8 + 18m^7 - 8m^6$.
28. $a^7 - 7a^6 + 21a^5 - 35a^4 + 35a^3 - 21a^2 + 7a - 1$.
29. $a^3 - b^3 - c^3 - 3abc$.
30. $-x^8 + 4x^6y^2 - 6x^4y^4 + 4x^2y^6 - y^8$.

V. f. Page 30.

1. $a^2 + a - 6$.
2. $a^2 - 13a + 42$.
3. $x^2 + x - 20$.
4. $b^2 - 2b - 24$.
5. $y^2 - 8y + 7$.
6. $a^2 - 10a + 9$.
7. $c^2 - c - 20$.
8. $x^2 - 12x + 27$.

9. $y^2 + 3y - 28$.
10. $a^2 - 9$.
11. $x^2 - 13x + 40$.
12. $a^2 - 49$.
13. $k^2 - 12k + 36$.
14. $a^2 - 25$.
15. $c^2 + 14c + 49$.
16. $p^2 - p - 90$.
17. $z^2 - 3z - 40$.
18. $x^2 - 81$.
19. $x^2 - ax - 6a^2$.
20. $a^2 - 4b^2$.
21. $x^2 - 8xy + 16y^2$.
22. $a^2 + 8ac + 16c^2$.
23. $c^2 - 10cd + 25d^2$.
24. $p^2 - 4q^2$.
25. $6x^2 - 5x - 6$.
26. $6x^2 + x - 1$.
27. $25x^2 - 4$.
28. $9x^2 - 4a^2$.
29. $36x^2 - 6ax - 2a^2$.
30. $49x^2 + 14xy - 3y^2$.

VI. a. Page 32.

1. $2x$.
2. $2a^4$.
3. $5a^3$.
4. $3b^4$.
5. $-x^2y$.
6. $-xy^2$.
7. $-2pq^2$.
8. $-3m^2n$.
9. l^2m.
10. $8x^6$.
11. $-5z^6$.
12. a^3.
13. $-q$.
14. $7x$.
15. $-8xyz$.
16. -2.
17. 9.
18. $-2k^2t^4$.
19. $-5a^2c^5$.
20. y^3.
21. $24abc$.
22. $5a^4b^2$.
23. $3x - 2$.
24. $5a^2 - 7b^2$.
25. $6p - 3q$.
26. $3x^2 - 5x$.
27. $-x + y + z$.
28. $-10a^2 + 5ab - 1$.
29. $-x^2 - 9ax + 4$.
30. $-a^2 + 3ab + 2b^2$.

VI. b. Page 34.

1. $a + 1$.
2. $b + 1$.
3. $x + 3$.
4. $y + 2$.
5. $x + 6$.
6. $x + 4$.
7. $p - 5$.
8. $q - 8$.
9. $a - 5$.
10. $m + 13$.
11. $x - 5a$.
12. $a - 3b$.
13. $-x + 3$.
14. $x - 21$.
15. $x - 8$.
16. $5x + 1$.
17. $3x + 7$.
18. $4a + 3x$.
19. $5x - 6y$.
20. $3a + 7c$.
21. $6p - q$.
22. $2m - 7n$.
23. $3a - 4b$.
24. $5x + 7y$.
25. $7p - 8q$.
26. $4x^2 + 2x + 1$.
27. $2x^2 - 3x + 2$.
28. $x^2 + 3ax + 3a^2$.
29. $3x^2y - 5xy^2 + 4y^3$.
30. $4x^2 - 7$.

VI. c. Page 36.

1. $a-2$.
2. $x-3$.
3. $y+4$.
4. $3m-1$.
5. $3a+2$.
6. $2k-3$.
7. $2x-5$.
8. $2x+3a$.
9. $2x-5y$.
10. $3c-2d$.
11. x^2-3x+2.
12. $10a^2-3a-12$.
13. $x-4$; rem. $x-1$.
14. $3a+2$.
15. $3m-5$.
16. $2x+3a$; rem. $3a^3$.
17. $3y-1$.
18. $2a+1$.
19. $3x^2+2x-4$; rem. $3x-4$.
20. p^2-3p+2; rem $2p+3$.
21. $7x^2+5x-3$; rem. 20.
22. $-a^3-2a^2-3a-4$.
23. $x-2a$.
24. y^2+3y+9.
25. $x^2-2xy+2y^2$.
26. $3a^2+4a+2$.
27. a^4+4a^2+8.
28. $4x^2-6x+9$.
29. $4m^2+14m+9$.
30. $3x^2-4x+5$; rem. $2x+7$.
31. $3a+2b+c$.
32. $-3x-2y+z$.
33. $2c-d-3$.
34. $-3p+4q-5$.
35. x^2-xy+y^2; rem x^2.
36. x^3+x-y; rem $-y^3$.
37. $-a+b^3-3$.
38. x^5-x^4+x-1; rem. -2.
39. $2a^3-4a^2+4c-2$; rem. 4.
40. $x^6+2x^4+x^3+4x^2-2x+1$.

VII. a. Page 39.

1. $3a-b$.
2. $-a+5b$.
3. $-5b$.
4. $4a-6$.
5. $2x+y$.
6. $2a+b+c$.
7. $-x+y+z$.
8. $-x+3y$.
9. $3b$.
10. $-5n+p$.
11. $-2b-2c$.
12. $-8x-17y$.
13. $4p-q$.
14. $2x^2+y^2$.
15. m^2.
16. $2x-4a+4b$.
17. $5a-b$.
18. $-7q^2$.
19. $-x$.
20. $2a$.
21. $2q$.
22. $4x$.
23. $-a^2+8b^2-9c^2$.
24. $-a$.

VII. b. Page 41.

1. $x+2y$.
2. $5y$.
3. $22-8x$.
4. $2x$.
5. $3x-9$.
6. $3-5x$.
7. $127x-315$.
8. $6xy^2$.
9. $7x-3y-3$.
10. $2y+4z$.
11. $a^2+x^2-4y^2-z^2$.
12. $x-4y$.
13. $a-2b+3c-3d+3e$.
14. 0.
15. $p+21q$.
16. $3x-4y$.

17. $415 - 98x$. **18.** $25 - a$.

19. $2ab + b^2$. **20.** $6x + 2y$.

21. $5x + 7$. **22.** $-50x$.

23. $42x^2 + 216xy + 30y^2$.

24. (1) $(a-1)x^4 + (2-b)x^3 + (2-c)x^2$.

(2) $-(1-a)x^4 - (b-2)x^3 - (c-2)x^2$.

25. (1) $(a^2 - c)x^3 + (a - b - 5)x^2$. (2) $-(c - a^2)x^3 - (5 - a + b)x^2$.

Miscellaneous Examples II. Page 42.

1. $3a + 5c$. **2.** $2y$.

3. c. **4.** $210x^8y^{11}$.

5. $q - p; q^2 + 5pq$. **6.** $1 + x - 2x^2$.

7. $4a^3 - 4a^2b - 9ab^2 + 9b^3$. **8.** $\frac{1}{3}$.

9. $16ax - 13xz$. **10.** $4a - 5b + 5c; 23$.

11. $2x^3 - ax^2 - 5x + 5$. **12.** $-6x^3yz + 8x^2y^3z^2 - 4x^4y^2z^4$.

13. $-75x - 120$. **14.** $x^2 + xy + y^2$.

15. $6x^3 + 7x^2y - 66xy^2 - 112y^3$. **16.** $3e + 3f$.

17. $x^2 + 3x + 2$. **18.** -1.

19. $21 - 72x; 64x - 18$. **20.** $x^2 - 2x + 3$.

21. $5x^3 + 2x^2$. **22.** (1) 5; (2) 10; (3) 8.

23. $49x^4 - x^2y^2 + 4xy^3 - 4y^4$. **24.** $a^5 - 3a^3 + 3a^2 - 10$.

25. (1) $b - c = a + 7$. (2) $3(a + 2b) = bc - 5$.

26. c^2. **27.** $x^8 + x^4y^4 + y^8$.

28. $2a + 3b - c$. **29.** (1) 0; (2) 31.

30. $(a + c)$ cm. **31.** $a + b - c$.

32. $4a - 2b; -7$. **33.** $1 + 2x + 3x^2 + 4x^3$.

34. $9x^4 - 18x^3y + 3x^2y^2 + 6xy^3 + y^4$.

35. (1) $3x - y - 2z$. (2) $3b - 7a = 5cd$. (3) $(m + n)(m - n) = m^2 - n^2$.

36. 2.

VIII. a. Page 45.

1. 1. **2.** 6. **3.** 6. **4.** 24.

5. 12. **6.** 96. **7.** 24. **8.** 36.

9. −10. **10.** 12. **11.** 6. **12.** 3.

13. 12. **14.** 10. **15.** 12. **16.** −3.

17. 2. **18.** −6. **19.** 5. **20.** −3.

21. 6. **22.** 48.

VIII. b. Page 48.

1. $-3m - \frac{1}{2}n.$ **2.** $a.$

3. $\frac{2}{3}a + \frac{3}{2}b - \frac{5}{6}c.$ **4.** $\frac{1}{4}a^2 - \frac{2}{3}ab + \frac{1}{2}b^2.$

5. $\frac{1}{6}x^3 - \frac{1}{9}x^2y + \frac{1}{4}xy^2 - \frac{1}{6}y^3.$ **6.** $\frac{1}{4}x^3 + \frac{1}{72}x + \frac{1}{12}.$

7. $\frac{2}{3}x^2 + xy + \frac{3}{2}y^2.$ **8.** $a - \frac{1}{3}b.$

9. $\frac{1}{12}x + \frac{11}{6}y.$ **10.** $\frac{1}{4}y^3 + \frac{1}{4}y^2 + \frac{1}{4}y + \frac{1}{4}.$

11. $\frac{1}{4}x^2 - \frac{1}{2}xy + \frac{1}{4}y^2 - \frac{1}{9}z^2.$ **12.** $-3a + b.$

13. $\frac{1}{2}x^2 - \frac{1}{3}x + \frac{1}{4}.$ **14.** $\frac{3}{4}x - \frac{3}{4}y.$

15. $\frac{4}{3}x^2 - \frac{4}{3}xy - \frac{1}{6}y^2.$ **16.** $\frac{2}{5}a^4 - \frac{13}{-7}\frac{6}{5}a^3x + \frac{8}{5}a^2x^2\ \frac{3}{10}ax^3 - x^4.$

17. $6a - \frac{1}{3}b - \frac{1}{2}.$ **18.** $6x^2 - \frac{27}{2}y^2 + 36y - 24.$

19. $\frac{3}{2}a^4 - \frac{1}{6}a^2b^2 + \frac{2}{3}ab^3 - \frac{2}{3}b^4.$ The values of the two expressions and the product are $\frac{9}{2}, -1, -\frac{9}{2}$ respectively.

20. $x^{\frac{3}{2}} - 2xy^{\frac{1}{2}} + 2x^{\frac{1}{2}}y - y^{\frac{3}{2}}.$ **21.** $x^{\frac{2}{3}} + x^{\frac{1}{3}}y^{\frac{1}{4}} + y^{\frac{1}{2}}.$

22. $x^{\frac{7}{12}}y + x^{\frac{1}{3}}y^{\frac{2}{3}} - x^{\frac{1}{4}}y^{\frac{4}{3}} - y.$ **23.** $a^{\frac{13}{6}} + a^{\frac{3}{2}}x^{\frac{2}{3}} - a^{\frac{2}{3}}x^{\frac{3}{2}} - x^{\frac{13}{6}}.$

24. $c^{-2} + 3c^{-1} + 1.$ **25.** $2x^{\frac{1}{3}}y^{-1} - 3 + 4x^{-\frac{1}{3}}y.$

26. $a^2x^{-4} - 2x^{-1} - 3a^{-2}x^2.$ **27.** $a^{\frac{1}{2}} - 2a^{\frac{1}{4}} - 1 + 2a^{-\frac{1}{4}} + a^{-\frac{1}{2}}.$

28. $3b - {}^{-1}x^2 - 3a^{-1}b^{-\frac{1}{3}}x^{\frac{5}{3}} + 3a^{-1}x^{\frac{4}{3}} - 3a^{-2}b^{\frac{2}{3}}x.$

29. $x^{\frac{1}{6}}y^{-\frac{1}{4}} - x^{-\frac{1}{6}}y^{\frac{1}{12}}.$ **30.** $a^4 - 2a^2 - 35 + 24a^{-2} - 4a^{-4}.$

31. $3x^{2a}y^{1-a} - y^{1+a} - 3y^{-1-a} + x^{-2a}\ y^{a-1}.$

VIII. c. Page 51.

1. $a^2 + 5ab - 2a + 25b^2 + 10b + 4.$ **2.** $x^2 - xy + xz + y^2 + yz + z^2.$

3. $a^2 + ab - a + b^2 + b + 1.$ **4.** $9c^2 + 6cd - 3c + 4d^2 + 2d + 1.$

5. $x^2 + x + 1.$ **6.** $a^2 - ab + b^2.$

7. $x^3 + ax^2 + a^2x + a^3.$ **8.** $x^3 - ax^2 + a^2x - a^3.$

9. $1 - a + a^2.$ **10.** $8 - 4b + 2b^2 - b^3.$

11. $a^4 - a^3b + a^2b^2 - ab^3 + b^4$. **12.** $a^4 + a^3b + a^2b^2 + ab^3 + b^4$.

13. $x^2 - 3xy + 9y^2$.

14. $a^5 - a^4x + a^3x^2 - a^2x^3 + ax^4 - x^5$.

15. $c^6 - c^5 + c^4 - c^3 + c^2 - c + 1$. **16.** $x^4 - x^2y^2 + y^4$.

17. The terms $2a^3b^2$ and $7a^3b^2$ are like; all the terms with the exception of $11a^4$ are homogeneous and of the fifth degree.

18. $7a^5bc^2 - a^5b^2c + 12ab^3c^4 - a^2b^5c$.

19. The product is $24x^4 - 46x^3y + 9x^2y^2 + 13xy^3 - 3y^4$.

20. $9a^4 - 12a^3b - 2a^2b^2 + 4ab^3 + b^4$.

21. $25a^6 - 9a^4b^2 + 6a^3b^3 - a^2b^4$.

22. Dividend $x^3 - y^3 - z^3 - 3xyz$; divisor $x - y - z$;
quotient $x^2 + xy + xz + y^2 - yz + z^2$.

IX. a. Page 56.

1. 3. **2.** 5. **3.** 2. **4.** 1.
5. 11. **6.** 3. **7.** –3. **8.** 2.
9. $4\frac{1}{2}$. **10.** $3\frac{1}{2}$. **11.** –5. **12.** 0.
13. $4\frac{1}{3}$. **14.** 0. **15.** $\frac{1}{11}$. **16.** –9.
17. 0. **18.** $\frac{1}{2}$. **19.** $\frac{1}{3}$. **20.** 3.
21. 2. **22.** 7. **23.** 3. **24.** 2.
25. $4\frac{1}{2}$. **26.** 2. **27.** 5. **28.** $\frac{1}{2}$.
29. 3. **30.** $1\frac{1}{2}$. **31.** –2. **32.** $1\frac{2}{3}$.
33. 13. **34.** $10\frac{1}{2}$. **35.** 32. **36.** 5.
37. 7. **38.** 10. **39.** $1\frac{2}{3}$. **40.** 5.
41. 3. **42.** 9. **43.** 18. **44.** –6.
45. 7. **46.** –8. **47.** 5. **48.** 6.
49. $-\frac{3}{2}$. **50.** $\frac{2}{3}$.

IX. b. Page 59.

1. 3. **2.** –13. **3.** 1. **4.** 2.
5. 2. **6.** $5\frac{1}{2}$. **7.** 11. **8.** 12.
9. –8. **10.** $\frac{1}{3}$. **11.** $\frac{2}{5}$. **12.** $-\frac{11}{2}$.

13. 10. **14.** –6. **15.** $-\frac{1}{7}$. **16.** 1.

17. 7. **18.** $\frac{1}{7}$. **19.** 17. **20.** –10.

21. 6 . **22.** 9. **23.** 2. **24.** –4 .

25. 11. **26.** 15. **27.** 8. **28.** 7.

29. –4 . **30.** $3\frac{1}{7}$. **31.** $2\frac{1}{2}$. **32.** –16.

33. 9. **34.** 60. **35.** 12. **36.** $-\frac{11}{13}$.

37. $1\frac{2}{5}$. **38.** 3.

X. a. Page 62.

1. $x-5$. **2.** $15-y$. **3.** $7-a$. **4.** $b-6$.

5. $\frac{a}{5}$. **6.** $\frac{3}{a}$. **7.** $3x$. **8.** $4x$.

9. $x-10$. **10.** $75-x$. **11.** x. **12.** $\frac{p}{m}$.

13. $\frac{2y}{x}$. **14.** $a-8$. **15.** $x+6$. **16.** $30-y$.

17. $4x$. **18.** $15x$. **19.** $2ax$. **20.** x^5.

21. p^x. **22.** Rs. ny. **23.** Rs. $\frac{x}{n}$. **24.** $\frac{y}{2}$.

25. $\frac{100y}{x}$. **26.** $10n$. **27.** $(500-n)$. **28.** $\frac{1500}{p}$.

29. $\frac{5000}{y}$. **30.** $\frac{100y}{x}$. **31.** $100p-36x$. **32.** $\frac{100x}{y}$.

33. $\frac{x}{10}$. **34.** pq km. **35.** $\frac{m}{n}$ km. **36.** $\frac{y}{x}$.

X. b. Page 64.

1. $a, a+1, a+2$. **2.** $b-3, b-2, b-1, b$.

3. $c-2, c-1, c, c+1, c+2$. **4.** $2n+1$.

5. $2n-2$. **6.** $(2x-1)(2x+1)(2x+3)$.

7. $x-15$ years. **8.** $n-x$ years.

9. $y-2x$ years. **10.** $40+x$ years.

11. $2x-10$ years. **12.** $(100m-75)=(n+75)$.

13. $(13+x)=4(25-x)$. **14.** $\frac{30}{x}$.

15. $\frac{50x}{y}$. **16.** $\frac{pq}{15}$ hours.

17. $\frac{120x}{7}$ km.
18. $\left(\frac{x}{30}+\frac{y}{10}\right)$ hours.
19. $\frac{5x^2}{y}$.
20. $\frac{q}{pr}$ days.
21. $ab + c$.
22. $x - yz$.
23. $\frac{m-r}{n}$.
24. $\frac{9n}{10}$.
25. $100(x - y) + z - 25$.
26. $52x - \frac{3}{25}y$.
27. Rs. 6.
28. $\frac{z}{xy}$.

XI. a. Page 67.

1. 9.
2. 3.
3. 4.
4. 12,15.
5. 11. 19.
6. 5, 15.
7. 6, 13.
8. 9, 17.
9. *A* Rs. 35, *B* Rs. 65.
10. *A* Rs. 12, *B* Rs. 20, *C* Rs. 34.
11. *A* Rs. 21, *B* Rs. 17, *C* Rs. 34.
12. *A* Rs. 31, *B* Rs. 23, *C* Rs. 19.
13. 30, 45.
14. 112, 10.
15. 6. 16. 4.
17. 6. 18. 56.
19. 18, 30.
20. *A* Rs. 48, *B* Rs. 24, *C* Rs. 4.
21. *A* Rs. 219, *B* Rs. 73, *C* Rs. 219.
22. *A* 48, *B* 32 years.
23. *A* 42, *B* 50, *C* 18 years.
24. 7, 8.
25. 15, 16.

XI. b. Page 69.

1. Rs. 2.
2. Rs. 7.
3. *A* Rs. 27, *B* Rs. 1.
4. *A* Rs. 27, *B* Rs. 9.
5. Father 32 years, Son 8 years.
6. *A* 45 years , *B* 25 years.
7. 25 years.
8. *A* 20 years, *B* 10 years.
9. Father 33 years, Son 9 years.
10. 20 men, 30 women.
11. Rs. 1.10.
12. 24 kg, 26 kg.
13. 22 days.
14. Rs. 25.7.
15. 18×50 paise, 45×25 paise and 180×10 paise.
16. Coffee 12 kg, Tea 12 kg.
17. Rs. 688.
18. 168, 72.
19. 48 years, 9 years, 3 years.
20. *A* Rs. 25, *B* Rs.17, *C* Rs. 28.
21. 36.
22. 360.
23. 128.
24. Tea Rs. 4, sugar 30 paise.
25. Port Rs. 32. 20, Sherry Rs. 21.40.
26. 18 boys, 5 girls,
27. Rs.11. 16.
28. *A* Rs. 2.21, *B* Rs. 4.42, *C* Rs.6.63.
29. 98 paise.
30. Coffee Rs. 2.50, Tea Rs. 3.
31. Flour 3, Wheat 10 bags.
32. 1.75 kg.
33. 6 carts, 14 wagons.
34. 6 hectares 84 ares.
35. 47 ares 96 centiares, 23 ares. 72 centiares.

XII. a. Page 73.

1. ab^2. 2. x^2y^2. 3. bc. 4. $2x$.
5. a^2bc. 6. $3ab$. 7. $2xy$. 8. $5y^3$.
9. $6abc^2$. 10. $7x^2yz^3$. 11. $2a$. 12. xy.
13. $7b$. 14. $5x^2$. 15. $17xyz$. 16. ab^2c^2.

XII. b. Page 74.

1. $3xy^3z$. 2. a^2b^4c. 3. $6x^3y^2z$.
4. $12a^2bx^4$. 5. $20a^4b^2c^3$. 6. $4abxy$.
7. lmn. 8. $6x^2y^2z^2$. 9. $12xyz$.
10. $7p^2q^3r$. 11. $75x^2yz^3$. 12. $63a^2b^3c$.
13. $162a^3b^5$. 14. $210a^2c^5x^6yz$. 15. $60a^2b^3x^2y$.
16. $216p^3q^3r^4$.

In each of the following examples, the H. C. F. stands first, the L. C. M. second.

17. $ab, 12a^4b^3$. 18. $5x^2y, 15x^3y^2z^5$.
19. $2a^2, 8a^4b^3c^7$. 20. $19xy, 228ax^2y^2z^7$.
21. $16a^4bc, 96a^7b^3c^5$. 22. $p, 102m^3np^4$.
23. $7, 1176a^4b^4c^3$. 24. $11x, 3630a^2b^5cx^4y^3z^7$.

XII. c. Page 75.

1. $\frac{1}{2b}$. 2. $\frac{a}{3b}$. 3. $\frac{c}{3b}$. 4. $\frac{1}{4ac}$.
5. $\frac{z^2}{x^2y^2}$. 6. $\frac{4n}{5l}$. 7. $\frac{2y^3}{3xz^3}$. 8. $\frac{3a^2}{4b^2c}$.
9. $\frac{5abc}{6}$. 10. $\frac{a^2z^3}{3y^2}$. 11. $\frac{5y^2}{12x^2}$. 12. $\frac{mnp}{5}$.
13. $\frac{3p^2m^2}{5k}$. 14. $\frac{3a}{5bx^2}$. 15. $\frac{8a^2c^2}{11z}$. 16. $\frac{z}{5x}$.

XII. d. Page 76.

1. $\frac{ab^2}{y}$. 2. $\frac{2c}{b^2d^2}$. 3. $\frac{xz^2}{6ay^2}$. 4. cx^2.
5. $\frac{c}{a}$. 6. $\frac{5c}{2b^2}$. 7. $\frac{3acd^2}{2b^3}$. 8. $\frac{pqxy}{6b}$.
9. $3a^2$. 10. $\frac{y}{2}$. 11. $\frac{18ax^5z}{5b^3}$. 12. $\frac{7b}{4a}$.

XII. e. Page 77.

1. $\frac{x, 4x}{2a}$. 2. $\frac{3y, 2y}{3b}$. 3. $\frac{15a, 8a}{10c}$.
4. $\frac{x, 2ay}{2y}$. 5. $\frac{5m, 12m}{20n}$. 6. $\frac{x^2, 6ay}{3xy}$.
7. $\frac{ab, 2a}{b^2}$. 8. $\frac{xy, 9x}{3y^2}$. 9. $\frac{ay, bx, by}{by}$.
10. $\frac{a^2, b^2, 2a^2b}{ab}$. 11. $\frac{6ab, a^2, b^2}{2ab}$. 12. $\frac{a, b, c}{abc}$.
13. $\frac{3az, 2bx, 6cy}{6xyz}$. 14. $\frac{m^2q, n^2q, mnp}{mnq}$.

XII. f. Page 78.

1. $\frac{5a}{6}$. 2. $\frac{7b}{12}$. 3. $\frac{x}{20}$.
4. $\frac{5y}{6}$. 5. $\frac{6a-5b}{30}$. 6. $\frac{5m-4n}{40}$.
7. $\frac{3p+q}{21}$. 8. $\frac{5a-3b}{12}$. 9. $\frac{ay+bx}{xy}$.
10. $\frac{bx-ay}{by}$. 11. $\frac{6ab+4a}{9b}$. 12. $\frac{2ab-x}{6}$.
13. $\frac{5a}{24}$. 14. $\frac{5x}{4}$. 15. $\frac{az+2ax+3ay}{xyz}$.
16. $\frac{y}{30}$. 17. $\frac{2ab+a^2-b^2}{ab}$. 18. $\frac{aq^2+bpq-cp^2}{p^2q^2}$.
19. $\frac{a^3-x^3}{a^2}$. 20. $\frac{m^3-2n^3}{2m^2}$. 21. $\frac{a^2-3b^2}{b^2}$.
22. $\frac{k^6-p^6}{k^2}$. 23. $\frac{2dx-3xy}{2y^2}$. 24. $\frac{ab-2a^2}{2b^2}$.

XIII. a. Page 82.

1. $x = 13, y = 6$. 2. $x = 14, y = 9$.
3. $x = 1, y = 10$. 4. $x = 12, y = 12$.
5. $x = 3, y = -3$. 6. $x = 19, y = -6$.
7. $x = 5, y = 7$. 8. $x = 13, y = 1$.
9. $x = 1, y = 6$. 10. $x = 7, y = 4$.
11. $x = 3, y = -2$. 12. $x = 12, y = 5$.
13. $x = 5, y = 2$. 14. $x = 11, y = -8$.
15. $x = 2, y = -3$. 16. $x = \frac{108}{5}, y = \frac{144}{5}$.

17. $x = -4, y = 10.$
18. $x = 8, y = 3.$
19. $x = 1, y = -1.$
20. $x = 6, y = 5.$
21. $x = 9, y = -7.$
22. $x = 7, y = 8.$
23. $x = 9, y = 15.$
24. $x = -2, y = -3.$
25. $x = 7, y = 5.$
26. $x = 1, y = -1.$
27. $x = -3, y = 3.$
28. $x = 5, y = 6.$
29. $x = -5, y = -1.$
30. $x = -9, y = 5.$
31. $x = 3, y = -2.$
32. $x = 10, y = 7.$
33. $x = -5, y = 6.$

XIII. b. Page 84.

1. $x = 6, y = 8.$
2. $x = 2, y = 7.$
3. $x = 3, y = 5.$
4. $x = -10, y = 4.$
5. $x = -2, y = -3.$
6. $x = 5, y = -4.$
7. $x = 12, y = 15.$
8. $x = -1, y = -1.$
9. $x = 4, y = -6.$
10. $x = -3, y = -5.$
11. $x = 20, y = -4.$
12. $x = 0, y = 0.$
13. $x = 4, y = 5.$
14. $x = 4, y = -5.$
15. $x = 7, y = 8.$
16. $x = -3, y = -6.$
17. $x = -4, y = 4.$
18. $x = 20, y = -12.$
19. $x = 2, y = 3.$
20. $x = \frac{1}{4}, y = \frac{1}{5}.$
21. $x = 5, y = -\frac{1}{2}.$

XIII. c. Page 86.

1. $x = 1, y = 2, z = 5.$
2. $x = 6, y = 1, z = 1.$
3. $x = 4, y = 5. z = 6.$
4. $x = 6, y = 10, z = 9.$
5. $x = y = z = 3.$
6. $x = 5, y = -6, z = -7.$
7. $x = -2, y = 2, z = 2.$
8. $x = 4, y = -5, z = 8.$
9. $x = 20, y = -10, z = 1.$
10. $x = 7, y = -4, z = 3.$
11. $x = 2, y = -1, z = 5.$
12. $x = 0, y = 3, z = -4.$
13. $x = 7, y = 9, z = 5.$
14. $x = -6, y = -4, z = 8.$
15. $x = y = z = -6.$
16. $x = 4, y = 3, z = -2.$

XIV. Page 89.

1. 33, 21.
2. 74, 23.
3. 33, 18.
4. 55, 29.
5. Cow Rs. 221, sheep Rs.39.
6. Horse Rs. 312, Cow Rs.234.
7. *A* 37 years, *B* 24 years.

8. A 28 years, B 52 years.

9. $C\ 3\frac{3}{4}$ km., $D\ 4\frac{1}{2}$ km.

10. Train 31 km, Coach 7 km.

11. 18×50 paise, 23×25 paise.

12. 22×10 paise, 32×2 paise.

13. Wagon $2\frac{1}{2}$ tonnes, cart $1\frac{1}{2}$ tonnes.

14. Boy Rs. 3. 10, Girls Rs. 2.48.

15. 84.

16. 36.

17. 54.

18. 88.

19. 750×10 paise , 300×5 paise , 500×2 paise.

20. 30×50 paise, 20×25 paise, 20×5 paise.

21. Man Rs. 10, Woman Rs. 8, Boy Rs. 6, Girls Rs. 2.

22. Coffee Rs. 2.55, Sugar Rs.2.55.

23. $15 \times$ Rs. 1,81×25 paise.

24. Man Rs. 2.50, Woman Rs. 1.50.

25. Bag 1.15 kg, Box 2.325 kg.

26. 68. 5 ares, 70.8 ares.

27. 52 kg, 31.5 kg.

XV. a. Page 92.

1. a^4b^2.

2. $9a^2c^6$.

3. $25x^2y^4$.

4. $36b^6c^4$.

5. $16a^4b^2c^6$.

6. $9x^4y^{10}$.

7. $4a^4b^6c^2$.

8. $9d^2x^8$.

9. $\frac{a^4c^2}{b^2d^6}$.

10. $\frac{4x^2z^6}{y^4}$.

11. $\frac{9a^6}{16b^4}$.

12. $\frac{25}{49x^2y^4}$.

13. $\frac{64p^4q^{10}}{9}$.

14. $\frac{m^4n^{12}}{81x^2y^8}$.

15. $\frac{1}{16x^4y^2z^6}$.

16. $\frac{9p^2q^4r^6}{25a^4x^2}$.

17. $8x^3$.

18. $27a^3b^6$.

19. $64x^9$.

20. $-27a^6b^3$.

21. $-64x^9y^6$.

22. $-b^6c^3d^9$.

23. $-216y^{12}$.

24. $-64p^9q^{15}$.

25. $\frac{1}{p^{12}r^9}$.

26. $-\frac{8}{a^3b^6c^9}$.

27. $-\frac{27x^6}{64y^3z^9}$.

28. $-\frac{8x^9}{27}$.

29. a^4b^8.

30. $-x^{10}y^5$.

31. $64m^{12}n^{18}$.

32. $-x^{21}y^{14}$.

33. $\frac{1}{243a^{10}}$.

34. $\frac{16a^{12}x^4}{81b^4y^8}$.

35. $-\frac{a^{21}}{2187}$.

36. $\frac{64a^{12}}{729}$.

XV. b. Page 94.

1. $x^2 + 4xy + 4y^2$.
2. $x^2 - 4xy + 4y^2$.
3. $a^2 + 6ab + 9b^2$.
4. $4a^2 - 12ab + 9b^2$.
5. $9a^2 + 6ab + b^2$.
6. $x^2 - 10xy + 25y^2$.
7. $4m^2 + 28mn + 49n^2$.
8. $81 - 18x + x^2$.
9. $4 - 4ab + a^2b^2$.
10. $a^2b^2c^2 + 2abc + 1$.
11. $a^2b^2 - 2abcd + c^2d^2$.
12. $4a^2b^2 + 4abxy + x^2y^2$.
13. $1 - 2x^2 + x^4$.
14. $9 + 12pq + 4p^2q^2$.
15. $x^4 - 6x^3 + 9x^2$.
16. $4a^2 + 4a^2b + a^2b^2$.
17. $a^2 + b^2 + c^2 + 2ab - 2ac - 2bc$.
18. $a^2 + b^2 + c^2 - 2ab - 2ac + 2bc$.
19. $4a^2 + b^2 + c^2 + 4ab + 4ac + 2bc$.
20. $4x^2 + y^2 + z^2 - 4xy - 4xz + 2yz$.
21. $x^2 + 9y^2 + 4z^2 + 6xy - 4xz - 12yz$.
22. $x^4 + 2x^3 + 3x^2 + 2x + 1$.
23. $9x^2 + 4p^2 + q^2 + 12px - 6qx - 4pq$.
24. $1 - 4x - 2x^2 + 12x^3 + 9x^4$.
25. $4 - 12x + 13x^2 - 6x^3 + x^4$.
26. $x^2 + y^2 + a^2 + b^2 + 2xy + 2ax - 2bx + 2ay - 2by - 2ab$.
27. $m^2 + n^2 + p^2 + q^2 - 2mn + 2mp - 2mq - 2np + 2nq - 2pq$.
28. $4a^2 + 9b^2 + x^2 + 4y^2 + 12ab + 4ax - 8ay + 6bx - 12by - 4xy$.

XV. c. Page 94.

1. $p^3 + 3p^2q + 3pq^2 + q^3$.
2. $m^3 - 3m^2n + 3mn^2 - n^3$.
3. $a^3 - 6a^2b + 12ab^2 - 8b^3$.
4. $8c^3 + 12c^2d + 6cd^2 + d^3$.
5. $x^3 + 9x^2y + 27xy^2 + 27y^3$.
6. $x^3 + 3x^2yz + 3xy^2z^2 + y^3z^3$.
7. $8x^3y^3 - 12x^2y^2 + 6xy - 1$.
8. $125a^3 + 150a^2 + 60a + 8$.
9. $x^6 - 3x^4 + 3x^2 - 1$.
10. $8x^6 + 12x^4y^2 + 6x^2y^4 + y^6$.
11. $8a^9 - 36a^6b^3 + 54a^3b^6 - 27b^9$.
12. $64y^6 - 144y^4 + 108y^2 - 27$.

XVI. a. Page 96.

1. $3x^2y$.
2. $5a^3b^2$.
3. $7cd^3$.
4. a^3bc^8.
5. $6x^3y^{18}$.
6. $4x^4$.
7. x^2y^3z.
8. $3p^3q^6$.
9. $\frac{2x^3}{4a^2}$.
10. $\frac{a^{18}}{6}$.
11. $\frac{4x^{32}}{5}$.
12. $\frac{12}{a^6}$.

13. x^2y^3. 14. $-a^2b$. 15. $2x^9$.

16. $-3x^3$. 17. $-\frac{b^9}{3}$. 18. $\frac{2a^3b^4}{y^5}$.

19. $\frac{5a^3x^7}{3c^2}$. 20. $-\frac{4a^9b}{x^3}$. 21. xy^3.

22. a^4x^3. 23. $-x^4y^6$. 24. $2a^7$.

25. a^3b^2. 26. pq^3. 27. $-x^5y^8$.

28. $3xy^8$. 29. $2ab^2c^5$.

XVI. b. Page 99.

1. $a-4$. 2. $x+7$. 3. $8+3x$.

4. $5-3m$. 5. $6n^2-7$. 6. $9+8y^3$.

7. $x^3-3y^4z^4$. 8. $2ab^2-3c^5$. 9. $\frac{1}{2}x-3y^3$.

10. $\frac{3a}{b}+\frac{4c}{d}$. 11. $\frac{3a}{5b}-\frac{5b}{3a}$. 12. $\frac{4x^2}{7y}+\frac{7y^2}{4x}$.

13. $4x^2-4x+1$. 14. $5-3a+2a^2$. 15. $3a^4-2a^2-1$.

16. $5p^2-3p-11$. 17. $2x^2+2x-1$. 18. $6a^2-9a+10$.

19. $a+b-c$. 20. $yz-zx+xy$. 21. $a^2-a+\frac{1}{4}$.

22. $\frac{a}{3}-2x+\frac{x^2}{2}$. 23. $3m^2+\frac{1}{2}n+\frac{3}{4}$. 24. $3x^2-12x+2a$.

25. x^4-2x^3+3x-1. 26. $a-3b-c$. 27. $\frac{m^2}{n^2}-\frac{m}{n}+2$.

28. $\frac{3a}{b}-1-\frac{b}{a}$.

XVI. c. Page 102.

1. $a+4$. 2. $2x+1$. 3. $4x-3$.

4. $2p^2-3$. 5. $m-6$. 6. x^2+2y^2.

7. $1-c+c^2$. 8. $2+3m+m^2$. 9. $6-k+3k^2$.

10. $2y^2+4y-3$. 11. $4+4k+k^2$. 12. $x-2y-z$.

XVII. a. Page 103.

1. $x(x+a)$. 2. $a(2a-3)$. 3. $a^2(a-1)$.

4. $a^2(a-b)$. 5. $3m(m-2n)$. 6. $p^2(1+2q)$.

7. $x^2(x^3-5)$. 8. $y(y+x)$. 9. $5a^2(1-5b)$.

10. $12x(1+4xy)$. 11. $5c^3(2-5cd)$. 12. $27(1-6x)$.

13. $xy(xyz^2+3)$. 14. $17x(x-3)$. 15. $a(2a^2-a+1)$.

16. $3x(x^2 + 2a^2x - a^3)$.

17. $7p^2(1 - p + 2p^2)$.

18. $2b^2(2b^3 + 3a^2b - 1)$.

19. $xy(x^2y^2 - xy + 2)$.

20. $13a^3b^2(2b^3 + 3a)$.

XVII. b. Page 104.

1. $(x + y)(x + z)$.

2. $(x - z)(x + y)$.

3. $(a + 2)(a + b)$.

4. $(a + c)(a + 4)$.

5. $(a + x)(2 + x)$.

6. $(3 + p)(q - p)$.

7. $(a - b)(m - n)$.

8. $(a - y)(b - y)$.

9. $(p + r)(q - r)$.

10. $(2m + n)(x + y)$.

11. $(x - 2y)(a - b)$.

12. $(2a + 3b)(a - c)$.

13. $(a + b)(c^2 + 1)$.

14. $(c^2 - 2)(a - b)$.

15. $(a - 1)(a^2 + 1)$.

16. $(2x + 3)(x^2 + 1)$.

17. $(ax - by)(a + 2)$.

18. $(a + bc)(xy - z)$.

XVII. c. Page 106.

1. $(x + 1)(x + 2)$.

2. $(y + 2)(y + 3)$.

3. $(y + 3)(y + 4)$.

4. $(a - 1)(a - 2)$.

5. $(a - 2)(a - 4)$.

6. $(b - 3)(b - 2)$.

7. $(b + 6)(b + 7)$.

8. $(b - 5)(b - 8)$.

9. $(z - 9)(z - 4)$.

10. $(x - 8)(x - 7)$.

11. $(x - 9)(x - 6)$.

12. $(z + 11)(z + 4)$.

13. $(b - 6)(b - 6)$.

14. $(a + 7)(a + 8)$.

15. $(a - 9)(a - 3)$.

16. $(x + 5)(x + 4)$.

17. $(x - 9)(x - 1)$.

18. $(x - 8)(x - 8)$.

19. $(y - 17)(y - 6)$.

20. $(y - 19)(y - 5)$.

21. $(y + 27)(y + 27)$.

22. $(a + 3b)(a + 7b)$.

23. $(a + b)(a + 11b)$.

24. $(a - 11b)(a - 12b)$.

25. $(m^2 + 7)(m^2 + 1)$.

26. $(m^2 + 2n^2)(m^2 + 7n^2)$.

27. $(2 - x)(3 - x)$.

28. $(6 - a)(9 - a)$.

29. $(13 + y)(1 + y)$.

30. $(27 - a)(8 - a)$.

XVII. d. Page 107.

1. $(x + 2)(x - 1)$.

2. $(x - 3)(x + 2)$.

3. $(x - 5)(x + 4)$.

4. $(y - 2)(y + 6)$.

5. $(y + 7)(y - 3)$.

6. $(y - 9)(y + 4)$.

7. $(a + 11)(a - 3)$.

8. $(a - 15)(a + 2)$.

9. $(a+12)(a-11)$.
10. $(b-15)(b+3)$.
11. $(b+17)(b-3)$.
12. $(b+13)(b-3)$.
13. $(m-8)(m+7)$.
14. $(m+7)(m-12)$.
15. $(m-7)(m+8)$.
16. $(p+5)(p-13)$.
17. $(p-9)(p+12)$.
18. $(p-10)(p+11)$.
19. $(x-6)(x+8)$.
20. $(x-15)(x+8)$.
21. $(x-12)(x+11)$.
22. $(y^2-3)(y^2+16)$.
23. $(y-8x)(y+12x)$.
24. $(y+14x)(y-7x)$.
25. $(a^2-8b^2)(a^2+9b^2)$.
26. $(a+16b)(a-15b)$.
27. $(2-a)(7+a)$.
28. $(5-b)(7+b)$.
29. $(8-b)(12+b)$.
30. $(9-b)(8+b)$.

XVII. e. Page 109.

1. $(2a+1)(a+1)$.
2. $(3a+1)(a+1)$.
3. $(4a+1)(a+1)$.
4. $(a+2)(2a+1)$.
5. $(a+3)(3a+1)$.
6. $(2a+1)(a+3)$.
7. $(5a+2)(a+1)$.
8. $(2a+5)(a+2)$.
9. $(2a+3)(a+2)$.
10. $(x+4)(2x+1)$.
11. $(x+3)(2x-1)$.
12. $(x+2)(3x-1)$.
13. $(y+1)(3y-2)$.
14. $(y-3)(3y+2)$.
15. $(y+5)(2y-1)$.
16. $(2b+1)(b-3)$.
17. $(2b+3)(3b-1)$.
18. $(b+3)(2b-5)$.
19. $(4m-3)(m+2)$.
20. $(2m-3)(2m+1)$.
21. $(3m+1)(2m-3)$.
22. $(2x-5y)(2x+y)$.
23. $(3x-2y)(2x-y)$.
24. $(6x-y)(x-2y)$.
25. $(3a-2b)(4a-3b)$.
26. $(3a+2b)(2a-3b)$.
27. $(6a-b)(a+6b)$.
28. $(2+y)(1-2y)$.
29. $(3-y)(1+8y)$.
30. $(4-y)(2+5y)$.
31. $(4-3x)(1+5x)$.
32. $(2-3a)(3-2a)$.
33. $(7+b)(4-5b)$.

XVII. f. Page 111.

1. $(a+3)(a-3)$.
2. $(a+7)(a-7)$.
3. $(a+9)(a-9)$.
4. $(a+10)(a-10)$.
5. $(x+5)(x-5)$.
6. $(x+12)(x-12)$.
7. $(8+x)(8-x)$.
8. $(9+2x)(9-2x)$.
9. $(2y+1)(2y-1)$.
10. $(y+3a)(y-3a)$.

11. $(2y + 5)(2y - 5)$.
12. $(3y + 7x)(3y - 7x)$.
13. $(2m + 9)(2m - 9)$.
14. $(6a + 1)(6a - 1)$.
15. $(k + 8l)(k - 8l)$.
16. $(3a + 5b)(3a - 5b)$.
17. $(11 + 4y)(11 - 4y)$.
18. $(11 + 6x)(11 - 6x)$.
19. $(5 + c^2)(5 - c^2)$.
20. $(ab + xy)(ab - xy)$.
21. $(7a^2 + 10b)(7a^2 - 10b)$.
22. $(8x + 7z)(8x - 7z)$.
23. $(2pq + 9)(2pq - 9)$.
24. $(a^2b^2c + 3)(a^2b^2c - 3)$.
25. $(x^3 + 2a^2)(x^3 - 2a^2)$.
26. $(x^2 + 5z^2)(x^2 - 5z^2)$.
27. $(a^5 + pq^2)(a^5 - pq^2)$.
28. $(4a^8 + 3b^3)(4a^8 - 3b^3)$.
29. $(5x^6 + 2)(5x^6 - 2)$.
30. $(a^3b^4c^2 + 3x)(a^3b^4c^2 - 3x)$.
31. $70 \times 8 = 560$.
32. $100 \times 2 = 200$.
33. $1002 \times 1000 = 1002000$.
34. $100 \times 64 = 6400$.
35. $500 \times 50 = 25000$.
36. $1000 \times 872 = 872000$.

XVII. g. Page 112.

1. $(a-b)(a^2 + ab + b^2)$.
2. $(a+b)(a^2 - ab + b^2)$.
3. $(1 + x)(1 - x + x^2)$.
4. $(1 - y)(1 + y + y^2)$.
5. $(2x + 1)(4x^2 - 2x + 1)$.
6. $(x - 2z)(x^2 + 2xz + 4z^2)$.
7. $(a + 3b)(a^2 - 3ab + 9b^2)$.
8. $(xy - 1)(x^2y^2 + xy + 1)$.
9. $(1 - 2a)(1 + 2a + 4a^2)$.
10. $(b - 2)(b^2 + 2b + 4)$.
11. $(3 + x)(9 - 3x + x^2)$.
12. $(4 - p)(16 + 4p + p^2)$.
13. $(5a + 1)(25a^2 - 5a + 1)$.
14. $(6 - b)(36 + 6b + b^2)$.
15. $(xy + 7)(x^2y^2 - 7xy + 49)$.
16. $(10x + 1)(100x^2 - 10x + 1)$.
17. $(8a - 1)(64a^2 + 8a + 1)$.
18. $(abc - 3)(a^2b^2c^2 + 3abc + 9)$.
19. $(2x - 7)(4x^2 + 14x + 49)$.
20. $(x + 6y)(x^2 - 6xy + 36y^2)$.
21. $(x^2 - 3z)(x^4 + 3x^2z + 9z^2)$.
22. $(m - 10n^2)(m^2 + 10mn^2 + 100n^4)$.
23. $(a - 9b)(a^2 + 9ab + 81b^2)$.
24. $(5a^2 + 8b)(25a^4 - 40a^2b + 64b^2)$.

XVII. h. Page 114.

1. $(x + y + z)(x + y - z)$.
2. $(x - y + z)(x - y - z)$.
3. $(a + 2b + c)(a + 2b - c)$.
4. $(a + 3c + 1)(a + 3c - 1)$.
5. $(2x - 1 + a)(2x - 1 - a)$.
6. $(a + b + c)(a - b - c)$.
7. $(2a + b - 1)(2a - b + 1)$.
8. $(3 + a + x)(3 - a - x)$.

APPENDIX ON EASY GRAPHS

[*Arts.* 1-7 *may be read as soon as the student has had sufficient practice in substitutions involving negative quantities. Arts.* 8-21 *may be read after Simultaneous Equations of the first degree. Subsequent articles should be postponed until the student is acquainted with quadratic equations.*]

1. DEFINITION. Any expression which involves a variable quantity x, and whose value depends on that of x, is called a **function of x**.

Thus the expression $3x + 8$ will have different values if different values are substituted for x, and is called a function of x of the first degree.

Similarly, $2x^2 + 6x - 7$, $x^3 - 2x + 1$ are functions of x of the second and third degrees respectively.

2. The words "function of x" are often briefly, expressed by the symbol $f(x)$. If two quantities x and y are connected by a relation $y = f(x)$, by substituting a series of numerical values for x we can obtain a corresponding series of values for $f(x)$, that is, for y.

Since in such a case the values of y *depend upon* the different values selected for x, it is sometimes convenient to call x the **independent variable**, and y the **dependent variable**.

3. Consider the function $x(9 - x^2)$, and let its value be represented by y; so that $y = x(9 - x^2)$.

Then, when $x = 0$, $y = 0 \times 9 = 0$,

when $x = 1$, $y = 1 \times 8 = 8$,

when $x = 2$, $y = 2 \times 5 = 10$,

when $x = 3$, $y = 3 \times 0 = 0$,

when $x = 4$, $y = 4 \times (-7) = -28$,

and so on.

By proceeding in this way we can find as many values of the function as we please. But we are often not so much concerned with the actual values which a function assumes for different values of the variable as with *the way in which the value of the function changes.* These variations can be very conveniently represented by a **graphical** method which we shall now explain.

4. Two straight lines XOX′, YOY′, are taken intersecting at right angles in *O*, thus dividing the plane of the paper into four spaces XOY, YOX′, X′OY′, Y′OX, which are known as the first, second, third and fourth quadrants respectively.

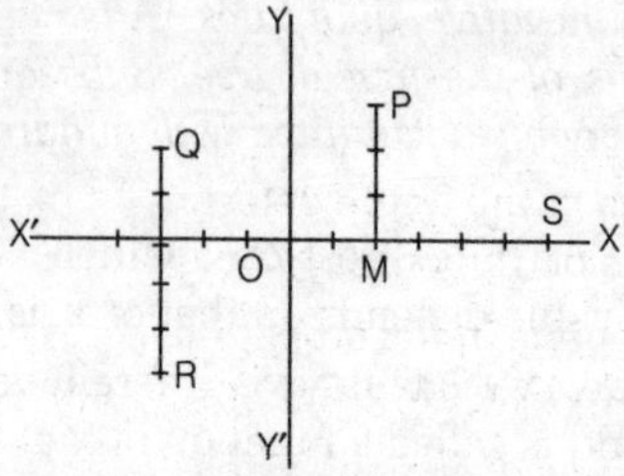

FIG. 1

The lines X′OX, YOY′ are usually drawn horizontally and vertically; they are taken as lines of reference and are known as the **axis of x and y** respectively. The point O is called the **origin**. Values of *x* are measured from O along the axis of *x*, according to some convenient scale of measurement, and are called **abscissae**, *positive* values being drawn to the right of O along OX, and *negative* values to the *left* of O along OX′.

Values of *y* are drawn parallel to the, axis of *y*, from the ends of the corresponding abscissae, and are called **ordinates**. These are *positive* when drawn *above* X′ X, *negative* when drawn *below* X′ X.

5. Suppose $y=3$, when $x=2$. To express this relation graphically we first mark off OM, 2 units in length, along OX; then at M we draw MP, 3 units in length, perpendicular to OX and above it. Thus the position of a point P is determined. Similarly, any pair of corresponding values of *x* and *y* will determine a point relatively to the axes.

6. The abscissa and ordinate of a point taken together are known as its **coordinates**. A point whose coordinates are *x* and *y* is briefly spoken of as "the point (x, y)."

The process of marking the position of a point, by means of its coordinates is known as **plotting the point**.

Example. Plot the points
(i) $(-3, 2)$; (ii) $(-3, -4)$; (iii) $(6, 0)$.

(i) We proceed as in Art. 5, but since *x* is negative we first take 3 units to the *left* of O. That is along OX′, then 2 units at right angles to OX′ and above it. The resulting point Q is in the second quadrant. See Fig. 1.

(ii) Here we may briefly describe the process as follows. Take 3 steps to the *left*, then 4 *down*; the resulting point **R** is in the third quadrant.

(iii) Take 6 steps to the *right*, then *no step! either up or down* from OX. Thus the resulting point **S** is on the axis of **X**.

Note. The coordinates of the origin are $(0, 0)$.

7. In practice it is convenient to use squared paper. Two intersecting lines should be chosen as axes, and slightly thickened to aid the eye, then one or more of the length-divisions may be taken as the linear unit.

We shall generally use paper ruled to tenths of a centimetre but for greater clearness a larger scale will sometimes be adopted.

Example 1. Plot the points (5, 2), (−3, 2), (−3, − 4), (5, − 4) on squared paper.

Find the area of the figure determined by these points, assuming the divisions on the paper to be quarters of a centimetre.

Taking the points in the order given, it is easily seen that they are represented by P, Q, R, S in Fig. 2, and that they form a rectangle which contains 48 squares. Each of these is $\frac{1}{16}$ or .0625 part of a *square* centimetre. Thus the area of the rectangle is 3 square centimetres.

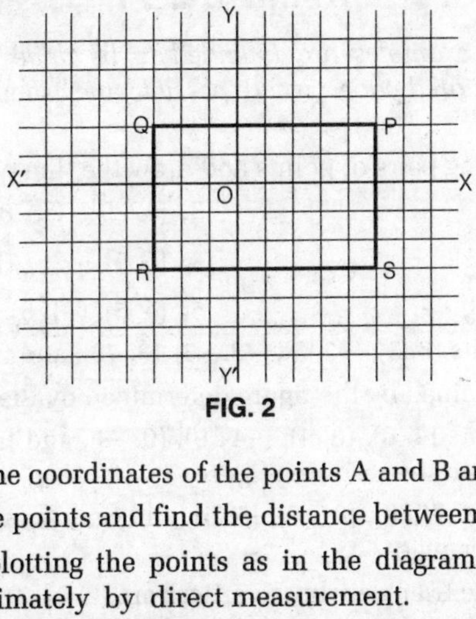

FIG. 2

Example 2. The coordinates of the points A and B are (7, 8) and (−5, 3): plot the points and find the distance between them.

After plotting the points as in the diagram, we may find AB approximately by direct measurement.

Or we may proceed thus:

Draw through B a line part to XX′ to meet the ordinate of A at C. Then ACB is a rt. angled Δ in which BC = 12, and AC = 5.

Now $\mathbf{AB^2 = BC^2 + AC^2}$

$$= 12^2 + 5^2$$

$$= 144 + 25$$

$$= 169$$

∴ AB = 13.

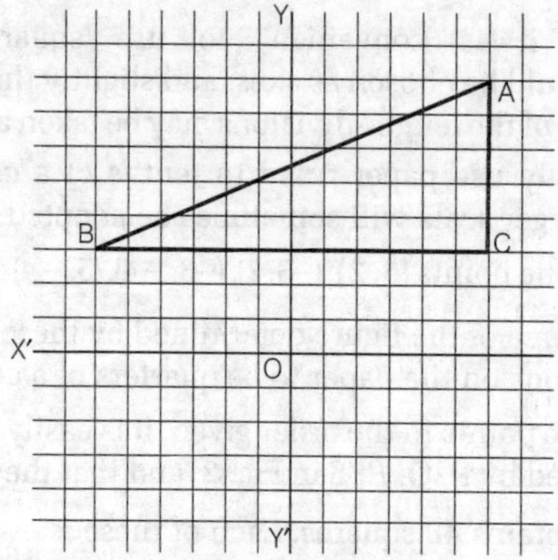

FIG. 3

EXAMPLES I

[*The following examples are intended to be done mainly by actual measurement on squared paper; where possible, they should also be verified by calculation.*]

Plot the following pairs of points and draw the line which joins them:

1. (3, 0), (0, 6). **2.** (–2, 0), (0, – 8).

3. (3, – 8), (–2, 6). **4.** (5, 5), (–2, –2).

5. (–2, 6), (1, –3). **6.** (4, 5), (–1, 5).

7. Plot the points (3, 3), (–3, 3), (–3, – 3), (3, –3), and find the number of squares contained by the figure determined by these points.

8. Plot the points (4, 0), (0, 4), (–4 , 0), (0, –4), and find the number of units of area in the resulting figure.

9. Plot the points (0, 0), (0, 10), (5, 5), and find the number of units of area in the triangle.

10. Shew that the triangle whose vertices are (0, 0), (0, 6), (4, 3) contains 12 units of area. Shew also that the points (0, 0), (0, 6), (4, 8) determine a triangle of the same area.

11. Plot the points (5, 6), (–5, 6), (5, –6), (–5, – 6). If each unit is supposed to represent one millimetre, find the area of the figure in square centimetres.

12. Plot the points (1, 3), (–3, – 9), and shew that they lie on a line passing through the origin. Name the coordinates of other points on this line.

13. Plot the following points, and shew experimentally that each set lie in one straight line.

(i) (9, 7), (0, 0), (–9, –7); (ii) (–9, 7), (0, 0), (9, –7).

Explain these results theoretically.

14. Plot the following pairs of points; join the points in each case, and measure the coordinates of the mid-point of the joining line.

(i) (4, 3), (12, 7); (ii) (5, 4), (15, 16).

Shew *why* in each case the coordinates of the mid-point are respectively *half the sum of the abscissae* and *half the sum of the ordinates* of the given points.

15. Plot the following pairs of points; and find the coordinates of the mid-point of their joining lines.

(i) (0,0), (8, 10); (ii) (8, 0), (0, 10);

(iii) (0, 0), (−8, −10); (iv) (−8, 0), (0, −10).

16. Plot the following points, and calculate their distances from the origin.

(i) (15, 8); (ii) (−15, −8);

(iii) (2.4 cm, .7 cm); (iv) (−.7 cm, 2.4 cm).

Check your results by measurement.

17. Plot the following pairs of points, and in each case calculate the distance between them.

(i) (4, 0), (0, 3); (ii) (9, 8), (5, 5);

(iii) (15, 0), (0, 8); (iv) (10, 4), (−5, 12);

(v) (20, 12), (−15, 0); (vi) (20, 9), (−15, −3).

Verify your calculation by measurement.

18. Plot the eight points (0, 5), (3, 4), (5, 0), (4, −3), (−5, 0), (0, −5), (−4, 3), (−4, −3), and shew that they are all equidistant from the origin.

19. Plot the two following series of points;

(i) (5, 0), (5, 2), (5, 5), (5, −1), (5, −4);

(ii) (−4, 8), (−1, 8), (0, 8), (3, 8), (6, 8).

Shew that they lie on two lines respectively parallel to the axis of y, and the axis of x. Find the coordinates of the point in which they intersect.

20. Shew that the points (−3, 2), (3, 10), (7, 2) are the angular points of an isosceles triangle. Calculate and measure the lengths of the equal sides.

21. Explain by a diagram why the distances between the following pairs of points are all equal.

(i) $(a, 0)$, $(0, b)$; (ii) $(b, 0)$, $(0, a)$; (iii) $(0, 0)$, (a, b).

22. Draw the straight lines joining

(i) $(a, 0)$ and $(0, a)$; (ii) $(0, 0)$ and (a, a);

and prove that these lines bisect each other at right angles.

23. Find the perimeter of the triangle whose vertices are the points (7, 0), (0, 24), (−10, 0).

24. Draw the figure whose angular points are given by $(0, -3)$, $(8, 3)$ $(-4, 8)$, $(-4, 3)$, $(0, 0)$.

Find the lengths of its sides, taking the points in the above order.

25. Plot the points $(13, 0)$, $(0, -13)$, $(12, 5)$, $(-12, 5)$, $(-13, 0)$, $(-5, -12)$, $(5, -12)$. Find their locus, (i) by measurement, (ii) by calculation.

26. Plot the points $(2, 2)$, $(-3, -3)$, $(4, 4)$, $(-5, -5)$, shewing that they all lie on a certain line through the origin. Conversely, shew that for *every* point on this line the abscissa and ordinate are equal.

27. If $y = 2x + 10$, find the values of y when x has the values 0, 1, 3, -2, -5. Plot the five points determined by these values, and shew experimentally that they lie on a straight line. Where does the line meet the axes?

28. By giving different values to x find by trial a series of points whose coordinates satisfy the equation $2y = 5x$. Shew that they all lie on a straight line through the origin.

[*It will be convenient here to take two-tenths of at centimetre as the unit.*]

Graph of a Function

8. Let $f(x)$ represent a function of x, and let its value be denoted by y. If we give to x a series of numerical values we get a corresponding series of values for y. If these are set off as abscissae and ordinates respectively, we plot a succession of points. If *all* such points were plotted we should arrive at a line, straight or curved, which is known as the **graph** of the *function* $f(x)$, or the **graph** of the *equation* $y = f(x)$. Thus the graph of the *function* $2x - 5$ is the same as the graph of the *equation* $y = 2x - 5$.

The variation of the *function* for different values of the variable x is exhibited by the variation of the *ordinates* as we pass from point to point.

In practice a few points carefully plotted will usually enable us to draw the graph with sufficient accuracy.

9. The student who has worked intelligently through the preceding examples will have acquired for himself some useful preliminary notions which will be of service in the examples on simple graphs which we are about to give. In particular, before proceeding further he should satisfy himself with regard to the following statements:

(i) The coordinates of the origin are $(0, 0)$.

(ii) For every point on the axis of x the value of y is 0.

Thus the graph of $y = 0$ *is the axis of* x.

(iii) For every point on the axis of y the value of x is 0.

Thus the graph of $x = 0$ *is the axis of* y.

(iv) The graph of all points which have the same abscissa is a line parallel to the axis of y. Thus on page 6, Ex. 19, (i) gives a line parallel to the axis of y, and this line is the graph of $x = 5$.

(v) The graph of all points which have the same ordinate is a line parallel to the axis of x. Thus on page 6, Ex. 19, (ii) gives a line parallel to the axis of x, and this line is the graph of $y = 8$.

(vi) The distance of any point **P** (x, y) from the origin is given by **OP**$^2 = x^2 + y^2$. (See Ex. 18, p. 5.)

Example 1. Plot the graph of $y = x$.

When $x = 0$, $y = 0$; *thus the origin is one point on the graph.*

Also, when $x = 1, 2, 3, \ldots -1, -2, -3, \ldots$

$y = 1, 2, 3, \ldots -1, -2, -3, \ldots$.

Thus the graph passes through O, and represents a series of points each of which has its ordinate equal to its abscissa, and is clearly represented by the straight line **POP′** in Fig. 4.

Example 2. Plot the graph of $y = x + 3$.

Arrange the values of x and y as follows:

x	3	2	1	**0**	−1	−2	**−3**	...
y	6	5	4	**3**	2	1	**0**	...

By joining these points we obtain a line **MN** parallel to that in **Example 1.**

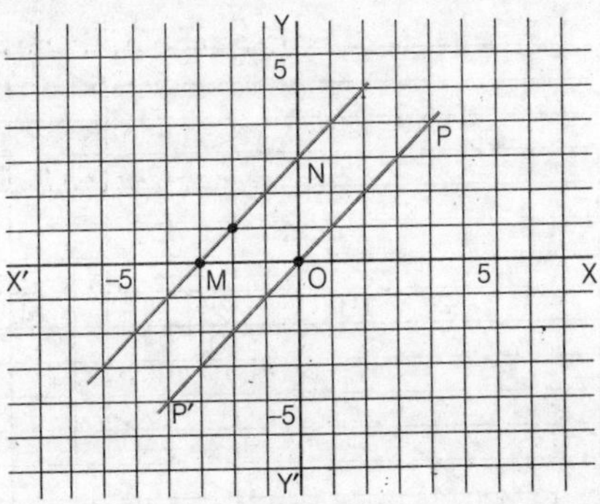

FIG. 4

The results printed in bold type should be specially noted and compared with the graph. They shew that the distances **ON, OM** (usually called the *intercepts on the axes*) are obtained by separately putting $x = 0$, $y = 0$ in the equation of the graph.

Note. By observing that in Example 2 each ordinate is 3 units greater than the corresponding ordinate in Example 1, the graph of $y = x + 3$ may be obtained from that of $y = x$ by simply producing each ordinate 3 units in the positive direction.

In like manner the equations

$$y = x + 5,\ y = x - 5$$

represent two parallel lines on opposite sides of $y = x$ and equidistant from it, as the student may easily verify for himself.

Example 3. Plot the graphs represented by the equations:

(i) $3y = 2x$; (ii) $3y = 2x + 4$;
(iii) $3y = 2x - 5$.

First put the equations in the equivalent forms:

(i) $y = \frac{2x}{3}$; (ii) $y = \frac{2x}{3} + \frac{4}{3}$;

(iii) $y = \frac{2x}{3} - \frac{5}{3}$;

and in each case find values of y corresponding to

$$x = -3, -2, -1, 0, 1, 2, 3.$$

For example, in (i) we have the following values of y:

$$y = -2, -\frac{4}{3}, -\frac{2}{3}, 0, \frac{2}{3}, \frac{4}{3}, 2.$$

In plotting the corresponding points it will be found convenient to take *three* divisions of the paper as our unit.

The graphs will be found to be as in Fig. 5.

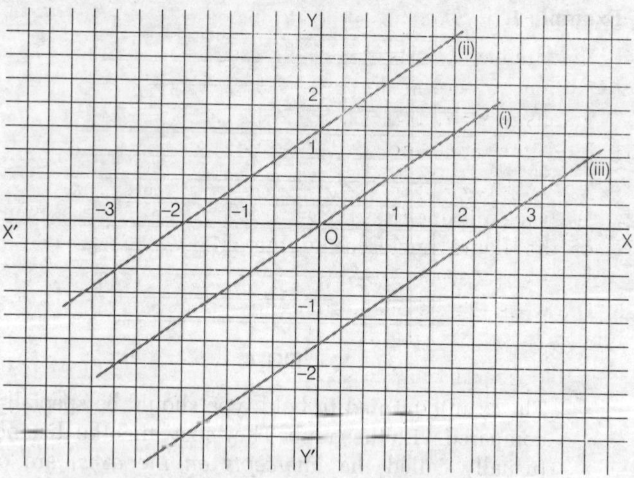

FIG. 5

Each graph should be verified in detail by the student.

EXAMPLES II

[*Examples 1-18 are arranged in groups of three; each group should be represented on the same diagram so as to exhibit clearly the position of the three graphs relatively to each other.*]

Plot the graphs represented by the following equations:

1. $y = 5x$. **2.** $y = 5x - 4$.

3. $y = 5x + 6$. **4.** $y = -3x$.

5. $y = -3x + 3$. **6.** $y = -3x - 2$.

7. $y + x = 0$. **8.** $y + x = 8$.

9. $y + 4 = x$. **10.** $4x = 3y$.

11. $3y = 4x + 6$. **12.** $4y + 3x = 8$.

13. $x - 5 = 0$. **14.** $y - 6 = 0$.

15. $5y = 6x$. **16.** $3x + 4y = 10$.

17. $4x + y = 9$. **18.** $5x - 2y = 8$.

19. Shew by careful drawing that the three last graphs have a common point whose coordinates are 2, 1.

20. Shew by careful drawing that the equations

$x + y = 10$, $y = x - 4$

represent two straight lines at right angles.

21. Draw on the same axes the graphs of $x = 5$, $x = 9$, $y = 3$, $y = 11$. Find the number of units of area enclosed by these lines.

22. Taking .5 cm as the unit of length, find the area included between the graphs of $x = 7$, $x = -3$, $y = -2$, $y = 8$.

23. Find the area included by the graphs of $y = x + 6$, $y = x - 6$, $y = -x + 6$, $y = -x - 6$.

24. With one millimetre as linear unit, find in square centimetres the area of the figure enclosed by the graphs of $y = 2x + 8$, $y = 2x - 8$, $y = -2x + 8$, $y = -2x - 8$.

25. Draw the graphs of the following equations: $x + y = 5$, $2x - y = 10$, $2x + 3y = -30$, $3y - x = 15$.

If the paper is ruled to quarters of a centimetre, shew that the graphs include an area of 9.375 sq cm.

10. The student should now be prepared for the following statements:

(i) For all numerical values of a the equation $y = ax$ represents a straight line through the origin.

If a is positive x and y have the same sign, and the line lies in the first and third quadrants; if a is negative x and y have opposite signs, and the line lies in the second and fourth quadrants.

In either case a is called the **slope** of the line.

(ii) For all numerical values of a and b the equation $y = ax + b$ represents a line parallel to $y = ax$, and cutting off an intercept b from the axis of y.

The graph of $y = ax + b$ is fixed in position as long as a and b retain the same values.

If a alone is altered, the line will have a different direction but will still cut the axis of y at the same distance (b) from the origin.

If b alone is altered, the line will still be parallel to $y = ax$, but will cut the axis of y at a different distance from the origin, further or nearer according as b is greater or less.

Since the values a and b fix the position of the line we are considering in any one piece of work, they are called the **constants** of the equation.

Note. The *slope* of $y = ax + b$ is the same as that of $y = ax$.

(iii) From the way in which the plotted points are determined from an equation, it follows that the graph passes through all points whose coordinates satisfy the equation, and through no other points.

11. Since every equation involving x and y only in the first degree can be reduced to one of the forms $y = ax$, $y = ax + b$, it follows that *every simple equation connecting two variables represents a straight line*. For this reason an expression of the form $ax + b$ is said to be a **linear function** of x, and an equation such as $y = ax + b$ or $ax + by + c = 0$, is said to be a **linear equation**.

Example. Shew that the points (3, –4), (9, 4), (12, 8) lie on a straight line, and find its equation. Assume $y = ax + b$ as the equation of the line. If it passes through the first two points given, their coordinates must satisfy this equation.

Substituting $x = 3$, $y = -4$, we have $-4 = 3a + b$ ... (i)

Again, substituting $x = 9$, $y = 4$, we have $4 = 9a + b$ ... (ii)

By solving equations (i) and (ii) we obtain $a = \frac{4}{3}$, $b = -8$.

Hence $y = \frac{4}{3}x - 8$, or $4x - 3y = 24$, is the equation of the line passing through the first two points. Since $x = 12$, $y = 8$ satisfies this equation, the line also passes through (12, 8). This example may be verified graphically by plotting the line which joins *any two* of the points and showing that it passes through the third.

12. Since a straight line can always be drawn when *any* two points on it are known, in drawing a *linear* graph only two points need be plotted. The points where the line meets the axes can be readily found by putting $y = 0$, $x = 0$, successively in the equation, and these two points will always suffice, though they are not always the best to select.

Example. Draw the graph of $4x - 3y = 13$.

If we find the intercepts on the axes we have

when $y = 0$, $x = -\frac{13}{4}$ (intercept on the x-axis),

and when $x = 0$, $y = -\frac{13}{3}$ (intercept on the y-axis).

As both the these value involve fractions of the unit, it would be difficult to draw the line with sufficient accuracy.

In such a case it is better to find by trial *integral* values of x and y which satisfy the equation.

Thus when $x = 1$, $y = -3$, and when $y = 1$, $x = 4$.

The graph can now be drawn by joining the points $(1, -3)$, $(4, 1)$.

Application to Simultaneous Equations

13. When there is only one simple equation connecting x and y, it is possible to find as many pairs of values of x and y as we please which satisfy the given equation. We now see that this is equivalent to saying that we may find as many points as we please on any given straight line. If, however, we have two *simultaneous* equations between x and y, there can only be one pair of values which will satisfy both equations. This is equivalent to saying that two straight lines can have only one common point.

Example. Solve graphically the equations:

(i) $3y - x = 6$, (ii) $3x + 5y = 38$.

In (i) the intercepts on the axes are -6, 2. Thus the line is found by joining **P**$(-6, 0)$ and **P′** $(0, 2)$.

In (ii) when $x = 1$, $y = 7$, and when $y = 1$, $x = 11$.

Thus the line is found by joining **Q** $(1, 7)$ and **Q′** $(11, 1)$.

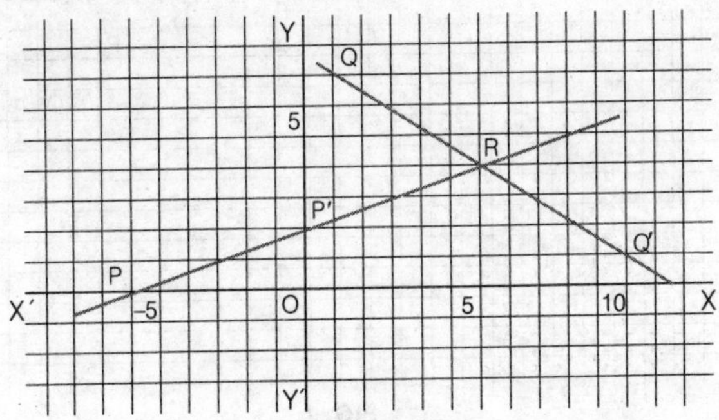

FIG. 6

It is seen from the diagram that these lines intersect at the point **R** whose coordinates are 6, 4. Thus the solution of the given equations is $x = 6$, $y = 4$.

The student should verify this result by solving the equations algebraically by any of the methods applicable to simultaneous equations.

14. It will now be seen that the process of solving two linear simultaneous equations is equivalent to finding the coordinates of the point at which their graphs meet.

Example. Draw the graphs of

(i) $5x + 6y = 60$, (ii) $6y - x = 24$, (iii) $2x - y = r$;

and shew that they represent three lines which meet in a point.

In (i) when $y = 0$, $x = 12$; when $x = 0$, $y = 10$.

Thus the intercepts on the axes are 12 and 10, and the graph is the line **PP′**.

In (ii) when $x = 0$, $y = 4$; when $x = 12$, $y = 6$, and the graph is the line joining **Q**(0, 4) to **Q′** (12, 6).

In (iii) when $x = 0$, $y = -7$; when $x = 8$, $y = 9$ and the graph is the line joining **R**(0, −7) to **R′** (8, 9).

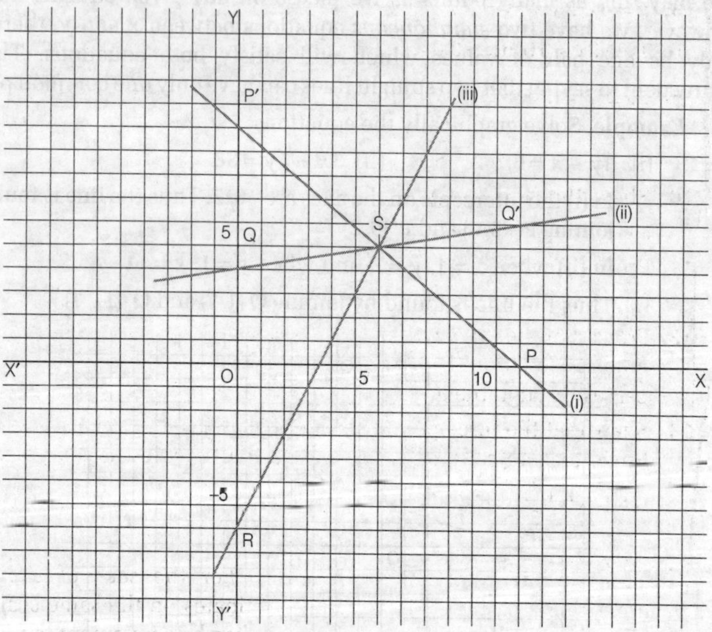

FIG. 7

From the diagram it is evident that these three lines all pass through the point **S** whose coordinates are 6, 5.

15. Two simultaneous equations lead to no finite solution if they are inconsistent with each other. For example, the equations

$$x + 3y = 2, 3x + 9y = 8$$

are inconsistent, for the second equation can be written $x + 3y = 2\frac{2}{3}$, which is clearly inconsistent with $x + 3y = 2$. The graphs of these two equations will be found to be two parallel straight lines which have no finite point of intersection.

Again, two simultaneous equations must be independent. The equations $4x + 3y = 1, 16x + 12y = 4$

are not independent, for the second can be deduced from the first by multiplying throughout by 4. Thus *any pair of values* which will satisfy one equation will satisfy the other. Graphically these two equations represent two coincident straight lines which of course have an unlimited number of common points.

EXAMPLES III

Solve the following equations graphically:

1. $y = 2x + 3, y + x = 6$.

2. $y = 3x + 4, y = x + 8$.

3. $y = 4x, 2x + y = 18$.

4. $2x - y = 8, 4x + 3y = 6$.

5. $3x + 2y = 16, 5x - 3y = 14$.

6. $6y - 5x = 18, 4x = 3y$.

7. $2x + y = 0, y = \frac{4}{3}(x + 5)$.

8. $2x - y = 3, 3x - 5y = 15$.

9. $2y = 5x + 15, 3y - 4x = 12$.

10. Shew that the straight lines given by the equations $9y = 5x + 65$, $5x + 2y + 10 = 0$, $x + 3y = 11$ meet in a point. Find its coordinates.

11. Prove by graphical representation that the three points (3, 0), (2, 7), (4, –7) lie on a straight line. Where does this line cut the axis of y?

12. Prove that the three points (1, 1), (–3, 4), (5, –2) lie on a straight line. Find its equation. Draw the graph of this equation, shewing that it passes through the given points.

13. Shew that the three points (3, 2), (8, 8), (–2, –4) lie on a straight line. Prove algebraically and graphically that it cuts the axis of x at a distance $1\frac{1}{3}$ from the origin.

16. Measurement on Different Scales. For the sake of simplicity we have hitherto measured abscissae and ordinates on the same scale, but there is no necessity for so doing, and it will often be convenient to measure the variables on different scales suggested by the particular conditions of the question.

For example, in drawing the graph of $y = 11x + 6$,

when x has the values $-2, -1, 0, 1, 2, 3$,

the corresponding values of y are $-16, -5, 6, 17, 28, 39$.

Thus some of the ordinates are much larger than the abscissae, and rapidly increase as x increases.

On plotting these points with x and y measured on the same scale, it will be found that with a small unit the graph is inconveniently placed with regard to the axes. If a larger unit is employed the graph requires a diagram of inconvenient size.

[The student should prove this for himself experimentally.]

The inconvenience can be obviated by measuring the values of y on a considerably smaller scale than those of x.

For example, let us take $\frac{1}{8}$ of a centimetre as unit for y and 2.5 cm as unit for x; then the graph of $y = 11x + 6$ will be as in Fig. 8, in which the line has been drawn by joining the points (0, 6), (2, 28).

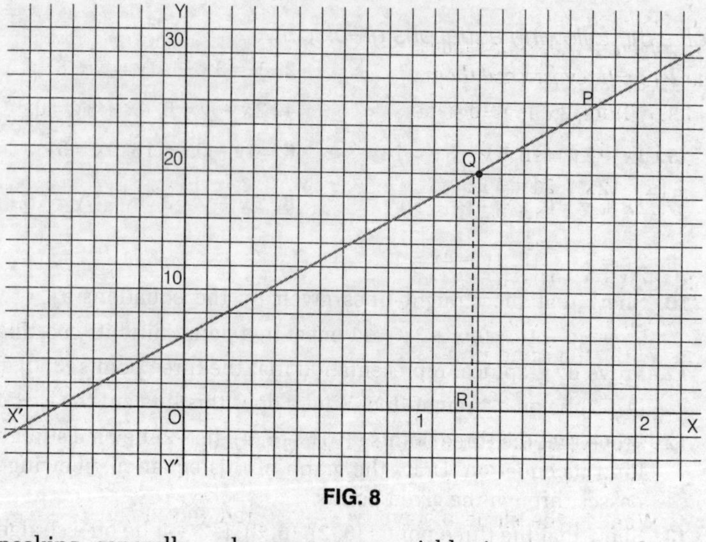

FIG. 8

Speaking generally, whenever one variable increases much more rapidly than the other, a small unit should be chosen for the rapidly increasing variable and a large one for the other.

17. When a graph has been accurately drawn from plotted points, it can be used to *read off* (without calculation) corresponding values of the variables at intermediate points. Or if one coordinate of a point on the graph is known the other can be found by measurement. Sometimes, of course, results so obtained will only be approximate, but, as will be seen later, some of the most valuable results of graphical methods are arrived at in this way. The process is known as **interpolation.**

Example. From the graph of the expression $11x + 6$, find its value when $x = 1.8$. Also find the value of x which will make the expression equal to 20.

Put $y = 11x + 6$, then the graph is that given in Fig. 8. Now we see that $x = 1.8$ at the point **P**, and here $y = 26$, nearly,

Again, $y = 20$ at the point **Q**; and $x =$ **OR** $= 1.28$, approximately. In obtaining this last result we observe that **OR** is greater than 1.2 and less than 1.3, and we mentally divide the tenth in which **R** falls into *ten* equal parts (*i.e.* into *hundredths of the unit*) and judge as nearly as possible how many of these hundredths are to be added to 1.2.

EXAMPLES IV

[*In some of the following Examples the scales are specified; in others the student is left to select suitable units for himself. When two or more equations are involved in the same piece of work, their graphs must all be drawn on the same scale. In every case the units employed should be marked on the axes.*]

1. By finding the intercepts on the axes draw the graphs of

(i) $15x + 20y = 6$;

(ii) $12x + 21y = 14$.

In (i) take 1 inch for unit, and in (ii) take six-tenths of an inch as unit. In each case explain why the unit is convenient.

2. Solve $y = 10x + 8$, $7x + y = 25$ graphically.

[Unit for x, one inch; for y, one-tenth of an inch.]

3. With the same units as in Ex. 2 draw the graph of the function $\frac{36 - 5x}{3}$. From the graph find the value of the function when $x = 1.8$; also find for what value of x the function becomes equal to 8.

4. On one diagram draw the graphs of $y = 5x + 11$, $10x - 2y = 15$,

What is the slope of these graphs? Find the length of the y-axis intercepted between them.

5. Draw the graphs of the equations: $3.4x + 5y = 17$, $x - y = 0.8$, $y - 0.5x = 0.45$; and shew that they all pass through one point.

6. Draw the triangle whose sides are represented by the equations : $3y - x = 9$, $x + 7y = 11$, $3x + y = 13$; and find the coordinates of the vertices.

7. With three centimetres as unit draw the triangle whose sides are given by the following equations, and find its vertices, $10y + 2x = 31$, $y = 3.5x$, $5y - 2x = 6.5$.

8. I want a ready way of finding approximately 0.866 of any number up to 10. Justify the following construction. Join the origin to a point **P** whose coordinates are 10 and 8.66 (three centimetres being taken as unit); then the ordinate of any point on **OP** is 0.866 of the corresponding abscissa. Read off from the diagram,

0.866 of 3, 0.866 of 6.5, 0.866 of 4.8, and $\frac{1}{0.866}$ of 5.

18. The last example gives a simple illustration of a graph used as a "ready reckoner." We shall now work two other examples of this kind.

Example 1. Given that 5.5 kilograms are roughly equal to 12.125 pounds, shew graphically how to express any number of pounds in kilograms. Express $7\frac{1}{2}$ lbs. in kilograms, and $4\frac{1}{4}$ kilograms in pounds.

Let y kilograms be equal to x pounds, then evidently we have $y = \frac{5.5}{12.125}x$, which is the equation of a straight line *through the origin*. Hence measuring pounds horizontally and kilograms vertically the required graph is obtained at once by joining the origin to the point whose coordinates are 12.125 and 5.5.

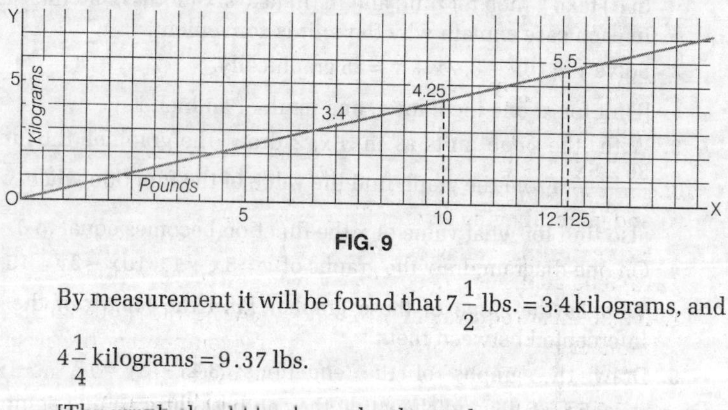

FIG. 9

By measurement it will be found that $7\frac{1}{2}$ lbs. $= 3.4$ kilograms, and $4\frac{1}{4}$ kilograms $= 9.37$ lbs.

[The graph should be drawn by the student on a larger scale.]

Example 2. The expenses of a school are partly constant and partly proportional to the number of boys. The expenses were ₹6500 for 105 boys, and ₹ 7420 for 128. Draw graph *a* to represent the expenses for any number of boys; find the expenses for 115 boys, and the number of boys that can be maintained at a cost of ₹7100.

If the total expenses for x boys are represented by ₹ y, the variable part may be denoted by ₹ ax, and the constant part by ₹ b. Hence x and y satisfy a linear equation $y = ax + b$, where a and b are constant quantities. Hence the graph is a straight line.

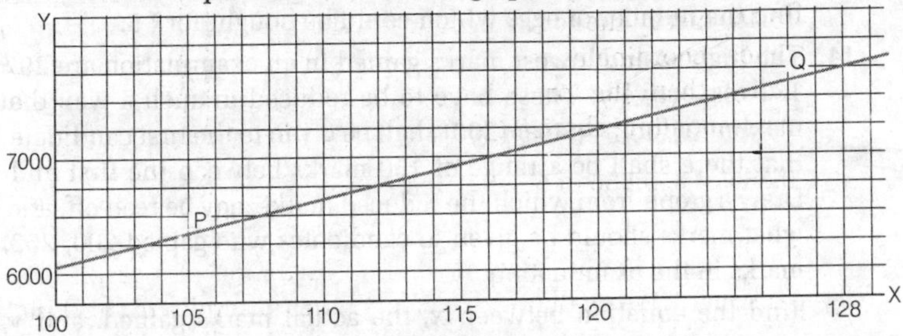

FIG. 10

As the numbers are large, it will be convenient if we begin measuring ordinates at 6000, and abscissae at 100. This enables us to bring the requisite portion of the graph into a smaller compass. When $x = 105$, $y = 6500$; and when $x = 128$, $y = 7420$. Thus two points **P** and **Q** are found, and the line **PQ** is the required graph.

By measurement we find that when $x = 115$, $y = 6900$; and that when $y = 7100$, $y = 120$. Thus the required answers are ₹ 6900, and 120 boys.

EXAMPLES IV (*Continued*)

9. Given that 6.01 yards = 5.5 metres, draw the graph shewing the equivalent of any number of yards when expressed in metres. Shew that 22.2 yards = 20.3 metres, approximately.

10. Draw a graph shewing the relation between equal weights in grains and grams, having given that 18.1 grains = 1.17 grams.

Express (i) 3.5 grams in grains.

(ii) 3.09 grains as a decimal of a gram.

11. If 3.26 in. are equivalent to 8.28 cm, shew how to find graphically the number of inches corresponding to a given number of centimetres. Obtain the number of inches in a metre, and the number of centimetres in a yard. Find the equation to the graph.

12. The highest marks gained in an examination were 136, and these are to be raised so that the maximum is 200. Shew how this may be done by means of a graph, and read off, to the nearest integer, the final marks of candidates who scored 61 and 49 respectively.

13. A man buys 100 eggs for ₹ 3.75 and has to pay ₹ 1.25 for carriage. He wishes to sell them so as to gain 15 per cent, on his whole outlay. Draw a graph to shew to the nearest paise the selling price of any number of eggs up to 100, and read off the price of 65. From the graph find the number of eggs which could be bought for ₹ 5.

14. The highest and lowest marks gained in an examination are 297 and 132 respectively. These have to be reduced in such a way that the maximum for the paper (200) shall be given to the first candidate, and that there shall be a range of 150 marks between the first and last. Draw a graph from which the reduced marks may be read off, and find what marks should be given to candidates who gained 200, 262, 163 marks in the examination.

    Find the equation between x, the actual marks gained, and y, the corresponding marks when reduced.

15. For a certain book it costs, publisher Rs. 1000 to prepare the type and Re. 1 to print each copy. Find an expression for the total cost in rupees of x copies. Make a diagram on a scale of 3 cm to 1000 copies, and 3 cm to Rs. 1,000 to shew the total cost of any number of copies up to 5000. Read off the cost of 2500 copies, and the number of copies costing Rs. 5250.

19. In all the cases at present considered the graph has been a straight line obtained by first selecting values of x and y which satisfy *an equation of the first degree*, and then drawing a line so as to pass through the plotted points. The method is quite general, and it is easy to see that it may be applied when the variables are connected by an equation *which is not linear.* In such a case it will be found that a line drawn through the plotted points will take the form of some *curve* differing in shape according to the equation which connects the variables. Before discussing such cases we may observe that, whenever two variable quantities depend on each other so that a change in one produces a corresponding change in the other, we can draw a graph to exhibit their variations without knowing any algebraical relation between them, *provided that we are furnished with a sufficient number of corresponding values accurately determined.*

But we frequently have to deal with cases in which a limited number of corresponding values of two variables have been obtained by observation or experiment. In such cases the data may involve inaccuracies, and consequently the position of the plotted points cannot be absolutely relied on. Moreover, we cannot correct irregularities in the graph by plotting other points selected at discretion. One method of procedure is to join successive points by *straight* lines. The graph will then be represented by an irregular broken line, sometimes with abrupt changes of direction as we pass from point to point.

In cáses where no great accuracy of detail is required this simple method is often used to illustrate statistical results. A familiar instance is a Weather Chart giving the height of the barometer at equal intervals of time.

The chief disadvantage of this method is that, although it gives a general idea of the total change that has taken place between the plotted points, it furnishes no accurate information with regard to intermediate points.

Example. The readings of a thermometer taken at intervals of 2 hours beginning at 10 a.m. were 62.5°, 64°, 69.6°, 69°, 66.5°, 65.7°. Draw a chart to show the changes of temperature.

Measuring degrees vertically and hours horizontally, with the scales indicated on the diagram, we obtain the broken line **PQRSTV** shown in Fig. 11.

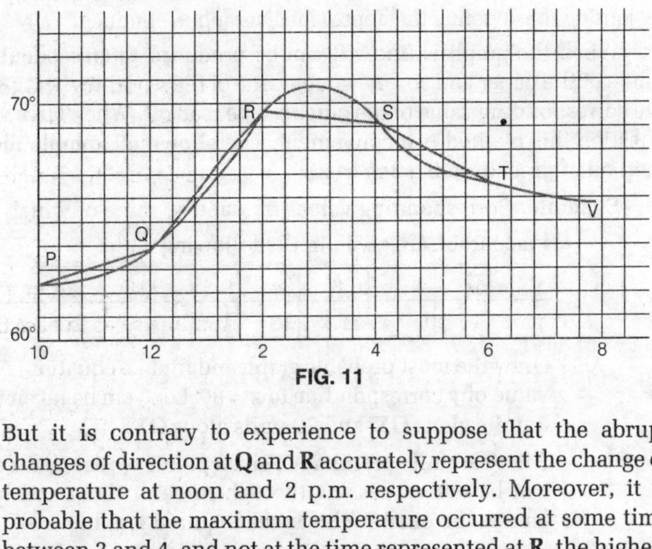

FIG. 11

But it is contrary to experience to suppose that the abrupt changes of direction at **Q** and **R** accurately represent the change of temperature at noon and 2 p.m. respectively. Moreover, it is probable that the maximum temperature occurred at some time between 2 and 4, and not at the time represented at **R**, the highest of the plotted points. Now if the chart had been obtained by means of a self-registering instrument, the graph (representing change from instant to instant instead of at long intervals) would probably have been somewhat like the continuous waving curve drawn through the points previously registered. From this it would appear that the maximum temperature occurred shortly before 3 p.m., and that **TV** (which represents a very gradual change) is the only portion of the broken line which records with any degree of accuracy the variation in temperature during two consecutive hours.

20. Although in the last example we were able to indicate the form of the curved line which from the nature of the case *seemed most probable*, it is evident that any number of curves can be drawn through a limited number of plotted points. In such a case the best plan is to draw a curve to lie as evenly as possible among the plotted points, passing through some perhaps, and with the rest fairly distributed on either side of the curve. As an aid to drawing an even continuous curve (usually called a *smooth* curve), a thin piece of wood or other flexible material may be bent into the requisite shape, and held in position while the line is drawn. A contrivance known as "Brooks' Flexible Curve" will often be found useful. When the plotted points lie approximately on a straight line, the simplest plan is to use a piece of tracing paper or celluloid on which a straight line has been drawn. When this has been placed in the right position the extremities can be marked on the squared paper, and by joining these points the approximate graph is obtained.

When the graph is linear it can be produced to any extent within the limits of the paper and so any value of one of the variables being determined, the corresponding value of the other can be read off. When large values are in question this method is inconvenient; the following Example illustrates the method of procedure in such cases.

Example. Corresponding values of x and y, some of which are slightly inaccurate, are given in the following table:

x	1	4	6.8	8	9.5	12	14.4
y	4	8	12.2	13	15.3	20	24.8

Draw the most probable graph and find its equation. Also find the value of y corresponding to $x = 80$. Let 3 cm be taken to represent 5 units along **OX**, and 20 units along **OY**.

After carefully plotting the given points we see that a straight line can be drawn passing through three of them and lying evenly among the others. This is the required graph.

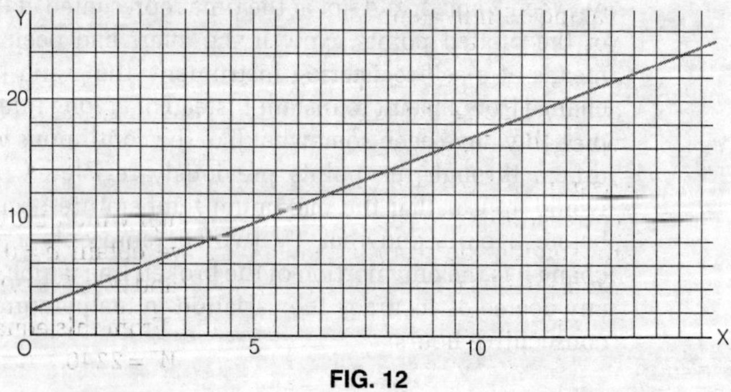

FIG. 12

Assuming $y = ax + b$ for its equation, we can find the values of a and b by substituting the coordinates of two points through which the line passes.

Thus putting $x = 4$, $y = 8$, we obtain $8 = 4a + b$;

again, when $x = 12$, $y = 20$, we have $20 = 12a + b$.

By solving these equations we obtain $a = 1.5$, $b = 2$.

Hence the equation of the graph is $y = 1.5x + 2$, and the coordinates of any number of points on the line may now be found by trial. Thus when $x = 80$, $y = 122$.

21. We shall now give an Example to illustrate a method common in the laboratory or workshop, the object being to determine the law connecting two variables when certain simultaneous values have been found by experiment or observation.

Example. In a certain machine P is the force in grammes weight required to raise a weight of W in grammes. The following corresponding values of P and W were obtained experimentally:

P	* 3.08	3.9	6.8	8.8	9.2	* 11	13.3
W	21	36.25	66.2	87.5	103.75	120	152.5

By plotting these values on squared paper draw the graph connecting P and W, and read off the value of P when $W = 70$. Also determine a linear law connecting P and W; find the force necessary to raise a weight of 310 gm and also the weight which could be raised by a force of 180.6 grammes weight.

As the page is too small to exhibit the graphical work on a convenient scale we shall merely indicate the steps of the solution, which is similar in detail to that of the last example.

Plot the values of P vertically and the values of W horizontally. Taking 15 mm as unit for P, and 3 mm as unit for W, it will be found that a straight line can be drawn through the points corresponding to the results marked with an asterisk, and lying evenly among the other points. From this graph we find that when $W = 70$, $P = 7$.

Assume $P = aW + b$, and substitute for P and W from the values corresponding to the two points through which the line passes. By solving the resulting equations we obtain $a = 0.08$, $b = 1.4$. Thus the linear equation connecting P and W is $P = 0.08W + 1.4$.

This is called the **Law of the Machine**. From this equation, when $W = 310$; $P = 26.2$ and when $P = 180.6$, $W = 2240$.

Thus a force of 26.2 gm wt. will raise a weight of 310 gm; and when a force of 180.6 gm wt. is applied the weight raised is 2 kg 240 gm.

[The student should verify all the details of the work for himself.]

Note. The equation of the graph is not only useful for determining results difficult to obtain graphically, but it can always be used to check results found by measurement.

Example 2. The following table gives statistics of the population of a certain country, where **P** is the number of millions at the beginning of each of the years specified.

Year	1830	1835	1840	1850	1860	1865	1870	1880
P	20	22.1	23.5	29.0	34.2	38.2	41.0	49.4

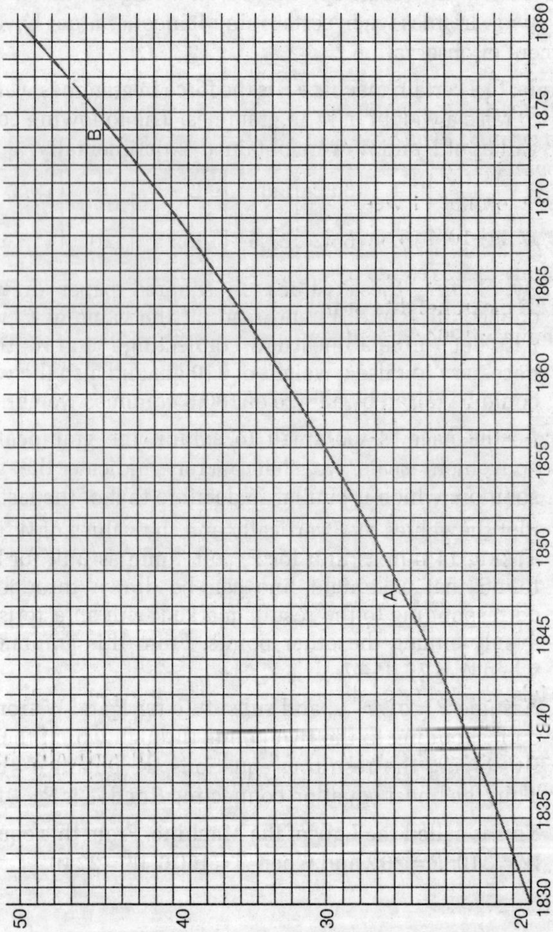

FIG. 13

Let t be the time in years from 1830. Plot the values of P vertically and those of t horizontally and exhibit the relation between P and t by a simple curve passing fairly evenly among the plotted points. Find what the population was at the beginning of the years 1848 and 1875.

Take 3 mm as unit in each case; also it will be convenient if we begin measuring abscissae at 1830, and ordinates at 20.

The graph is given in Fig. 13 on the back page; it will be seen that it passes exactly through the extreme points and lies evenly among the others.

The populations in 1848 and 1875, at the points **A** and **B** respectively, will be found to be 27.8 millions and 45.3 millions.

Examples V

[In Examples 1-4 the plotted points may be joined by straight lines. In other cases the graph is to be a straight line or smooth curve lying evenly among the plotted points.]

1. In a term of 11 weeks a boy's places in his Form were as follows:

8, 6, 11, 10, 9, 6, 6, 4, 2, 1, 1.

Shew these results by means of a graph.

2. The mean heights of the barometer in inches for the first 10 days of January 1904, recorded at the Royal Observatory, were as follows:

29.21, 29.12, 29.00, 29.25, 29.37, 29.26, 29.46, 28.83, 28.66, 28.76.

Exhibit these variations by means of a chart.

3. The highest and lowest prices of Consols for the years 1895 to 1904 were as follows:

Year	'95	'96	'97	'98	'99	'00	'01	'02	'03	'04
Highest	$108\frac{1}{8}$	$113\frac{7}{8}$	$113\frac{7}{8}$	$113\frac{3}{8}$	$111\frac{1}{2}$	$103\frac{1}{4}$	$97\frac{7}{8}$	$97\frac{7}{8}$	$93\frac{5}{8}$	$91\frac{1}{4}$
Lowest	$103\frac{1}{2}$	$105\frac{1}{8}$	$110\frac{5}{8}$	$106\frac{3}{4}$	$97\frac{3}{4}$	$96\frac{3}{4}$	91	$92\frac{5}{16}$	$86\frac{7}{8}$	85

Make a chart to shew these variations graphically on the same diagram.

[A convenient scale will be: 3 cm to Rs. 10 vertically, beginning at 85, and 1.5 cm to 1 year horizontally.]

4. Make a chart to shew the variations in French Imports and Exports (in billions of rupees), for the years 1896 to 1903 inclusive, from the following data:

Imports	50.1	53.3	51.3	53.0	53.6	51.2	50.6	49.9
Exports	20.6	19.5	20.5	22.2	25.8	23.7	22.2	23.1

5. Corresponding values of x and y are given in the following table:

x	3	6.5	12	14	21	28.6	31.5
y	4	4.8	6.7	7	8.5	11	11.5

Draw the most probable graph, and find its equation. Find the value of x when $y = 11.5$ and the value of y when $x = 10$.

6. Plot on squared paper the following measured values of x and y, and determine the most probable equation between x and y:

x	3	5	8.3	11	13	15.5	18.6	23	28
y	2	2.2	3.4	3.8	4	4.6	5.4	6.2	7.25

7. Corresponding values of x and y are given in the following table:

x	1	3.1	6	9.5	12.5	16	19	23
y	2	2.8	4.2	5.3	6.6	8.3	9	10.8

Supposing these values to involve errors of observation, draw the graph approximately, and determine the most probable equation between x and y. Find the correct value of y when $x = 19$, and the correct value of x when $y = 2.8$.

8. At different ages the mean after-lifetime ("expectation of life") of males, calculated on the death rates of 1871-1880, was given by the following table:

Age	6	10	14	18	22	26	27
Expectation	50.38	47.60	44.26	40.96	37.89	34.96	34.24

Draw a graph to shew the expectation of any male between the ages of 6 and 27, and from it determine the expectation of persons aged 12 and 20.

9. The following table gives approximately the circumferences of circles corresponding to different radii:

C	15.7	20.1	31.4	44	52.2
r	2.5	3.2	5	7	8.3

Plot the values on squared paper, and from the graph determine the diameter of a circle whose circumference is 12.1 cm and the circumference of a circle whose radius is 2.8 cm.

10. For a given temperature, C degrees on a Centigrade are equal to F degrees on a Fahrenheit thermometer. The following table gives a series of corresponding values of F and C:

C	– 10	– 5	0	5	10	15	25	40
F	14	23	32	41	50	59	77	104

Draw a graph to shew the Fahrenheit reading corresponding to a given Centigrade temperature and find the Fahrenheit readings corresponding to 12.5°C and 31°C.

By observing the form of the graph find the algebraical relation between F and C.

11. If W is the weight in grammes required to stretch an elastic string till its length is l centimetres, plot the following values of W and l.

W	2.5	3.75	6.25	7.5	10	11.25
l	8.5	8.7	9.1	9.3	9.7	9.9

From the graph determine the unstretched length of the string and the weight the string will support when its length is 12 centimetres.

12. In a certain machine P is the force in gm wt. required to raise a weight of W gm. The following corresponding values of P and W were obtained experimentally.

P	2.8	3.7	4.8	5.5	6.5	7.3	8	9.5	10.4	11.75
W	20	25	31.7	35.6	45	52.4	57.5	65	71	82.5

Draw the graph connecting P and W, and read off the value of P when $W = 60$. Also determine the law of the machine, and find from it the weight which could be raised by a force of 31.7 gm wt.

13. The keeper of a hotel finds that when he has G guests a day his total daily profit is ₹ R. If the following numbers are averages obtained by comparison of many days, accounts determine a simple relation between R and G.

G	21	27	29	32	35
R	– 1.8	2	3.2	4.5	6.6

For what numbers of guests would he just have no profit?

14. A man wishes to place in his catalogue a list of a certain class of fishing rods varying from 3 metres to 5.3 metres in length. Four sizes have been made at prices given in the following table:

300 cm	392 cm	478 cm	533 cm
Rs. 7.50	Rs. 11	Rs. 15.50	Rs. 19

Draw a graph to exhibit prices for rods of intermediate lengths, and from it determine the probable prices for rods of 333 cm and 422 cm in length.

15. In the Clergy Mutual Assurance Society the premium (Rs. P) to insure Rs. 1000 at different ages is given approximately by the following table:

Age	20	22	25	30	35	40	45	50	55
P	18	19	20	23	27	31	36	44	55

Illustrate the same statistics graphically and estimate to the nearest rupee the premiums for persons aged 34 and 43.

16. The connection between the areas of equilateral triangles and their bases (in corresponding square and linear units) is given by the following table:

Area	.43	1.73	3.90	6.93	10.82	15.59
Base	1	2	3	4	5	6

Illustrate these results graphically and determine the area of an equilateral triangle on a base of 2.4 metres.

17. A manufacturer has priced a certain set of lathes; the largest sells at Rs. 1760 and the smallest at Rs. 400. He wishes to increase his prices so that the largest will sell at Rs. 2000 and the smallest at Rs. 500. By means of a graph find an algebraical relation between the new price (P) and the old price (Q) and find to the nearest rupee the new prices of lathes originally priced at Rs. 1500, at Rs. 1255, and at Rs. 780.

18. The mean temperature on the first day of each month, on an average of 50 years, had the following values:

Jan. 1,	37°;	May 1,	50°;	Sept. 1,	59°;
Feb 1,	38°;	June 1,	57°;	Oct. 1,	54°;
Mar. 1,	40°;	July 1,	62°;	Nov. 1,	46°;
April 1,	45°;	Aug. 1,	62°;	Dec. 1,	41°;

Represent these variations by means of a smooth curve.

[The difference of length of different months may be neglected.]

19. The price in rupees of a standard weight of silver on January 1st in each of the ten years 1091-1900 was

2.70, 2.40, 2.16, 1.74, 1.80, 1.86, 1.68, 1.62, 1.62, 1.68.

Draw a smooth curve shewing its value approximately at any time during these ten years.

20. Work the following three exercises graphically as if in each case one alone were given, taking in each case the simplest supposition which the information permits.

(i) The total yearly expense in keeping a school of 100 boys is Rs. 21,000; what is the expense for 175 boys?

(ii) The expense is Rs. 21,000 for 100 boys, Rs. 30,500 for 200 boys; what is it for 175 boys?

(iii) The expenses in three cases are known as follows:

Rs. 21,000 for 100 boys, Rs. 26,500 for 150 boys, Rs. 30,500 for 200 boys. What is the probable expense for 175 boys?

21. A manufacturer wishes to stock a certain article in many sizes; at present he has five sizes made at the prices given below:

Length in cm	50	67.5	82.5	112.5	135
Price in rupees	8.25	10.86	15	26.25	36.36

Draw a graph to shew suitable prices for intermediate sizes, and find what the prices should be when the lengths are 75 cm and 115 cm.

22. The salary of a clerk is increased each year by a fixed sum. After 6 years' service his salary is raised to Rs. 1280, and after 15 years to Rs. 2000. Draw a graph from which his salary may be read off for any year, and determine from it (i) his initial salary, (ii) the salary he should receive for his 21st year.

23. By measuring time along **OX** (3 cm for 1 hour) and distance along **OY** (3 cm for 10 kilometres), shew that a line may be drawn from **O** through the points (1, 8), (2, 16), (3, 24), ... to indicate distance travelled towards **Y** in a specified time at 8 kilometres per hour.

A starts from London at noon at 8 kilometres per hour; two hours later *B* starts at 12 kilometres per hour. Find graphically at what time and at what distance from London *B* overtakes *A*. At what times will *A* and *B* be 8 kilometres apart? If *C* goes after *B*, starting at 3 pm at 15 kilometres per hour, find from the graphs

(i) The distance between *A*, *B* and *C* at 5 pm.

(ii) The time when *C* is 8 kilometres behind *B*.

24. With the same conditions as in Ex. 23, shew how to draw a line from **Y** to indicate distance travelled from **Y** towards **O** at 6 kilometres per hour.

If **O** and **Y** represent two towns 45 kilometres apart, and if *A* walks from *Y* to O at 6 kilometres per hour while *B* walks from **O** to **Y** at 4 kilometres per hour, both starting at noon, find graphically their time and place of meeting.

Also read off from the graphs

(i) the times when they are 15 kilometres apart;

(ii) *B*'s distance from **Y** at 6.15 pm.

25. At 8 a.m. *A* starts from **P** to ride to **Q** which is 48 kilometres distant. A the same time *B* sets out from **Q** to meet *A*. If *A* rides at 8 kilometre per hour, and rests half an hour at the end of every hour, while walks uniformly at 4 kilometres per hour, find graphically

(i) the time and place of meeting;

(ii) the distance between *A* and *B* at 11 am;

(iii) at what time they are 14 kilometres apart.

22. We shall now give some graphs of functions of higher degree tha the first.

Example. Draw the graph of $y = x^2$.

This is one of the most useful and interesting graphs the student wil meet with;

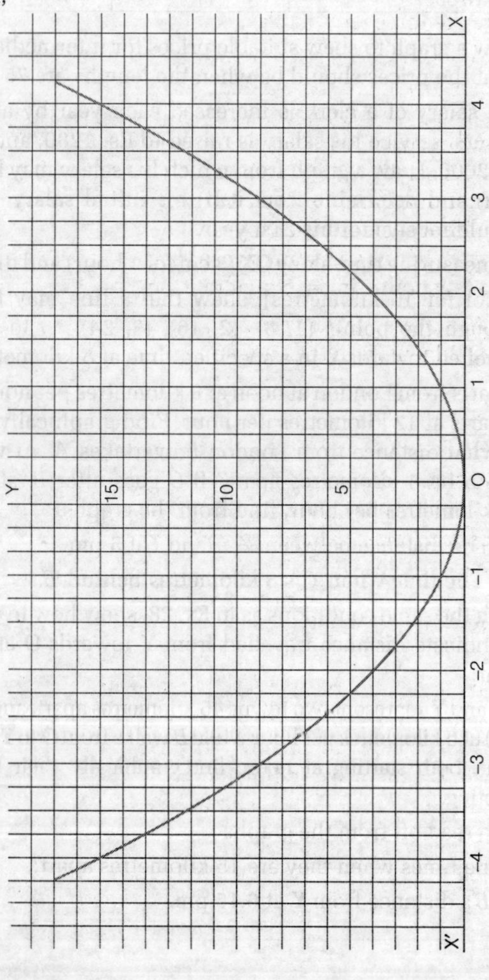

FIG. 14

it is, therefore, important to plot the curve carefully on a suitable scale.

Take 0.4 of an inch as unit for x, and 0.1 of an inch for y, then *positive* values of x and y may be tabulated as follows:

x	0	0.5	1	1.5	2	2.5	3	3.5	4	...
y	0	0.25	1	2.25	4	6.25	9	12.25	16	...

Now if we take the following *negative* values of x

$$-0.5, -1, -1.5, -2, -2.5, -3, -3.5, -4 \ldots$$

we shall obtain the same series of values for y as before.

If the points we have now determined are plotted and connected by a continuous line drawn freehand, we shall obtain the curve shewn in Fig. 14. This curve is called a **parabola**.

There are three facts to be specially noted in this example.

(i) Since from the equation we have $x = \pm\sqrt{y}$, it follows that for every value of the ordinate we have two values of the abscissa, *equal in magnitude and opposite in sign*. Hence the graph is symmetrical with respect to the axis of y; so that after plotting with care enough points to determine the form of the graph in the first quadrant, its form in the second quadrant can be inferred without actually plotting any points in this quadrant. At the same time, in this and similar cases beginners are recommended to plot a few points in each quadrant through which the graph passes.

(ii) We observe that all the plotted points lie above the axis of x. This is evident from the equation; for since x^2 must be positive for all values of x, every ordinate obtained from the equation $y = x^2$ must be positive.

In like manner the student may shew that the graph of $y = -x^2$ is a curve similar in every respect to that in Fig. 14, but lying entirely below the axis of x.

(iii) As the numerical value of x increases that of y increases very rapidly. Hence, as there is no limit to the values which may be selected for x, it follows that the curve extends upwards and outwards to an infinite distance in both the first and second quadrants.

23. Any equation of the form $y = ax^2$, where a is constant, will epresent a parabola. If a is a positive integer, the curve will be as in Fig. 14 out will rise more steeply in the direction of **OY**. If a is a positive fraction, we hall have a flatter curve, extending more rapidly to right and left of **OY**. If a s negative, the curve will lie below the x-axis, and will be steeper or flatter han the graph of $y = x^2$, according as a is greater or less than unity. In every ase the axis of x is a tangent to the curve at the origin.

24. We shall now discuss the graphs of some quadratic function of the form $ax^2 + bx + c$. It will be found that the curve is always a parabola differing in shape and position according to the values of a, b, c.

Example. Find the graph of $y = 2x + \frac{x^2}{4}$. Here the following arrangemen will be found convenient.

x	3	2	1	0	− 1	− 2	− 3	− 4	− 5	− 6	− 7	− 8	− 9
$2x$	6	4	2	0	− 2	− 4	− 6	− 8	− 10	− 12	− 14	− 16	− 18
$\frac{x^2}{4}$	2.25	1	.25	0	.25	1	2.25	4	6.25	9	12.25	16	20.25
y	8.25	5	2.25	0	− 1.75	− 3	− 3.75	− 4	− 3.75	− 3	− 1.75	0	2.25

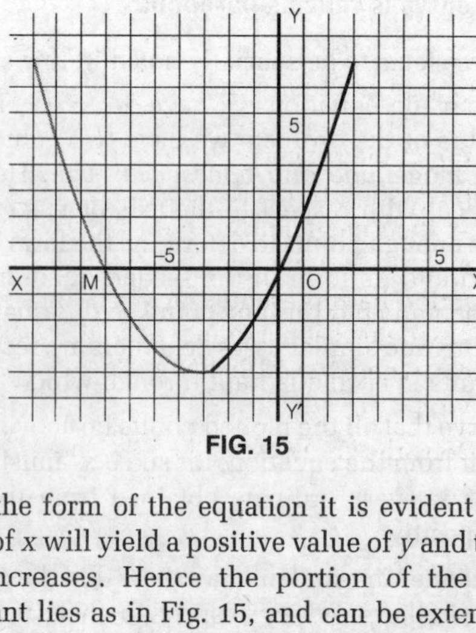

FIG. 15

From the form of the equation it is evident that every positive value of x will yield a positive value of y and that as x increases y also increases. Hence the portion of the curve in the first quadrant lies as in Fig. 15, and can be extended indefinitely in this quadrant. In the present case only two or three positive values of x and y need be plotted, but more attention must be paid to the results arising out of the negative values of x. It is found that the values of y are negative between $x = 0$ and $x = -8$ When $x = -8$, $y = 0$, and the curve crosses the x-axis; after this the values of y are positive.

25. In the last Example, since the value of $\frac{x^2}{4} + 2x$ is represented by y, the *expression* $\frac{x^2}{4} + 2x$ has a zero value when the ordinate is zero. Thus we can obtain the roots of the *equation* $\frac{x^2}{4} + 2x = 0$ by reading off the values of x at the points where the curve cuts the x–axis. These are $x = 0$, $x = -8$, a the points **O** and **M**.

We can apply this method to an equation of any degree. Thus if any function of x is represented by $f(x)$, a solution of the equation $f(x) = 0$ may be obtained by plotting the graph of $y = f(x)$, and then measuring the intercepts made on the axis of x. These intercepts are values of x which make y equal to zero, and are therefore roots of $f(x) = 0$.

26. In the graph of $y = x^2$ (Fig. 14) it will be noticed that as we pass from right to left along the curve the ordinate is constantly decreasing until it becomes zero at **O**; after this the ordinate begins to increase. The point at which this change takes place in a graph is known as a **turning point**. Thus the origin is a turning point of $y = x^2$, and of all curves represented by an equation of the form $y = ax^2$. Again in Fig. 15 there is a turning point at the point $(-4, -4)$. In each of these cases the algebraically least value of the ordinate is found at the turning point.

27. If a function gradually increases till it reaches a value a, which is algebraically greater than neighbouring values on either side, a is said to be a **maximum value** of the function.

If a function gradually decreases till it reaches a value b, which is algebraically less than neighbouring values on either side, b is said to be a **minimum value** of the function.

Let the function be represented by $f(x)$, then when $y = f(x)$ is treated graphically, it is evident that maximum and minimum values of $f(x)$ occur at the turning points, where the ordinates are algebraically greatest and least in the immediate vicinity of such points.

Example. Draw the graph of $y = 3 - 4x - 4x^2$. Hence find the roots of the equation $4x^2 + 4x - 3 = 0$. Shew that the expression $3 - 4x - 4x^2$ is positive for all real values of x between 0.5 and -1.5, and negative for all real values of x outside these limits. Also find the maximum value of $3 - 4x - 4x^2$.

Take the unit for x four times as great as that for y, and use the following table of values:

x	2	1.5	1	0.5	0	-0.5	-1	-1.5	-2	-2.5
$-4x$	-8	-6	-4	-2	0	2	4	6	8	10
$-4x^2$	-16	-9	-4	-1	0	-1	-4	-9	-16	-25
y	-21	-12	-5	0	3	4	3	0	-5	-12

After plotting these points we have the graph given in Fig. 16.

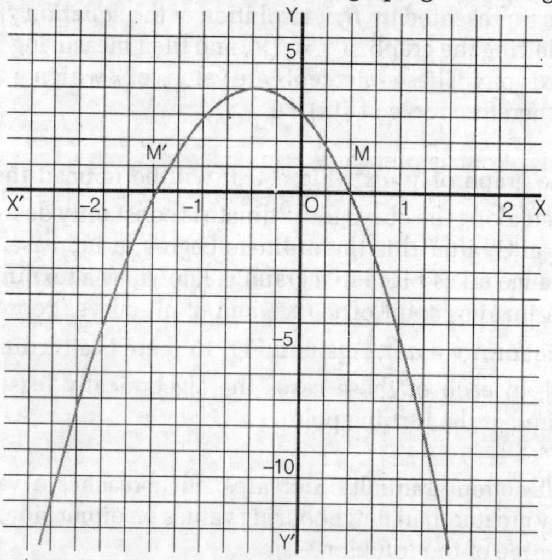

FIG. 16

The roots of the equation $4x^2 + 4x - 3 = 0$ are the values of x which make y equal to 0. These are found at the points **M** and **M′** where the curve cuts the x-axis. Thus the required roots are 0.5 and – 1.5.

Again between the points **M** and **M′** the graph lies above the x-axis; that is, the value of y, or $3 - 4x - 4x^2$, is positive so long as x lies between 0.5 and – 1.5, and is negative for other values of x.

The maximum value of the expression $3 - 4x - 4x^2$ is the value of the greatest ordinate in the graph, namely, 4. This may also be obtained algebraically as follows:

$$3 - 4x - 4x^2 = 3 + 1 - (1 + 4x + 4x^2) = 4 - (1 + 2x)^2.$$

Now $(1 + 2x)^2$ must be positive for all real values of x except $x = -\frac{1}{2}$, in which case, it vanishes and the value of the expression reduces to 4, which is the greatest value it can have.

Note. Another method of dealing with examples of this class will be found in Art. 32.

EXAMPLES VI

1. Draw the graphs of

   (i) $y = x^2$, (ii) $y = 8x^2$.

   In (i) take 1 cm as unit for x, 5 mm as unit for y.

   In (ii) .... 3 cm .... x, 3 mm .... y.

2. On the same scale as in Ex. 1 (ii) draw the graph of $y = 16x^2$. Shew that it may also be simply deduced from the graph of Ex. 1 (ii).

3. Plot the graph of $y = x^2$, taking 3 cm as unit on both axes, and using the following values of x, $-0.4, -0.3, -0.2, -0.1, 0, 0.1, 0.2, 0.3, 0.4$.

4. Draw the graphs of $y = x^2$ and $x = y^2$, and shew that they have only one common chord. Find its equation.

5. From the graphs and also by calculation, shew that $y = \frac{x^2}{8}$ cuts $x = -y^2$ in only two points and find their coordinates.

6. Draw the graphs of

   (i) $y^2 = -4x$; (ii) $y = 2x - \frac{x^2}{4}$;

   (iii) $y = \frac{x^2}{4} + x - 2$.

   In each case give the coordinates of the turning points.

7. Draw the graph of $y = x + x^2$. Shew also that it may be deduced from that of $y = x^2$.

8. Shew (i) graphically, (ii) algebraically, that the line $y = 2x - 3$ meets the curve $y = \frac{x^2}{4} + x - 2$ in one point only. Find its coordinates.

9. Find graphically the roots of the following equations to 2 places of decimals.

   (i) $\frac{x^2}{4} + x - 2 = 0$; (ii) $x^2 - 2x = 4$;

   (iii) $4x^2 - 16x + 9 = 0$.

   From the graphs deduce solutions of

   (iv) $\frac{x^2}{4} + x - 2 = 6$; (v) $x^2 - 2x = 8$;

   (vi) $4x^2 - 16x + 9 = -6$.

10. On a large scale draw the graph of $x^2 - 7x + 11$; hence find the roots of the equation $x^2 - 7x + 11 = 0$, and the minimum value of the expression $x^2 - 7x + 11$.

11. Find the minimum value of $x^2 - 2x - 4$, and the maximum value of $5 + 4x - 2x^2$.

12. Draw the graph of $y = (x-1)(x-2)$ and find the minimum value of $(x-1)(x-2)$. Measure, as accurately as you can, the values of x for which $(x-1)(x-2)$ is equal to 5 and 9 respectively. Verify algebraically.

13. Show graphically that the expression $x^2 - 2x - 8$ is negative for all values of x between -2 and 4, and positive for all value of x outside these limits.

28. The distance from the origin of any point **P** (x, y) is given by the relation $\mathbf{OP}^2 = x^2 + y^2$. Hence any equation of the form $x^2 + y^2 = a^2$, where a is constant, represents a circle, of radius a, whose centre is at the origin, since every point (x, y) which satisfies the equation is at a constant distance a from the origin.

Example. Solve graphically the simultaneous equations

(i) $x^2 + y^2 = 41$, (ii) $y = 2x - 3$.

The graph of (i) is a circle. Since the equation is satisfied by $x = 4, y = 5$ (the point **P**), the graph may bedrawn by describing a circle with centre **O** and radius **OP**.

The graph of (ii) is a straight line, which cuts the axes at the points (1.5,0), (0, –3).

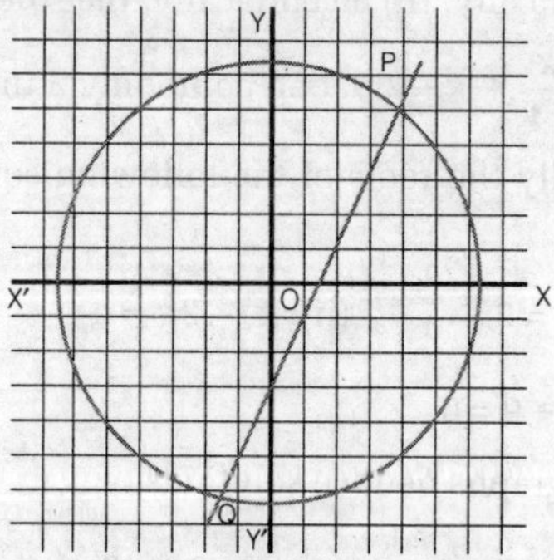

FIG. 17

This line produced cuts the circle at **P** and **Q**. The coordinates of these points are (4, 5) and (– 1.6, – 6.2); thus the solution of the equations is given by

$$x = 4, y = 5, \text{ and } x = -1 \cdot 6, y = -6 \cdot 2.$$

Infinite and Zero Values

29. Consider the fraction $\frac{a}{x}$ in which the numerator a has a *certain fixed value*, and the denominator is a *quantity subject to change;* then it is clear that the smaller x becomes, the larger does the value of the fraction $\frac{a}{x}$ become.

For instance, $\frac{a}{\frac{1}{10}} = 10a, \frac{a}{\frac{1}{1000}} = 1000a, \frac{a}{\frac{1}{1000000}} = 1000000a$.

By making the denominator x sufficiently small the value of the fraction $\frac{a}{x}$ can be made as large as we please; that is, if x is made *less than any quantity that can be named,* the value of a/x will become *greater than any quantity that can be named.*

A quantity less than any assignable quantity is called **zero** and is denoted by the symbol 0.

A quantity greater than any assignable quantity is called **infinity** and is denoted by the symbol ∞.

We may now say briefly

when $x = 0$, *the value of* $\frac{a}{x}$ is ∞.

Again, if x is a quantity which gradually increases and finally becomes *greater than any assignable quantity*, the fraction becomes *smaller than any assignable quantity*. Or more briefly

when $x = \infty$, *the value of* $\frac{a}{x}$ *is* 0.

It should be observed that when the symbols for zero and infinity are used in the sense above explained, they are subject to the rules of signs which affect other algebraical symbols. Thus we shall find it convenient to use a concise statement such as "when $x = +0, y = +\infty$" to indicate that when a *very small and positive* value is given to x, the corresponding value of y is *very large and positive.*

Example. Find the graph of $xy = 4$. Shew that it consists of two infinite branches, one in the first and the other in the third quadrant.

The equation may be written in the form $y = \frac{4}{x}$,

from which it appears that when $x = 0, y = \infty$ and when $x = \infty, y = 0$. Also y is positive when x is positive, and negative when x is negative. Hence the graph must lie entirely in the first and third quadrants.

Take the positive and negative values of the variables separately.

(1) *Positive values:*

x	0	1	2	3	4	5	6	...	∞
y	∞	4	2	$1\frac{1}{3}$	1	.8	$\frac{2}{3}$	...	0

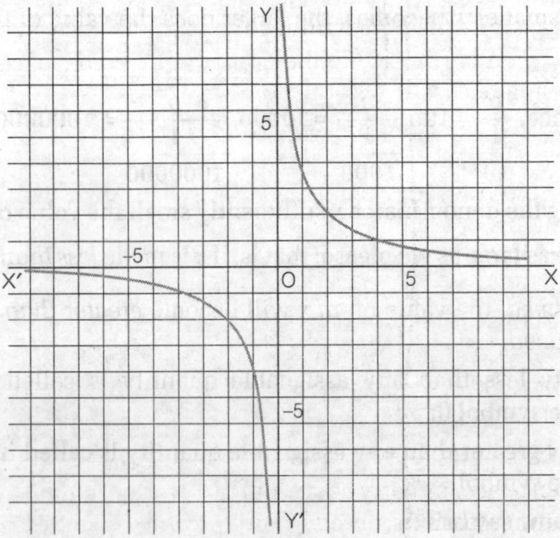

FIG. 18

Graphically these values shew that as we recede further and further from the origin on the x-axis in the positive direction, the values of y are positive and become smaller and smaller. That is, the graph is continually approaching the x-axis in such a way that by taking a sufficiently great positive value of x we obtain a point on the graph as near as we please to the x-axis but never actually reaching it until $x = \infty$. Similarly, as x becomes smaller and smaller the graph approaches more and more nearly to the positive end of the y-axis, never actually reaching it as long as x has any finite positive value, however small.

(2) *Negative values:*

x	-0	-1	-2	-3	-4	-5	...	$-\infty$
y	$-\infty$	-4	-2	$-1\frac{1}{3}$	-1	$-\cdot 8$	...	-0

The portion of the graph obtained from these values is in the third quadrant as shown in Fig. 18, and exactly similar to the portion already traced in the first quadrant. It should be noticed that as x passes from $+0$ to -0 the value of y changes from $+\infty$ to $-\infty$. Thus the graph which in the first quadrant has run away to an infinite distance on the positive side of the y-axis, reappears in the third quadrant coming from an infinite distance on the negative side of that axis. Similar remarks apply to the graph in its relation to the x-axis.

This curve is known as a **rectangular hyperbola**. Any equation of the form $xy = c$, where c is constant, will give a graph similar in form to that in Fig. 18.

30. When a curve continually approaches more and more nearly to a line without actually meeting it until an infinite distance is reached, such a line is said to be an **asymptote** to the curve. In the above case each of the axes is an asymptote.

31. In the simpler cases of graphs, sufficient accuracy can usually be obtained by plotting a few points, and there is little difficulty in selecting points with suitable coordinates. But in other cases, and especially when the graph has infinite branches, more care is needed. The most important things to observe are (1) the values for which the function $f(x)$ becomes zero or infinite; and (2) the values which the function assumes for zero and infinite values of x. In other words, we determine the *general character* of the curve in the neighbourhood of the origin, the axes, and infinity. Greater accuracy of detail can then be secured by plotting points at discretion. The selection of such points will usually be suggested by the earlier stages of our work.

The existence of symmetry about either of the axes should also be noted. When an equation contains no *odd* powers of x, the graph is symmetrical with regard to the axis of y. Similarly, the absence of odd powers of y indicates symmetry about the axis of x. [Compare Example in Art. 22.]

Example. Solve the following pairs of equations graphically:

$$\text{(i)} \quad \left.\begin{array}{r} x - y = 2 \\ xy = 35 \end{array}\right\}; \qquad \text{(ii)} \quad \left.\begin{array}{r} x^2 + y^2 = 74 \\ xy = 35 \end{array}\right\}.$$

In each case we shall require the graph of $xy = 35$. Proceeding as in the example of Art. 29, we find that the curve is a rectangular hyperbola lying in the first and third quadrants.

In (i) $x - y = 2$ is a straight line **QS** making intercepts 2 and -2 on the axes.

In (ii) $x^2 + y^2 = 74$ is a circle. Since the equation is satisfied by $x = 5$, $y = 7$, the graph can be drawn by finding this point (**P**), and describing a circle with centre **O** and radius **OP**.

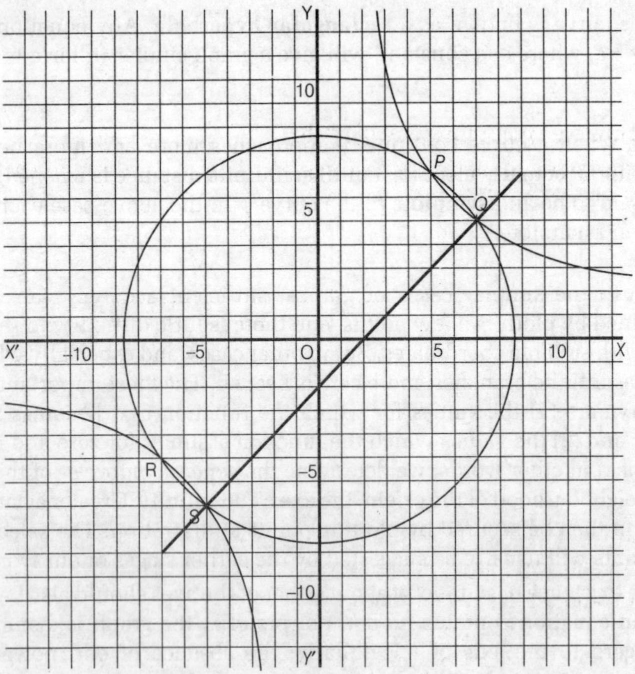

FIG. 19

The roots of (i) are the coordinates of **Q** and **S**; that is,

$$x = 7, \; y = 5; \text{ or } x = -5, \; y = -7.$$

The roots of (ii) are the coordinates of **P**, **Q**, **R**, and **S**; that is,

$$x = 5, \; y = 7; \; x = 7, \; y = 5;$$

$$x = -7, \; y = -5 \;; \; x = -5, \; y = -7.$$

32. Combination of two graphs. The method employed in the example on page 224 is quite general, and may be applied to functions of the third or higher degree, but the same results may often be more readily obtained by combining two graphs in the manner illustrated below.

Example. Solve the equation $2x^2 - x - 3 = 0$ graphically. Between what values of x is the expression $2x^2 - x - 3$ positive?

Write the equation in the form $x^2 = \frac{x}{2} + \frac{3}{2}$.

Put $y_1 = x^2$ .... (i), and $y_2 = \frac{x}{2} + \frac{3}{2}$. ... (ii)

and plot the graphs of these equations, taking the x-unit twice as great as the y – unit.

For (i) we may use the values:

x	0	± 0.5	± 1	± 1.5	± 2
y	0	0.25	1	2.25	4

Thus we obtain the parabola **POQ**.

The intercepts of (ii) on the axes are —3, 1, 5; thus the graph of (ii) is the straight line **PQ**.

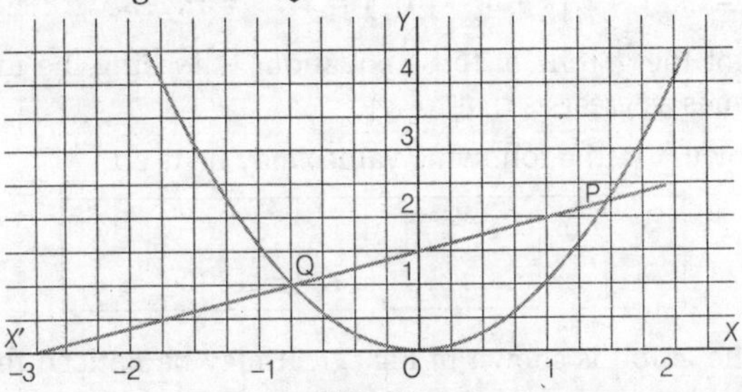

FIG. 20

At the points of intersection, **P** and **Q**, the ordinates of (i) and (ii) are equal, that is, $y_1 = y_2$; and the values of x at these points are 1.5 and – 1. Hence for these values of x, we have

$$x^2 = \frac{x}{2} + \frac{3}{2}, \text{ or } 2x^2 - x - 3 = 0.$$

Thus the roots of the equation $2x^2 - x - 3 = 0$ are furnished by the abscissae of the common points of the graphs of $y = x^2$ and

$$y = \frac{x}{2} + \frac{3}{2}.$$

Again, the expression $2x^2 - x - 3$ is positive or negative according as y_1 is greater or less than y_2. From the graph we see y_1 is less than y_2 between **Q** and **P**, that is, between $x = -1$ and 1.5, and y_1 is greater than y_2 for all other values of x. Hence $2x^2 - x - 3$ is positive for all values of x except such as lie between – 1 and 1 · 5.

33. The solution of the last example might have been effected equally well by drawing the graphs of $y = 2x^2$ and $y = x + 3$. But if a number of quadratic equations have to be solved graphically it is convenient to reduce them to the form $x^2 = px + q$ as a first step. The graph of $y = x^2$ can then be plotted once for all on a suitable scale, and the line $y = px + q$ can be readily drawn for different values of p and q.

Equations of higher degree may be treated by a similar method. For example, the solution of such equations as

$$x^3 = px + q, \text{ or } x^3 = ax^2 + bx + c$$

can be made to depend on the intersections of $y = x^3$ with the straight line $y = px + q$, or with the parabola $y = ax^2 + bx + c$.

Example. Find the real roots of the equations:

(i) $x^3 - 2.5x - 3 = 0$; (ii) $x^3 - 3x + 2 = 0$.

Here we have to find the points of intersection of

(i) $y = x^3$; $y = 2.5x + 3$; (ii) $y = x^3$, $y = 3x - 2$.

Plot the graphs of these equations, choosing the unit for x five times as great as that for y.

For $y = x^3$ the following values may be used:

x	0	± 0.5	± 1	± 1.5	± 2
y	0	± 0.125	± 1	± 3.375	± 8

The graph is shewn in Fig. 21. It may be noticed that the curve touches the x-axis at **O**, it crosses the axis at this point, and has symmetry in opposite quadrants.

The line $y = 2.5x + 3$ joins the points (0, 3) and (2, 8), and meets $y = x^3$ only at the point **P** whose abscissa is 2. Thus 2 is the only real root of equation (i).

Again $y = 3x - 2$ joins the points (1, 1) and (0, –2); it *touches* $y = x^3$ at **Q** where $x = 1$, and cuts it at **R** where $x = -2$. Corresponding to the former point equation (ii) has *two equal* roots Thus the roots are 1, 1, – 2.

GRAPHS OF THE SECOND OR HIGHER DEGREE

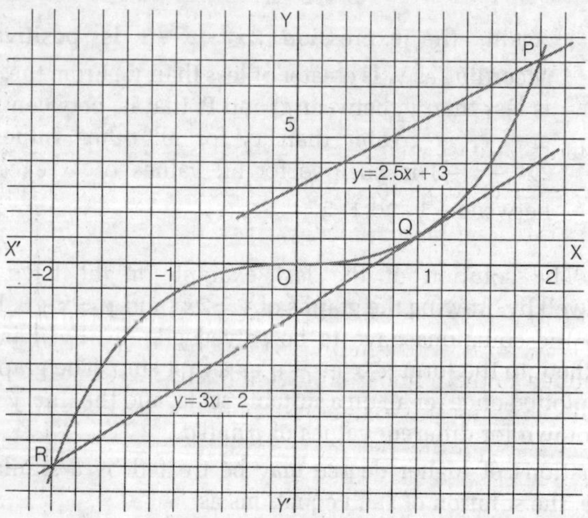

FIG. 21

EXAMPLES VII

1. Solve the following equations graphically:

(i) $x^2 + y^2 = 53, y - x = 5;$

(ii) $x^2 + y^2 = 100, x + y = 14;$

(iii) $x^2 + y^2 = 34, 2x + y = 11;$

(iv) $x^2 + y^2 = 36, 4x + 3y = 12.$

[Approximate roots to be given to one place of decimals.]

2. Plot the graphs of $x^2 + y^2 = 25$, $3x + 4y = 25$, and examine their relation to each other where they meet. Verify the result algebraically.

3. By the method of Art. 32 find graphically the roots of the following equations to two places of decimals:

(i) $\frac{x^2}{4} + x - 2 = 0;$ (ii) $x^2 - 2x = 4;$

(iii) $4x^2 - 16x + 9 = 0.$

4. Solve graphically the equation $3 + 6x = x^2$, and find the maximum value of the expression $3 + 6x - x^2$.

5. Shew by the method of Art. 32 that the expression $4x^2 + 4x - 3$ is negative of all real values of x between 0.5 and – 1.5, and positive for all real values of x outside those limits.

6. Draw the graphs of x^2 and of $3x + 1$. By means of them find approximate values for the roots of $x^2 - 3x - 1 = 0$.

7. Shew graphically that the expression $x^2 - 4x + 7$ is positive for all real values of x.

8. On the same axes draw the graphs of

$y = x^2, y = x + 6, y = x - 6, y = -x + 6, y = -x - 6.$

Hence discuss the roots of the four equations

$x^2 - x - 6 = 0, x^2 - x + 6 = 0, x^2 + x - 6 = 0, x^2 + x + 6 = 0.$

9. If x is real, prove graphically that $5 - 4x - x^2$ is not greater than 9; and that $4x^2 - 4x + 3$ is not less than 2. Between what values of x is the first expression positive?

10. The reciprocal of a number is multiplied by 2.25 and the product is added to the number. Find graphically what the number must be if the resulting expression has the least possible value.

11. Shew graphically that the expression $4x^2 + 2x - 8.75$ is positive for all real values of x except such as lie between 1.25 and – 1.75. For what value of x is the expression a minimum?

12. Solve the following pairs of equations graphically:

(i) $x^2 + y^2 = 15$, $xy = 36$; (ii) $x + y = 3$, $xy = 18$. (iii) $x^2 + y^2 = 13$, $xy = 6$.

13. From a graphical consideration of the following pairs of simultaneous equations:

(i) $x^2 + y^2 = a$, $xy = b$; (ii) $x + y = a$, $xy = b$.

explain why (i) has either *four* solutions or none, while (ii) has *two* solutions or none.

14. Draw the graph of $y = x^3$ between $x = -2$ and $x = 2$, taking 3 cm as unit on each axis.

15. From the graphs of $y = x^3$ and $y = 3x$ shew graphically that the roots of $x^3 - 3x = 0$ are approximately $-1.73, 0$, and 1.73.

[Take 3 cm as unit on each axis.]

16. Find graphically the real roots of the equations:

(i) $x^3 + x - 2 = 0$; (ii) $x^3 - 7x + 6 = 0$.

17. Taking 3 cm as unit, plot the graph of $y = x^3 - 3x$, taking the following values of x: $0, \pm .2, \pm .4, \pm .6, \pm .8, \pm 1, \pm 1.2, \pm 1.4, \pm 1.6 \pm 1.8, \pm 2$.

Find the turning points, and the value of the maximum or minimum ordinates between the limits given. Verify the result of Ex. 15.

18. On the diagram of Ex. 17, draw the graph of $y + 2 = 0$, and thus verify the solution of the equation $x^3 - 3x + 2 = 0$ given in the Examples on page 44.

19. On the same scale as on page 44, draw the graphs of $y = x^3$, and of $y = 2x^2 + x - 2$. Hence find the roots of the equation $x^3 - 2x^2 - x + 2 = 0$.

20. Taking the x-unit ten times as great as the y-unit, plot the graphs of $x^3 - 4x^2$ and of $5x - 14$. Hence find the roots of the equation $x^3 - 4x^2 - 5x + 14 = 0$ to three significant figures.

21. If p is a positive quantity, shew graphically that the equation $x^3 + px + q = 0$ can only have one real root.

Miscellaneous Applications of Graphs

34. When two quantities x and y are so related that a change in one produces a proportional change in the other, their variations can always be expressed by an equation of the form $y = ax$, where a is constant. Hence in all such cases the graph which exhibits their variations is a straight line through the origin, and only one other point is required to determine the graph. For instance, such examples as deal with work and time, distance and time (when the speed is uniform), quantity and cost of material, principal and simple interest at a given rate per cent., may all be illustrated by linear graphs through the origin.

Note. It must be admitted that solutions of this kind are often very artificial, and they should be regarded mainly as exercises in ingenuity. The graphical treatment of a quite simple problem may often prove cumbrous and elaborate in detail, and in such a case a straight forward arithmetical or algebraical solution is to be preferred. For example, it is an unprofitable waste of time and skill to devise graphical solutions for certain types of easy problems which at most require only a few lines of very simple Arithmetic or Algebra. When, however, the answer to a question involves several allied results (as in Examples V, 23-25) a graphical method is often useful and interesting.

Example 1. P and **Q** are two towns 30 km apart. At 1 p.m. *X* starts to walk from **Q** to **P** at 3 km an hour, and after walking two hours finds it necessary to run back for his watch. This he does at $6\frac{2}{3}$ km per hour, and after a delay of 6 minutes he again starts from **Q** at 4 km per hour. Meanwhile γ starting from **P** at 1 p.m. sets out for **Q** at 4 km per hour; after walking for two hours, he spends half an hour with a friend from whom he borrows a bicycle on which he continues his journey at 12 km per hour. Draw graphs to shew the position of each man relative to **P** and **Q** at any time between 1 p.m. and 5.30 p.m. Also from the graphs find

(i) when and where ***X*** and γ meet;

(ii) at what times respectively they were 18 km and 8 km apart. In Fig. 22, on the opposite page, time is measured horizontally (3 cm to 1 hour), and distance vertically (3 cm to 10 km). Thus each division on the horizontal axis represents 6 minutes and each division on the vertical axis stands for 1 km.

The graph shewing the course of *X* is drawn downwards from **Q**; similarly, γ's course is shewn by a graph drawn upwards from **P**.

At 3 p.m. *X* has gone 6 km, therefore if **A** is taken 1.8 cm below the point which marks 3 p.m., **QA** is his graph for the first 2 hours.

To get back to **Q** at $6\frac{2}{3}$ km per hour will take $6 \div 6\frac{2}{3}$, or $\frac{9}{10}$ of an hour. Hence **B** is the next point on his graph.

The delay at **Q** before he starts again at 4 km per hour at 4 p.m. is represented by **BC**, which denotes 6 minutes. If **D** is taken 1.2 cm, representing 4 km, vertically below 5 p.m., the line **CDE** completes the graph.

For γ's graph measure 2.4 cm vertically above 3 p.m. to **F**; then, since he walks 8 km in 2 hours, **PF** is the first stage of the graph.

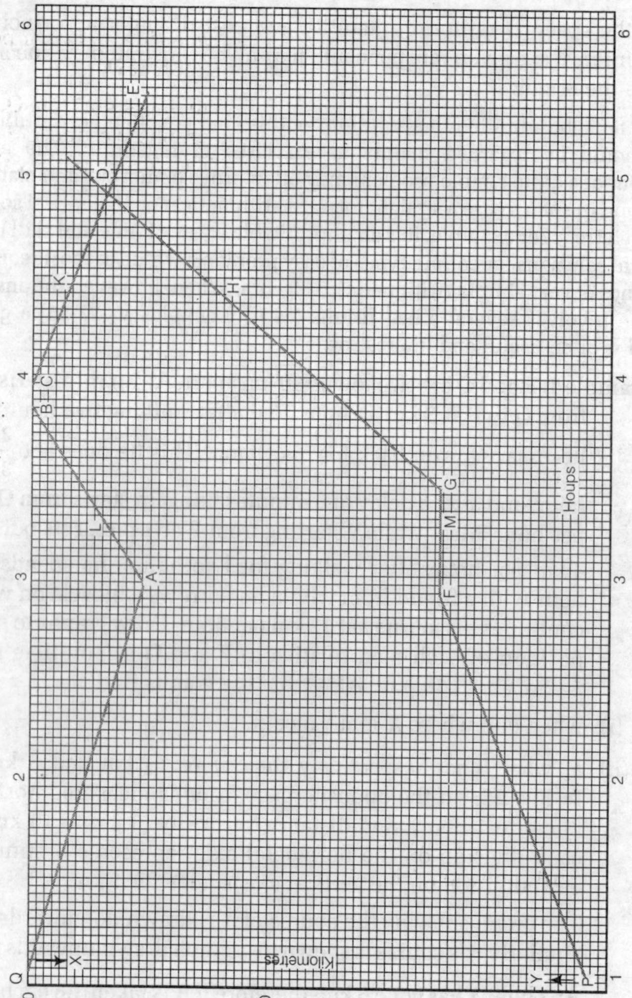

Fig. 22

The next half-hour is spent without advance towards **Q**; therefore the corresponding portion of the graph is **FG**.

GH represents the course of the bicycle ride at 12 km per hour, and it will be found that it cuts *X*'s graph at **D**.

Hence the point of meeting is at **D**, which is 4 km from **Q**, and the time is 5 p.m. By inspection of the graphs we find **LM** and **KH** represent 18 and 8 km respectively. The corresponding times are 3.3 and 4.5 hours; that is, *X* and γ are 18 and 8 km apart at 3.18 p.m. and 4.30 p.m. respectively.

They were also 18 km apart, approximately, at 18 min. before 3.

Note. The solution has here been given in full to illustrate and enforce the general principle on which the linear graphs depend. Solutions may usually be presented with less detail, and the results quickly obtained from a well-drawn diagram on a suitable scale.

Example 2. A, **B**, and **C** run a race of 300 metres. *A* and *C* start from scratch, and *A* covers the distance in 40 seconds, beating *C* by 60 metres. *B*, with 12 metres' start, beats A by 4 seconds. Supposing the rates of running in each case to be uniform, find graphically the relative positions of the runners when *B* passes the winning post, Find also by how many metres *B* is ahead of *A* when the latter has run three-fourths of the course.

In Fig. 23 let time be measured horizontally (1.5 cm to 10 seconds), and distance vertically (3 cm to 60 metres). **O** is the starting point for *A* and *C*; take **OP** equal to 0.6 cm, representing 12 metres, on the vertical axis; then **P** is *B*'s starting point.

A's graph is drawn by joining **O** to the point which marks 40 seconds. From this point measure a vertical distance of 3 cm downwards to **Q**. Then since 3 cm represents 60 metres, **Q** is *C*'s position when *A* is at the winning post, and **OQ** is *C*'s graph.

Along the time-axis take 5.4 cm to **R**, representing 36 seconds; then **PR** is *B*'s graph.

Through **R** draw a vertical line to meet the graphs of *A* and *C* in **S** and **T** respectively. Then **S** and **T** mark the positions of *A* and *C* when *B* passes the winning post.

By inspection **RS** and **ST** represent 30 and 54 metres respectively. Thus *B* is 30 metres ahead of *A*, and *A* is 54 metres ahead of **C**.

Again, since *A* runs three-fourths of the course in 30 seconds, the difference of the corresponding ordinates of *A*'s and *B*'s graphs after 30 seconds will give the distance between *A* and *B*. By measurement we find **VW** = 1.35 cm which represents 27 metres.

The student is recommended to draw a figure for himself on a scale twice as large as that given in Fig. 23.

35. When a variable quantity y is partly constant and partly proportional to a variable quantity x, the algebraical relation between x and y is of the form $y = ax + b$, where a and b are constant. The corresponding graph will therefore be a straight line; and since a straight line is completely determined when the positions of two points are known, it follows that, in all problems which can be illustrated by linear graphs, it is sufficient if the data furnish for each graph two independent pairs of simultaneous values of the variable quantities.

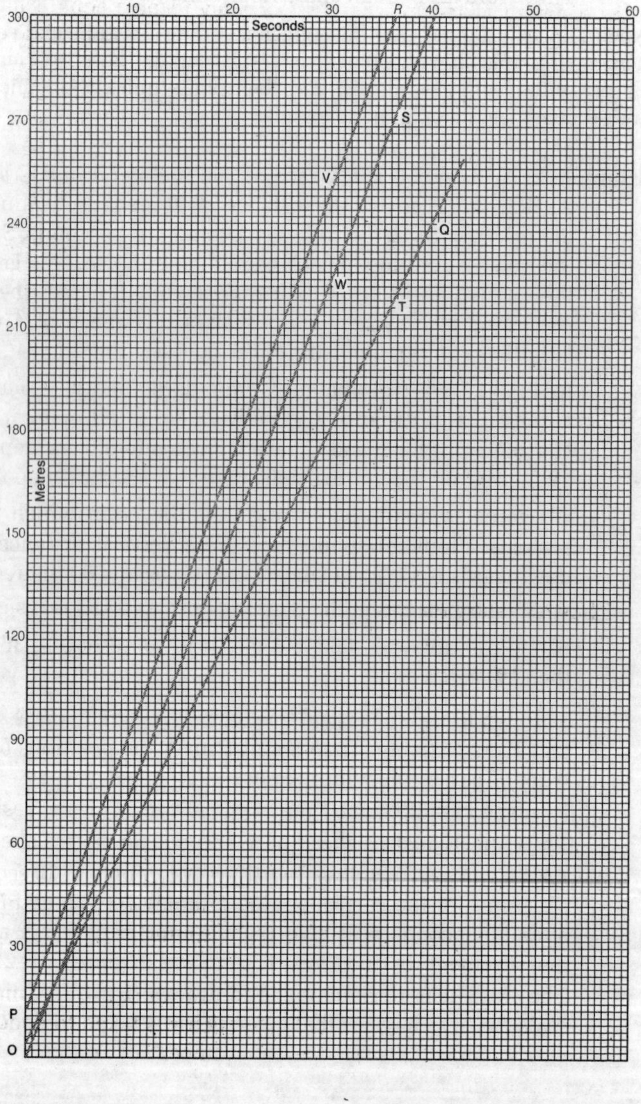

Some easy examples of this kind have already been given in Examples IV. See pages 18-20. We shall now work out two more examples.

Example 1. In a certain establishment the clerks are paid an initial salary for the first year, and this is annually increased by a fixed bonus, the initial salary and the,bonus being different in different departments. **A** receives Rs. 1300 in his 10th year, and Rs. 2200 in his 19th. **B**, in another department, receives Rs. 1400 in his 5th year, and Rs. 1800 in his 13th. Draw graphs to shew their salaries in different years. In what year do they receive equal salaries? Also find in what year *A* earns the same salary as that received by *B* for his 21st year.

In Fig. 24 let each horizontal division represent **1** year; and let the salaries be measured vertically, beginning at 1300, with one division to represent Rs. 20.

If salary at the end of x years is denoted by Rs. y, it is evident that in each case we have a relation of the form $y = ax + b$, where a and b are constant. Thus the variations of time and salary may be represented by linear graphs.

Since no bonus is received for the first year, $x = 8$, when $y = 1300$, and $x = 18$, when $y = 2200$. Thus the points **P** and **Q** are determined, and by joining them we have the graph for *A*'s salary. Similarly, the graph for *B*'s salary is found by joining **P′** (41,400) and **Q′** (121,800).

These lines have the same ordinate and abscissa at **L**, where $x = 16$, $y = 2000$. Thus *A* and *B* have the same salary when each have served 16 years, that is, in their 17th year. Again, *B*'s salary at the end of 20 years is given by the ordinate of **M**, which is the same as that of **Q** which represents *A*'s salary after 18 years.

Thus *A*'s salary for his 19th year is equal to *B*'s salary for his 21st year.

Example 2. Two sums of money are put out at simple interest at different rates per cent. In the first case the Amounts at the end of 6 years and 15 years are Rs. 2600 and Rs. 3500 respectively. In the second case the Amounts for 5 years and 20 years are Rs. 3300 and Rs. 4200. Draw graphs from which the Amounts may be read off for any year, and find the year in which the Principal with accrued Interest will amount to the same in the two cases. Also from the graphs read off the value of each Principal.

When a sum of money is at simple interest for any number of years, we have Amount = Principal + Interest,

where "Principal" is constant, and " Interest" varies with the number of years. Hence the variations of Amount and Time may be represented by linear graph in which x is taken to denote the number of years, and y the number of rupees in the corresponding Amount.

Here, as the diagram is inconveniently large, we shall merely indicate the steps of the solution which are similar in detail to those of the last example. The student should draw his own diagram.

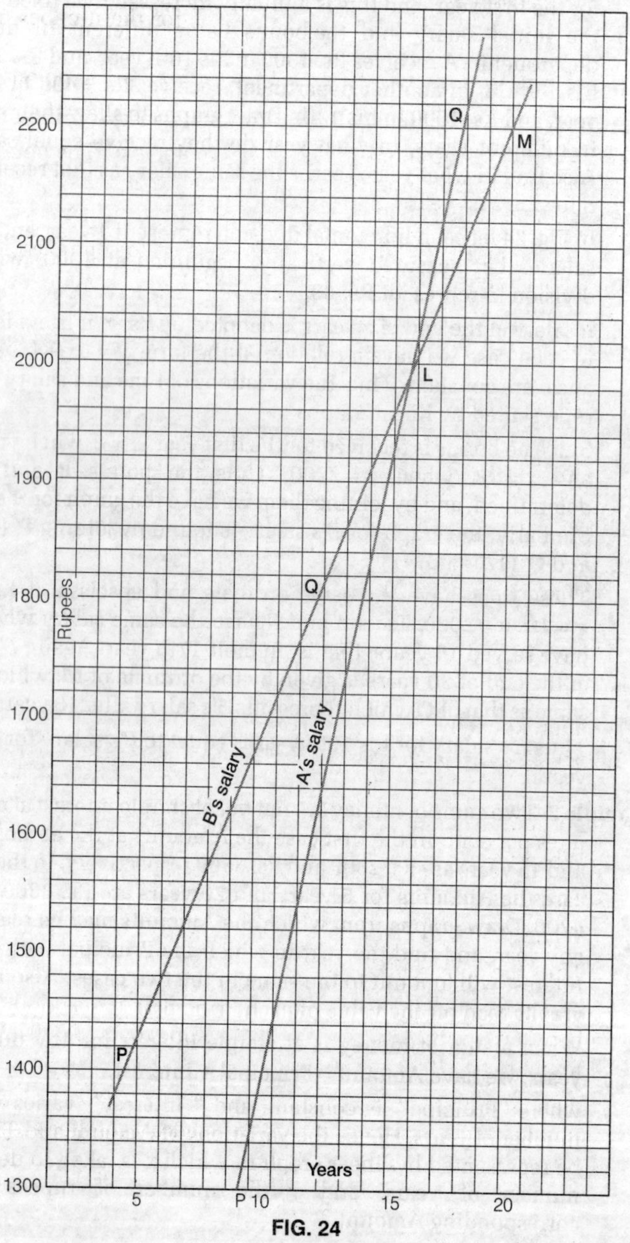

FIG. 24

Measure time horizontally (3 cm to 10 years), and Amount vertically (3 cm to Rs. 400) beginning at Rs. 2600.

The first graph is the line joining **L** (62,600) and **M** (153, 500). The second graph is the line joining **L′** (53,300) and **M′** (204,200). In each of these lines the ordinate of any point gives the Amount for the number of years given by the corresponding abscissa.

Again **LM, L′ M′** intersect at a point **P** where $x = 25$, $y = 4500$. Thus each Principal with its Interest amounts to Rs. 4500 in 25 years.

When $x = 0$ there is no Interest; thus the Principals will be obtained by reading off the values of the intercepts made by the two graphs on the y-axis. These are Rs. 2000 and Rs. 3000 respectively.

Note. To obtain the result $y = 2000$ it will be necessary to continue the y-axis downwards sufficiently far to shew this ordinate.

36. Some of the ordinary processes of Arithmetic lend themselves readily to graphical illustration. For example, the graph of $y = x^2$ may be used to furnish numerical square roots. For since $x = \sqrt{y}$, if a series of numbers are represented by ordinates, the corresponding abscissae will give the square roots of those numbers. Similarly, cube roots may be found from the graph of $y = x^3$.

Example. Draw a graph to find the cube roots of 10 and 14 correct to 3 places of decimals.

The cube root of 10 is a little greater than 2; hence it will be sufficient to plot the graph of $y = x^3$, taking $x = 2 \cdot 1,\ 2 \cdot 2,\ 2 \cdot 3,\ 2 \cdot 4, \ldots$

The corresponding ordinates are $9 \cdot 26$, $10 \cdot 65$, $12 \cdot 17$, $13 \cdot 82$, ... approximately.

When $x = 2$, $y = 8$, Take the axes through this point, and let the units for x and y be 30 cm said 1.5 cm respectively. The requisite portion of the curve is shewn in Fig. 25.

When $y = 10$, by measurement we find $x = 2 \cdot 154$.

Thus the cube root of $10 = 2 \cdot 154$.

When $y = 14$, by measurement $x = 2 \cdot 410$.

Thus the cube root of $14 = 2 \cdot 410$.

The graph may be used to read off the cube roots of all numbers between 8 and 14. For example, the cube roots of $8 \cdot 6$ and 13 are found to be $2 \cdot 050$ and $2 \cdot 350$.

Note. Solutions of this kind can only be regarded as a further *illustration* of the graphical method. As a *substitute* for arithmetical evolution they serve no useful purpose.

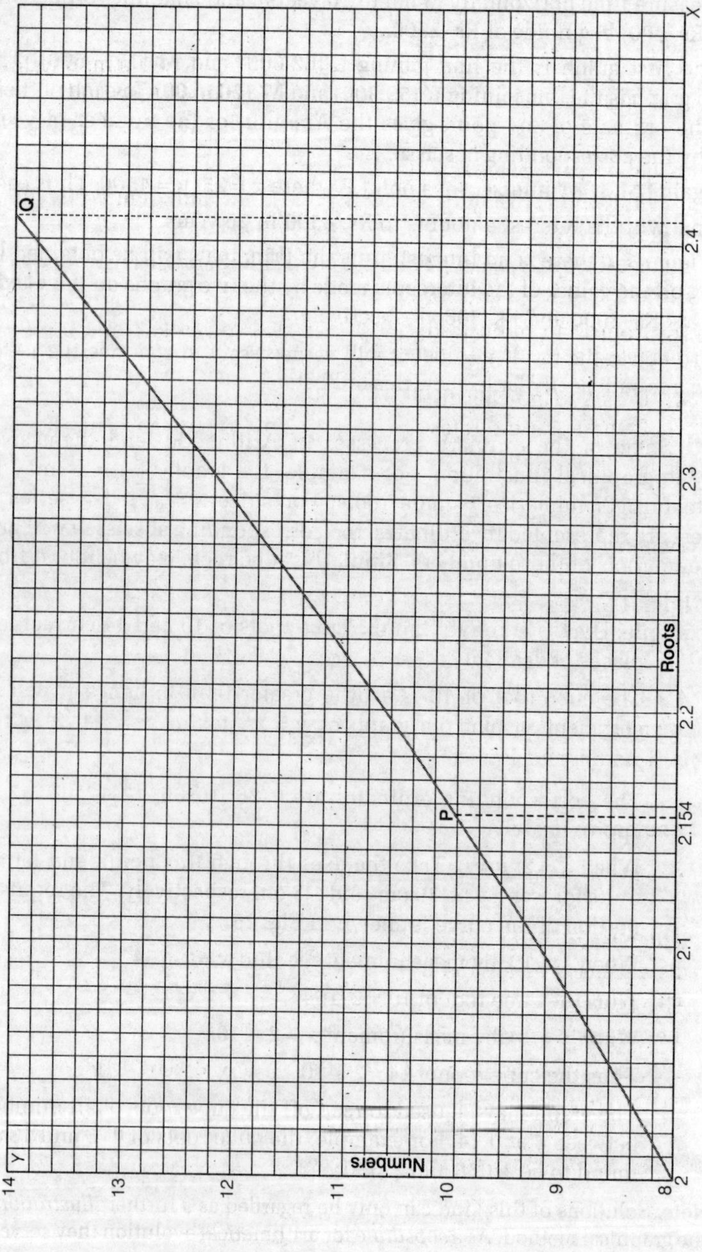

FIG. 25

EXAMPLES VIII

1. At noon A starts to walk at 6 km an hour, and at 1.30 p.m. B follows running at 8 km an hour. When will B overtake A? Also find

(i) when A is 5 km ahead of B;

(ii) when A a 3 km behind B.

[Take 3 cm horizontally to represent 1 hour, and 3 cm vertically to represent 10 km.]

2. By measuring time along **OX** (3 cm for 1 hour) and distance along **OY** (3 cm for 10 km) shew how to draw lines

(i) from **O** to indicate distance travelled towards **Y** at 12 km per hour;

(ii) from **Y** to indicate distance travelled towards **O** at 9 km per hour. If these are the rates of two men who ride towards each other from two places 60 km apart, starting at noon, find from the graphs when they are first 18 km from each other. Also find (to the nearest minute) their time of meeting.

3. Two cyclists ride to meet each other from two places 95 km apart. A starts at 8 a.m. at 10 km per hour, and B starts at 9.30 a.m. at 15 km per hour. Find graphically when and where they meet, and at what times they are $37\frac{1}{2}$ km apart.

4. A, on a cycle, and B, on a scooter, start at the same time from town **P** to town **Q**, A riding 4 km per hour, B riding 9 km per Hour. B reaches **Q** in 4 hours, and immediately rides back to **P**. After 2 hours rest he starts again for **Q** at the same rate. How far from **P** will he overtake A, who has in the meantime rested $6\frac{1}{4}$ hours?

5. At what distance from **A**, and at what time, will a train which leave **A** for **B** at 2.33 p.m., and goes at the rate of 35 km per hour, meet a train which leaves **B** at 1.45 p.m. and goes at the rate of 25 km per hour, the distance between **A** and **B** being 80 km?

Also find at what times the trains are 24 km apart, and how far apart they are at 4.9 p.m.

6. A, B, and C set out to walk from **P** to **Q** at 5, 6, and 4 km per hour respectively. C starts 3 minutes before, and B 7 minutes after A. Draw graphs to shew (i) when and where A overtakes **C**; (ii) when and where **B** overtakes A;

(iii) C's position relative to the others after he has walked 45 minutes.

[Take 3 cm horizontally to represent 10 minutes, and 3 cm to the kilometre vertically.]

7. **X** and **Y** are two towns 70 km apart. At 8 · 30 a.m. *A* starts to walk from *X* to **Y** at 8 km per hour; after walking 16 km he rests for an hour and then completes his journey on a scooter at 20 km per hour. At 9 · 48 a.m. *B* starts to walk from **Y** to **X** at 6 km per hour; find when and where A and *B* meet. Also find at what times they are $6\frac{1}{2}$ km apart.

8. *A* can beat *B* by 20 metres in 120, and *B* can beat *C* by 10 metres in 50. Supposing their rates of running to be uniform, find graphically how much start *A* can give *C* in 120 metres so as to run a dead heat with him. If *A*, *B*, and *C* start together, where are *A* and *C* when *B* has run 80 metres?

9. *A*, *B*, and *C* run a race of 200 metres. *A* gives *B* a start of 8 metres, and *C* starts some seconds after *A*. *A* runs the distance in 25 seconds and beats *C* by 40 metres. *B* beats *A* by 1 second, and when he has been running 15 seconds he is 48 metres ahead of *C*. Find graphically how many seconds *C* starts after *A*. Shew also from the graphs that if the three runners started level they would run a dead heat, [Take 3 cm to 40 metres, and 3 cm to 10 seconds.]

10. A scooter-rider has to ride 75 km. He rides for a time at 18 km per hour and then alters his speed to 30 km per hour, covering the distance in $3\frac{1}{2}$ hours. At what time did he change his speed?

11. *A* and *B* ride to meet each other from two towns **X** and **Y** which are 60 km apart. *A* starts at 1 p.m., and *B* starts 36 minutes later. If they meet at 4 p.m., and *A* gets to **Y** at 6 p.m., find the time when *B* gets to *X*, Also find the times when they are 22 km apart. When *A* is half-way between **X** and **Y**, where is *B* ?

12. The distance between two towns **A** and **B** is 119 km; if I were to set out at noon by cycle from **A**, going at 26 km the first hour and decreasing my rate by 3 km each successive hour, find graphically how long it would take me to reach **B**. Also find approximately the time at which I should reach **C**, which is 48 km from **B**.

13. At 8 a.m. *A* begins to cycle at 20 km per hour, and an hour and a half later *B*, starting from the same point, follows at 10 km per hour. After riding 36 km, **A** rests for 1 hr. 24 min., then rides back at 9 km per hour. Find graphically when and where he meets *B*. Also find (i) at what time the riders were 21 km apart, (ii) how far *B* will have ridden by tho timo *A* gets back to his starting point.

14. I row against a stream flowing 750 metres per hour to a certain point, and then turn back, stopping 1 km short of the place whence I originally started. If the whole time occupied in rowing is 2 hr. 10 min. and my uniform speed in still water is 2.25 km per hr., find graphically how far upstream I went.

[Take 3 cm horizontally to represent 1 hour, and 3 cm to 1 km vertically.]

15. One train leaves town **A** at 3 p.m. and reaches town **B** at 6 p.m.; a second train leaves town **B** at 1·30 p.m. and arrives at town **A** at 6 p.m.; if both trains are supposed to travel uniformly, at what time will they meet? Shew from a graph that the time does not depend upon the distance between **A** and **B**.

16. At 7·40 a.m. the ordinary train starts from town **P** and reaches town **Q** at 11·40 a.m.; the express starting from **Q** at 9 a.m. arrives at **P** at 11·40 a.m.: if both trains travel uniformly, find when they meet. Shew, as in Ex. 15, that the time is independent of the distance between **P** and **Q**, and verify this conclusion by solving an algebraical equation.

17. A boy starts from home and walks to school at the rate of 10 metres in 3 seconds, and is 20 seconds too soon. The next day he walks at the rate of 40 metres in 17 seconds, and is half a minute late. Find graphically the distance to the school, and shew that he would have been just in time if he had walked at the rate of 20 metres in 7 seconds.

18. The annual expenses of a Convalescent Home are partly constant and partly proportional to the number of inmates. The expenses were Rs. 3840 for 12 patients and Rs. 4320 for 16, Draw a graph to shew the expenses for any number of patients, and find from it the cost of maintaining 15.

In a rival establishment the expenses were Rs. 3750 for 5, and Rs. 4450 for 15 patients. Find graphically for what number of patients the cost would be the same in the two cases.

19. A body is moving in a straight line with varying velocity. The velocity at any instant is made up of the constant velocity with which it was projected (measured in cm per second) diminished by a retardation of a constant number of cm per second in every second. After 4 seconds the velocity was 320, and after 13 seconds it was 140. Draw a graph to shew the velocity at any time while the body is in motion.

A second body projected at the same time under similar conditions has a velocity of 450 after 5 seconds, and a velocity of 150 after 15 seconds. Shew graphically that they will both come to rest at the same time. Also find at what time the second body is moving 100 cm per second faster than the first, and determine from the graphs the velocity of projection in each case.

20. To provide for his two infant sons, a man left by his will two sums of money as separate investments at different rates of interest, on the condition that the principal sums with simple interest were to be paid over to his sons when the amounts were the same. After 5 years the first sum amounted to Rs. 4510, and after 15 years to Rs. 5330. After 10 years the second sum amounted to Rs. 4320, and after 20 years to Rs. 5440. Draw graphs from which the amounts may be read off for any year, and find after how many years the sons were entitled to receive their legacies.

Also determine from the graphs what the original sums were at the father's death.

21. Two vessels, *A* and *B*, are travelling at varying speeds. *A*'s rate in any hour after the first is made up of a constant number of kilometres *increased* by a number of kilometres which is a constant fraction of the number of hours completed before that hour. *B*'s rate in any hour after the first is made up of a constant number of kilometres *decreased* by a number of kilometres which is a constant fraction of the number of hours completed before that hour. In the 8th and 24th hours *A* travels 7 kilometres and 15 kilometres respectively. In the 5th and 38th hours *B*'s rates are 23 kilometres and 12 kilometres. Draw graphs to shew the rates of each vessel for any hour, and find in what hour they are travelling at the same rate.

Find *A*'s rate in the 38th hour and B's in the 35th. Shew also that in the 10th hour *B*'s speed is twice that of *A*.

22. In a certain examination the highest and lowest marks gained in a Latin paper were 153 and 51. These have to be reduced so that the maximum (120) is given to the first candidate, and the minimum (30) to the lowest. This is done by reducing all the marks in a certain ratio, and then increasing or diminishing them all by the same number. In a Greek paper the highest and lowest marks were 161 and 56; after a similar adjustment these become 100 and 40 respectively. Draw graphs from which all the reduced marks may be read off, and find the marks which should be finally given to a candidate who scored 102 in Latin and 126 in Greek.

Shew also that it is possible in one case for a candidate to receive equal marks in the two subjects both before and after reduction. What are the original and reduced marks in this case?

23. The table below shews the distance from London of certain stations, and the times of two trains, one up and one down. Suposing each run to be made at a constant speed, shew by a graph the distance of each train from London at any time, using 3 cm to represent 32 km, and 9 cm, to represent an hour.

Distance in km

London,	arrive depart		4.30 p. m.		7.0 p.m.
8 · 8 Willesden,		↓	4.38 ...	↑	(No intermediate stop.)
			4.42 ...		
			5.50 ...		
105·6 Northampton,	arrive depart		5.54 ...		5.0 p.m.
180 · 8 Birmingham,			7.0		

At what point do they pass one another, and how far is each from London at 5.30? Which of the three runs by the stopping train is the fastest?

24. Taking 3 cm as unit for x, and 1.5 cm as unit for y, draw the graph of $y = x^2$, and employ it to find the squares of 0.72, 1·7, 3·4; and the square roots of 7·56, 5·29,9·61.

25. Draw the graph of $y = \sqrt{x}$ taking the unit for y five times as great as that for x.

By means of this curve check the values of the square roots found in Ex. 24.

26. Draw a graph which will give the square roots of all numbers between 25 and 36, to three places of decimals.

[Take the origin at the point 5, 25, and use the same units as in the Example of Art. 36.]

27. From the graph of $y = x^3$ (on the scale of the diagram of Art. 36) find the values of $\sqrt[3]{9}$ and $\sqrt[3]{9.8}$ to 4 significant figures.

28. A boy who was ignorant of the rule for cube root required the value of $\sqrt[3]{14.71}$. He plotted the graph of $y = x^3$, using for x the values 2.2, 2.3,2.4 2.5 2.5, and found 2.45 as the value of the cube root. Verify this process in detail. From the same graph find the value of $\sqrt[3]{13.8}$ to two places of decimals.

29. Draw a graph which will give the cube roots of all numbers between 27 and 64 correct to 3 places of decimals.

Read off the cube roots of 44, 60; and the cubes of 3.42, 3.659.

Answers

I. PAGE 226

7. 36. **8.** 32.

9. 25. **11.** 1.2 sq. cm.

12. $y = 3x$. Any point whose ordinate is equal to three times its abscissa.

14. (i) (8·5); (ii) (10, 10).

15. (i) (4, 5); (ii) (4, 5); (iii) (– 4, – 5); (iv) (– 4, – 5).

16. (i) 17; (ii) 17; (iii) 2.5 cm; (iv) 2.5 cm.

17. (i) and (ii) 5; (iii) and (iv) 17; (v) and (vi) 37.

19. The lines are $x = 5$, $y = 8$. The point (5, 8).

20. 10. **23.** 68 units.

24. 10, 13, 5, 5, 3.

25. A circle of radius 13 whose centre is at the origin.

27. 10, 12, 16, 6, 0. At the points (0, 10), (– 5, 0).

II. PAGE 231

21. 32 units of area.
22. 25 sq cm.
23. 72 units of area.
24. 0.64 sq cm.

III. PAGE 235

1. $x = 1, y = 5$.
2. $x = 2, y = 10$.
3. $x = 3, y = 12$.
4. $x = 3, y = -2$.
5. $x = 4, y = 2$.
6. $x = 6, y = 8$.
7. $x = -2, y = 4$.
8. $x = 0, y = -3$.
9. $x = -3, y = 0$.
10. $x = -4, y = 3$.
11. At the point (0, 21).
12. $3x + 4y = 7$

IV. PAGE 237

2. $x = 1$, $y = 18$.
3. 9; 2·4.
4. 5 in each case. 18·5 units.
5. 2·5, 1·7.
6. (3, 4), (4, 1), (– 3, 2).
7. (3, 25), (0·84, 2·94), (0·42, 1·47).
8. 2·60, 5·63, 4·16, 5·77.
10. (i) 54·1 grains; (ii) 0·2.
11. 39·3; 91·6; $y = 0.393x$.
12. 90; 72;
13. Rs. 3·74 ; 87.
14. 112; 168; 78. $y = \frac{10}{11}x - 70$.
15. $y = 1000 + x$; Rs. 3500; 4250.

V. Page 245

5. $11y = 3x + 35$. 30·5; 5·9.
6. $y = 0{\cdot}21x + 1{\cdot}37$.
7. $y = 0{\cdot}4x + 1{\cdot}6$. 9·2; 3.
8. 45·96; 39·40.
9. 3·85 cm; 17·6 cm.
10. 54·5° F. 86·9° F. $F = 32 + \frac{9}{5}C$.
11. 8·1 cm; 24·375 gm.
12. 8·6 gm. wt.; $P = 0{\cdot}14W + 0{\cdot}2$; 225 gm wt.
13. $P = 0.6G - 14{\cdot}4$; 24.
14. Rs. 13; Rs. 18·25.
15. Rs. 26; Rs. 34.
16. 2·49 sq metres.
17. $P = 1{\cdot}1Q + 60$, Rs. 1710; Rs. 1440; Rs. 920.
20. (i) Rs. 36750; Rs. 28125; (iii) Rs. 28600.
21. Rs. 12·75; Rs. 19·87.
22. Rs.800; Rs. 2400.
23. 6 p.m., 48 km from London. At 4 and 8 p.m.
(i) B 4 km behind A; C 6 km behind B.
(ii) 4·20 p.m.

24. 4·30 p.m., 18 km from **O**.

(i) At 3 and 6 p.m. (ii) 20 km.

25. (i) 1 p.m., 28 km from **P**; (ii) 20 km; (iii) 11·30 a.m.

VI. PAGE 255

4. $y = x$.

5. (0, 0), (– 4, 2).

6. (i) (0, 0); (ii) (4, 4); (iii) (– 2, – 3).

8. (2, 1).

9. (i) 1·46, – 5·46; (ii) 3·24, – 1·24; (iii) 3·32, 0·68; (iv) 4, – 8;

(v) 4, – 2; (vi) 1·5, 2·5.

10. 2·38, 4·62; – 1·25.

11. – 5; 7.

12. –0.25, 3·79, – 0.79; 4·54, – 1·54.

VII. PAGE 263

1. (i) $x = 2$, or – 7; $y = 7$, or – 2. (ii) $x = 8$, or 6; $y = 6$. or 8.

(iii) $x = 3$, or 5·8; $y = 5$, or – 0·6. (iv) $x = 5·2$, or – 1·4; $y = – 3·0$, or 5·8.

2. The straight line $3x + 4y = 25$ *touches* the circle $x^2 + y^2 = 25$ at the point (3, 4).

3. (i) 1·46, – 5·46. (ii) 3·24, – 1·24; (iii) 3·32, 0·68.

4. 6·46, – 0·46. 12.

6. 3·30, – 0·30.

9. – 5 and 1.

10. 1·5.

11. – 0·25.

12. (i) $x = 12$, or 3; $y = 3$, or 12; (ii) $x = 6$, or – 3; $y = 3$, or – 6.

(iii) $x = 2, 3, – 3, – 2$; $y = 3, 2, – 2, – 3$.

16. (i) 1; (ii) 1, 2, 3.

17. Maximum ordinate (2) and minimum ordinate (– 2) at the points (– 1, 2), (1, – 2).

19. – 1, 1, 2.

20. 1·59, 4·41, – 2.

VIII. PAGE 273

1. 6 p.m.; (i) 3·30 p.m.; (ii) 7·30 p.m.

2. (i) 2 p.m.; 2·52 p.m.

3. 47 km from *A*'s starting place at 12·42 p.m., 11·12 a.m. and 2·12 p.m.

4. 27 km.

EXAMPLES VIII

1. At noon A starts to walk at 6 km an hour, and at 1.30 p.m. B follows running at 8 km an hour. When will B overtake A? Also find

(i) when A is 5 km ahead of B;

(ii) when A a 3 km behind B.

[Take 3 cm horizontally to represent 1 hour, and 3 cm vertically to represent 10 km.]

2. By measuring time along **OX** (3 cm for 1 hour) and distance along **OY** (3 cm for 10 km) shew how to draw lines

(i) from **O** to indicate distance travelled towards **Y** at 12 km per hour;

(ii) from **Y** to indicate distance travelled towards **O** at 9 km per hour. If these are the rates of two men who ride towards each other from two places 60 km apart, starting at noon, find from the graphs when they are first 18 km from each other. Also find (to the nearest minute) their time of meeting.

3. Two cyclists ride to meet each other from two places 95 km apart. A starts at 8 a.m. at 10 km per hour, and B starts at 9.30 a.m. at 15 km per hour. Find graphically when and where they meet, and at what times they are $37\frac{1}{2}$ km apart.

4. A, on a cycle, and B, on a scooter, start at the same time from town **P** to town **Q**, A riding 4 km per hour, B riding 9 km per Hour. B reaches **Q** in 4 hours, and immediately rides back to **P**. After 2 hours rest he starts again for **Q** at the same rate. How far from **P** will he overtake A, who has in the meantime rested $6\frac{1}{4}$ hours?

5. At what distance from **A**, and at what time, will a train which leave **A** for **B** at 2.33 p.m., and goes at the rate of 35 km per hour, meet a train which leaves **B** at 1.45 p.m. and goes at the rate of 25 km per hour, the distance between **A** and **B** being 80 km?

Also find at what times the trains are 24 km apart, and how far apart they are at 4.9 p.m.

6. A, B, and C set out to walk from **P** to **Q** at 5, 6, and 4 km per hour respectively. C starts 3 minutes before, and B 7 minutes after A. Draw graphs to shew (i) when and where A overtakes **C**; (ii) when and where **B** overtakes A;

(iii) C's position relative to the others after he has walked 45 minutes.

[Take 3 cm horizontally to represent 10 minutes, and 3 cm to the kilometre vertically.]